Psychology

THE SCIENCE OF MENTAL LIFE

Psychology

THE SCIENCE OF MENTAL LIFE

BY GEORGE A. MILLER

—————◆—————

HARPER MODERN SCIENCE SERIES
EDITED BY JAMES R. NEWMAN

HARPER & ROW / PUBLISHERS
NEW YORK AND EVANSTON

ACKNOWLEDGMENTS

We would like to express appreciation to the several authors and publishers who permitted us to quote from their works or reproduce their illustrations. Explicit citations are given at the points where such material is used.

TO E. G. BORING

CONTENTS

viii   *Contents*

PREFACE

In this book I have tried to explain what the science of psychology is like and how it got that way. Because psychology is large in its scope and grows larger every year, I obviously could not phrase my explanation in the form of an exhaustive catalogue. I have instead been selective, both with respect to current status and past history. I have tried to scatter my selections widely in order to represent several different areas of psychology, but I have neglected the more technological and applied aspects of the science. Selectivity—some might call it bias—is unavoidable in a modest volume such as this; I mention it so that everyone will understand clearly that modern psychology includes a great deal more than I have been able to describe or appraise, or even to mention, in these pages. Readers who would like to explore the subject further may find that the suggestions for further reading at the end of the book will help them to get a proper start.

A great many people have helped to make this book possible; the simplest way for me to acknowledge my intellectual debts in this enterprise is to recount some of its history.

The book, or something like it, was James R. Newman's idea. Originally, in 1958, he wanted something predominantly historical and he wanted Professor Edwin G. Boring to write it. But when that proved impossible, Boring suggested that I might be able to do the job. I was indeed interested. I was then planning a course of lectures in psychology at the introductory level, and I imagined that such a writing assignment might fit nicely into my schedule. But I doubted my competence as an historian. It took several conversations with Boring before I saw how to handle that part of it. The course I finally adopted—as an examination of the present table of contents will make clear—was to arrange the various topics approximately in the historical order in which psychologists developed them and to insert half a dozen biographical essays at appropriate points into this introductory survey, thus serving both Newman's purposes and my own simultaneously. I knew that Boring's admirable writings on the history of psychology would give me a good start, and when he agreed to criticize my final product, I decided to try it. Three years later I had finished the job and Boring kept his promise. He went over the manuscript with all the wisdom and enthusiasm that have always characterized his editing. And it is well that he did. He managed to protect the reader from some of my more questionable interpretations of history, and even from a few downright mistakes. Thus, in addition to Newman's and my own efforts, Boring's vast scholarship has also contributed to the present volume. It gives me considerable pleasure to acknowledge my debt and express my affection by dedicating the book to him. It goes without saying, of course, that any mistakes that may have slipped by us all are uniquely my own, and that the dedication in no sense deprives Boring of his right to take issue with what is written here.

When I began this job I did not intend to work three years at it. In 1958–59 I took leave of absence from Harvard University in order to spend the year at the Center for Advanced Study in the Behavioral Sciences, in Stanford, California. There I intended to enjoy the climate, to write this book, to talk to other behavioral scientists, and to read everything in sight. I did get a good start on the writing, but before the year was over I was attracted into other enterprises with Eugene Galanter and Karl Pribram. Although our discussions together eventually influenced many of the chapters in this book, at the time they provided an irresistible distraction from Mr. Newman's project.

In the fall of 1959, therefore, I arrived back at Harvard with a half-written manuscript and no leisure at all. At this point Professor Jerome S. Bruner came to my rescue; he agreed to collaborate with me on that introductory course I had been working toward. Together we developed a series of lectures that has now become a Harvard General Education course entitled "Psychological Conceptions of

Man." Bruner proposed many important improvements in my original plan, and the course, as it is now taught, is different both in scope and conception from the present volume. Nevertheless, many of the passages published here would sound familiar to any students who may have listened carefully to certain of my lectures. I believe that the writing is clearer as a direct consequence of that preliminary exposure. There is nothing quite so helpful as a student's puzzled frown for indicating that the argument has slipped a cog.

Finally, at the Harvard Center for Cognitive Studies, during the summer of 1961, I was able to find time to finish a job that had already dragged on far too long. For their patience and support through long months of delay, publisher and editor alike have won my deep appreciation.

This brief history indicates some of my major debts in this enterprise: James R. Newman, E. G. Boring, Eugene Galanter, Karl Pribram, J. S. Bruner, and several hundred Harvard and Radcliffe students have earned my fondest gratitude. In addition, I would like particularly to thank both Dr. Richard Herrnstein and Professor Paul F. Lazarsfeld for many helpful and interesting discussions of the history of psychology. And, finally, in this as in all the books I have written, my wife Katherine made indispensable contributions by typing, editing, listening, and understanding.

GEORGE A. MILLER

Harvard Center for Cognitive Studies

CHAPTER I

PSYCHOLOGY, SCIENCE,

AND MAN

Several years ago a professor who teaches psychology at a large university had to ask his assistant, a young man of great intelligence but little experience, to take over the introductory psychology course for a short time. The assistant was challenged by the opportunity and planned an ambitious series of lectures. But he made a mistake. He decided to open with a short definition of his subject. When the professor got back to his classroom two weeks later he found his conscientious assistant still struggling to define psychology.

An alternative approach is to assume at the very outset that everybody knows, more or less, what psychology is all about. "Psychology," said William James in the first sentence of his classic text, "is the science of mental life." Although this definition no longer means what it did when James wrote *The Principles of Psychology* in 1890, it is relatively familiar and mercifully short. We can use it to launch our discussion of psychology without prolonged introductions.

Psychology is the science of mental life. The key words here are *science* and *mental*.

Our conception of what a science of mental life should be has changed considerably since James's time. In 1890 mental life seemed to be a well-defined thing. No one doubted that a mind was there waiting for scientists to study it. But today, after seventy years of trying to study it scientifically, we are less certain. No longer is it self-evident what a psychologist means when he says that he studies mental life. The modern mind seems to be concealed from view, a mental iceberg floating nine-tenths hidden in a vague, unconscious sea; even its owner can do little more than guess which way it will drift next. At the time James wrote, scientific psychology was very young and the mental life that psychologists had been able to study was largely limited to the *conscious* mental life of *sane, well-educated, adult, Western European, human* beings. Today, every one of the restrictions implied by those adjectives has been removed. As the science of mental life developed, its base broadened to include children, animals, preliterate peoples, the mentally retarded, the insane. It is not obvious that all these newcomers share anything we could call a mental life, in the sense understood during the nineteenth century.

At the time James wrote, his claim that psychology was a science was little more than an expression of hope and enthusiasm. In 1890 scientific psychology was still a possible future development. A few men had begun to ask what they might do to make this branch of philosophy more empirical in its methods and conceptions. A few small laboratories had been founded, a few methods of measurement had been adopted, a few preliminary results had been reported. Whipped together with physiology, philosophy, and great common sense in the delightful Jamesian prose, the result was engaging and full of promise, but still a good deal less than a true science of the mind.

Scientific methods, however, are notoriously successful. Since James wrote his *Principles* there has been a remarkable growth in both the quantity and the quality of scientific research on psychological problems. Today when we say that psychology is a science we support the claim with several impressive accomplishments. Indeed, the rapid development of this young science has disrupted the daily pattern of our lives in scores of ways.

Scientific accomplishments usually affect us on at least two levels. On the one hand, scientific knowledge provides a foundation for technological advances, for the solution of practical problems that arise in the daily affairs of ordinary people. In this aspect, science is something that we exploit, just as we would exploit a natural resource. Many people think that this is all there is to science; they are confused by distinctions between scientists and engineers, between science and technology. But in its essence, science is something more than a useful art. Science has understanding, as well as control, as one of its aims. Thus science affects us at a deeper level by changing the way we understand the world we live in. Scientific advances mold our vision of reality, our fundamental and often unspoken set of assumptions about how the world *really* runs and what people are *really* like. Such effects of science are less tangible than the technological ones, but it is perilous to assume they are less important.

Like all sciences, psychology has influenced our lives on both levels. It has given us technical tricks and it has changed our conception of human nature.

When new fields of scientific activity first take form they begin, almost necessarily, with things and ideas that are part of the common experience of all men. During this early period of growth the science is widely intelligible, and the discoveries it makes can be understood, argued, resisted, supported, or ridiculed by millions of people. At a later stage the science may become more precise, may achieve deeper insight or soar to greater heights of intellectual virtuosity, but it will never again have quite the same impact on the average man's view of himself and the world around him. At this later stage the science may be supported for the technical miracles it mysteriously provides, but it is no longer a living reality to more than a handful of specialists. As its technological impact on society tends to increase, its impact on the common understanding often fades into the background.

Psychology is currently passing through its initial stage. It is still intelligible to most people. It is not unusual to hear a layman say, "I'm something of a psychologist myself, and I think . . ." What he thinks is often subtle and interesting and would not embarrass a more professional practitioner. In order to stay alive among our fellow men, we must all be psychologists. Of course, survival requires us to be mathematicians, physicists, chemists, and biologists, too, but there the distance has grown too great; no layman claims brotherhood without a prolonged initiation ritual conducted at some accredited university. It was not always so. There was a time when Everyman was a physicist, when Shakespeare would interrupt a play to argue against the heliocentric theory of the universe, just as a modern playwright may digress to illustrate or to oppose some new psychological theory today. It is in this initial stage of development that a science is most visible, most controversial, and most likely to change our vision of reality.

In spite of psychology's youth, however, the little knowledge it has painfully gained has fed a thousand different human needs. In some quarters demand has so far outrun supply that many psychologists fear their science has been oversold to an overwilling public. Yet even when we try to be conservative in our appraisal, it is plain that the new psychotechnology has already changed the way we live.

Consider our public schools. Everyone in the United States has felt the influence of modern psychology through its effects on our educational system. Indeed, there was a time when our schools seemed little more than a vast laboratory to test the psychological theories of John Dewey. The modern teacher has tried to use psychology—he has thumbed many a textbook ragged in search of the psychological principles underlying good teaching. Frequently the answer he seeks is not to be found, and the educator's pressing responsibilities to the young force him to extrapolate far beyond the established facts of scientific psychology; he hopes his guesses will be more intelligent if he tries to use psychology. Psychologists have tried to find answers for him. They have carefully explored a variety of conditions that affect how quickly a child can learn. They have painstakingly charted the stages of mental and social development. They have developed better techniques for measuring the progress of the child and the effectiveness of the teaching. They have provided counselling and guidance services outside the classroom. And they have given teachers that indispensable tool, the intelligence test. Yet all this is far too little, for the teacher's needs are great and vitally important.

The mention of intelligence tests is a reminder of another area of psychotechnology, the mental testing business. It is a sizable business. It has been estimated that in 1960 there were 130 million psychological tests given to our school children, or approximately three tests for every child from the first grade through college.

Mental tests, like the airplane, are part of our heritage from World War I. Before that time the tests were given individually to school children, and they tested nothing but intelligence. During the war, however, psychologists in the U. S. Army developed a pencil-and-paper test of adult intelligence that could be given to thousands of draftees—the famous Army Alpha Test—and so the large-scale testing procedures became firmly established in the public's consciousness. After that the testers began to branch out. They began to test aptitudes, to classify interests, to evaluate achievements. Now they can pigeonhole your personality, assess your emotional stability, your masculinity, your imagination, executive potential, chances of marital bliss, conformity to an employer's stereotype, or ability to operate a turret lathe. Whatever you plan to do, there seems to be a psychological test you should take first. Citizens who resent the many hours spent answering pointless questions are apparently in the minority, since enterprising newspapers and magazines have found that they can boost sales by providing daily or weekly questionnaires for their readers to answer. The flood of tests that has poured out across the nation has included many frauds—tests that are poorly conceived, confusingly phrased, completely unstandardized, and never validated. Psychologists have maintained reasonable professional standards among themselves, but it is not always easy to restrain the amateurs —it is as if everyone who bought a knife became a surgeon. Yet, in spite of these problems, the mental testing movement in the United States has managed to perform a needed service for both the individual and the community.

Once the Army saw how useful psychologists could be in the assessment of men, it began to discover other problems of a similar nature. Soon the psychologist became a familiar member of the military team. For example, during World War II much highly technical military equipment was developed that had never existed before. In the developmental stages it often seemed that no one less gifted than Superman would be able to operate the equipment. The task of making the equipment fit the man was tackled by psychologists, who were able to contribute their knowledge of what a human eye could see or a human ear could hear, how far and how fast a human hand could move, how much interference and distraction a human mind could overcome. Psychologists can help to design trainers and simulators, to plan training programs, to select men who are likely to succeed in each type of job. Moreover, in addition to man-machine problems, the military services have a vast range of psychological problems in the area known as mental health, where psychologists work together with psychiatrists to maintain morale and to heal the mentally wounded. A military branch is a small society unto itself

—each application of psychology in our larger society has its parallel in this more limited world of warriors.

One large and active sector of psychotechnology goes under the trade name of industrial psychology. Many of industry's concerns are similar to the Army's—how to select men who will be successful at different types of jobs, how to train workers to do their jobs better. Industrial psychologists have worked on the problem of fatigue: how should intervals of rest and work be alternated to give the greatest output with the least fatigue for the worker? The discovery that an employer often got less for his money from a laborer who worked a ten-hour day than from the one who worked an eight-hour day helped to change management's attitude toward many of labor's demands. Questions of fatigue lead quickly into questions of morale; industrial psychologists have worried mightily over this important factor. And morale, in turn, leads into questions of emotional adjustment. Clinical psychologists and psychiatrists have found their niche in the industrial scene, with a consequent reduction, so it is claimed, in illness, absenteeism, and accidents. Even the executives have succumbed to the psychologist's charms, and many a firm's management has been overhauled on the recommendation of a psychological consultant. There are people who feel that if the traditionally hard-headed American businessman is enough convinced of the usefulness of psychology to spend his own dollars on it, then there must be something to it after all!

A possible reason why some businessmen are willing to tolerate a psychologist underfoot is that they may have made a good profit by following his advice about advertising and selling the company's product. The psychologist has been keenly interested in techniques of persuasion, and his discoveries have colored our advertising, propaganda, politics, and entertainment as these are distributed broadside through our mass media of communication. And by probing around in the consumer's unconscious, a psychologist may turn up some useful information for the advertising agency. Just how far one can go in shaping the public mind with a television screen is debatable. But it is apparent that there are both good and bad ways to advertise; psychologists can often help distinguish between them in advance.

Business is not the only place where careful attention is paid to surveys of public opinion. Government agencies have used polls for years to guide our public policies; politicians are particularly sensitive to fluctuations in their popularity with the voters. And feedback from the grass roots is just one of several ways that social psychology is involved in the processes of government. For example, in 1954 psychological evidence was used in the United States Supreme Court decisions against racial segregation in the public schools, where it was held that separate but equal facilities for both races were impossible because the psychological consequences of segregation were too great a handicap for the minority group. The Court's decision rested as much on a point of psychology as on a point of law.

This recital could be extended for several pages. Psychological dogma influences the way we discipline our children, manage our businesses, and run our marriages. Studies of abnormal behavior modify our conception and treatment of mental illness, incompetence, perversion, criminality, and delinquency. The priest and the rabbi agree in their use of psychological techniques to guide their flocks to salvation. Novels, plays, and movies now feature psychological themes as one of their standard formulas. Psychological drugs have already changed the situation in our mental hospitals, and more are yet to come. Wherever people are involved, psychology can be useful—and that is almost everywhere. Whether we like it or not, the practical application of psychology to our daily affairs is already in an advanced stage.

It must be admitted, however, that not every application of psychology is firmly grounded in scientific evidence. Those who apply psychology to the dynamic processes of an evolving society often jump to conclusions that make their laboratory colleagues tremble and turn pale. But when decisions must be made here and now, they must be made in the light of the evidence at hand, no matter how fragmentary and inconclusive that may be. In the past the same decisions had to be made with even less help; today the man who must take the responsibility can at least console himself that he tried to be intelligent, that his guess was informed by whatever evidence existed. The sun will not stand still while he discovers and verifies every fact he needs to know. He works by guess and hunch and intuitive feel, searching always for what will work, for what will meet the present needs. By a shrewd mixture of intelligence, science, and salesmanship, the applied psychologists have given us better answers to hundreds of practical questions. And they will improve those answers just as fast as our growth in basic, scientific psychology permits.

But, if those are some of the practical consequences of scientific psychology, what are some of the impractical ones? What subtler influences has psychology had upon our contemporary attitudes toward life and the universe? Those subtler effects are not easily converted into 8 per cent investments, yet there is a sense in which they are more deeply significant than any merely technological advances.

Scientific psychology educates public psychology. It informs and enriches the picture of man that we all share and that guides so much of our daily conduct. It modifies the public image that is taken for granted in our literature, in our schools, in our theatres, in art and music, in religion and government. It has been said that if human nature ever changes, it is because we learn to see ourselves in a new way. Our feeling for right and wrong, our sense of what is comic and what is tragic, our judgment of what will perish and what will survive are shaped and reshaped by our silently assumed psychology.

Consider, for example, the shadow that our implicit psychology casts on our conception of power, of how human behavior is controlled, of how man is governed. In every age the standards by which laws are written and enforced, goals are set, promises are kept or broken, actions are judged and rewards are given derive from a loose consensus about human nature, about the gap between what is humanly desirable and what is humanly possible. Change man's image of himself and you send a jar reverberating through the foundations of his society. Those who sit in positions of power are particularly sensitive to tremors in the structure that supports them. They will not let man move from the center of the universe or evolve from a monkey without protest. And their protest can be passionate and merciless.

The extent to which the political system of a country can affect the kind of psychology carried on there is eloquent testimony to the investment that our rulers have in our public image of human nature. Psychologists in the United States during World War II were appalled to see their colleagues in Germany twist psychology to support the Nazi's fantastic claims of racial superiority. The history of Russian psychology also illustrates this danger. The leaders of the revolution were slow at first to recognize the importance of psychology; but by 1923 it was clear that Russian psychology, if it wanted to survive, would have to base its theories on materialistic philosophy. For a brief period, therefore, the official image of Soviet man was that of a physiological robot. When a government decides to impose its preconceived views, science, which is never easy, can become virtually impossible.

Our concern here, however, is not with direct interactions between psychology and government, but with the indirect influence psychology can exert by modifying slowly the opinions that every man holds of himself and his neighbors. What are these influences? A citizen should find it in his own interest to learn which way he is being pushed. Where does scientific psychology seem to lead? What image of man is the psychologist trying to promote? Unfortunately—or, perhaps, fortunately—no simple answer will suffice, for there are many psychologists and many different images.

There is a general scientific ethos shared by most psychologists. They expect to base their image of man on empirical knowledge, not upon political dogma or traditional opinion or divine revelation or esthetic appeal. Once this much is said, however, it is difficult to continue until we know which psychologist we are talking about. There are many ways to be scientific, there are many different psychological problems to be studied, and there are innumerable ways to fit our scraps of evidence together into an image of man. It is not easy to see just which part of this complicated enterprise we should take hold of first.

One approach to scientific psychology is through its history; we can go back to the nineteenth century and try to recapture some of the enthusiasm and confidence with which scientific methods were first applied to the human mind. Everyone recognizes, of course, that the analytical methods of science can work miracles when applied to nonliving systems. With living systems, however, scientific successes have been more modest. And with man, the most complicated of all living systems, it was not immediately obvious to everyone that the methods could be applied at all.

The modern psychologist's faith that scientific methods can be applied to the mental life of human beings is inherited from the nineteenth century, a time when science looked bigger than the universe itself.

CHAPTER II

WILHELM WUNDT, PSYCHOLOGIST

Psychology became an experimental science during the closing decades of the nineteenth century, at a time when European thought was dominated by *positivism*. In its narrowest sense positivism was the philosophy of Auguste Comte, who invented the term as a name for his ambitious work, *The Positive Philosophy*. Comte's aim was to provide a systematic survey of all knowledge. In order to cope with so large an enterprise, he had to limit himself strictly to facts whose truth was unquestionable, whose validity was insured by the recognized methods of science. Some men would have regretted this limitation, but Comte considered it one of the great merits of his work. It was acceptance of these limitations to which he gave the name, positivism.

Once invented, however, the term soon came to be used rather loosely to describe any discussion of human beings phrased in the language of natural science. That is the broader sense intended here.

Positivism is positive in a polemical sense, meaning that it is not metaphysical. Any speculation about transcendental powers, hidden essences, or ultimate causes is dismissed as sophistry and illusion. The worst insult a positivist can give is to call you a metaphysician. A positive philosophy accepts as real only those things that can be known. Everything that is mere conjecture, unsupportable by argument or observation, must be rejected. Philosophy must be based squarely on knowledge. A theory that cannot be tested by an appeal to facts is mere humbug. In particular, if nothing recommends a

10

hypothesis except the satisfaction and comfort it can provide, commit it to the flames! This attitude inevitably gives offense to those who cherish their religious beliefs.

The men who tried to maintain this hardheaded, no-nonsense philosophy in every situation discovered that certain other philosophical ideas were particularly appealing. On the one hand, the positivists were powerfully attracted to the *empiricists,* who believed that the only source of true knowledge about the universe is sensory experience—what can be seen, heard, felt, tasted, or smelled, or what can be inferred about the relations between, or invariances among, such sensory facts. Thus when a positivist said that he based his philosophy on knowledge, what he usually meant was that he based it on the evidence of his senses, the kind of evidence that had proved so spectacularly successful in the natural sciences.

Positivists also found strong support—sometimes more than they wanted—from the *materialists,* who believed that everything in the universe can be understood in terms of the properties of matter and energy, and reduced to descriptions expressed in centimeters, grams, and seconds. Materialists usually believe that all the phenomena of consciousness will eventually be explained by the laws of physics and chemistry. Thus in psychological arguments they tend to focus attention on the anatomy and physiology—the structure and function —of the brain.

And from still another direction, the positivists—especially Comtean positivists—had a very close tie with the *evolutionists.* It is a part of Comte's theory that civilization evolves through three stages: the theological, the metaphysical, and the positive. These stages represent an evolutionary theory of society. It is not surprising, therefore, that Comte's followers were among the first to support Darwin's theory of biological evolution when it appeared in 1859. They, with Herbert Spencer and Thomas Huxley, grafted Darwin's theory onto the positive philosophy.

Thus positivism found strong allies. Empiricism, materialism, and evolutionism were the philosophical foundations of a scientific revolution that was rapidly changing the nineteenth-century man's conception of himself and his world. Because psychology became an experimental science during this period, all three of these great traditions contributed to it, nourished it, and helped to define its problems and its methods.

Of these three traditions, empiricism was probably the most important during the initial development of scientific psychology. Empiricism has played a dual role in the history of psychology, for it provides both a *method* to increase knowledge and a *theory* about the growth of the mind. As a method, empiricism means that we learn by making observations, by having new experiences, by conducting experiments. As a psychological theory, empiricism means that a child's mind at birth is a blank slate upon which experience will write. It is possible, of course, to apply the empirical method without subscribing to an empiricist theory of the mind—but the historical fact is that men who subscribed to one often believed the other as well. If you hold an empiricist theory about the growth of the mind, you are likely to see the empirical method as the only possible way for anyone to acquire knowledge—the scientist, philosopher, child, or plain man. An empiricist theory of the mind is particularly useful to support and explain the success of empirical methods in modern science.

Empirical methods are sometimes contrasted with rational methods of acquiring knowledge. In this context, the empirical method is said to be inductive, whereas the rational method is deductive. The empiricist theory, on the other hand, has generally been contrasted with a *nativist* theory of the mind; the empiricist says that a child must learn everything through experience, and the nativist replies that some things are inherited and must be present at birth.

Although it is possible to find clear anticipations of empiricism —it was Aristotle, after all, who coined the famous metaphor about the baby's mind being a blank slate—its greatest thrust was felt in the writings of the seventeenth-century British philosopher John Locke. Locke deeply admired Isaac Newton and tried to develop a philosophy based, like Newton's science, on observable things and events.

In his great *An Essay Concerning Human Understanding* (1690), Locke defended the premise that all ideas originate in experience:

> Let us then suppose the mind to be, as we say, white paper void of all characters, without any ideas:—How comes it to be furnished? Whence comes it by that vast store which the busy and boundless fancy of man has painted on it with an almost endless variety? Whence has it all the *materials* of reason and knowledge? To this I answer, in one word, from EXPERIENCE. In that all our knowledge is founded; and from that it ultimately derives itself. Our observation, employed either

about external sensible objects, or about the internal operations of our minds, perceived and reflected on by ourselves, is that which supplies our understandings with all the *materials* of thinking. These two are the fountains of knowledge, from whence all the ideas we have, or can naturally have, do spring.[1]*

A newborn infant must acquire his ideas of this world by observing what goes on around him; the limits of his understanding are set by the limits of his senses and his reason.

Locke's argument was immediately successful, and empiricism rapidly became the dominant philosophy of the eighteenth century. Its influence extended into every intellectual nook and cranny; into education, into social, political, and economic theory. Its effect on psychology was only one aspect of this broad and influential movement.

We can summarize briefly the major implications for psychology: First, of course, empiricism places enormous emphasis upon the processes of *sensation,* for the senses are the doors to the mind through which all knowledge of the world must pass. The British— always the most loyal adherents to an empiricist position—have forever baffled their Continental friends by their faith in perception as the cornerstone of all philosophical truth. Second, empiricism usually leads to analysis into *elements,* analysis of conscious experience into the simple ideas that are the basic building blocks of the mind. The simple ideas—blueness, loudness, saltiness, the odor of turpentine —are sensory elements into which the more complicated ideas can eventually be analyzed. Third, empirical analysis into elements creates a need for a corresponding conception of empirical synthesis into compounds—a theory of *association* whereby simple elements can combine to form more complicated elements. As the empiricists developed their doctrine, the importance of associative processes became more and more obvious; there was much debate over rival sets of laws describing how associations are formed. Fourth, empiricism emphasizes the importance of *conscious* processes in knowledge—of perceptions and images—and neglects the possibility that mental processes might not always be immediately apparent to their host. Fifth, it is a theory about the *individual* mind; social implications are not considered. All minds are created free and equal. An individual mind is a private, personal thing, completely independent of all other

* Superior numbers refer to Notes beginning on page 355.

private, personal minds and free to enter into any contracts or agreements with others that suit its own purposes.

Even in its youth empiricism made easy alliances with materialism. A worthy precursor of positivistic thinking about the human mind was provided by a British physician, David Hartley, who in 1749 explained in his *Observations on Man* how our ideas become associated with one another. It is simply a matter of resonance. According to Hartley, an idea is a vibration in the nerves. By resonance, one vibration sets off another. Thus he explained how one idea can lead to another, and so proposed a material basis for the empiricist theory of the mind.

By the second half of the nineteenth century, of course, physiological theories had advanced well beyond Hartley's mechanical vibrations in the nerves; by then it was clear that chemical and electrical processes were involved. But the general purpose of the endeavor did not change. Materialists are never satisfied that they understand something until they can explain it in terms of the properties of material substances. Their task is to find a materialistic basis for everything, including thought, that takes place in the human body. This was the program for physiology during the nineteenth century —and by 1870 the doctrine that all human acts can be explained by physico-chemical principles had completely captured the thinking of physiologists and physicians.

Sensory physiology developed quite rapidly during the nineteenth century. Physiologists who studied the nervous system scored some of their earliest successes with the receptor organs and with the sensory nerves leading from the receptors to the brain. The bulk of this work was done in Germany—G. T. Fechner, Hermann Ludwig von Helmholtz, Ewald Hering were among the leaders—but the work bore an interesting relation to the empiricist philosophy of England. The Germans knew how the receptors worked; the British knew why they were important. Given the positivistic spirit of the times it was inevitable that the two lines of thought should converge. When this happened, psychology became an experimental science.

Wilhelm Wundt, the son of a Lutheran pastor, was born in 1832 at Neckarau, a suburb of Mannheim, in the German state of Baden.[2] His childhood was solemn and studious. When he was eight years old, his schooling became the responsibility of his father's assistant, a vicar whose room Wilhelm shared. The boy formed a deep attachment to his mentor, who received the affection normally reserved for parents, and when the vicar was called to a neighboring town, Wilhelm went with him. There is no record of any other boyhood friends, no foolish pranks or young adventures, no boisterous laughter or silly giggles—only study, reading, work, and more study. So far as one can tell, he was a humorless, indefatigable scholar from the day of his birth.

The Wundts were not a wealthy family, and Wilhelm had to consider how he would support himself. He decided to become a physician. It would enable him to earn a living and to study science simultaneously. At Heidelberg, therefore, he studied anatomy, physiology, physics, chemistry, and medicine, and slowly discovered that the medical profession was not for him. He had instead the luckiest of gifts, a calling, something he loved to do, and he determined to answer it by becoming an academician. The fact that his subject was physiology was accidental, and almost incidental. His real goal was to satisfy a lifelong lust for scholarship. He took his doctorate in medicine at Heidelberg in 1856 and was then habilitated as *Privatdozent* in physiology.

In 1858 Hermann Ludwig von Helmholtz, soon to become the greatest physiologist in the world, moved to Heidelberg. Young Wundt received an appointment as his assistant. But it was dreary work; Wundt was responsible for drilling the sudden influx of new students in their laboratory fundamentals. After a few years of this routine he resigned in order to resume his former position. The years spent in the same laboratory with Helmholtz did not inspire him to novel achievements in physiology. Indeed, it was during this period that he lost interest in pure physiology and began to question the positivistic philosophy. He was finding himself intellectually, deciding his position, and laying out the program of work that would occupy him for the rest of his life. For six decades, long after he had left Heidelberg to become the famous professor at Leipzig, Wundt followed this program with persistence and unremitting energy.

What Wundt did was to look at the psychological problems posed by the British philosophers with the eyes of a man trained in the traditions of German physiology. The notion that psychology could become a science of observation and experiment had been stated clearly and explicitly by the British philosopher John Stuart Mill in

his *Logic* as early as 1843, but it required a person who really knew
how observation and experiments are made to bring it off. Wundt was
that person.

Wilhelm Wundt

It would be wrong, however, to think of Wundtian psychology as
a simple union of empiricist British philosophy and materialist German physiology. Wundt was not willing to reduce the mind to a
physical process in the brain, nor was he willing to abandon metaphysics as empty nonsense. Thus, even though positivism had created
an intellectual atmosphere in which it seemed reasonable to be scientific about everything, even consciousness, the founder of this new
science thought of himself as in revolt against the positivistic spirit
of his day. In this respect Wundt anticipated some aspects of the up-
heaval of the 1890's when a great flood of genius—Weber, Durkheim,
Sorel, Pareto, Freud, James, Dewey, Croce, Bergson—broke free
at last from the constrictions positivism had placed on social and
psychological thought.

The program to which Wundt devoted his life was first published
in the introduction to his book, *Contributions to the Theory of Sensory Perception,* in 1862. The body of the book—a summary of the
medical psychology of perception—is of little value a century later.
But the introduction is interesting. It sets forth three projects that the
young physiologist invented: to create an experimental psychology,
to create a scientific metaphysics, and to create a social psychology.
He then set to work with what may have been the most tireless pen

in the whole history of German scholarship. By 1920, some fifty thousand pages later, his projects were complete and he could permit himself to die.

The sheer bulk of his writing made Wundt almost immune to criticism. A critic would be outwritten, evaded by qualifications, and buried under mountains of detail. Wundt's theories were more like classification schemes than like systems of functional relations; they tended to be loosely knit and almost impossible either to prove or to disprove. There was no vital center to his thought where an opponent could slay him with a single blow. "Cut him up like a worm," said William James, "and each fragment crawls." The same quality makes it impossible to summarize his work or reduce it to a simple formula.

For Wundt, psychology involved the analysis of consciousness into elements, the determination of the manner in which these elements are connected, and the determination of the laws of connection. This conception he borrowed from the British empiricists. Just as chemists had analyzed matter into atoms and anatomists had analyzed living systems into cells, psychologists, he decided, must analyze mind into the elementary sensations and feelings that make it up. Wundt once summarized this thesis in a ponderous, German way:

> All the contents of psychical experience are of a composite character. It follows, therefore, that *psychical elements,* or the absolutely simple and irreducible components of psychical phenomena, are the products of analysis and abstraction. . . . As a result of psychical analysis, we find that there are *psychical elements of two kinds.* . . . The elements of the objective contents we call *sensational elements,* or simply *sensations:* such are a tone, or a particular sensation of heat, cold, or light, if in each case we neglect for the moment all the connections of these sensations with others, and also their spatial and temporal relations. The subjective elements, on the other hand, are designed as *affective elements,* or *simple feelings.* . . . The actual contents of psychical experience always consist of various combinations of sensational and affective elements, so that the specific character of a given psychical process depends for the most part, not on the nature of its elements, so much as on the union of these elements into a composite psychical compound.[3]

Since the contents of psychical experience at any given instant are likely to be rather complex, the variety of ways to analyze them into

elements, to classify and relate those elements to one another provided material for almost endless subtleties and fine distinctions—a
realm in which the patient, scholarly, encyclopedic Wundt was grand
master.

Yet his purpose was as straightforward as his arguments were complicated. His first goal was to establish psychology as a science. By
1874, the year he moved to Leipzig as professor of philosophy, the
hard-working Wundt was well along toward his goal. That year
the first edition of his *Physiological Psychology* was published. In the
preface he said, "The work which I here present to the public is an
attempt to mark out a new domain of science." This book, which he
rewrote and expanded five times, was Wundt's masterpiece. It firmly
established psychology as a laboratory science with its own problems
and its own experimental methods. This scientific version became
known as "the new psychology," in order to distinguish it from "the
old psychology" that had been produced in the philosopher's armchair.

When a living system is studied from the outside, it is physiology.
According to Wundt, when we study a living system from the inside,
it is psychology. The only way we can study a living system from
within is by self-observation, or *introspection*. Of course, the most
remarkable thing about introspection is that we can do it at all—but
Wundt could shed no more light on that accomplishment than we
can today. So he accepted it as given and went on to ask what could
be learned from it.

We learn little about our minds from casual, haphazard self-
observation, just as we learned little about mechanics from centuries
of casual, uncontrolled observation of falling bodies. It is essential
that observations be made by trained observers under carefully speci-
fied conditions for the purpose of answering well-defined questions.
To Wundt, "scientific" meant "experimental"; if psychology was to
become a science, it would have to use its introspective approach in
an experimental situation in a laboratory where all conditions could
be precisely controlled and repeated. Only in the special environment
of a laboratory could the elusive elements of conscious experience
be analyzed accurately.

At Leipzig Wundt presented the odd spectacle of a professor of
philosophy who gave scientific demonstrations during his lectures.
How else could an ex-physiologist make his point? These demonstrations became such an important part of his thinking that in 1879

he started his own laboratory—the world's first formal laboratory of psychology. And as he began to train young philosophers to use the scientific method, it became necessary to find some place to publish their results. In 1881 he started a magazine called the *Philosophische Studien,* the first effective journal for experimental psychology. With a handbook, a laboratory, and a scholarly journal, the new psychology was well under way.

In his prime, *Herr Geheimrat* Professor Doctor Wilhelm Wundt was tall, thin, slightly stooped, with a large head, a pleasant face, and a full beard. He wore thick, dark glasses and could use only part of the vision of one eye during the last half of his life. In spite of this handicap, he worked with unflagging zeal. He seems to have had no capacity for boredom. In the morning he worked at home on the many books that remain his monument, read student theses, and edited his journal. In the afternoon he took a walk, and attended examinations or visited his laboratory. On his arrival at the laboratory, he went directly to his private room, where he held conferences. Some days he toured the laboratory and inspected the experiments. His lectures were given at four o'clock, well after dark during the winter months. As a professor he enjoyed a high social standing and easy financial circumstances, a position of privilege granted all German professors before World War I. His security and his family made life seem both cheerful and productive.

Wundt was the most popular lecturer at Leipzig; the largest lecture hall was never large enough to hold all those who wanted to hear him. One of his most famous students, E. B. Titchener—who later disseminated Wundtian psychology to America from his professorial chair at Cornell University—recalled vividly the great man's classroom manner. Wundt would appear at exactly the correct minute—punctuality was essential—dressed all in black and carrying a small sheaf of lecture notes. He clattered up the side aisle to the platform with an awkward shuffle and a sound as if his soles were made of wood. On the platform was a long desk where demonstrations were performed. He made a few gestures—a forefinger across his forehead, a rearrangement of his chalk—then faced the audience and placed his elbows on the bookrest. His voice was weak at first, then gained in strength and emphasis. As he talked his arms and hands moved up and down, pointing and waving, in some mysterious way illustrative. His head and body were rigid, and only the hands played back and forth. He seldom referred to the few jotted notes. As the clock struck the end of the hour he stopped and, stooping a little, clattered out as he had clattered in.

The work done in his new laboratory and published in his new journal extended in several directions. Most of it, of course, concerned sensation and perception, particularly vision and hearing; perception was the problem considered fundamental in Wundt's empirical philosophy. In these experiments Wundt was able to exploit the methods of measurement devised by that eccentric genius, Gustav Theodor Fechner, and he had the famous Fechner Law to guide him.[4] In every respect, the analysis of perceptual processes into their elements was the simplest and most profitable line to follow in the new psychology. Next most popular were the studies of reaction time, for these seemed to provide a way to measure the speed of thought.

Psychology cannot be constructed entirely in terms of elementary sensations and their modes and levels of integration. The field of consciousness, said Wundt, has a small, bright area at its center; he directed some of his students into research on the problems of attention. Other students attempted to study association and memory. Still others introspected on their feelings and emotions. The six rooms of his little laboratory buzzed with the discoveries and arguments of the students as they applied analytic introspection to one problem after another.

One series of experiments on attention used a metronome, an instrument for marking exact time in music. As all music students know, a metronome produces clearly audible clicks at regular intervals; the rate of the clicks can be adjusted to suit the tempo of the music. Wundt's listeners were asked to form rhythmic groupings of the clicks and to report their conscious experiences. The introspective method used in such experiments is simple to describe, but it requires considerable training and self-discipline to use. Stimuli—in this case the sequence of clicks—are presented while the subject pays careful attention to all that he notices. When stimulation ends, the subject gives a full verbal report. In an experiment on attention, the subject may be interested in whether a particular pattern of clicks can be held in consciousness as a unitary whole. However, exactly the same source of stimulation can be used to investigate other aspects of conscious experience.

Consider how he worked: Wundt reported from his own introspections that at the end of a rhythmic row of beats he had the impression of an agreeable whole. That is, some rhythmic patterns are more pleasant, more agreeable than others. He concluded from this self-observation that part of the experience of any pattern of beats is a subjective feeling of pleasure or displeasure, a feeling that can be located somewhere along a continuum ranging from the agreeable to the disagreeable. While he listened to the clicks, however, he detected another kind of feeling about them. As he expectantly awaited each successive click he felt a slight tension; after the anticipated click occurred he felt relief. This alternation between tension and relief was clearest when the clicks came at a slow rate. In addition to a pleasure-displeasure continuum, therefore, his feelings seemed to have a tension-relief dimension. But that was not all. When the rate of the clicks was increased, he said, he felt mildly excited; when the rate slowed, he had a quieting feeling. In this way, by patiently varying the speed of the metronome and carefully noting his subjective experience—his sensations and feelings—Wundt teased out three distinct and independent dimensions: agreeableness-disagreeableness, strain-relaxation, excitement-calm. Every conscious feeling, he said, can be located somewhere in three-dimensional space (see Figure 1).

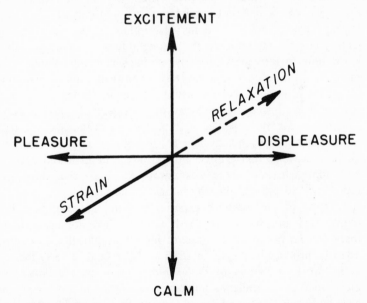

Fig. 1. Wundt's tri-dimensional theory of feeling. Every feeling is supposed to be located somewhere in this space.

This was the kind of introspective evidence on which he based his hotly disputed tri-dimensional theory of feeling. Emotions, he argued, are complex combinations or patterns of these elementary conscious feelings, and each elementary feeling can be completely described by stating its position along each one of three dimensions. History has dealt harshly with his effort to reduce emotions to conscious contents of the mind: emotions may involve feelings, people may be able to make judgments based on those feelings, but it is not possible to say that emotions are *nothing but* feelings. Wundt's analysis ignored the meaning of the situation in which the emotion is experienced.

Nevertheless, Wundt's introspections held a great fascination for his students. Who would have guessed that anything as familiar as one's own mind could harbor all these shadowy and unexpected elements? Who could guess what other pumpkins might turn into coaches when examined with the marvelous inner eye? Wundt's talent for making the perfectly familiar seem completely novel and mysterious—by stripping off its meaning and cutting it up in pieces—was the source of both his strength and his weakness as a psychologist.

Note how hard it is to disprove his claims. If your own introspections give you a different result, how can you decide who is right? Perhaps you misunderstood his description of his experience; perhaps you paid attention to the wrong things; perhaps you do not know how to introspect properly; perhaps you and Wundt are not made the same way; and so on. His experiments, unlike experiments elsewhere in science, do not insure agreement among all those who witness them. Introspective observation is essentially private, and disagreements cannot be settled by repeated observations.

But scientific psychology had to start somewhere. It was not obvious in advance that a direct attack on the mind would not be the best approach. And there was always the hope that introspective reports would parallel the physiological indicators.

In spite of his eccentric experimentalism, however, Wundt was a professor of philosophy. With scientific psychology flourishing, therefore, he began next to record his philosophical convictions. In 1880 he produced a *Logic,* in 1886 an *Ethic,* and in 1889 the crown of his work, a *System of Philosophy.* Today these massive monuments to Wundt's tireless scholarship hold little interest for psychologists and even less for philosophers. But that he could argue against the prevailing positivism and in favor of a greater emphasis on metaphysical problems in philosophy shows how far he had outgrown his student days. His conception of scientific metaphysics was simply a contradiction in terms to any good positivist.

It was during this time—his "philosophical decade"—that the first of a long string of students from America began to appear in Leipzig. Upon arrival they found themselves apprenticed to the perfect model of a German professor. At their first conference he would appear holding a list of research topics. Taking the students in the order in which they stood—there was no question of their being seated—he assigned one topic to each. He supervised their work on these topics most carefully; when the thesis was completed he held complete power of acceptance or rejection. If part of the work failed to support his theories, it might be instantly deleted. German scientific dogmatism was no myth, and it flourished undisguised in the little laboratory at Leipzig.

The last of Wundt's three lifetime projects was to create social psychology. This he did with characteristic industry in the ten volumes of his *Elements of Folk Psychology* which appeared during the last twenty years of his life. The concept of *Volk* which had gradually emerged during Germany's struggle for political unification now seemed ripe for psychological exploitation. Thus he moved even further away from positivism; in his view, the collective, social, folk mind transcended the individual minds that composed it. The folk mind manifested itself in languages, art, myths, social customs, law, and morals—cultural works that an individual never makes in isolation.

This opinion had an important implication, for it divided his science of psychology into two parts, the experimental and the social. According to Wundt, the simpler mental functions—sensation, perception, memory, simple feelings—can be studied by laboratory experiments on the minds of individuals. But the higher mental processes involved in human thinking are so strongly conditioned by linguistic habits, moral ideas, and ideological convictions that scientific experiments are impossible. Human thinking, he said, can be explored only by the nonexperimental methods of anthropology, sociology, and social psychology. Thinking cannot be understood through the analysis of logic, for it is too often illogical; and it is too complicated to be studied by simple introspection on the mental events that accompany it. Only by studying the *products* of thought as these have accumulated during man's history can we hope to understand thinking.

Wundt's observation that social products, especially language, play a central role in all of the more complicated mental processes of an educated, adult human being is both true and important. But the conclusion he based on this observation—that complicated mental processes cannot be studied experimentally—has not stood the test of time. Other psychologists have proved that experiments can be done on the so-called higher mental processes. The proof is the experiments themselves. It was necessary to burst through the rigid, introspective limits that Wundt had set for his new science, to devise new methods and invent new theories; this was done. Almost before it was properly born, therefore, scientific psychology began to evolve and to expand.

Wundt's genius was the kind Thomas Edison described—1 per cent inspiration and 99 per cent perspiration. One cannot help marveling at Wundt's energy and endurance over a period of sixty years. Yet it is his first achievement—the creation of a scientific, experimental psychology—that must command our greatest respect. His later work is now largely forgotten. His philosophy was undistinguished, and his social psychology came too late.

It was his experimental psychology, and his enormous scholarship, exhibited in three fat volumes, that made Wundt's influence felt. Where Mill only talked about doing psychological experiments, Wundt did them. He conducted them in a laboratory that he designed for the purpose, published them in his own journal, and tried to incorporate them into a systematic theory of the human mind. And he trained his students well; they founded more laboratories and continued to experiment. As a direct result of his labors, psychology was provided with all the trappings of a modern science. For that service, all psychologists, even those who bitterly opposed his theories, are permanently indebted to the indefatigable Wilhelm Wundt.

CHAPTER III

———————•————

LEVELS OF AWARENESS

Consciousness is a word worn smooth by a million tongues. Depending upon the figure of speech chosen it is a state of being, a substance, a process, a place, an epiphenomenon, an emergent aspect of matter, or the only true reality. Maybe we should ban the word for a decade or two until we can develop more precise terms for the several uses which "consciousness" now obscures. Despite all its faults, however, the term would be sorely missed; it refers to something immediately obvious and familiar to anyone capable of understanding a ban against it. Of course, some of our problems may arise from the fact that we must use consciousness to understand consciousness. Turning a tool on itself may be as futile as trying to soar off the ground by a tug at one's bootstraps. Perhaps we become confused because whenever we are thinking about consciousness, we are surrounded by it, and can only imagine what consciousness is *not*. The fish, someone has said, will be the last to discover water.

A psychologist's difficulties in formulating a definition for consciousness are similar to a biologist's difficulties in defining life. Although biology is the science of life, most biologists confess they do not know what life is. They are sure life is not a substance—not a material thing—but a process, or group of processes, that occurs in some things and not in others. And biologists agree with one another rather well about which things are alive and which are not. The defining properties of the system are the clue. There must be a steady

25

turnover of materials and energy, a process called metabolism; the system must be capable of reproducing itself; it must be capable of growing; and it must be capable of responding to energies in the world around it. Whenever all these properties are present, a biologist can be confident the system is living. On this planet, at least.

But, it may be asked, is life nothing more than a list of properties? Isn't something missing? As to this question biologists disagree. There is nothing more, some may say; for life is a process which emerges whenever a sufficiently complex chunk of matter is organized in a certain way. If one criticizes this use of the concept of emergence because it seems to sneak unscientific notions in through the back door, the biologist may argue that emergence is not something new and mysterious that he has just invented. Your lap emerges when you sit down; stand up and it goes away. The emergence of life in a system of properly organized molecules (which are not themselves alive) is no more mysterious than the emergence of a bridge game in a group of four properly idle people. According to this theory, one of the biologist's tasks is to study the conditions that must be satisfied before a physical system will exhibit this property and come to life.

But there are people who cannot accept such a theory of life. To them life is something more than a physico-chemical equation. What that something more may be, however, is itself a problem that provokes disagreement. Some say that life exists, just as matter exists, but it transcends any physical methods of isolation or examination. One could know everything there is to know about physics and chemistry, it is argued, and yet never suspect that life existed.

There are biologists who dislike a physico-chemical theory of life because it seems to reduce biology to a branch of physics. Other biologists wish to leave room for new discoveries whose nature cannot at present be imagined; only a fool claims to know everything. Some of those who object to an emergent materialism do so because they believe in the divine origin of life. And some of the nicest people object to materialism because it offends their personal dignity as living organisms. So crass a doctrine destroys all the poetic beauty of living things. What is missing from the scientific definition of life is life itself. But, of course, how many potential chemists have lost interest when they discovered that the formula for water was not wet?

A biologist's discussion of life can be compared to a psychologist's discussion of consciousness. Most psychologists confess they do not know what consciousness is. They are sure it is not a substance—a material thing—but a process, or group of processes, which occurs in some objects and not in others. And they can sometimes agree, though not nearly as well as the biologists, about which things are conscious and which are not. Their approach is to define the properties the system must have to qualify, and to search for them. But admittedly there is no consensus as to the defining characteristics.

What properties might be included? Should we require that a conscious system be able to perceive, to remember, to feel emotions, to think? These are excellent psychological processes, but they lead us directly to the question: What *use* do we expect to make of the list? Do we, for instance, expect to stand in front of a tree, or a computing machine, or a boulder, and ask if it is conscious? If so, we will have to ask about its perceptions, memories, feelings, and thoughts. To question these properties will raise more problems than it settles. If a poet believes that a river is conscious because it perceives a path downhill, because it remembers how to reach the sea, because it becomes angry during the spring floods and thinks long, solemn, majestic thoughts in summer, do you see any argument to dissuade him? How can we distinguish a metaphorical from a literal use of such words as perception, thought, feeling? And if we cannot foresee perfect agreement about so obvious a matter as the consciousness of a river, imagine the quarrel that will arise over the doubtful cases.

Possibly there are other properties easier to agree upon. For instance, should we insist that a system be alive before we will say it is conscious? That decision alone would settle many puzzling problems. It would, for instance, deny the existence of any divine Consciousness to watch over us. And, passing from the sublime to the ridiculous, a decision that only living organisms can be conscious would settle once and for all whether any computing machine, however clever, could be conscious. And we could say definitely that social groups have no collective consciousness. Indeed, if we took this step, we should then go on to the next and limit the domain of consciousness to living animals. It is unlikely that the study of botany would be impeded by a decision that all plants were lacking in consciousness. Consciousness seems to go along with mobility in living systems.

Further criteria could be considered. For instance, we might insist that a conscious system be one capable of reacting to its own reactions. A stone can react: kick it and it moves. But it does not make this movement the occasion for another reaction. A human being will do something and talk about it; his speech is a reaction to his own earlier behavior, and one usually accepts what he says as evidence that he was conscious of what he was doing. Of course, engineers can build clever electromechanical devices, called servomechanisms, which also respond to their own responses, so we should probably not make this our only criterion.

Another property that a conscious system should probably have is an ability to profit from experience, to learn and to remember. This requirement does not eliminate many members of the animal kingdom, however; so far as we know, they all can modify their behavior to some extent as a result of experience. And here, again, modern technology can produce many inorganic devices that remember. A magnetic tape recorder, for example, can remember the acoustic waves it hears far better than any human listener can.

We could continue in this way to accumulate recognizable properties to use in testing for the presence of consciousness. But notice something odd about them. Each seems to come back to processes or functions that can also be performed in various mechanical, electrical, or chemical ways.[1] As in the biological case, this argument seems to move toward a definition of consciousness in terms of an emergent property of sufficiently complex physico-chemical systems. It is all too easy to foresee the complaints that will arise—indeed, have already arisen repeatedly—when an intelligent layman is told that his consciousness is merely the side effect of a chemical reaction going on in his brain. The battles fought on this ground are too grisly to recall.

It should be plain, however, that psychologists are not as far along with consciousness as biologists are with life. We are still not sure whether we should say that an earthworm, or a cockroach, or a catfish, or a robin, or a cat, or a monkey is conscious. One feels intuitively that a paramecium is not conscious and that a chimpanzee probably is. But where along the branching experiments of evolution does consciousness intrude? The more one struggles with this question, the more clearly one recognizes that there is an important difference between a definition of life and a definition of consciousness.

A biologist can say that a system is alive or not alive. It is a form of hangman's humor to joke about being only a little bit dead. The case is not so open-and-shut when we talk about consciousness. It is more natural to admit to degrees of consciousness. A man is more conscious than a cat, perhaps, but the cat is more conscious than a frog, and so on. The proposition is not completely clear, but neither is it completely senseless.

Although a meaningful way to decide which of two animals is the more conscious is nowhere near at hand, some progress has been made in determining degrees of consciousness within a single individual from one moment to the next. Begin with the familiar fact that man, like many other animals, follows a daily cycle of sleeping and waking. Within every span of twenty-four hours we expect to find his state change from highly conscious to deeply unconscious. The sleep cycle is the most obvious change in behavior that we could ever hope to find. Consequently, there should be, and there are, many bodily changes that accompany these extreme swings in consciousness, bodily changes that we can measure and relate to a person's verbal report about his level of awareness. Thus the bodily changes, if selected judiciously, can give us indicators of the degree of consciousness at any moment.

One simple way to gauge the depth of sleep is to produce a sound that grows progressively louder until it wakes the sleeper. (The difference between normal sleep and a drugged state is that the person in normal sleep can always be roused by sufficiently intense stimulation.) The intensity needed to awaken him is then a measure of how deeply he slept. With this technique it is a simple matter to show that the depth of sleep fluctuates considerably during the night.

A more complicated technique is to take an electroencephalogram, a recording of the electrical activity in the brain. Fortunately, it is not necessary to make a hole in the sleeper's skull to accomplish this purpose. Electrodes placed on the scalp can pick up enough, with the help of special amplifiers, to record what is going on inside. These records of brain waves were first investigated by Hans Berger in 1929; since then thousands of technical papers have been published on the subject.[2]

Brain waves show periodic oscillations at various frequencies ranging from one cycle per second or even lower (the so-called delta waves) up to 45 or 50 cycles per second. These rhythmic waves tend to change in various ways according to what the person is doing. If a person relaxes with his eyes closed and lets his attention wander vacantly, alpha waves will usually occur—electrical fluctuations of about 0.00005 volts at a frequency around 10 cycles per second. But give him a problem to think about, or let him open his eyes, and the alpha waves disappear, to be replaced by the smaller, faster beta waves, which oscillate at 20 to 25 cycles per second. This is illustrated in Figure 2.

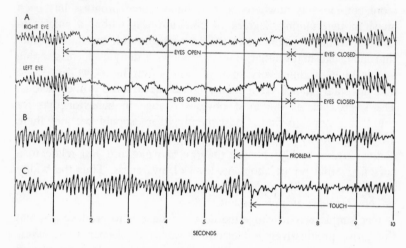

Fig. 2. Brain waves show the shift from alpha waves (about 10 per second) when the person is resting, to smaller, faster beta waves (A) when the eyes are open, (B) when solving a problem in mental arithmetic, or (C) when responding to other sensory stimuli. (From J. C. Eccles, The physiology of imagination, *Scientific American,* September, 1958.)

There are several theories about the source of brain waves. One line of speculation goes like this: In order to give waves large enough to be measured through the skull, a large portion of the brain must be linked together so that it is all active and inactive simultaneously. This synchrony only occurs when the brain is not disturbed by signals coming to it from the sense organs. Thus when the level of consciousness is low, as in resting or in sleep, we should find large, slow brain waves—as if the brain cells were marking time, waiting to be used. At higher levels of awareness, this pattern would break up, different parts of the brain would become involved in various activities with different characteristic rhythms, and the result would be smaller, faster brain waves. This line of argument seems to account for the gross phenomena that have been observed.

As a person falls asleep, his level of awareness goes through several successive stages; these can usually be recognized from an examination of the brain waves. As he becomes drowsy and his thoughts tend to drift, his brain waves begin to get slower. As he begins to doze lightly "sleep spindles" appear, short bursts of periodic waveform. As he sinks into deep sleep, his brain will produce large and slow delta waves. These various levels are illustrated in Figure 3.

There are many differences among individuals, and sometimes patterns of electrical activity occur which cannot be explained. But a beginning has been made. The brain waves enable us to assert with

EXCITED

RELAXED

DROWSY

ASLEEP

DEEP SLEEP

50 µv.

1 SEC

Fig. 3. Brain waves characteristic of the different stages along the continuum from excitement to deep sleep. (From H. H. Jasper, Electroencephalography, in W. Penfield and T. C. Erikson [eds.], *Epilepsy and Cerebral Localization.* Springfield, Ill.: Thomas, 1941.)

some conviction that a person who has been hypnotized is not asleep, because his brain waves do not show the sleeping pattern. They enable us to study the conditions under which dreams occur. And in addition to such special applications in psychology, the waves are an invaluable tool to the physician when disease or damage has interfered with the brain's normal functioning.

Dreaming is a particularly interesting phenomenon to study with these techniques. Is a person conscious or unconscious when he dreams? Common sense says that he is somewhere in between, conscious of the dream but unconscious of the world around him, and the evidence from brain waves tends to support this opinion. In the course of a night's sleep a person will fall rapidly into a very sound sleep for about an hour, and gradually become more active as the brain waves get more rapid. The sleeper will come close to waking and then slip back again into deeper sleep. These fluctuations in the depth of sleep take about ninety minutes, and they continue throughout the night. They are shown graphically in Figure 4. It is during periods of light sleep, when a person is most easily roused, that dreams will occur.

The occurrence of dreams can be detected easily by an observer.[3] A faint light on a dreamer's eyes will show that his eyeballs are moving rapidly to and fro, as though he were watching some scene which he "sees" projected on the inside of his eyelids. (These eye move-

Fig. 4. Episodes of dreaming alternate with periods of deeper sleep. This hypothetical function shows the depth of sleep as a function of the number of hours the person had been sleeping. On the average, episodes of dreaming last longer as the night wears on.

ments can also be detected and recorded with the same kind of electronic equipment used to record brain waves.) If the sleeper dreams of a tennis match, his eyes move back and forth from left to right. If he dreams that he is picking up basketballs and throwing them through a hoop over his head, his eyes move up and down. If he is watching some action near by, his eyes make large, irregular movements. At the same time that the eyes start to move, the pattern of the brain waves usually indicates lighter sleep; moreover, the sleeper's heart may begin to pound and he may begin to breathe more rapidly—common symptoms of an emotional experience. A person awakened during one of these periods of rapid eye movements is likely to have a dream to report; if he is awakened at other times, during deep sleep, he does not. When awakened from deep sleep, he is often bewildered. He may have any of a variety of emotions to report. He may be sure that he had been dreaming, but not be able to recall the dream. Or he may feel that he was not asleep at all. But he seldom reports dreams and those few that he does report are probably remembered from periods of dreaming earlier in the night. According to the objective evidence, everyone is a dreamer—but not everyone can recall his dreams.

Considerations such as these encourage psychologists to think of consciousness as more-or-less, rather than all-or-none. There is a gradual change of psychological state that runs from the deepest sleep up through dream states, quiet resting, perceptual awareness, symbolic manipulation, and finally to states of strong emotion. Corresponding to these psychological changes is a sequence of physiological changes that seem to correspond to increasing arousal, or activation, as shown by brain waves, muscular tension, hormonal activity, etc.[4]

Neurophysiologists who study the brain have located centers deep in the oldest part of it where sleep and wakefulness seem to be regulated. This part has been called the ascending reticular activating system. When this system is functioning, the brain waves become desynchronized, just as they do during states of conscious activity and attention. When the activating system is not functioning, however, information from the sense organs does not get relayed on to the higher centers in the cortex of the brain, and a state of sleep results. Exactly how the activating system works is a very complicated matter, but it is obviously important for controlling the level of activity everywhere in the nervous system. Beginning in the 1950's the discovery and exploration of these control systems quickly became one of the most exciting areas of research on the brain.

It is easier for us to sleep in dark, quiet, warm places because these conditions cause little excitation of the sense organs, and thus reduce the amount of nervous activity affecting the lower centers in the brain —a relative quiescence we have since childhood associated with falling asleep. When the activity of the lower centers is decreased and they no longer support the activity of the higher centers, the brain falls into the slow, rhythmic activity that is characteristic of brain waves during sleep. In order to remain awake and alert, therefore, it would seem that we need to have a great many things going on around us and affecting our perceptions in striking ways.

If we are going to stay alert, our environment must keep surprising us. The surprises may be small, but something at least mildly unexpected is needed to keep us on our toes. It is not enough merely to have energy falling on our eyes, ears, skin, or other receptors; the critical feature is that the pattern of those energies must keep changing in unforeseen ways. If one makes continuous physiological measurements of the brain waves, the pulse, the electrical resistance of the skin, and the like, it is possible to follow the fluctuations as a person drifts into lower levels of awareness or is suddenly jolted to attention. Physiological indicators show increasing habituation whenever the person can formulate some kind of expectation, some internal model for what is going on around him; arousal occurs when his internal model disagrees with external reality.[5] And in general the larger the disagreement, the larger the arousal.

At McGill University in Montreal, a group of psychologists under the leadership of D. O. Hebb tried to discover what would happen to people deprived of a normally varying sensory input.[6] The investigators paid college students to stay in a quiet cubicle on a comfortable bed for twenty-four hours a day. The students wore goggles that admitted light, but the light was diffused and they could not recognize any patterns. And they wore cardboard cuffs, extending beyond the fingertips, which permitted free movements of their joints but little tactual perception. Their plight is pictured in Figure 5. Students would stay for periods of two to six days before they quit and demanded to be let out. At regular intervals the psychologists would ask some questions over an intercommunication system and would give simple psychological tests.

Fig. 5. Experimental cubicle constructed to study the effects of perceptual isolation. The subject wears a plastic visor to limit his vision, cotton gloves and cardboard cuffs to restrict what he can touch, and hears only the noise of a fan and an air conditioner above him. Wires attached to his scalp make it possible to record his brain waves. Communication between the subject and the experimenter is possible over a system of microphones and loudspeakers. The room is always lighted and, except for brief intermissions to eat or go to the toilet, the subject lies on the bed twenty-four hours a day until he can stand it no longer. (From W. Heron, The pathology of boredom, *Scientific American*, January 1957.)

Different persons reacted in different ways, of course, but nobody really enjoyed being isolated. After a student had caught up on his sleep and thought—or tried to think—about some of his personal problems, the isolation became extremely boring.

The tests showed that as time wore on problems became harder to solve; the students reported that they were unable to concentrate. The most striking result was the occurrence of hallucinations. At first the symptoms were rather slight; when they closed their eyes they noticed that their visual field was light, not dark. After staying in the cubicle somewhat longer they began to see dots of light, lines, or simple geometrical patterns. Still later these developed into something like wallpaper patterns. Then came isolated objects, without backgrounds. And finally, for a few persons, there were integrated scenes usually containing dreamlike distortions. In general, the students were surprised by the hallucinations, which were a new experience for them. Then they were amused or interested to discover what they would see next. Later some of them complained that the vividness interfered with sleep. Auditory and bodily hallucinations also occurred, but were less frequent. When the students finally left the cubicle they were apt to be mildly confused and their intelligence test scores were temporarily lower.

These studies of the effects of reduced stimulation emphasize the dual role of sensory events. Our senses not only give us specific information about our environment, but they also have a nonspecific function in maintaining the normal waking organization of the brain. If we do not use our sensory systems for a period of time, they do not work as efficiently as they normally would. It is as though perception is a skill which begins to decline when not exercised.

The same changes in the brain waves which we have described for man have been found in other animals. In fact, it is probably easier to tell from a record of the brain waves whether an animal is awake or asleep than it is to tell whether it is a man or a monkey. One assumes that if the monkey's behavior and his bodily processes show the same pattern as man's, then the monkey must also go through the same daily cycles of sleep and waking, of consciousness and unconsciousness. We cannot be certain, for the monkey will not talk. On the other hand, so long as he does not talk, he will not contradict us. Since neither proof nor disproof is possible, one must appeal to other criteria, such as simplicity and consistency, to support the view that consciousness is not a uniquely human characteristic.

Granted certain assumptions, it may someday be possible to say something intelligible about the degree of consciousness achieved by different animals. Already there is much we can say about variations in the level of awareness in man. But even with the most delicate scientific instruments our observations are woefully coarse and indirect. We have been using the term "conscious" to describe a general state of an organism. A description of the consciousness of an alert human being that tells us no more than we can read from his brain waves must seem to an intelligent layman to be a rather poor joke. We know vastly more about our conscious minds than any electric meter can show. Recall the exquisite sensitivity with which Virginia Woolf or James Joyce display a human mind and you will appreciate the gap that exists. Even for our more limited scientific needs, however, the faithful description of a human consciousness requires techniques far more sophisticated than any we are likely to find in a physiological laboratory. We shall want to say, for example, that even when we are most highly conscious there is much going on in our minds that we are not directly aware of. In some sense not yet defined we are both conscious and unconscious at the same time. The oldest meter in the world cannot measure such a contradiction! Before we can understand these higher levels of consciousness, therefore, we will have to come at the problem again from a different direction.

———— ◆ ————

CHAPTER IV

THE SELECTIVE FUNCTION
OF CONSCIOUSNESS

Are there any obvious facts about consciousness, any propositions that every educated adult in our culture would have to accept?

A few, perhaps. No doubt everyone agrees that consciousness is filled with well-organized objects, events, and symbols; consciousness refers to things that exist outside itself. Everyone agrees that the content of consciousness changes from one moment to the next. And we all must agree that we cannot think about everything at once. Everyone would probably agree that changes in consciousness are continuous; there is no succession of discrete photographs, but a stream that flows from one state of consciousness to the next. Probably we would agree also that consciousness is filled with relations; we continually judge the good-or-bad, the more-or-less, the before-or-after of one particular conscious object in terms of, or relative to, other objects.

Such statements merely list things that intelligent people already understand and that stupid people will never be interested in. However, of all these simple statements, and many others that might be added, there is one that stands out as being central to the psychologist's task: *Consciousness is selective.* We are constantly swimming through oceans of information, far more than we could ever notice and understand; without some effective way to select what is important, we would surely drown.

No one has described the selective function of consciousness more eloquently than William James in his famous chapter on "The Stream of Thought." The following summary paragraph is still worth careful reading:

> Looking back, then, over this review, we see that the mind is at every stage a theatre of simultaneous possibilities. Consciousness consists in the comparison of these with each other, the selection of some, and the suppression of the rest by the reinforcing and inhibiting agency of attention. The highest and most elaborated mental products are filtered from the data chosen by the faculty next beneath, out of the mass offered by the faculty below that, which mass in turn was sifted from a still larger amount of yet simpler material, and so on. The mind, in short, works on the data it receives very much as a sculptor works on his block of stone. In a sense the statue stood there from eternity. But there were a thousand different ones beside it, and the sculptor alone is to thank for having extricated this one from the rest. Just so the world of each of us, howsoever different our several views of it may be, all lay embedded in the primordial chaos of sensations, which gave the mere *matter* to the thought of all of us indifferently. We may, if we like, by our reasonings unwind things back to that black and jointless continuity of space and moving clouds of swarming atoms which science calls the only real world. But all the while the world *we* feel and live in will be that which our ancestors and we, by slowly cumulative strokes of choice, have extricated out of this, like sculptors, by simply rejecting certain portions of the given stuff. Other sculptors, other statues from the same stone! Other minds, other worlds from the same monotonous and inexpressive chaos! My world is but one in a million alike embedded, alike real to those who may abstract them. How different must be the worlds in the consciousness of ant, cuttlefish, or crab![1]

Phrases such as these should roll forward majestically into a lecture hall of thousands of upturned faces, hushed and waiting. They are too large in their conception for a scientist's laboratory, too spacious in their style for a scholar's study. How could anyone more forcefully express his conviction that consciousness is at all times primarily a *selecting* agency? It selects not only what we do, but how we see, as well. Could a listener doubt he had heard the Truth?

Of course, there are always cynics—suspicious people who charge that eloquence flourishes where the evidence is weakest. If you select one world and your friend selects another, they say, there must be some meaningful consequence; you must bump into each other, or have violent arguments, or be mutually invisible, or *something*. How do we get a scientific grip on James's ideas and force them to lead us toward some outcome, some measurement?

To critics who will settle for nothing short of proof, there is little to say. But for those willing to consider examples, there are many at hand. The dots in Figure 6 will group and regroup themselves, shifting as we move our eyes about from point to point. Or look up at the stars on a clear night and try to imagine how men came to see there Aries the Ram, Taurus the Bull, Gemini the Twins, and all the other zodiacal constellations that encircle the sky; try to imagine how many

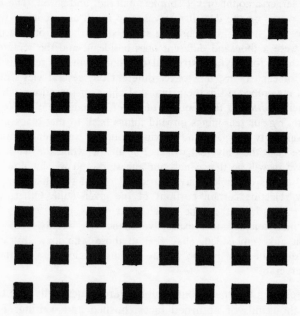

Fig. 6. A regular grid of dots can show a variety of patterns.

alternative organizations might have been selected from the same monotonous and inexpressive chaos. Or drop ink onto paper haphazardly, then fold the paper to produce a symmetrical design. You will recognize many familiar objects in the ink blot, and your friends will recognize different ones. Twenty years after James wrote about the selective nature of consciousness, the Swiss psychiatrist Herman

Rorschach recognized that the choices people make when they recognize things in such patterns reflect significant aspects of personality; the result was his famous ink-blot test.[2] It is an example of a *projective test,* so-called because the person unwittingly projects himself into his perception of the environment. James said that all perceptions are, at some stage in our development, similarly selected from an assortment of alternative perceptions we might have had instead.

An inkblot of the sort used by Rorschach.

Rhythm provides an illustration of James's thesis. Some of the earliest scientific observations reported from the first laboratory of experimental psychology—the laboratory founded by Wundt at the University of Leipzig—concerned the perception of rhythmic patterns.[3] In order to reproduce those early experiments we require an accurate metronome. If the metronome is constructed correctly, every click will be the same as every other click, and every interval between clicks will be the same duration as every other interval.

A metronome generates a steady train of clicks, yet no one hears it as a steady train; the listener imposes a rhythmic pattern of his own choosing, in common time, triple time, or whatever he prefers. Two different listeners can be exposed to exactly the same steady train of acoustic pulses, yet hear them in entirely different patterns. The consequence of imposing a rhythmic organization is to make some clicks sound louder than others and to make some intervals sound longer than others, although we know such impressions are illusory. In William James's metaphor, a rhythmic pattern is the psychological sculpture that we carve as we will from the indifferent clicks of the clock.

We can make several different observations of our conscious selection of a pattern for these clicks, but we need a collaborator. One person should control the metronome (he is the *experimenter*), and the other person should be free to concentrate on his perception of the clicks (he is the *subject* in the experiment). With two persons, try the following test: The experimenter sets the metronome going at a medium rate, say, one click a second or a little slower, and lets it run for, say, exactly ten separate clicks. Then after a short pause he lets it run again for exactly the same number of clicks, or for one more or one less. A subject who listens attentively to these two strings of clicks will recognize immediately whether they were the same. It is not a matter of counting the clicks as they occur; the recognition of the pattern is direct and immediate. It is similar to the visual difference between a triangle and a square; the distinction can be drawn immediately, without counting the sides. Or, to put the point differently, the two strings of clicks are perceived as complete wholes, and one whole is compared with the other. (It should be noted, however, that the rate is important. If the metronome is too slow, the pattern falls apart. If it is too fast, no rhythm is perceived.)

The space we call "here" and the time we call "now" are not infinitesimal, like mathematical points. They have extension, they cover a span in space and in time. The size of that span is an important feature of consciousness. How much we include in here-now is not a question we can refer to experts on physical space and time; it is determined by the way our minds work, by the limitations of our own consciousness. The psychologist must find his own method to measure the size of the clear focus of consciousness that we call our attention.

We can use a metronome to estimate the temporal duration of here-now. Phrase the matter in terms of clicks: How many clicks of a metronome can a subject hold together in consciousness? The answer depends on the speed of the clicks and also on the way the clicks are rhythmically grouped. The early German psychologists (who tried it with clicks coming about once a second) found that when they grouped the clicks by pairs:

click-click—*click*-click—*click*-click—*click*-click,

the maximum number they could hold in mind at once was sixteen, or eight pairs of clicks. However, if they adopted a more complicated rhythmic pattern:

CLICK-click—*click*-click—*CLICK*-click—*click*-click,

they could appreciate a total of forty clicks at one time before the pattern broke apart. With the complicated pattern, one rhythmic chunk consists of eight clicks, and five of these chunks can be grasped in consciousness at once. The additional span—forty instead of sixteen—is attributable to the more complicated rhythm, which in turn was achieved by having four intensities of emphasis. (A curious fact reported by Wundt and his students was that they were unable to differentiate more than four grades of emphasis.)

Other exercises are possible with a metronome, but we have seen enough to demonstrate the point. Consciousness is free, within limits, to select whatever pattern you like. While one is listening to waltz time, a neighbor can hear the same clicks in march time. This depends on what one selects through the "reinforcing and inhibiting agency of attention."

William James was not thinking merely of rhythmic patterns. Clicks are just one way to illustrate the selections we must make in order to maintain a conscious organization of the world around us. As a matter of fact, James disliked this example, since the clicks of a metronome are so discrete and independent. He preferred to describe consciousness as a stream that flows continuously, not as a succession of discrete ideas or sensations. Even so, the clicks exemplify James's thesis that everything in your consciousness must have a pattern and a meaning that are peculiarly your own. In William James's theory, the selection of that pattern is the central task of consciousness.

Now we introduced the metronome in order to conciliate the cautious critics who felt that if James was talking about anything real, this reality must make an observable difference in the way the world runs. If we have saved James from their wrath, however, we have done it by offering an even better target. Any self-respecting cynic should now be eager to attack, not James, but Wundt! "How in the name of science can anyone refer to such shenanigans as an *experiment!*" The critic is red in the face; suppose we listen to his complaints.

"In the first place," he assails Professor Wundt, "how can you say that eight pairs, or five octuplets, or any other aggregates set a limit to consciousness? When I listen I am uncertain as to the exact instant my conscious whole breaks down; it doesn't break so much as crumble and fade away. Perhaps you were counting unconsciously. Am I supposed to accept your work just because you are a famous professor? Suppose I summon up all the prestige I can muster and use it to tell the next subject that his limit will be just half of what you claim. Will he dare to contradict me? Is your result so clear and inevitable that we can rule out any possible distortions caused by the suggestibility of the subject? There is no way to check on the subject, to decide whether he is fooling us, and himself as well. If you admit his subjective reports as if they were scientific evidence, you will have no criterion left whereby to exclude prejudice, authority, or revelation. You would undermine the very foundations of modern science!"

Our critic is here launching into a familiar argument, so we need not record his hoarse shouts in every indignant detail. At the heart of the problem lies the privacy of the experience that Wundt reports; the experience is something to which he claims special, immediate, personal, privileged access. But no one has ever built anything scientific out of private experience. Science has achieved its remarkable success only because it has insisted inflexibly that it must be public, impersonal, explicit, symbolic. Reports of private, subjective experiences—even when carefully controlled in the manner prescribed by Wundt—provide no basis for sure agreement. The clicks of the metronome are relatively innocent, but in more interesting and only slightly more complex situations the introspective reports obtained from subjects in different laboratories simply do not agree. Introspectors have a notorious talent for finding in their minds almost anything they look for. Even Wundt's own students, all trained to introspect in the same way in the same laboratory, frequently disagreed with each other and with the master.

This situation became so disturbing, as a matter of fact, that such men as I. P. Pavlov in Russia and J. B. Watson in the United States attracted much favorable attention and support when they claimed that consciousness does not exist; that if it does exist, one cannot make a science out of it; and that if one could, it would have to be a science of behavior, not of consciousness. The persistence of such mentalistic confusion is due, they said, to the lack of an adequate physiology of the brain. The assault upon Wundt's introspective method was so successful that even today, half a century later, some psychologists feel slightly sinful when they permit themselves to refer to the mind, consciousness, attention, sensation, etc. Consciousness may exist, in some metaphorical sense of existence, yet it has no effect upon the physiological processes in the body. Can a shadow carry stones?

But this is only one line our critic can take. There are others. He might ask Professor Wundt, "What about differences among people? Surely you cannot believe that everyone will give the same report. What of those people—most Africans, musicians generally and tympanists in particular—who spend years of loving study on beautifully intricate and complex rhythmic patterns? Or, at the other extreme, what about young children or animals? Are they not different from a dignified and elderly *Gelehrter?* How elastic are the limits? How does the ability to organize rhythmic patterns vary as a function of other things?" One doubts whether Wundt considered these questions; if so, they did not interest him. It remained for Francis Galton in England, James McKeen Cattell in the United States, Alfred Binet in France, and many other psychologists all over the world to discover and develop the importance of individual differences.

Finally, a critic always has recourse to the devastating question, "So what? Suppose all you say is true. Even suppose it is true for everybody, everywhere. What then? What of poetry and work, of love and death and beauty? What of everything that really matters? The dust on your metronome, *Herr Professor,* is six feet deep. While we yearn to understand the deep, throbbing forces that drive us headlong through our modern jungles, you sit at your metronome counting clicks. It is better to count the leaves on trees, for then at least you get fresh air and exercise for your pains."

Critics who reject the significance of Wundt's observations may reject psychology completely—at best, they turn from Wundt to seek a psychology more directly relevant to their own lives. They may be curious about the phenomena of their personal consciousness, yet feel that to reduce those phenomena to the status of metronome clicks is a preposterous distortion. These were the rebels who found Henri Bergson in France, Sigmund Freud in Austria, and Carl Jung in Switzerland such a welcome relief.

These criticisms of Wundt suggest some of the directions taken by modern psychologists. For the moment, however, it is important to establish that, in spite of all the objections, the observations reported by Wundt were essentially correct.

Attention is not some superstitious fiction; its effects can be demonstrated by physiological techniques every bit as objective and scientific as any used by Pavlov or Watson. For example, it is possible to record the electrical activity of the auditory nerve of a cat. If one presents repeated clicks to a relaxed and drowsy cat, one can record repeated pulses of neural activity in the cat's ear. But now distract the cat's attention. Let the cat smell the odor of fish, or let it glimpse mice constrained in a glass beaker. Once the cat begins to pay active attention to what its nose or its eyes are reporting, the neural pulses from its ear almost completely disappear. When the acoustic clicks become irrelevant the cat seems not to respond to them in any way. The central mechanism of attention is so powerful and effective that when one kind of information has been selected, the other receptor organs are simply turned off.[4]

Moreover, rhythmic grouping is a universal fact about people; all cultures have some form of rhythmic performance such as music or dancing. Of course, there are individual differences, but for the average adult in our culture, the numerical values given by Wundt for the conscious span are approximately correct. There are several ways to measure such spans, some more objective than others, but all give similar results. As a matter of fact, Wundt was aware of other possible methods; he himself cites them in support of his studies with the metronome.

Consider some of the possible methods. Suppose we ask subjects to sit in a darkened room where they can watch a projection screen. On the screen we flash briefly a picture of round, black dots against a white background. The number of dots can vary from two or three up to a hundred or more. The pattern of the dots is always different, always haphazard. The exposure time for the random pattern of dots will be of the order of a tenth of a second, long enough for a clear view of the pattern but too short for subjects to move their eyes to a second fixation point in the pattern. (The device used for producing these brief exposures is called a tachistoscope.) On the basis of one short glance a subject must guess how many dots there were in the pattern.

Up to five dots, perhaps six, subjects are never in doubt and almost never wrong. They do not need to count the separate dots; they see the number directly. For seven or more dots, however, subjects begin to make mistakes; the larger the number of dots, the bigger their errors are likely to be. There is a sharp break in their performance, a break that occurs in the neighborhood of six dots.[5] This value, six, can be taken as a measure of the span of attention. It should be compared with the five to eight rhythmic chunks Wundt reported when listening to clicks of a metronome. It can also be compared with the six positions for the points that are used in Braille printing for the blind. Six points are as many as the blind person can recognize accurately by touch. Since the values for visual dots, auditory clicks, and tactual points are all so similar, one argues that it is not the sense organs—eye, ear, or skin—that set the limit. Instead, the limitation is imposed centrally, at a point in the nervous system where all the different senses converge to pass through the same bottleneck. It is, so the argument goes, our attention, not our sense organs, that is limited.

Another way to measure the momentary capacity of consciousness is to ask a subject to repeat something he has just heard or just read. This task is frequently included on tests of intelligence. The tester says, "Listen to the following numbers, and when I am through repeat them back in the same order." He then gives two numbers. If the subject repeats them both, in the right order, the examiner goes on to three, then to four, to five, and so on, until the subject begins to make mistakes. The number of digits he can, on the average, repeat perfectly after one presentation is his span of immediate memory. The test is not diagnostic for superior adults; a very long span of immediate memory is not a reliable indication of superior intelligence. However, an unusually short span, two or three digits only, is a fairly reliable indication of mental deficit. As a rough figure, people of average intelligence can repeat six or seven digits without error. Note that this value is once more in the range we have learned to expect.

The span of immediate memory is not greatly affected by the kind of symbols we use to test it. If we ask a subject to repeat letters of the alphabet, we again find that he makes mistakes when there are more than about six or seven. Indeed, if we use short words taken at random from the dictionary, his span will be about five. This last result is particularly interesting, since the five words will be composed of some fifteen or twenty letters. That is to say, when the letters do not spell anything, but are chosen at random and so must be recalled individually, we can hold six or seven in mind at once, but if the letters spell words, we can recall three times as many. The situation is analogous to the rhythmic groups of the metronome, where the number of clicks that could be held together varied from sixteen to forty depending upon the way they were grouped.

How grouping helps to increase the amount of information that we can keep in mind at any instant can be explored as follows: Ask a generous and cooperative friend to let you test his span of immediate memory. First test him with ordinary digits, as above. Then test him with haphazard sequences of two words, "yes" and "no." The span for the average person is about eight or nine of these binary items. For example,

no, no, no, yes, no, yes, yes, no, no

is as far as most people can go before they become confused and fail to remember accurately.

Now teach your friend the following code:

no-no-no	= 0	yes-no-no	= 4
no-no-yes	= 1	yes-no-yes	= 5
no-yes-no	= 2	yes-yes-no	= 6
no-yes-yes	= 3	yes-yes-yes	= 7

Make him practice it for thirty minutes. When he can snap it out quite automatically, test his span again. This time, however, instruct him to group the words into triplets as he listens to them, to recode the triplets as numbers, and to remember the number. When the time comes to recite he should simply translate back again from numbers into words. This new procedure, which requires the subject to group the items, turns the sample sequence given above into "no-no-no," "yes-no-yes," and "yes-no-no," which in turn is recorded as 054. The number 054 is easily remembered. In fact, we already know how many digits he can remember, and since each digit is worth three "yes" answers or "no" answers, we can predict how long a sequence of "yes" answers and "no" answers he will now be able to reproduce. A typical result is to increase his span from eight or nine up to twenty-one or twenty-four binary items.[6]

This trick of recoding one set of symbols into another is used by computing engineers. They must examine long rows of small lights which may be on or off according to the internal state of the computing machine. It is difficult to remember a pattern of lights if each light is regarded as a separate item of information. Therefore, people who work around the machines quickly memorize a little code, similar to the one given here, which enables them to group the lights and so to remember many more of them at one time.

Grouping clicks of the metronome into rhythmic feet, grouping letters of the alphabet into words, grouping rows of lights into coded triplets, share the feature that they enable us to make better use of our span of consciousness, to hold more information in mind at one time. This same economy works in our favor when we express our experiences in words and then remember the words, rather than the raw experience itself. We insulate ourselves from the world around us by a curtain of language. The reward is a greater efficiency in dealing with patterns, with organized parts of the world. It is the language we speak more than anything else we do, that represents the particular sculpture we have carved out of "the primordial chaos of sensations."

Notice that the selective function of consciousness and the limited span of attention are complementary ways of talking about the same thing. If there were no limits on the variety of information that we could contemplate simultaneously, there would be little cause to talk about selectivity. The fact that our minds are limited, critically limited to a minuscule allotment of seven psychological units at a time, forces us to use each symbol as effectively as possible. When a problem is too complex to fit into a man's consciousness, various elements of the problem must convene and elect symbols to represent them. And if there are still too many component parts, the elected symbols must themselves group together and elect more symbols to represent them at a still higher level in the hierarchy. Because consciousness is limited, we must consolidate and symbolize. How we choose to consolidate and symbolize is our style of selection, our way of comprehending this segment of our universe.

Cartoon of POGO, by Walt Kelly

When we look at a picture of an unfamiliar landscape or a group of people we usually feel that we grasp it in consciousness as a whole, as a unified experience. Yet when we must answer questions about it, we are chagrined to discover that we did not see much after all. If we have only a single, brief glance, we will not be able to name more than about five or ten things that were in the picture. We may, for example, correctly recall that there was a horse in the picture, yet have no notion whether it was facing to the right or to the left.

But what if we have a prolonged look and can move our eyes over the entire scene? As we scan the picture our eyes do not glide smoothly along, but jump rapidly from one fixed position to the next. Sudden changes in the point of fixation can be recorded by special cameras, and it has been found that we make about three or four fixations per second when viewing a complex picture. A finite period of time is required in order to stop paying attention to one part of a picture and to start paying attention to another.

Some interesting records of eye movements have been made by Russian psychologists; two examples are shown in Figure 7. A. L. Yarbus recorded a person's eye movements while looking at pictures. Yarbus made the records by reflecting a beam of light from one eyeball onto sensitized paper; since the eyeball is not a perfect sphere, each movement altered the angle of reflection. His records show that normal eye movements tend to trace out the outlines of the scene being viewed. The picture of the young girl is almost redrawn by the viewer's eyes; the major details of the forest scene are clearly revealed. Each discontinuity in the recorded trace indicates a place where the person's eyes paused briefly to inspect the picture. The continuous lines show the very swift movements between resting points. Russian psychologists have used such records to diagnose effects of brain injuries; unlike the normal records shown here, the records produced by patients with brain damage may be irregular and show little relation to the contours of the picture.

Records of eye movements show clearly that the unified, integrated experience we get when we look at a scene is something we must actively construct out of dozens of short, quick snapshots aimed at different parts of it. Our attention shifts rapidly from one point to another until gradually we become familiar with all the parts and the relations among them.

Fig. 7. Records of eye movements show which parts of a picture receive the most attention. (From *New York Times,* April 24, 1960.)

William James, in the passage that has guided our discussion of consciousness and attention, pointed out that attention both selects and suppresses; attention is both a reinforcing and an inhibiting agency. If you choose one line of thought, you necessarily reject others. If you remember one episode, you are not remembering other episodes. The collection of symbols and feelings that are potentially available to consciousness, but that are temporarily unconscious, form part of what is usually called the preconscious mind. These momentarily rejected but potentially conscious ideas prove that we cannot identify mind with consciousness. The contents of the preconscious system are both mental and nonconscious, so we are forced to recognize that there is more to the mind than meets the inner eye.

A crude example, recommended only by its simplicity, is provided by our friend who, a few pages back, learned to group and recode sequences of "yes" and "no." In the particular sequence given as an example, he would be conscious that the three triplets, "no-no-no," "yes-no-yes," and "yes-no-no" occurred. But he would not be aware that "no-no-yes" also occurred. When he recalls the sequence correctly, of course, he will necessarily say "no, no, yes," as part of it, but if we ask him whether or not he said "no, no, yes," he cannot be certain until he has repeated the sequence with a new orientation toward it. Until he has done this, he is not aware of what he said. We should not make a mystery of the phenomenon; the particular triplet occurs out of step with the grouping he used. He was not thinking about the grouping in these terms.

One can say, with James and many other psychologists, that the ideas and the organizations that a person chooses will actively *suppress* his awareness of other ideas and other organizations. But we should remember that this is a figure of speech. We are not required to conjure up some vigilant demon who actively shoves things downward out of sight. Suppression is accomplished more subtly, as a necessary consequence of the fact that attention is limited and selective. When repressive demons seem to be at work, we have passed beyond the normal processes of preconscious thought into the darker regions of the unconscious mind.

Processes of preconscious organization and selection are critically important in creative thinking. Somehow, by free association or by the confluence of many simultaneous streams of thought, preconscious processes enable us to leap to intuitive conclusions that we are able to verify or disprove consciously only after slow, tedious, step-by-step argument and deduction. "Preconscious mentation," a psychiatrist has said, "is the Seven-league Boot of intuitive creative functions."[7]

What determines how the preconscious will work, what contents and patterns it will present to consciousness, how much freedom or constraint it will enjoy? Rigorous answers cannot be given. One supposes that what we pay attention to—the middle-sized things that populate the center of our minds—are in large measure determined by the way we are built, both genetically and habitually. We pay attention to sudden noises or unexpected flashes of light because we are born with reflex reactions to such stimuli; we group the sounds of speech in certain ways because we have learned to speak and understand the language they represent. But over and beyond those relatively stable patterns of selection and organization there still remains, even in the sophisticated adult, an area of freedom where personal needs, interests, motivations are allowed to act.

An advertising man, after spending more than a billion dollars of his client's money to find out what makes people notice something, concluded that we allocate our attention to different categories of information according to how important we judge them to be. There is a limit to what we are willing to notice and remember about tires, tobacco, or toothpaste; advertisers compete for their share of the very small amount we care to know about their type of product. The advertising man developed this view of an average consumer: "It is as though he carries a small box in his head for a given product category. The box is limited either by his inability to remember or his lack of interest. It is filled with miscellaneous data, and, when a new campaign forces in more, some data are forced out, and the box spills over."[8] An effective advertisement may increase an advertiser's share of the box, but it will not increase the size of the box itself. The size of each box is a basic parameter of the preconscious system, one not likely to be much affected by bright colors and catchy tunes.

It is probably worth making a distinction between preconscious *contents*—symbols and feelings that could be conscious but momentarily are not—and preconscious processes—operations and transformations that seem to be necessarily unconscious. Thinking is a good example of a preconscious process. The fact that the process of thinking has no possible access into consciousness may seem surprising at first, but it can be verified quite simply. At this moment, as you are now reading, try to think of your mother's maiden name.

What happened? What was your conscious awareness of the process that produced the name? Most persons report they had feelings of tension, of strain unrelated to the task, and then suddenly the answer was there in full consciousness. There may have been a fleeting image or two, but they were irrelevant. Consciousness gives no clue as to where the answer comes from; the processes that produce it are unconscious. It is *result* of thinking, not the process of thinking, that appears spontaneously in consciousness.[9]

Look across the room at a chair.

Did you see it as a chair? Or did you see it as a mosaic of isolated sensations that had to be consciously welded into a coherent perception?

The fact that the perceptual object was so immediately present in consciousness implies that the many operations you had to perform upon the visual information were all unconscious. Helmholtz noticed this more than a century ago when he spoke of the unconscious inferences or unconscious conclusions that are always involved in perception. Of course, the average person ordinarily remains ignorant of all the work he does when he recognizes a chair. In order to convince him, we must ask him to describe a machine that would recognize objects the same way he does. Then he begins to appreciate what a complicated process must be operating.

What is true of thinking and of perceiving is true in general. We can state it as a general rule: No activity of mind is ever conscious. In particular, the mental activities involved in our desires and emotions are never conscious. Only the end products of these motivational processes ever become known to us directly. The impulses behind our actions can only be inferred from their conscious and behavioral consequences.

Take dreams as an example. Dreams can provide a highly imaginative, sometimes truly creative synthesis of the events of the day, of remembered episodes, personal associations, desires, passions. The synthesis is often cleverly contrived, as you will discover if you attempt to decipher some of your own dreams. In order to interpret them, the basic assumption you must make is that nothing in your dreams occurs accidentally. Everything can be explained in terms of your personal history. Often—but not always—the events and people that occur in your dreams do not mean what they seem to mean on the surface, but turn out on closer analysis to stand as symbols for something else, usually something less pleasant for you to contemplate. Whether the dream symbols are introduced to disguise a disturbing idea or whether they represent the same kind of psychological processes involved in slang or figures of speech is still a matter for argument. But the point is that dream episodes are fabricated by a kind of thinking whose end product appears spontaneously, surprisingly, during sleep. "The interpretation of dreams," said Sigmund Freud, "is the royal road to a knowledge of the unconscious activities of mind."

Then there is hypnosis. Under hypnosis a subject temporarily allows another person, the hypnotist or operator, to plan for him, to manage his thoughts and images. During this period the operator may tell the subject that after he returns to normal he will do something without remembering why. The commonest demonstration is posthypnotic amnesia; a subject is told that he will remember nothing that went on during the time he was hypnotized. Thereafter the subject's unwillingness to explore this part of his memory is similar to the avoidance of unpleasant, painful facts by normal, unhypnotized persons. These avoided ideas are kept out of consciousness. But they can return when the proper signal is given, or when the proper occasion occurs for them to take effect. Thus a hypnotist may tell the subject to trip and stumble accidentally against the first bald man he sees after he awakens. The awakened subject has no reportable memory of this instruction, he behaves quite naturally in every way; but when the signal—the bald man—appears, the subject stumbles against him, apologizes, and goes on unaware that his stumbling was not accidental.

Hypnotists should always make clear to a subject when the suggestion will be completed. Even if it is not acted upon, the hypnotist cannot assume that it was ignored. In any case, he must cancel it, terminate it. The sort of difficulties that can arise are illustrated in this story:[10] A hypnotist attempted to produce a blister on the right forearm of a young woman by suggesting to her that he was applying a piece of red-hot metal to it. The suggestion apparently had no effect, and the hypnotist went on to other things, forgetting to cancel the blister-producing idea. The patient went home, but re-

turned several days later suffering from a burn on her right forearm
where a blister had formed on the very spot previously chosen by
the hypnotist. The patient had no memory of the suggestion. She
had "accidentally" spilled scalding water on her arm when lifting
a pot with her left hand to make coffee. The accident finally termi-
nated a suggestion that the hypnotist thought had been completely
ineffectual. Similar stories can be adduced by any experienced hypnotist.

Still another source of evidence is the fact that life is full of accidents that can not possibly be wholly accidental, but seem to be
determined by causes unknown to the actor. The posthypnotic accidents just mentioned illustrate the mechanism whereby such events
can occur, but hypnotism is not a necessary precondition. Sigmund
Freud filled a book, *The Psychopathology of Everyday Life,* with
examples of the forgotten name, the mispronounced word, the inadvertently broken promise, the misplaced wedding ring, the unexpectedly favorable (but unfortunately inaccurate) balance in the
bank account, and so on, all normal occurrences with definite and
discoverable causes that the person did not consciously recognize.
The motives often revealed by these little slips are so widely recognized today that the "Freudian slip" has become an established fact
even in lay psychology. Not every slip requires a Freudian explanation, but many do.

These are but a few of the reasons for believing that a person
cannot be conscious of all his mental processes. Many other reasons
can be cited: Drugs are known that relax some people and put them
into a state in which they can recall emotionally disturbing episodes
that they cannot recall under normal circumstances. Physiological
measurements reveal the occurrence of emotional responses to particular events, emotions that have no representation in the person's
conscious experience. And so on and on.

I have described these mental operations as preconscious; they
influence conscious contents and reflect the person's efforts to cope
with his environment. Medical psychologists, however, recognize
another kind of nonconscious process, more rigid, more compulsive,
more maladaptive. These are unconscious mechanisms. They manifest themselves most clearly in the abnormal behavior of neurotic
and psychotic patients—unfortunate persons no longer able to lead
productive lives. Difficulty with the selective and organizing functions

of consciousness is a common symptom of neurosis. Sometimes emotionally disturbing ideas are stubbornly rejected; at other times they break through and interrupt every effort at concentration. Thus the neurotic unconscious seems to block the normal flow of preconscious processes. Unconscious processes typically have their own dynamism, independent of the situation in which the person finds himself; they are wounds that never healed, losses never mitigated, remnants of the ancient battles of childhood. These are realms explored by psychoanalysis.

It was not very long ago—less than a century—that mind and consciousness were regarded as one and the same. As soon as one begins to examine consciousness, however, one realizes that it is selective, that there is a preconscious system of rejected options. But only in the twentieth century have we begun to appreciate how vast this nonconscious region is, how much we rely on the intuitive leaps of preconscious thought, how crippled we can be by the scars of unconscious wounds.

Our ideas about nonconscious mental activities are still open for debate and revision. Some psychologists split the questions up one way, some another. But most psychologists who have tried to peer beyond consciousness know well that they can find in this elastic concept almost anything they want. The preconscious and the unconscious are repositories for all the processes that psychologists assume *must* exist to explain what people do. Some psychologists assume that the nonconscious contains a seething mass of passion and desire. Or it is full of instincts, or habits, or all the tacit mental functions that are performable, not knowable. But, whatever else may be hidden in these dark recesses, one can be sure there will always be room left for the psychologist's theories. For it is only through theory, never through direct awareness, that one discovers the nonconscious mind.

Two passengers leaned against the ship's rail and stared at the sea. "There sure is a lot of water in the ocean," said one. "Yes," answered his friend, "and we've only seen the top of it."

CHAPTER V

WILLIAM JAMES, PHILOSOPHER

"The modern movement known as pragmatism," wrote Ralph Barton Perry, "is largely the result of James's misunderstanding of Peirce." It is one of the rare passages in his distinguished biography, *The Thought and Character of William James,* where Perry seems less than fair to his hero. James understood quite well how his life-long friend, Charles S. Peirce, defined pragmatism. But James imposed a personal stamp on his friend's invention. A more accurate summation, perhaps, is that Peirce provided a tool that James used in ways Peirce could not accept. And so it happened that pragmatism, the most characteristic philosophic expression of the American mind, was born with two heads.

Three, really, if we count John Dewey's. According to Morton White, "Peirce is the pragmatic philosopher of science, James the pragmatic philosopher of religion, and Dewey the pragmatic philosopher of morals." But White adds a warning that, "It is not always the same pragmatism that they apply to these different problems."[1] What the three philosophers had in common was not so much a specific set of doctrines as an attitude of mind, a general way of defining and attacking problems. In details they could hardly be expected to agree—three more different personalities than the eccentric, creative, sometimes deliberately obscure Peirce, the urbane, eloquent, almost evangelistic James, and the systematic, discursive, democratic, but often dull Dewey can scarcely be imagined. That they could tolerate one another was a tribute to their common vocation.

The name and the doctrine of pragmatism first saw light in the early 1870's when Peirce explained his ideas to "The Metaphysical Club," a group that included Peirce, James, Wendell Holmes, Chauncey Wright and several other defiant, young intellectuals around Harvard at the time. Peirce published his argument in 1878 in one of his least obscure papers, "How to Make Our Ideas Clear." His original, careful but cumbrous statement of the pragmatic rule for attaining clarity was: "Consider what effects, which might conceivably have practical bearings, we conceive the object of our conception to have. Then, our conception of these effects is the whole of our conception of the object." "Practical bearings" are the crucial words. What, for example, is electricity? According to Peirce, our whole conception of electricity is our conception of the practical effects of electricity.

As Peirce formulated pragmatism, it was a method of getting at the meanings of our ideas. To discover the meaning of a statement, one must translate it into a hypothesis to the effect that if such-and-such an operation is performed, such-and-such experiences will ensue. The meaning of the statement, "John is six feet tall," becomes clear when we translate it into the hypothesis, "If you count the number of times a foot rule can be placed end-to-end between the floor and the top of his head when he is standing erect, you will find that the result is six."

Peirce's approach to meaning contrasts sharply with the traditional approach of British empiricists. In the eighteenth century Bishop Berkeley, for example, held that the meaning of any statement is the mental image we form of it. The meaning of "John" is the image of John. The meaning of "John is six feet tall" is the image of John tucked into an image of the six-foot span. The image theory of meaning involved British empiricists in absurd difficulties. For example, what is the meaning of triangle? It is your mental image of a triangle. But your image must be an image of a particular triangle—isosceles, equilateral, scalene, right-angled, obtuse—whereas the meaning of triangle in general is all and none of these simultaneously. Therefore, said Berkeley, it is impossible to have an abstract idea! It was this sort of nonsense Peirce explicitly and emphatically denied. The meaning of triangle is contained in the hypothesis, "If one examines the sides one discovers there are three, intersecting, straight lines," and in the hypothesis, "If one counts the number of angles, one sees that there are three," and in the hypothesis, "If one adds up the number of degrees in the angles, one sees that there are 180 degrees," and so forth. Whether or not an abstract image can be found in the furniture of the mind is entirely irrelevant, said the pragmatic Peirce, to the meaningfulness of the concept. In 1878 the mind was still being analyzed into elementary sensations, images, and feelings by Berkeley's intellectual descendents; Peirce's contribution to logic was therefore potentially of considerable significance for psychology.

Without William James, however, it is unlikely that Peirce's pragmatism could have affected psychology for another fifty years or so. It would probably have remained, like so many of Peirce's creative insights, buried in obscurity, awaiting exhumation by the patient editors who compiled and published many of his papers in 1930, sixteen years after his death. But James appreciated Peirce's concept, transformed it, assimilated it into his own thinking, and made it part of the large and motley assortment of ideas he accepted in his philosophic vision of a pluralistic universe. Where Peirce was often obscure—sometimes even deliberately obscure—James was brilliantly clear and interesting, with a gift of apt metaphor seldom equalled in science or literature. And so the pragmatic thesis was spread abroad in the most persuasive manner possible. It was so persuasive, in fact, that Peirce scarcely recognized that James's version derived from his own. To make the distinction explicit, Peirce renamed his own views "pragmaticism," which he hoped would be "ugly enough to be safe from kidnapers."

In 1907, James, in a book entitled *Pragmatism,* applied Peirce's maxim to the concept of truth. What is the meaning of a statement such as " 'John is six feet tall' is true"? Does it mean anything more than "John is six feet tall"? Following Peirce's advice, one tries to translate the statement into a hypothesis: If one performs such-and-such operations, such-and-such experiences will ensue. But how can this translation be made? There seem to be no reasonable operations that one can perform to test whether "*P* is true" is meaningful. Does that mean that "true" is meaningless by pragmatic standards? James argued that it was necessary to generalize the notion of an operation; not merely physical operations, but psychological operations must be permitted. To tell someone, "*P* is true," is to tell him that he can believe it. Still, this is only half the hypothesis: "If you believe *P,* then . . . ." Then what? What experiences should result from believing *P* if *P* is indeed true? Surely nothing evil or unfortunate can result from believing the truth. The complete hypothesis, therefore, must be *"P* is true" means "If you believe *P,* the effects will be satisfactory to you."

So long as the proposition *P* involved "John is six feet tall" or other correspondingly testable propositions, little harm could come from translating *"P* is true" in the way James advocated. But what if *P* were some such proposition as "There is a God"? This was exactly the class of statements James was most interested in, and his pragmatic formulation of truth enabled him to reintroduce into philosophy problems that the positivistic and materialistic thinkers of the nineteenth century had long since rejected. James argued that "There is a God" is true if, when one believes it, the results are satisfactory. Although he made the argument in erudite and subtle terms, the message that came through to the philosophically unsophisticated public who heard him was: "Anything is true if it works." To European ears this sounded as if the raw, backwoods Americans were trying to rationalize their preoccupation with material objects and financial profits or, at best, as if a new form of anti-intellectualism had taken root in the United States. A major trouble with James's theory of truth—a difficulty Peirce recognized immediately—was that the operation of believing and the consequence of satisfaction are personal, subjective, individualistic, whereas the customary definition of truth is public. James insisted that the truth he was talking about was a truth for the individual. Peirce insisted that the truth science requires is interpersonal. A scientific proposition is not simultaneously true for those who believe it and false for those who do not—it is either true or false, and one group or the other must be wrong. Of course, Peirce was not in favor of an idealistic Absolute Truth; but James's alternative was so completely relative that it seemed to Peirce a fatal mistake.

If Peirce invented pragmatism and James popularized it, John Dewey applied it—that is, he applied pragmatism to social problems in general and to education in particular. In Dewey's hands, the new philosophy emphasized experimental approaches to all problems, logical and ethical as well as scientific. He began with a biological conception of man, the conception of an organism trying to adapt to, or come to terms with, its environment. When difficulties are encountered it becomes necessary for the organism to stop and think.

An emphasis on the instrumental nature of thought was one of Dewey's most characteristic contributions to the pragmatic tradition; his own version of pragmatism he called instrumentalism. In this biological orientation Dewey remained close to the views James expressed in *The Principles of Psychology*. In his pragmatism, however, Dewey seemed to favor Peirce. Dewey's interest in social processes, for example, made him agree with Peirce that truth must be publicly, socially determined, not set by the whim of an individual.

Whereas Peirce had said that operational thinking is necessary to discover the meaning of any scientific conception, Dewey argued that operational thinking is necessary to judge the *value* of any thing or activity. A thing is not valuable merely because one happens to enjoy it; in order to assign value to it, one must conduct carefully controlled experiments, just as a scientist would conduct experiments to determine its meaning. Evaluations are a form of empirical knowledge, not essentially different from other forms of knowledge, which must be constructed by operational and experiential techniques.

Dewey's pragmatic theory of value made him a philosopher of morals—and it was this interest in moral issues that spurred him to lead the growing movement to reform the American school system.[2] The schools Dewey had known as a boy were kept, not taught, by untrained appointees of the local politicians. Discipline was maintained by physical force. Children sat silently with their hands folded on top of their desks and listened to teacher. Occasionally they would be called to recite a lesson by rote, but no questions were tolerated. No one knew what subjects could or should be taught. The only principle that guided the choice of topics was the implicit assumption that they must not be related to the child's world outside of the schoolroom—the purpose of education was to make a child appreciate a set of cultural products entirely alien to his own life.

When Dewey began his attack on this principle he did so from an urgent conviction that what is most important in education is its moral purpose. Discipline, natural development, culture, social efficiency are moral traits—marks of a person who is a worthy member of the society that education is designed to further. Dewey wanted the schools to instill in children the best of American ideals. Unfortunately, the American ideal of the good mixer somehow became dominant over the American ideal of individualism; intellectual excellence became second in importance to life adjustment. In Dewey's own lifetime "Learning by doing" had degenerated into an empty slogan and progressive education passed into scornful disrepute.

From 1896, when he opened his first experimental school at the University of Chicago, until his death in 1952, John Dewey was the foremost spokesman for progressive education; he saw it as a race between intelligence and catastrophe. Although he has often been criticized irresponsibly by people who have not read his books or understood his ideas, we should remember that it was John Dewey more than any other single individual who gave the United States a public school system intelligently planned to support a democratic government. If progressive education was a failure, the fault was not one of conception, but of execution.

The significance of these philosophical innovations for the development of psychology in America appeared first in the formation of the Chicago school of philosophy and psychology. As philosophers, the members of the Chicago school were known as pragmatists; as psychologists, they were *functionalists*. Although James through his writings provided much of the inspiration, it was Dewey who directly instigated the work of the functional psychologists. On the psychological scene at that time their principal competitor was the Wundtian experimental psychology imported from Leipzig. Whereas the Wundtians attempted to analyze the structure of the mind, the American psychologists, under the influence of evolutionism and pragmatism, directed most of their attention to its functions.

Dewey's instrumentalism asserted that the function of the mind is to guide behavior. While structuralists focused exclusively on the mind as the proper subject of psychological study, functionalists permitted the mind to share the spotlight with its "practical effect," with the behavior that resulted from mental processes.

The consequences of this shift in emphasis were important. One consequence was that functionalism could readily absorb studies of animal behavior as a part of psychology; the studies of cats in a puzzle box that E. L. Thorndike (1898) conducted at Columbia, the studies at Johns Hopkins by H. S. Jennings (1897) on adaptive processes in protozoa, R. M. Yerkes's (1907) investigations at Harvard of the dancing mouse, W. S. Small's (1900) studies of the rat in a maze at Clark, J. B. Watson's (1907) work at Chicago on

the somesthetic cues in maze learning by rats—these were but a few
of many experimental studies of animal behavior that accorded with
functionalism, but were of little interest to psychologists who, following Wundt, had made introspection the indispensable tool of their
science.

By broadening the definition of psychology, the American functionalists were able to incorporate studies of animals, of children, of
the mentally retarded and the insane, and of primitive, preliterate
peoples. And they were able to supplement introspection by other
methods of collecting data; physiological experiments, mental tests,
questionnaires, and descriptions of behavior all became legitimate
sources of information in the study of psychological processes. By
the time of Wundt's death in 1920 the purely introspective, experimental science he had founded in Leipzig was merely a small part
of, and had been overshadowed by, the larger and more pragmatic
American science of psychology. Ten years later the victory of the
functional psychologists was complete. In the U.S. today functional
psychology *is* psychology.

The liberating effects of enlarging the science of mental life to
include a science of behavior were so striking that some workers
tried to jettison the mind entirely and to define psychology as the
study of behavior, pure and simple. This possibility had been latent
for several years before John B. Watson opened his campaign for
behaviorism in 1913. If Watson had not been so inept as a philosopher, he might have offered behaviorism as a pragmatic theory of
mind, comparable to Peirce's pragmatic theory of meaning, James's
pragmatic theory of truth, and Dewey's pragmatic theory of value.
The mind—the other chap's mind, at any rate—is something whose
existence is inferred entirely from the behavior we observe. "John is
conscious" must be translated into the hypothesis, "If I call to John,
he will answer," or, "If I stand in John's way, he will detour around
me," and so on. In short, if I present him with such-and-such stimuli, he will make such-and-such responses. To paraphrase Peirce,
"Consider what effects, which might conceivably have practical
bearings, we conceive the mind to have. Then, our conception of
these effects is the whole of our conception of the mind."

Watson did not put his argument in these terms; what he said,
instead, is that the aim of behavioristic psychology is to be able,
given the stimulus, to predict the response; or, to put it another way,

to be able on seeing the reaction take place, to define the stimulus that produced the reaction. Thus he emphasized the simple fact that everything we do consists ultimately of the motion of material objects from one place to another. No introspective inferences about any mysterious mind-stuff were required. Mental phenomena were reduced to the behavioral evidence from which they were inferred: sensation and perception were reduced to discriminative responses; learning and memory to conditioning and maintaining stimulus-response connections; thinking to talking and problem solving; motivation and value to choice behavior; emotion to activity of the autonomic nervous system, glands, and smooth muscles. Everything intangible was simply replaced by its most tangible manifestation. During the 1920's behaviorism became one of the major influences on psychological thought in the United States.

Behaviorism was not James's idea of psychology, and it is ironic that his pragmatic philosophy proved so hospitable to these materialistic ideas. Of course, James often spoke of behavior in a very modern sense, especially when he wrote about education and the formation of habits, but his outstanding gift as a psychologist lay in a very different realm. His sensitivity to the subtle nuances of his own conscious life and his ability to communicate what he experienced through electric metaphors in beautiful prose are unrivaled among scientific psychologists. A psychology without consciousness is a psychology without need for James's greatest talent.

William James was born in 1842 in New York, the first of five children. Second born was Henry, the novelist; third, Garth Wilkinson; fourth, Robertson; and last, Alice, who was only six years younger than William.

Their father, Henry James, Sr., was wealthy enough to live on his income, which left him the leisure to write tracts on Swedenborg and to be a devoted parent. He organized his family into one of the most high-spirited and exclusive debating clubs in all history; the atmosphere he created for them was vividly recalled by Edward Emerson:

> "The adipose and affectionate Wilkie," as his father called him, would say something and be instantly corrected or disputed by the little cock-sparrow Bob, the youngest, but good-naturedly defend his statement, and then, Henry (Junior) would emerge from his silence in

defence of Wilkie. Then Bob would be more impertinently insistent, and Mr. James would advance as moderator, and William, the eldest, join in. The voice of the moderator presently would be drowned by the combatants and he soon came down vigorously into the arena, and when, in the excited argument, the dinner knives might not be absent from eagerly gesticulating hands, dear Mrs. James, more conventional, but bright as well as motherly, would look at me, laughingly reassuring, saying, "Don't be disturbed, Edward; they won't stab each other. This is usual when the boys come home."[3]

It would be difficult to devise a better way to learn to think for one-self, or to learn that intellectual combat need not interfere with personal affection. Even when the children grew up their debate continued. Throughout their lives they wrote frequent, voluminous, fascinating letters that—fortunately for the many biographers attracted to this amazing family—they were wise enough to preserve for posterity.[4] Few families remain so close so long.

The schooling of this precocious brood seems to have been a series of accidents. Until he was nine William passed from one governess to another; then he started to school, but after he had tried several, his parents decided that American schools were not good enough, and in 1855 the family set off for Europe. For five years they traveled like a pack of intellectual gypsies through England, Switzerland, France, and Germany while the children absorbed the languages and any other aspects of European culture that took their fancy. Whatever else might be said for it, this unconventional program of studies left William anything but the backwoods American barbarian that his critics later assumed him to be. William James was literally a man of the world, and throughout his life he was, through reading, correspondence, and frequent journeys abroad, in constant contact with the best that England and the Continent could offer. The overseas voyages were in large part the result of a unique Jamesian formula; when someone in the family became ill he was sent not to a hospital, but to Europe. Since their health was seldom good, the Jameses all became great travelers.

In 1860 William announced that he was going to be an artist. His father was not a little grieved, for he had always counted on a scientific career for Willy. But he believed in liberty, so he agreed to take his family back to America and to William Morris Hunt. As the younger Henry expressed it, "We went home to learn to paint."

Fortunately, the vocational experiment was a complete success, and the autumn of 1861 found William a student of chemistry in the Lawrence Scientific School at Harvard. His teacher was Professor Charles William Eliot, who a few years later was to become Harvard's president. In later years Eliot recalled William as a very interesting and agreeable pupil, but not wholly devoted to the study of chemistry. He was inclined toward "unsystematic excursions" in unpredictable directions—his personal notebooks during those years ranged over the whole field of literature, history, science, and philosophy. After two years of chemistry, he decided that his interests lay more in the direction of natural history, and so, with the notion of coupling this with a possible medical career, he entered the Harvard Medical School.

A pencil-drawn self-portrait by William James, about 1866.

Except for his work under the saintly Jeffries Wyman, medical studies did not please William James. His first impressions were that there is a great deal of humbug in the practice of medicine. "With the exception of surgery, in which something positive is sometimes accomplished," he commented in a letter to his cousin, "a doctor does more by the moral effect of his presence on the patient and family, than by anything else. He also extracts money from them."

He kept at it, however, until the spring of 1865, when he took a year off to join the Thayer Expedition to Brazil. He saw the expedition up the Amazon as an opportunity to work with the famous Swiss-American zoologist, Agassiz, and to try out yet another possible career, biology. Once again the vocational experiment was instructive, and long before the expedition was over he knew that a life filled with careful collecting and orderly classifying was not for him. Somewhat reluctantly, he resumed medical studies. The subject was no more attractive to him than when he began it—indeed, he rather dreaded the prospect of becoming a doctor—but until he discovered something else that really would attract him as a career, there seemed no alternative to the medical school. His next choice would have to be the right one; his two previous mistakes were already more than he felt he should allow himself.

Not all choices are deliberate, however. James's future was shaped by ill health. Insomnia, digestive disorders, eye troubles, a weak back, and deep depressions combined to produce a new interruption of his medical studies. It was obvious to everyone that he was suffering from America; Europe was the only cure. In 1867 he went to Dresden and Berlin, where he took baths for his back, read widely in German and other literature, toyed with thoughts of suicide, displayed his loneliness and homesickness by the tremendous volume of his correspondence, and remained just as miserable as he had been at home. After a sojourn of almost two years he returned to Cambridge, took up his medical courses once again, and in the spring of 1869 received his degree. His M.D. was the only academic degree he ever acquired by passing the necessary examinations.

His spirits continued their steady decline, and the spring of 1870 found him in the deepest melancholy. His will to live was at its lowest ebb. He was in a fundamental spiritual crisis, paralyzed by a sense of moral impotence, soul-sick (as he realized) for lack of a philosophy to live by. By now positivism repelled him. It was in these dark months that he began to build his philosophy, not as an intellectual exercise, but as a desperate measure he could not avoid if he wanted to stay alive.

The turning point came when he discovered a number of essays on free will by Charles Renouvier. Renouvier convinced him that the activities of the mind have causal effects on the body—a possibility that the materialistic physiology of the day wholly rejected—and that these activities can be controlled by deliberate choice. "My first act of free will," he recorded in his diary at the time he first read Renouvier, "shall be to believe in free will." From then on James's philosophy was identified with his personal convictions. And his first conviction was that he must believe in the efficacy of the will, believe that by sheer belief he could cure himself.

His gospel of belief was a cheerful success. No one knows what cures mental illness; approximately two out of every three cases recover regardless of the therapy, or even, as in his case, without therapy. But whatever the reason, he was convinced that his personal difficulties had been relieved by philosophic insight, and the insight involved a new conception of freedom. Renouvier was perhaps the greatest individual influence on the development of James's thought, and with that help he slowly fought his way back to health and full activity once more.

By 1872 he was well enough to accept Eliot's offer of a teaching position—he agreed to teach physiology to the undergraduates in Harvard College. He proved to be a satisfactory teacher and having a job to do turned him away from further morbid self-examination. In 1875-76 he offered a course on "The Relations between Physiology and Psychology" which marked the first American introduction of the new, experimental psychology. The undergraduate version of that course, offered in the following year, was known as the "new Spencer elective," since it used as a text the 1200-page *Synthetic Philosophy* of Herbert Spencer. He was able to extract $300 from the Harvard Treasurer for use in purchasing laboratory and demonstrational equipment for the course, a munificence bestowed during the same year that Wundt established an informal demonstrational laboratory in Leipzig.

James had moved from pure physiology and anatomy into physiological psychology and, because psychology was at that time the responsibility of the Department of Philosophy, James's professorship was in philosophy, rather than physiology. Thus he continued his slow but inevitable migration away from medicine through physiology and psychology to philosophy.

In 1878, the year of his marriage, James agreed to write a text on psychology for Henry Holt & Co. He felt he could finish it in two years but, as a matter of fact, the composition of the book took twelve—and Holt waited. The manuscript grew in close connection with the author's classroom instruction, and an animated, polemical style was a natural result. The chapter on "Habit" is an excellent example, one that has been reprinted repeatedly in anthologies. It is, in fact, a lay sermon:

—Habit simplifies the movements required to achieve a given result, makes them more accurate and diminishes fatigue.

—Habit is the enormous flywheel of society, its most precious conservative agent. It alone is what keeps us all within the bounds of ordinance, and saves the children of fortune from the envious uprisings of the poor.

—In most of us, by the age of thirty, the character has set like plaster, and will never soften again.

—The great thing, in all education, is to make our nervous system our ally instead of our enemy. We must make automatic and habitual, as early as possible, as many useful actions as we can.

—In the acquisition of a new habit, or the leaving off of an old one, we must take care to launch ourselves with as strong and decided an initiative as possible. Never suffer an exception to occur until the new habit is securely rooted in your life.

—Seize the very first possible opportunity to act on every resolution you make, and on every emotional prompting you may experience in the direction of the habits you aspire to gain.

—Keep the faculty of effort alive in you by a little gratuitous exercise every day.

The chapter is full of wise advice to the young student. Of course, one might ask what manner of science this is. On what experiments did he base his generalizations? What scientifically controlled observations did he make? What laboratory procedures did he use to test his hypotheses? The answer would be, none whatsoever. James's psychology, at its best, came from his own sharp observations of the life around him. He approved of experimentation, he studied it and fostered it, but he did not do it himself. Yet in spite of its personal origins in his own experience, the chapter on habit is still read with profit by every new generation of students— although today it is assigned more often for courses in literature than in psychology.

In 1882, within a span of ten months, he lost both of his parents. In a family group so closely knit their deaths were profoundly felt, and it might have been expected that William would not easily withstand the emotional strain. Although his letters express his personal feelings, one searches through his work almost in vain for the effects of his bereavement. He had learned how to live with his feelings, how to rise above grief as well as depression, but one can speculate that it was not easy. In 1884 he published an article, "What is an Emotion?" that must have been conceived during his deepest grief and prepared for publication in the following year. It gives us some hint of the device he had discovered. "There is," he wrote, "no more valuable precept in moral education than this, as all who have experience know: if we wish to conquer undesirable emotional tendencies in ourselves, we must assiduously, and in the first instance cold-bloodedly, go through the *outward motions* of those contrary dispositions we prefer to cultivate."[5] If we act cheerful and kindly, those emotions will replace the depressions and sullenness we wish to be rid of. It is an application of the principle he had learned from Renouvier; we can will to believe what we should believe.

When the *Principles* appeared in 1890, the chapter on "The Emotions" continued this same line of thought. He had discovered in the meanwhile an article by the Danish physiologist C. Lange which agreed with his own views, and the theory has been known ever since as the *James-Lange theory of emotion*. The essence of it is captured in the following famous paragraph:

> Our natural way of thinking about these coarser emotions is that the mental perception of some fact excites the mental affection called the emotion, and that this latter state of mind gives rise to the bodily expression. My theory, on the contrary, is that *the bodily changes follow directly the perception of the exciting fact, and that our feeling of the same changes as they occur* is *the emotion*. Common-sense says, we lose our fortune, are sorry and weep; we meet a bear, are frightened and run; we are insulted by a rival, are angry and strike. The hypothesis here to be defended says that this order of sequence is incorrect, that the one mental state is not immediately induced by the other, that the bodily manifestations must first be interposed between, and that the more rational statement is that we feel sorry because we cry, angry because we strike, afraid because we tremble.[6]

In meeting his personal problem, he believed he could control his emotions by voluntarily initiating the bodily manifestations appropriate to them. For the scientific problem, the point was that he had proposed a physiological process associated with emotion, a proposal that could be tested experimentally in the laboratory. It was almost forty years before anyone proposed a better theory.

Even more deeply involved in the development of James's thinking, however, was a chapter in the *Principles* entitled "The Stream of Thought." That, too, started life as an article, "On Some Omissions of Introspective Psychology," published in the same journal and during the same year as the article on emotion.[7] The use of the term "omissions" in the title of the article indicates that James had found something in his own consciousness that his less observant predecessors had overlooked; the use of the term "stream" in the later title of the chapter indicates that the omission he had detected was of the fluid, fleeting, transient phases of consciousness that serve to link successive states in an on-going flow.

William James

British empiricists usually described their minds as if their consciousness were filled by a sequence of discrete, independent pictures flashed on some inner screen, each still and motionless, each connected to the next by some mechanical trick of association. Nothing could have seemed more artificial to James, who likened consciousness to a bird's life, made of an alternation of flights and perchings. This was his famous distinction between substantive and transitive parts of the stream of thought. The resting places are occupied by sensory images; the path of flight is filled with relations between the matters contemplated during the periods of rest. Previous introspective psychologists had failed to respect the transitive states—this was the omission he charged them with, the implications of which he went on to develop in detail.

His persistent concern with relations among conscious elements led him directly to the puzzling psychological question of the *self*. In every person's stream of consciousness there is a dichotomy between the *me* and the *not-me;* at the same time it is *I* who am aware of this dichotomy. With characteristic sensitivity to his inner life, James divided the self into *I* the knower and *me* the known. The *me* is simply an object like any object we might be conscious of, although it is obviously of supreme interest. It is the *I*, the active sense of personal identity, that poses the real puzzle. In associationistic psychology the self was somehow compounded of ideas, each separate, each ignorant of its mates, but sticking together and calling each other up according to certain laws. Such an account might suffice to explain the empirical *me*, but it was obviously inadequate to the judging *I*. The *I* that knows its own ideas cannot itself be one of those ideas. In addition to the ideas that are known, therefore, there must be an active ego that knows them, relates them in the stream of consciousness, and is the source of whatever unity and organization they possess.

His attempt to expand the contents of consciousness to include more than had hitherto been suspected—to include the relations among the elements and, therefore, the self as the necessary source of those relations—was in many ways characteristic of him. For one thing, it indicates the importance he set on experience as the source of our knowledge; he was above all an empiricist, a philosopher of experience, even though he did not fall into the narrower empiricism of his British predecessors. For another, it shows how he was able to open up, enlarge and enrich the content of psychology; he was forever expecting to find something more, something new and unexpected, and he tried to leave his theories open toward the future and the abundance it would bring. It demonstrates his sensitivity to mental subtleties and his ability to capture experience *sui generis* and to communicate it to another person. And it exhibits once again his eloquence, unfettered by pedestrian facts from the laboratory.

In 1904 James, by then a full-time philosopher, developed his empiricism one step further. "Everything real," he wrote, "must be experienceable somewhere, and every kind of thing experienced must somewhere be real."[8] In this "radical empiricism" he tried to redefine experience in a way that made it even broader than conscious experience, tried to categorize subjectivity in the mental sense and objectivity in the physical sense as particular modes of experience in his pure, phenomenal sense. His final philosophic step, in his pluralistic universe, was to identify experience with metaphysical reality. These philosophical adventures, although more important to his thinking than, say, his pragmatism, have not had the same degree of influence on subsequent generations of psychologists. But they are indicative of his continual effort to broaden the scope of his empiricism, to leave room for more than he could clearly see a need for at the moment. It was this attitude that made his psychology an ideal vehicle for a growing science that sought to include more and more phenomena within its scope.

After the fourteen hundred pages of the *Principles* had been published in 1890 he felt he had said all he knew about psychology and that he would turn to philosophy. He wanted someone else to take on the responsibility for psychology at Harvard. About this time Wundt viciously attacked a young psychologist named Hugo Münsterberg; in James's eyes no higher praise was possible. Harvard brought Münsterberg from Germany to teach the courses in psychology, and freed James for his work as a philosopher.

In 1892 James revised the two volumes of the *Principles* into the profitable "Briefer Version"—known to several generations of students as "Jimmy"—and he wrote some articles and reviews, but his major contributions to psychology seemed to have been made. His notes during the next few years were not without considerable interest, however. For example, in 1894 he was the first American to call attention to the work of Breuer and Freud.[9] But, to every psychologist's regret, it appeared that psychology was merely a bridge over which James intended to pass from medicine to philosophy, and that the *Principles* was to be his only payment for the privilege of passage.

But then in 1902 he published *The Varieties of Religious Experience*. It was a magnificent re-entry into the psychological arena—this time into a part of it that later psychologists were to call clinical psychology. *The Varieties* was written for his Gifford Lectures delivered in Edinburgh in 1901-1902. It was in part an act of filial piety—he wanted to understand a little more the value and meaning of religion in the sense his father had experienced it. And it was in part a working out of his own experiences; his crisis of 1870 was used to illustrate the state of the sick soul, and his personal "salvation" gave him a conception of the religious experience of being reborn. But in the main it was an expression of the psychological interests he had continued to pursue during the 1890's; interests in the exceptional mental states that characterize psychic experiences, mob violence, hypnosis, psychopathology. He was convinced that the real backbone of the world's religious life was not the carefully argued systems of theology, but a mass of concrete experience— voices, visions, responses to prayer, conversations with the unseen, changes of heart, deliverances from fear. And he was convinced that religion is something more primordial than reason but of equal authority, something intellectuals could omit from their theories of psychology only by distorting their conception of the nature of man.

Although psychiatrists and clinical psychologists have continued to be interested in the morbid mental states that he described in *The Varieties,* they have not made much use of his suggestion that faith can operate as a healing agent. A conversion experience can be a kind of cure, a source of change in the personality structure of the individual. The records of miracle cures attributed to religious faith are well documented. Every doctor has seen patients cured by placebos—sugar pills whose only healing powers derive from the patient's faith in the doctor and the science he represents.[10] Such cures are usually dismissed as the product of suggestibility, the implication being either that the patient was not really sick to begin with, or that he is not really cured after all, or that if he was sick and is cured, then some hocus-pocus occurred.

Although James continued to carry on a full load of lecturing and writing, his health was never good. *The Varieties of Religious Experience* was largely written in bed, where he was recovering from a grim, thirteen-hour scramble, when he was lost in the Adirondack Mountains. The ordeal aggravated a valvular lesion of his heart, and recovery was slow and not complete. The condition grew progressively more serious during the succeeding years and was eventually responsible for his death in 1910.

It is much easier to appreciate William James than to evaluate him. If one points to the thousands of students who read his books, to the inspiration he provided for Dewey and the functional psychologists at Chicago and Columbia, to the sensitivity with which he exposed to view a rich world of inner experience, to the intelligence of his arguments and the beauty of his prose, it is obvious that he was, and still is, the foremost American psychologist.

Yet there is another side, and many psychologists have pointed to it. James was really more of an artist than a scientist, a man who would not enter the laboratory and who disliked the paraphernalia of the careful experimenter. He paid no attention to the embryonic development of mental testing or to the early uses of statistical techniques in analyzing psychological data; he was far too much of an individualist ever to summarize a person by an integer. He had no interest in many of the developments that his own work made possible, and even his clinical pursuits were cast in a strangely unscientific context of religious belief. He is an immortal, a classic, a literary psychologist, a dim figure from the dusty past—yet, according to his critics, he is no longer a moving force on the current scene.

Perhaps the critics are right, but they are not wholly convincing. There are still those who read James for pleasure, who derive strength from him, and find in him still an impulse toward greater freedom. "Neither the whole of truth nor the whole of good is revealed to any single observer," he once said, "although each observer gains a partial superiority of insight from the peculiar position in which he stands." A partial superiority of insight is all he would have claimed for himself.

Fortunately, the final evaluation of William James as a scientist can wait for a time—his value as a wise and profoundly human being should suffice to keep his memory fresh for many years to come.

CHAPTER VI

---◆---

SUBJECTIVE YARDSTICKS

A great scientist, Lord Kelvin, once said, "When you cannot measure . . . your knowledge is of a meager and unsatisfactory kind." He was, of course, a physicist. You can be sure he was not a mathematician; mathematics is often regarded as a science, even as the Queen of the Sciences, yet it demands no skill for making measurements. Nor could he have been a logician, a botanist, a linguist, a psychoanalyst—there is a long list of creditable sciences that do not rely on measurements. But in physics the art of measurement is both elegant and essential. It would be difficult to imagine physical science shorn of clocks, balances, and meter sticks.

It is a bit ironic that Kelvin's proclamation is better known among social scientists than among natural scientists. Social science has always been a little defensive about its status, a little sensitive about its claim to be scientific. So when a great physicist announces that measurement is the key to scientific knowledge he is apt to receive more attention than he deserves. In truth, a good case could be made that if your knowledge is meager and unsatisfactory, the last thing in the world you should do is to make measurements. The chance is negligible that you will measure the right things accidentally. Nevertheless, many social and behavioral scientists, assured that measurement is the touchstone of scientific respectability, have rushed out to seek numbers before they knew what the numbers would mean.

Psychologists are by now reasonably well recovered from such

feelings of professional inferiority, but there are still a few who believe that good measurement is the highest mark of good science,
that deeper understanding lies always in the direction of greater
precision. One can still find psychologists making extravagantly
precise and elaborate measurements just to demonstrate how thoroughly scientific a psychologist can be. Some people will not admit
that if a thing is hardly worth doing, it is hardly worth doing well.

The worship of measurement for its own sake is not, to be sure,
a majority view. More common, but equally wrongheaded, is the
opposite opinion that measurement violates the dignity of man, that
numbers bruise the human spirit. At this extreme there seems to be
a fear that the paraphernalia of science will block our view of one
another and clutter our channels of direct, intuitive understanding.

Wisdom, as usual, lies somewhere between compulsion and re-
vulsion. The first sensible step is to acknowledge that measurement
is a means, not an end in itself.

Precise measurement is an indispensable part of the larger enterprise of understanding ourselves and our universe. The knowledge
so acquired is not a useless ornament of the educated mind; it sets
policy, guides action, and supports decision in every realm it touches.
But not all measurements are equally valuable. Measurements made
without a supporting context of theory or practical application seldom justify the time and money spent on them. To make measurements without knowing why is like buying gasoline without owning
a car. A blind faith that measurement is necessarily a good thing,
that someday somebody will provide a theory to explain every
conceivable measurement we might make, completely ignores the
delicate play between observation and analysis. Outside of a supporting framework of problems, facts, and theories measurement is
empty; inside such a framework it may unlock the secrets of the
universe.

The great virtue of measurement is that it enables us to bring
mathematics to bear on our problems. Once we have replaced the
objects or events we want to understand by numerical symbols, we
can proceed to operate on those symbols according to. the rules of
mathematics, rules developed and elaborated by the most brilliant
minds in history. We can borrow temporarily the intelligence of
Archimedes, Newton, or Gauss. It is not the numbers themselves
that we prize so highly, it is what the numbers enable us to do. And

what we can do with them is intimately related to the extent to which the rules of measurement we use exploit all the properties of the number system.

What is measurement? In its broadest definition, it means assigning numbers to things according to explicit rules.[1]

The level of refinement can vary tremendously. There are at least two ways to make more refined measurements. One is to reduce the errors, to be sure one assigns the right number to the thing measured. Another is more fully to specify the rules. Everyone recognizes the virtues of precision, but the importance of the rules is not as widely appreciated. Consider some of the different rules that can be applied.

In the broadest sense of our definition the assignment of numbers to the jerseys of football players can be called a form of measurement. In this case the rule for assigning numbers to things is very simple: No two players on the same team can have the same number. The rule is a little more complicated than that, as all football fans know, for low numbers are usually given to players in the backfield and each position in the line has its special decade. Even with this embellishment, however, the numbers serve only to identify the players. One would not ordinarily think of the numbers as measuring anything, in spite of the fact that they satisfy the weak conditions imposed by the definition. In this sense it could be said that even a botanist makes measurements, because the names he assigns to different plants serve much the same purpose as do the numbers worn by football players. We can think of the names as numbers written with a system of twenty-six, rather than ten digits. In this broadest possible sense of measurement numbers serve merely as names; we say we have a *nominal scale* of measurement.

Usually, however, we expect our measurements to exploit the ordered character of the number system. We expect something to increase or decrease as the numbers increase or decrease. The assignment of street numbers to houses is an example. As in the case of football players, no two objects—no two houses on the same street—can receive the same number. Street numbers therefore serve all the purposes served by a nominal scale. But that is not all. The rule for assigning street numbers is more explicit: The farther one goes along the street, the larger (or the smaller) the numbers become. If you are given two addresses on the same street, you discover in an instant in what order you will come upon them as you walk along. This more elaborate rule is a clear improvement over the football example, but it is still far short of what Kelvin had in mind. If you are given two addresses on the same street, you cannot tell whether the houses are side by side or three miles apart. All you know is their order. We call this an *ordinal scale* of measurement. Many kinds of psychological measurements are as crude as this: for example, our statements of preference among a set of objects or events.

Greater refinement is possible if, in addition to identifying and ordering the objects, the numbers also indicate the sizes of the intervals between objects. To have an *interval scale* one must be able somehow to determine whether the differences between objects are equal. Here at last is a form of measurement that is quantitative in the ordinary sense of the word. An interval scale must have a standard unit of measurement, a unit interval. The assignment of numbers to days by a calendar is an example of this kind of measurement. Every day has its separate name, thus all the properties of a nominal scale are preserved. The order of the numbers corresponds to the order of the days; accordingly, ordinal properties are preserved, too. Moreover, given any two dates, one can calculate directly how many days intervened between them.

Psychologists often try to create scales with equal intervals, but there is still much disagreement about acceptable methods. It is not possible to lay psychological phenomena end to end or to put them into a scale pan—to add them in the familiar sense that lengths or weights can be added—whence it is necessary to invent new procedures that differ from, but are logically equivalent to, the operations of physical measurement. But even if it were impossible for psychologists to construct interval scales (and it is not), measurement of the more primitive kinds would still be possible. And often the more primitive measures are sufficient for the decisions and inferences that concern us.

There is yet another stage of refinement possible in the measurement process. In addition to operations for determining identity, order, and a unit interval, operations are available for the determination of the equality of ratios. This sophistication presupposes a scale with a natural value that corresponds to zero. Physical scales—length, mass, density, voltage, etc.—frequently have such natural zero points. Psychological scales are seldom so well behaved. When it is possible to fix an appropriate zero point on an interval scale, it is called a *ratio scale*.

The social and behavioral sciences are sometimes criticized for not being able so to formulate their variables that they can be encompassed by ratio scales of measurement. The criticism unfortunately is true. However, much can be accomplished with the cruder varieties of scales. And as our understanding becomes less meager and unsatisfactory, we may be able to discover better methods than we have now.

Suppose we consider an example that will highlight some of the difficulties of psychological measurement. How is one to measure the psychological phenomenon of anxiety? Everyone knows the cruel bite of this emotion, everyone recognizes that it varies in intensity from moment to moment and from person to person. In principle, therefore, one should be able to use numbers to indicate how anxious a person is. But how to find the numbers?

One method exploits a reaction that physiologists discovered many years ago. When a normal person experiences a strong emotion, there is usually a decrease in the resistance to the passage of a weak electric current through his skin. All one has to do therefore is apply electrodes to his skin and measure its resistance. This is simple and convenient; many psychological experiments have relied on exactly this technique to measure emotional responses. There are things about it, however, that must be clearly understood. It is not a kind of *psychological* measurement; the quantity involved is electrical, the resistance measured in ohms. Anxiety, however, is not to be measured in ohms. S. S. Stevens has suggested that the measurement in ohms might better be called an *indicant*, rather than a measure of anxiety. An indicant is something that presumably correlates closely with what one would like to measure, and so can be substituted for a measure when the more direct approach is impossible. But it is necessary to assume that the indicant is valid, whereas a measure is valid by definition. There are many circumstances where psychologists have settled for indicants, but hope some day to find scales of measurement.

If we wish to be certain that our indicant of anxiety is valid, how should we proceed? A direct approach is to ask people to introspect on their anxiety, to report verbally how much anxiety they are feeling. These observations through the inner eye could then be used to check the electrical measurements on the ohmeter. Now, it is perfectly easy to get verbal reports from persons who are exposed to different kinds of threatening situations, but certain difficulties appear. For example, when a particular situation occurs and the person's skin resistance takes a sudden drop, his introspections may reveal nothing at all. His skin says one thing, his words another. Which are we to believe? We may not call the subject a liar. Psychologists have sometimes argued that the feeling of anxiety is so intolerable that the mind has subtle tricks for avoiding it. If so, the ohmeter may be reflecting a perfectly valid emotional reaction that is not directly accessible to consciousness. It would seem that we have encountered a problem where direct introspective report does not give us a true measure. Until someone thinks of some better procedure, therefore, we must measure anxiety in terms of skin resistance, breathing rate, heartbeat, and so on, all indicants, rather than direct measurements of emotion. Perhaps the problem will not be resolved by finding a true measure of emotion, but by redefining what we mean by emotion as a psychological phenomenon.

Measurement in psychology is not always as difficult as this example may suggest. There are subjective phenomena that submit with docility to a psychologist's yardsticks. Suppose, for example, that we apply our general ideas to the measurement of sensations. The intrinsic qualities of sensation—sourness, redness, middle C—can only be described and named. But certain aspects of sensations are variable, and the magnitude of those variations can be measured. Lights grow and fade in brightness, sounds swell and recede in loudness. How can these changes be measured? According to our definition, the problem is to assign numbers to sensations according to certain rules. This form of psychological measurement is the oldest, the most elaborately developed, the most precise, and, in the opinion of many generations of students, the dullest kind of measurement that psychologists perform.

Historically, sensation was the first problem of psychological measurement to be attacked in a systematic way; the results formed a major piece of evidence that psychology might someday develop into a real science. The problem was given particular emphasis because Wundt, following the British empiricists, considered sensations to be fundamental building blocks of the mind. If one could measure sensations, one could then measure any other perceptual phenomenon by analyzing it into these elementary, measurable components of experience.

The procedures used to measure sensations were developed during the nineteenth century by Weber, Fechner, Helmholtz, Wundt, Galton, and many others. They were so successful that it was many years before anyone suspected there might be something more to the study of perception than the straightforward task of measuring sensations. Even today the field of sensory psychology is a tidy little kingdom unto itself, a subscience concerned with physical aspects of the stimulus, with neurophysiological processes in the receptors and the sensory nerves, and with the experience or behavior of the stimulated organism. These sensory processes can be studied intensively by scientists who have little interest in the remainder of psychology and who would prefer to avoid anything that seems vague or intangible by comparison with the rigorous standards they maintain for the measurement of sensations.

The principal tool a sensory psychologist uses is a hypothetical entity called the threshold. A threshold is a boundary separating what we can experience from what we cannot. If a light is too dim to see, we say it is below the visual threshold; if a sound is too faint to hear, it is below the auditory threshold. Conversely, if the light energy or the sound energy is intense enough to trigger off some response, then it is above the threshold. Sometimes the threshold is referred to as the *limen;* stimuli that cannot be detected are subliminal, those that can be, supraliminal. But, whatever one calls it, the underlying idea is that our sense organs are not infinitely delicate, that there is a point separating physical energies that are adequate to excite the sense organs from those that are not. Because of this intimate relation implied between the physical and the psychological magnitudes, the techniques of measurement used by sensory psychologists are usually referred to as *psychophysical methods.*

Psychologists often speak as if the threshold were a hard and fixed value, as if stimuli greater than the threshold were always detected and stimuli less than the threshold were never detected. When we examine the matter more carefully, we are forced to recognize that a threshold is a statistical concept. A given level of physical energy may be perceived at one instant and not perceived a few moments later. Because of this characteristic unpredictability and uncertainty, one speaks of the *probability* of detecting a stimulus.

There are dozens of sources of this uncertainty: fluctuations in the metabolic processes that feed the sense organs, tiny mechanical differences in the orientation of the receptor, spontaneous activity in the nervous system, lapses of attention, coincidence of the stimulus with the thud of a heartbeat or the blink of an eyelid: how can one foresee which of these will work in favor of detection, which will oppose it at a given instant? It is a question of competing probabilities. When we measure a threshold, therefore, we look for the stimulus value that is missed as often as it is detected, that is, where the probability of detection is 0.50.

As a light gets dimmer and dimmer, the probability that one can see a short flash gradually diminishes. The task is to measure the probability at each stimulus intensity. A hypothetical example is graphed in Figure 8; as the stimulus value goes up, the proportion of times it is detected also increases. The stimulus value at which one can see the light half of the occasions it flashes, *i.e.,* the point at which the probability is ½, is usually taken as the statistical definition of the threshold.

We occasionally detect subliminal stimuli and miss supraliminal ones. Thus, for example, a subliminal advertisement is one that can be perceived less than half the times it is presented. Although there

Fig. 8. The proportion of the stimuli detected by the subject is plotted as a function of the stimulus intensity. The 50 per cent point is usually defined as the limen.

has been some irrational fear of what advertisers might do to us with subliminal tricks, it is probably fair to say that the public should be grateful for the relief such advertising provides. The more subliminal the advertising gets, the better most of us will like it. Perhaps someone will invent a subliminal billboard.

In order to measure the amount of stimulus energy required to reach the threshold, it is necessary to use physical equipment that presents energies—lights, sounds, tastes, and so on—in known amount to the receptor organs of the person or animal being tested. And it is necessary that the equipment should be able to vary the amount of energy over a range of values running from well below to far above threshold. The design, construction, maintenance, and operation of equipment having the necessary sensitivity and accuracy usually requires considerable scientific and engineering skill. Once the equipment is assembled and calibrated, a person—the subject—is brought into the situation and asked to report when he detects the presence of a stimulus. He may be instructed to report vocally, or to punch a key that signals when he has detected the stimulus. The specific instructions are quite important; if he is encouraged to be conservative in his judgments, he may appear to be rather insensitive, whereas if he is encouraged to guess, he may report many stimuli that were not really there. The way a subject balances his misses against his false reports can make a significant difference in the measured value of his threshold. Considerable training is often necessary before a subject can reliably maintain a fixed criterion of judgment in a psychophysical experiment.

Given a properly trained and carefully instructed subject, the threshold measurement can begin. In one of the standard procedures the experimenter presents a particular intensity of the stimulus, a value selected in advance, and records whether or not the subject responds to it. He then presents another value, also selected in advance in random fashion, and again notes the subject's response. This sequence is repeated again and again, each time with different values. In a typical experiment the investigator may select in advance eight or ten different intensities all in the region where he expects the threshold to lie. He continues the procedure until he has presented the subject with, say, 100 stimuli at each of the preselected intensities; 100 are needed at each intensity to get reliable estimates of the probabilities of detection. In all, therefore, 800 or

1,000 stimuli may be presented in the course of measuring a single threshold for a single subject. The proportion that the subject detects at each intensity is plotted, a curve is fitted to the points, and the threshold is estimated as in Figure 8. And this procedure must be repeated with other subjects until the investigator can be sure the value obtained is not attributable to the idiosyncrasies of a particular subject. Shortcuts are possible and are necessarily adopted for clinical tests—few patients are as amenable and uncomplaining as an experimental subject—but the laboratory measurement of a threshold value frequently requires several hours.

One reward for such painstaking labors, however, has been the discovery of man's amazing sensitivity to certain forms of energy. In the case of vision, for example, under optimal conditions a visual sensation will result if only five or ten quanta of blue light reach the layer of sensitive receptor cells in the retina. Since light quanta are the smallest possible packages of radiant energy, and since it is highly improbable that more than one of the five or ten packages fall on any single receptor cell, this result seems to imply that one light quantum is sufficient to activate one visual receptor cell! It is physically impossible to be more sensitive than this. And the ear is almost as good as the eye. A tone of 2,000 cycles per second can be heard when the movement of the air particles against the eardrum is smaller than the diameter of a hydrogen molecule. In olfaction, one part of mercaptan in fifty billion parts of air produces a detectable odor. It seems likely that our sense organs are, for some stimuli, as sensitive as is compatible with the conditions and requirements of life. If these organs were more sensitive, they would begin to respond to the random dance of molecules in the air and in the receptors themselves.

Measuring these minimum detectable amounts of energy, however, occupies only a small part of a sensory psychologist's time and effort. Of even greater interest to him is the measurement of *difference thresholds*—the smallest difference between two stimuli that can be detected. For example, two different intensities of light may be displayed side by side; if the viewer can detect a contour where one field stops and the other starts, he reports which side is brighter. Or two tones may be sounded, one after the other; a listener reports whether the second was louder or fainter than the first. Quite frequently the results of these experimental measurements of differential sensitivity—measurements of the fineness of resolution of our sensory equipment—can be interpreted more or less directly in terms of the anatomy and physiology of the receptors themselves. Psychophysics is a close relative of biophysics.

A wide variety of sensory differences has been subjected to this kind of testing. The results are contained in hundreds of different professional journals and are summarized in scores of handbooks.[2] The measurement can be represented best if we use symbols: Let M represent the magnitude of the weaker stimulus, and let $M + D$ represent the magnitude of the stronger stimulus. Thus D is the difference between the two intensities of stimulation, and it is D that the subject is trying to detect. As D gets smaller and smaller, approaching zero, the likelihood that a subject will detect it gets less and less; the threshold value of D can be estimated from such data. Let us use D' to designate the particular value of D that corresponds to the threshold. Then the results of thousands of measurements of difference thresholds can be summarized in a simple rule noted first by Ernst Heinrich Weber in 1834. In its details the rule is wrong, but it is so simple and so nearly true over such a wide range of conditions that it is still remembered and referred to as Weber's Law. The rule says that D', the size of D necessary for detection, increases as a direct function of the size of M. The stronger the stimulus, the larger the increment required. For example, if you strike a match in a room where a single candle is burning, the increment in illumination is quite obvious, but the same increment of light in a room where a thousand candles are burning is scarcely noticeable.

More precisely, Weber stated that the ratio, D'/M, is a constant for all values of M, the value of the constant varying from one sense modality to another. Today it is known that the ratio, D'/M, may change when M is extremely small or extremely large, but within the normal ranges of stimulation, Weber's Law is usually a reliable guide. Thus it can be said, for example, that the Weber fraction is approximately $1/100$ for the just noticeable difference in the brightness of a light and is approximately $1/10$ for the just noticeable difference in the intensity of a tone. The size of D', in absolute or in fractional terms, has been measured and tabulated for an amazing variety of situations, far more than we could survey here; the information exists and can be found in a good psychological library.

Now suppose we stand back a few paces from these meticulous measurements and try to understand why psychologists—and not only physiologists, doctors, or engineers—must be concerned with such things. Is it merely historical accident? British philosophers of empiricism long ago pointed to the senses as the source of all our knowledge about the universe; "Nothing is in the mind," they said, "that is not first in the senses." And in the materialist tradition, physiologists long ago developed techniques for measuring what the sense organs can do. Wundt adopted these two lines of thought as the foundation for his new science. Problems of sensory psychology have been handed down ever since from one generation of psychologists to the next. But some people feel that modern psychology has outgrown this problem and that from now on it should be left to physiologists.

Certainly the measurement of sensations no longer occupies the central position in psychology it once did. But it still provides essential information about important psychological concepts. It is, for example, absolutely fundamental to our understanding of the crucially important psychological concept of *similarity*. Similarity is the basis of our ability to recognize objects and group them in classes—chairs, books, ships, shoes, and sealing wax—each member of a class being related to, and therefore a symbol of, the others. This skill enables man to profit from experience, to recognize a new situation as similar to an old one. It would be impossible to give any coherent account of how people behave without somehow including the fact that they tend to generalize on the basis of similarity.

One important kind of similarity might be called sensory similarity. Sensory similarity is what we mean when we say that blue is more like green than red, or that a flute sounds more like a clarinet than like a trombone, or that tuna tastes more like chicken than like apple pie, and so on. If we can find a reasonable way to talk about these sensory similarities, perhaps we can generalize our ideas, extend them to more complex structural and semantic similarities.

What does a person mean when he says two sensations are similar? When he says that blue is more like green than like red, he may merely be repeating what he was taught to say. Perhaps his parents or his teachers told him that blue and green are similar; we cannot know what our subjects were taught about colors before they came to the laboratory. Perhaps this is all that similarity amounts to.

If we are convinced, however, that there is some other definition of similarity—a specific sense in which blue and green are *really* similar—we might approach the matter in the following way. Suppose one defines similar stimuli to be stimuli to which people tend to respond in the same way. Then the matter can be explored experimentally. A person can be instructed to make some response— raise his hand, call out, push a button, and so on—every time a blue light goes on. Then the investigator surprises the subject with lights of other colors. The response should occur more frequently— and more quickly and intensely—when green is unexpectedly substituted for blue than when red is. On performing this experiment, we discover, in truth, that the probability of response decreases as the similarity between the original and the test stimulus decreases. This measurement is generally referred to as determining a gradient of *stimulus generalization.*

Another convenient technique for measuring similarity is to ask people to name the colors that are shown them, and then to make the conditions of judgment so difficult that they are sure to make mistakes. To force the subjects to make mistakes the colors can be presented at low illuminations, or for very short periods of time, or at a rapid rate. Confusions will occur; we expect discrimination to fail first between blue and green, indicating that they are somehow closer together, or more alike, than blue and red.

In other words, the trick is to make *failure of discrimination* a measure of *similarity.* We will examine this trick in detail. Notice, however, that this equation between confusability and similarity is a definition, not a discovery.

The use of confusability to measure similarity goes back at least as far as 1860 when G. T. Fechner proposed to use the difference threshold—the just noticeable difference, or jnd—as a unit with which to measure the subjective magnitude of a sensation.

Fechner's argument went something like this: Suppose one wishes to measure how bright a particular sensation of light is for the person who experiences it. Obviously, one cannot use physical measurements of intensity to measure how it *looks;* the problem is to develop an independent measure of the psychological intensity of the sensation. This can be done as follows: First, measure how much the physical intensity of the light must be decreased before the subject is barely able to detect the difference. Then change the intensity of the light to this new, lower value and again measure the size of the difference threshold. Since both changes were just barely noticeable, Fechner assumed that they were subjectively equal. Now decrease the intensity again by a just noticeable amount. This process is repeated until finally the light is entirely invisible. Since every decrement was subjectively equal to every other decrement, the number of times one had to decrease the intensity of the light—the number of just noticeable differences in intensity—can be used as a measure of the subjective magnitude of the sensation.

Of course, the measure is not limited to this particular situation. Once one accepts Fechner's assumption that the just noticeable difference, the jnd, can be used as a standard unit of subjective measurement, one can count the number of jnd's between any two stimuli and use this number as a measure of their discriminability. The smaller the number of jnd's, the greater their similarity must be. In this way Fechner used confusability to measure similarity.

It should be apparent that the actual experimental operations involved in carrying out this measurement—measuring one difference limen after another until the absolute threshold is reached—are far too tedious to carry out every time a sensory magnitude is to be measured. Some short cuts are needed, and here, at last, mathematics can be useful. By certain relatively simple calculations many hours of tedious measurement can be avoided. Fechner assumed that Weber's Law was true, so that

$$\frac{\Delta M}{M} = \text{constant},$$

where now $\Delta M \ (= D')$ indicates the size of the increment in the stimulus magnitude M that is necessary to make the increment just detectable. Since Fechner assumed that all jnd's are subjectively equal, he could write

$$\Delta S = k \frac{\Delta M}{M},$$

where ΔS denotes the amount of change in the psychological magnitude of the sensation that results when the physical magnitude of the stimulus is changed by ΔM, and k is a constant of proportionality that depends upon the particular units of measurement one adopts. Now he could rewrite the equation as

$$\frac{\Delta S}{\Delta M} = \frac{k}{M},$$

which he then proceeded to solve by assuming that it was really a differential equation,

$$\frac{dS}{dM} = \frac{k}{M}.$$

As students of the calculus know, the solution of this equation is

$$S = k \, log_e \, M + c,$$

where c is the constant of integration and e the base of the natural logarithms. In this way he derived *Fechner's Law,* which states that (if we ignore the irrelevant constants) the subjective magnitude of a sensation is measured by the logarithm of the physical magnitude of its stimulus.

The reader should now be much impressed by how scientific all this sounds. Even if one does not understand the calculus, it is still a solemn thing to see it used. In the nineteenth century it seemed even more impressive; Wundt's new psychology could scarcely have achieved scientific recognition as quickly as it did without this fundamental and ingenious contribution from Fechner.

What kind of man was Gustav Theodore Fechner? In his fine history of experimental psychology, E. G. Boring says of him:

> He first acquired modest fame as professor of physics at Leipzig, but in later life he was a physicist only as the spirit of the *Naturforscher* penetrated all his work. In intention and ambition he was a philosopher, especially in his last forty years of life, but he was never famous, or even successful, in this fundamental effort that is, nevertheless, the key to his other activities. He was a humanist, a satirist, a poet in his incidental writings and an estheticist during one decade of activity. He is famous, however, for his psychophysics, and this fame was rather forced upon him. He did not wish his name to go down to posterity as a psychophysicist. He did not, like Wundt, seek to found experimental psychology. He might have been content to let experimental psychology as an independent science remain in the womb of time, could he but have established his spiritualistic *Tagesansicht* as a substitute for the current materialistic *Nachtansicht* of the universe. The world, however,

chose for him; it seized upon the psychophysical experiments, which Fechner meant merely as contributory to his philosophy, and made them into an experimental psychology.[3]

Fechner tells us that it was on the morning of October 22, 1850, while he was lying late in bed thinking about how he might combat the materialistic tendencies of his times, that the general outline of his idea occurred to him and he saw how he could use physical magnitudes of stimulation to measure subjective magnitudes of sensation. Thus October 22 is sometimes celebrated by psychologists— only half in jest—as the birthday of their science.

The irony of Fechner's achievement, however, was that he succeeded so well that what he was most interested in—sensation, mind, the subjective view of reality—became excess baggage. Instead of proving by empirical evidence that sensations were real because they could be measured in physical units, he provided a way to talk about them that was completely materialistic. A later generation would adopt his insight as part of a larger conviction that it is *discrimination,* not sensation, that must be measured. The psychology, at least in the spiritual sense Fechner meant the term, could be left out entirely. Perceptual similarity, so the argument runs, can always be reduced to objective questions of discrimination and confusability.

Today a psychologist tries to predict behavior generally. He does not limit himself to the subjective experience that a conscious, human adult is able to judge and to talk about. In this broader context, the study of discrimination has largely displaced the older study of sensation. Obviously, discrimination is an indispensable feature of intelligent behavior. Insofar as our receptors provide the information that guides our behavior, it is important for us to understand their capacities and their limitations. This broader perspective has, in general, had a refreshing effect on this branch of the psychological enterprise.

Consider briefly how the psychophysical methods have been generalized and extended far beyond the realms of sensory psychology. Late in the 1920's L. L. Thurstone, who taught psychophysics at the University of Chicago, became bored with what he was teaching. He admitted that psychophysics offered the satisfaction of clean and quantitative logic, a rare satisfaction for a psychologist to enjoy, but he could not convince himself that the sensations he was measuring so precisely were worth all the time and trouble he lavished on them. He decided to change what he was teaching and to use the same methods to measure something worthwhile. "Instead of asking a person which of two cylinders is the heavier," he said, "we might as well ask something interesting, such as, 'Which of these two nationalities do you in general prefer to associate with?' or, 'Which of these two offenses do you consider to be in general the more serious?' or 'Which of these two pictures or colored designs do you like better?' Questions of this sort of discrimination might be multiplied indefinitely, and if they could be handled with some sort of psychophysical logic, it is clear that we should have here the possibilities of objective description of more psychological significance than the sensory limen."[4] And so Thurstone put the study of attitudes on a quantitative basis.

Thurstone's transfer of psychophysical logic from sensations to attitudes was an important generalization, one that breathed new life into an old and often doddering subject. However, there are ways to measure similarity other than the one Fechner invented and Thurstone generalized; there are units of subjective measurement other than the jnd. Some of the other methods are much simpler, and they do not assume that you can get red by adding up various shades of pink.

Suppose we ask a subject to make direct, numerical estimates of the magnitudes of his sensations. One technique is to give a person a standard stimulus and tell him, "I want you to imagine that the magnitude of this is 100. Now, if this is 100, what number would you assign to the following stimuli?" A series of intensities are then presented and his numerical estimates are recorded and averaged with the estimates obtained from other subjects. The assumption that a subject is capable of making valid numerical estimates seems justified by the repeatability of his replies, by the agreement among different judges, and most of all by the internal consistency of the results obtained.

It is often the case that when some aspect of sensation has been measured both according to Fechner's method of jnd's and by some more direct assignment of numbers to magnitudes, the results obtained are not the same. Or, to put the best foot forward, sometimes the results of these two different methods of measurement are the same. When the two methods agree we feel that all is well and that our assumptions about an observer's ability to make direct numerical estimates must have been essentially correct.[5] But what can we say when the two disagree? And disagree systematically? Whereas the

Fechnerian argument makes sensory magnitude a logarithmic function of the stimulus magnitude, the newer methods of direct estimation indicate that it should be a power function

$$S = kM^n$$

where k and n are constants for any particular sense modality. Which law is the right one? The question is important because methods of measurement based on or patterned after both of these two methods —confusability and subjective estimation—have been widely used throughout all departments of scientific psychology.

Psychologists who work on these problems are far from unanimous about the proper way to resolve such discrepancies among different methods of measurement. At times their arguments become violent, proof enough for anyone who needed it that precise measurements do not always suffice to settle scientific disagreements. It is clear, however, that an old and venerable problem is still exciting interest, still leading us toward new concepts and methods of measurement that will eventually enrich many different fields of psychology.

CHAPTER VII

THE ANALYSIS OF PERCEPTIONS

You have three basins of water. In one the water is cold, in the second it is tepid, in the third hot. Put one hand into the cold water and the other into the hot. After you leave them immersed a minute or two you will discover that the difference in warmth disappears. When your two hands seem to be approximately the same neutral warmth, remove them both and plunge them into the remaining basin, the one containing the lukewarm water. Now the water here seems to have two temperatures at the same time, warm to one hand and cool to the other. But you *know* that the water must have a single temperature! It is not reasonable to say that the same water is both warm and cool simultaneously, even though it feels that way. Something has gone wrong with the usually reliable machinery for finding out about the world we live in.

The dilemma of the three basins was used by John Locke in 1690 as part of his argument that the apparent qualities of objects —warmth, for example—are not in the objects themselves, but in the minds of the persons who perceive the objects. The object is not warm, said Locke; it merely possesses the capacity of arousing the idea of warmth in us. If the warmth we perceive were truly in the object itself, as it appears to be, it would be impossible for us to perceive two different warmths in one object at the same time. Thus, Locke used the three basins to drive the wedge of his argument between the objective and the subjective views of reality.

In revisiting this ancient landmark today, however, we have a somewhat different purpose in mind. Our present interest in it derives from its usefulness as an example of why many psychologists persist in using two different terms, sensation and perception, to describe the way we are affected by events going on in the world around us.

When you first hear a strange language spoken, it is merely a rapid flow of sound. The voice is recognizable as human, but that is about all you get from it. When you have learned the language, however, the jumble of auditory sensations sort themselves out into phonemes, syllables, words, and phrases. Now you perceive the patterns that underlie and organize the flow of sounds. But there is still a third level that emerges when you learn the language, a conceptual level of meaning and reference. You not only learn to perceive what the sounds are, you learn to understand what they signify.

Are these three levels—sensation, perception, conception—really distinct modes of functioning? Do they appear in all our efforts to cope with reality? Are percepts and concepts always the result of learning? These are some of the basic questions we face when we try to analyze the processes of perception.

The gaps between sensation, perception, and conception have puzzled men at least since the time of Socrates. How can we discover the permanent, stable, reliable, true conception of ourselves and our world? How do we identify the solid, substantial reality that lies behind the shifting, deceptive, changing, fallible appearances presented to our senses? How do we build our image of the universe out of the conglomeration of stimuli that affect our sense organs? To build a world-that-is out of a world-that-seems-to-be is one of the great triumphs of childhood.

Some psychologists like to think of sensations as the basic data reported by the sense organs, data stripped as far as possible of all inference about their cause or their meaning. In the case of the three basins, our sensations are the feelings of cold, cool, warm, and hot wetness. Perceptions, on the other hand, may be affected by what we know of our environment from our past, as well as our present, experience with it. We perceive the water, not just the wetness. Ordinarily, we perceive the water to *be* warm, not merely to *feel* warm, though in the dilemma of the three basins our perception becomes confused and we seem to perceive two contradictory things at the same time.

The three basins

Notice that there is nothing confusing about our sensations: one hand feels warm and the other feels cool. The sensations are simple enough and quite straightforward, so the temptation is strong to begin with them when we try to explain what happens with the three basins. If we concentrate on our sensations and ignore perceptual and conceptual problems for the moment, the dilemma can be understood and explained quite simply. It is a typical example of a very general phenomenon, called adaptation. The fundamental fact is that if you wait long enough, and if the temperature is not too extreme, the skin tends to adapt to the temperature of its environment. When you sit down in a hot tub, at first you may think you have been scalded, but after a minute or two it seems comfortably warm and may even come to feel neutral in temperature. When you go swimming in a cold pool, you feel at first that you will surely freeze, but if you keep going it may become bearable, even neutral, in its apparent temperature. Once your skin has adapted to the environmental temperature, your judgment of warm or cool is relative to that adaptation level. That is to say, when the skin has become adapted to a particular temperature, any higher temperature will feel warm and any lower temperature will feel cool. The dilemma of the three basins is simply a clever trick to illustrate the phenomenon of adaptation in a striking manner.

When we take this approach to the problem, we are concerned only with the sensations of warm and cool, not with an inference about the real temperature of the water. We say only that the same sensations can be produced by different temperatures, depending upon what our skin has become accustomed to. Of course, once the process of sensory adaptation has been identified, it becomes an interesting problem in its own right. Many questions remain to be answered. For example, what are the limits within which complete adaptation can occur? (Below about 65° F. and above about 105° F. the water does not come to feel neutral even after long exposures.) How rapidly does adaptation take place? (If it is not complete in two or three minutes, it probably will never feel neutral.) Will a change of five degrees from the neutral point feel like an equal change in warmth regardless of what the neutral temperature was? (No. A 5° F. change in the middle of the range, say, at 85° F., is equivalent to an 8° F. change at the extremes.) Is adaptation a function of the size of the skin area that is exposed? (Yes. It takes longer for a larger area to adapt.) And so the questions about adaptation can be posed and answered by careful psychophysical experiments in the laboratory.[1] The fact remains, however, that these are questions about how the water feels, not about the actual physical temperature of the water. Calling the process adaptation does not resolve the underlying problem of the three basins.

If one takes this approach to the study of perception, one is likely to give special weight to sensations as the primitive elements out of which more complicated perceptions can be built, and on the basis of which inferences can be drawn about reality. Thus sensory processes are seen as simple and primary, whereas perceptual processes are complex and derivative. Wilhelm Wundt is a famous example of a psychologist who adopted this view. But it is a difficult view to defend. The trouble is that most people feel intuitively that the things and events are primary and, in some sense, simple. Sensations are, to them, the result of analyzing one's perceptions in a highly artificial way, and so are considered to be complex, derivative phenomena. Gestalt psychologists provide an excellent example of a view exactly opposite to Wundt's.[2]

The argument as to which comes first, sensation or perception, has consumed more time and attention than it deserves. However, the position a psychologist takes will affect the kind of research he does, and affect the development of the science.

For example, consider a traditional attitude toward the study of hearing. It was pointed out quite early by G. S. Ohm—who is usually remembered today for his studies of electricity—that the ear acts as an acoustic analyzer. That is to say, when two different frequencies of a vibration affect the ear simultaneously we hear them both at the same time and do not (as in color vision) perceive some synthetic compromise halfway between the two of them. Moreover, it was known that all complex sounds—noise, music, speech—can be analyzed into the sum of many simple sounds by means of techniques based on concepts developed by the nineteenth-century French mathematician J. B. J. Fourier. Since a complicated sound is the sum of several simple sounds, the sensation produced by a complicated sound must be the sum of the sensations produced by the several simple sounds. Therefore, the argument went, it is not necessary to study the perception of complex sounds. Consequently, nearly all the pioneer work on audition was focused on the study of pure, simple tones, for they were considered to be the sensory atoms out of which everything auditory is built. It was not until the development of the telephone that practical considerations overrode theoretical biases and a group of engineers at the Bell Telephone Laboratories began to study the perception of speech directly.[3] Acoustic analysis of the speech waves into simple components gave only a first approximation to what listeners could understand. Intelligibility is also a function of many psychological variables. Alertness, familiarity with the language, the meaning of the message, and the listener's expectations, all influence what is heard.

By way of contrast with a theory that builds up compound perceptions out of the simpler atoms of sensation, the gestalt psychologists ask us to consider the perception of melodies. We listen to a melody played in one key. Then it is repeated, but in a new key. We have no difficulty in recognizing it as the same melody; some of us may even be unaware that the pitch was different the second time through. Clearly, then, something besides our particular sensations of pitch must be involved when we recognize a tune. We cannot learn anything about a melody by studying its several notes in isolation. The search for conditions that determine our recognition of patterns, relations, and configurations represents a very different approach to the problem of perception.

The gestalt psychologists—Max Wertheimer, Wolfgang Köhler, Kurt Koffka, Kurt Lewin, Karl Duncker and many others—forced their colleagues to admit that a complex perception cannot be explained as a linear sum of the sensations that its parts arouse. Figure

9 shows an example of the kind of objections they raised.[4] A wheel rolls slowly across a room that is totally dark. A light attached to the rim of the wheel traces out the cycloid path in *a*. A light attached to the hub produces a simple horizontal line, as in *b*. But if we now attach lights to both the hub and the rim, we do not get a simple sum of the two lines, as in *c*. Instead, the motions of the two lights are related to one another to give the unified pattern suggested in *d*, where one light is now seen to revolve around the other; the cycloid path vanishes completely. This is but one of a large variety of examples that show how difficult it is to analyze perceptions into their sensory elements.

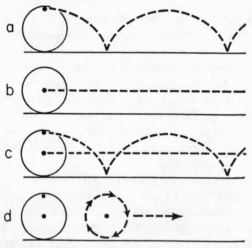

Fig. 9. In pitch darkness a wheel with lights on the rim *a* or the hub *b* rolls slowly along a table. When both lights are on, the perception is not the simple sum of the perception of each light alone: *a* + *b* does not equal *c*. The cycloid motion is lost and one light seems to rotate around the other, as in *d*. (From D. Krech and R. S. Crutchfield, *Elements of Psychology*. New York: Knopf, 1958.)

An alternative view of the matter is that perception and sensation are not essentially different processes. The difference lies not in what we experience but rather in the way we describe what we experience. Sensation and perception correspond to two languages people have for talking about their experience, about the information their sense organs are providing. When they talk about their sensations, they speak cautiously and try to say how their experience would appear to someone who had no conception of its true source or meaning. When they talk about their perceptions, they speak more freely without trying to distinguish what they sense from what they know must be the case. Of course, questions about how things *really* are are shot through with metaphysical pitfalls that could take many volumes to explore in detail; such scholarship will not detain us here.

The American psychologist J. J. Gibson has called the cautious, attentive approach *literal* perception, and the casual, familiar approach *schematic* perception. "In the course of practical behavior," he says, "perception is no more literal with respect to color, size, shape, and sequence than is necessary, since literal perception takes time and effort. The percept is reduced to a cue for action. But perception can become literal whenever the observer needs to discriminate. Under favorable conditions it can be surprisingly exact, as the experiments of the laboratory demonstrate. One can always look at a thing carefully if there is a reason to do so."[5] Thus an observer exercises control over the amount of detail he will take in, just as an artist might control the amount of detail he will include in a drawing. The smallest, most literal details are neither the first nor the easiest for us to appreciate.

Schematic perceptions are not merely less detailed; they are usually more meaningful, too. When an observer becomes cautious and attentive, he tries to jettison these meaningful aspects first. This is not always possible, but he tries anyhow. Coleridge said that esthetic appreciation demands a "willing suspension of disbelief." So does perception. If you become too suspicious, if you try to eliminate all your interpretations and expectations, your perceptual world will crumble into meaningless fragments.

Imagine that you are visiting a psychological laboratory—probably around 1915. As you walk in, a psychologist comes over and, without waiting for introductions, asks what you see on the table.

"A book."

"Yes, of course, it is a book," he agrees, "but what do you *really* see?"

"What do you mean, 'What do I *really* see'?" you ask, puzzled. "I told you that I see a book. It is a small book with a red cover."

The psychologist is persistent. "What is your perception *really?*" he insists. "Describe it to me as precisely as you can."

"You mean it isn't a book? What is this, some kind of trick?"

There is a hint of impatience. "Yes, it is a book. There is no trickery involved. I just want you to describe to me *exactly* what you can see, no more and no less."

You are growing very suspicious now. "Well," you say, "from this angle the cover of the book looks like a dark red parallelogram."

"Yes," he says, pleased. "Yes, you see a patch of dark red in the shape of a parallelogram. What else?"

"There is a grayish white edge below it and another thin line of the same dark red below that. Under it I see the table—" He winces. "Around it I see a somewhat mottled brown with wavering streaks of lighter brown running roughly parallel to one another."

"Fine, fine." He thanks you for your cooperation.

As you stand there looking at the book on the table you are a little embarrassed that this persistent fellow was able to drive you to such an analysis. He made you so cautious that you were not sure any longer what you really saw and what you only thought you saw. You were, in fact, as suspicious as the New England farmer who would admit only that, "It looks like a cow on this side." In your caution you began talking about what you saw in terms of sensations, where just a moment earlier you were quite certain that you perceived a book on a table.

Your reverie is interrupted suddenly by the appearance of a psychologist who looks vaguely like Wilhelm Wundt. "Thank you, for helping to confirm once more my theory of perception. You have proved," he says, "that the book you see is nothing but a compound of elementary sensations. When you were trying to be precise and say accurately what it was you really saw, you had to speak in terms of color patches, not objects. It is the color sensations that are primary, and every visual object is reducible to them. Your perception of the book is constructed from sensations just as a molecule is constructed from atoms."

This little speech is apparently a signal for battle to begin. "Nonsense!" shouts a voice from the opposite end of the hall. "Nonsense! Any fool knows that the *book* is the primary, immediate, direct, compelling, perceptual fact!" The psychologist who charges down upon you now bears a faint resemblance to William James, but he seems to have a German accent, and his face is so flushed with anger that you cannot be sure. "This reduction of a perception into sensations that you keep talking about is nothing but an intellectual game.

An object is not just a bundle of sensations. Any man who goes about seeing patches of dark redness where he ought to see books is sick!"

As the fight begins to gather momentum you close the door softly and slip away. You have what you came for, an illustration that there are two different attitudes, two different ways to talk about the information that our senses provide.

The notion that perceptions are built from sensations the way a wall is built of bricks is now generally recognized to be unsatisfactory. Ordinarily, the perception of an object is possible only because we are willing to go far beyond the sensory information we are given.[6] We are usually unaware how far we leap to reach a perceptual conclusion. The leap itself is, of course, unconscious. All such processes are unconscious; only their end product appears in consciousness and is accessible for introspective analysis. But even though our conscious experience is much the same, the way we describe it need not be. When we talk about our sensations, we are trying to talk about the information we must have had *before* we made the leap; when we talk about our perceptions, we are trying to talk about the same information *after* we have made the leap. The question as to which way of talking is truer, which more natural or more immediate, is an interesting one, but it is not essential that we decide it before we can proceed with our study of perception.

The leap that carries perception beyond sensation is often called, after Helmholtz, an unconscious inference, and the perception itself an unconscious conclusion. Inferences and conclusions sound very intellectual, and some people object to this way of talking about perception. We should clearly recognize that the inferences of perception are not the articulate, deductive inferences of a trained logician; they are more the tacit, inductive inferences of a gullible child.

Two processes, one that tries to test hypotheses, another that tries to integrate details, must cooperate for veridical perception. And each process, if given full sway, carries its own style and attitude with it. In the cautious, literal attitude we remain open to many hypotheses, we welcome evidence that will narrow the field. In the confident, schematic attitude we have already adopted our hypothesis, and we take all the evidence as consonant with it.

What does it mean to say that perception ordinarily goes beyond the information that the senses actually provide? Some examples are needed.

An interesting class of perceptual problems arises from the fact that the retina—the light-sensitive surface in the back of the eyeball where the optical image is projected—is a two-dimensional surface. The world we move around in has three dimensions. How are we able to perceive a three-dimensional world with a two-dimensional retina? It is easy to play tricks on such a device. For example, a small object nearby can cast exactly the same image onto the retina as a larger object farther away; this is a simple fact of projective geometry. In principle, therefore, it should be impossible to decide whether anything is a small object nearby or a large object in the distance. In fact, we manage to make these judgments of distance with considerable accuracy. How do we do it? The clues we use have been studied in great detail. For one thing, our two eyes give us slightly different images of the object, a fact that can be easily verified—what child has not spent hours fascinated by the discovery?—by covering first one eye and then the other. The nearer an object is, the larger will be the difference in its image in the two eyes. Thus the amount of

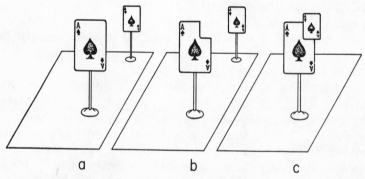

Fig. 10. If two playing cards, both of standard size but separated from a subject by different distances, as in *a*, are viewed with one eye against a dark background, they will cast different optical images on the retina of the eye. The smaller image will be judged to be farther away; relative size is a cue for the perception of distance. This judgment will be confirmed if the nearer card blocks the view of a corner of the distant card; interposition is another cue for the perception of distance. However, if a corner of the nearer card is carefully cut away, as in *b*, the distant card will now appear to be in front of the closer card, but will seem much smaller in size, as in *c*. In this case interposition is a more compelling cue than relative size. (From D. Krech and R. S. Crutchfield, *Elements of Psychology*. New York: Knopf, 1958.)

difference between the eyes provides information useful for judging distance. A much simpler kind of information is provided by the fact that near objects will block distant objects from view. Moreover, a distant object is likely to appear hazy, to move more slowly, to have less intense colors, to have finer surface texture, and so on and on.

In addition to all these sensory clues, however, we make considerable use of our prior knowledge of the object we are looking at. We know, for example, approximately how large shoes are. When we see a shoe, therefore, we can judge its distance in terms of its assumed size. It is possible, to be sure, that an energetic psychologist might construct a shoe six feet long. If he does, he can easily fool people about its distance, for no one normally expects to see shoes that size. In short, it is a part of our tacit assumption about the world that shoes—and people, trees, cigarettes, cars, and the like—regularly come in certain familiar sizes. When we judge distance, we use our knowledge of these sizes to infer the distance that would be appropriate.

Figure 11 makes the point. How far away you think the ball is depends on whether you think of the ball as a marble, a Ping-Pong ball, a billiard ball, or a large beach ball. Your *perception* changes directly as a function of your *conception* of the scene you are viewing.[7] In Chapter VIII we will pursue this topic further.

Our previous familiarity with the visual environment has such an important effect on what we see that many psychologists have used

Fig. 11. Where you see the ball will depend on what kind of ball you assume it is.

this familiarity as the basis for defending a distinction between sensation and perception. Sensations are unlearned, they say, but perceptions are the meanings we learn to attach to the patterns of sensation. The assumption that we have no unlearned perceptions is probably too strong, but it is certainly true that learning can account for many of the perceptual schemata we use. In the example of the three basins, our sensations of warmth and coolness are unaffected by previous learning; but there would be no perceptual illusion if we had not previously learned that a given volume of water must have a relatively uniform temperature. Many other perceptual phenomena can be accounted for by arguments similarly phrased in the language of learning.

But let us consider some more examples. Distance is not the only perceptual judgment one can study. For example, how bright is a particular surface? Your estimate depends not only upon the color you assign to the surface, but also upon the kind of light you think is falling on it. If you are misled in your estimate of the illumination, you will make an incorrect judgment of the brightness of the surface. The importance of a viewer's assumptions about the ambient illumination can be demonstrated by an amusing trick. Take two discs and paint one white, the other black. Hang them by black threads about a foot apart. Take a spotlight and focus it carefully on the black disc. Now dim the lights in the rest of the room until the black disc under the spotlight seems as bright as the white disc that has no special illumination. Put a screen up so that the spotlight is out of sight. The experimental situation is diagrammed in Figure 12. Now you are ready to test your friends. Call them into the room and ask them to judge which of the two discs is brighter. After they have looked and decided, you can reveal the source of illumination to them. One way to reveal it is to light a cigarette and blow smoke into the beam of the spotlight. Or move the screen. Or accidentally put your hand into the beam. The viewer will almost certainly have an "Oh, no!" reaction as the highly illuminated, apparently white disc is suddenly seen for what it is—a *black* surface! There is no change in the sensations aroused by the two discs, but the change in perception is like going from day to night. In this case no amount of meticulous introspection will enable us to isolate our sensations from their perceptual matrix.

And, incidentally, when the objects are withdrawn from the light beam the disc returns immediately to its original appearance. Simply knowing that the spotlight is there is not enough; we must see the illumination. So apparently our percepts are not completely at the mercy of our conceptual knowledge.

Fig. 12. Concealed illumination experiment. The person who does not know about the spotlight will judge the black and the white discs to have equal brightness. A small piece of paper thrust into the light beam, however, makes it obvious that the left disc is black.

Nevertheless, these examples of perceptual inference should suffice to make the point that our tacit assumptions about the nature of the perceived object can play an important role in determining what we see. The point can be made to look paradoxical, for it seems to imply that we must know what we are seeing before we can know what we see. But there is really no paradox. We often know partially, in advance, what we do not know completely. We know what kinds of things to expect in different situations, what actions or events are the most probable in a given place at a given time in the company of given people. We try to interpret any new experiences we have in such a way as to be consistent with our previous experience. Of course, when a strange psychologist takes you into the House of Unknown Horrors that he calls his laboratory and asks you to sit quietly in a dark room until you see or hear something, you are not likely to do much perceiving. It is doubtful that you could recognize your own face in such a context. In the strange and unpredictable world of the laboratory you may indeed try to retreat to the literal description of your sensations in order to communicate your experiences. Perhaps that is why psychologists who spend most of their time studying people in a laboratory environment often forget how much inference is involved in the perceptions that occur in more familiar settings, and how much aid a little advance information can furnish.

But no matter how cautious one tries to be, one cannot give a completely literal description of one's experience in the language of pure sensation. Some inferences about the nature of our world will always slip in to spoil the game. For example, it is difficult, probably impossible, to describe visual experience in terms of local patches of different colors and brightnesses without saying anything about the fact that these patches have boundaries, that there are relatively sharp discontinuities, contours, in the visual field, where one surface appears to stop and another begins. But these are not pure sensations. As the gestalt psychologists like to point out, these are *relations* among the parts of the whole visual field. The contour exists by virtue of a relation between two adjacent patches of colored surface. Instead of the relatively simple appreciation of color, one must make the more complicated judgment of a difference between two spatially distinct regions of color. That there is a space in which these colors exist, that there is a thing whose extent can be defined by its boundaries, are assumptions about the nature of the world we live in. The fact that they are assumptions whose validity we believe completely, and without which we would be unable to function, does not alter the fact that they are assumptions.

Contours define shapes, and shapes are much harder to describe than simple sensations. If the contours are three straight lines that bound a surface of relatively uniform color, one sees a triangle. But one does not speak about a sensation of triangularity in the same way one speaks about a sensation of redness. The difference between them is that the discussion of triangles must involve relational aspects of the total situation that can be ignored when one speaks of colors. For one thing, one speaks about the triangle as a unit, as a whole, as a thing. And for another, the perceived triangle stands out from the surrounding area; it forms a figure against a background. This figure-ground relation is so spontaneous and natural that one usually ignores it entirely. One way to appreciate its importance is to have the relation suddenly change. For example, in the upper half of Figure 13 you can see a white triangle against a black background;

Fig. 13. Figure and ground can often be organized in various ways: *a*, *b*, *c*, and *d* indicate four different organizations that we might expect to find if we could get a cross-section view. The easiest configuration to see is probably *a*, which represents a white triangle seen lying on top of a square black card that seems in turn to lie on top of the white page. However, figure and ground can also be organized as *b*, a square black card with a triangular hole lying on top of the page, or as *c*, a square hole cut in the white page to reveal a black background underneath it. The hardest to see is probably *d*, which is supposed to represent the "real" situation—black ink and white paper all in the same plane.

or you can see a black template lying on a white page, in which case the black area becomes the figure against a white ground, and so on. Four different ways of organizing this arrangement are indicated schematically in the lower half of Figure 13. As you stare at the figure, the figure-ground relations can switch back and forth almost, but not quite, at will. (Another example is shown in Figure 14, and left as an exercise for the reader.)

Fig. 14. What is this?

We see things and not the holes between them; this simple fact cannot be explained in a language of pure sensations. These configurational aspects of experience have been emphasized most strongly by gestalt psychologists. They argue that the perceptual field at any moment is highly organized, highly structured. If this statement has any meaning, it is that what we experience in one part of the perceptual field is related to what we experience in other parts. To talk about sensations as if they exist in isolation, or can be moved from one part of the field to another without changing, is, therefore, extremely artificial. As soon as a sensation takes its place as part of a perceptual whole, its character is changed by the other parts of the configuration.

Now we have considered principally examples of spatial configurations; but temporal configurations are equally interesting and important. For instance, motion is an example of organization in both time and space. We can obtain an impression of movement, of course, when nothing has moved, which is the basis for the motion picture; a sequence of still pictures is presented rapidly enough to produce the illusion of continuity. We can study the illusion more simply in the laboratory with two lights that go on briefly one after the other. If the lights are placed side by side, there will appear to be movement from one to the other. The effect has been called the phi phenomenon. A person who does not know how the lights are arranged may be convinced that a light went on in one spot, and then moved through the intervening space and stopped in the second spot, where it vanished. In other words, the observer reports light coming from the space between the two sources. It is not possible to speak about this transient light as emanating from nowhere, as if it were an independent atom of sensation, for it derives its existence entirely from the pattern or configuration of the two lights in space and time.

Most psychologists no longer try to reduce the perceptual world to sensory elements, nor assume that they can learn about complicated experiences by studying only the simple ones. More and more, psychologists who study perception are shifting away from their old question, "How can I analyze this perception into its basic atoms?" and are beginning to ask a different question, "How can I discover the transformations that a perceiver can impose upon the information he takes in?" And with each new step forward in understanding the transformations, one gains increased respect for both the complexity and the beauty of our perceptual machinery.

CHAPTER VIII

---◆◆---

SPACE

The world consists of more-or-less solid objects arranged irregularly in familiar, stationary, three-dimensional space. This organization of things in space seems common, natural, and inevitable. We all take it for granted; it is too banal for comment. When we stop to analyze it, however, this altogether familiar organization becomes a rich source of insight into the way our minds work.

Consider space. One does not literally *see* space, the way one sees surfaces, colors, contours, shadows; one *infers* it, either perceptually, conceptually, or both. Space is one of the abstract schemata we impose on our world in order to make experience more coherent and meaningful.

A spatial schema can take several different forms. Space can be flat, as in a child's drawing; with two-dimensional retinas in our eyes the wonder is that we so seldom see a flat world. Or space can be positional; this is probably the schema most used whenever we are interested in specifying the location of one thing relative to another. Or space can be the great container of all objects; that is the infinite system of absolute coordinates so valuable for classical physics.[1]

Which of these schemata is the true one? Prior to the time of Newton space was generally defined as a relation between objects. Empty space was thought to be meaningless, because space and place could be understood only in terms of the objects involved. But Newton boldly introduced the framework of absolute space and stated his laws of mechanics in terms of spatial coordinates that extend to infinity in all directions. Today we find Newton's system so natural and obvious that we are surprised to learn how bitterly his contemporaries objected to this metaphysical assumption that space, like God, was infinite. But no one could then find a way to deal with the inertia principle in terms of a relative schema. Not until Einstein's theory of relativity was it possible for physicists to give up the container concept and return to a simpler positional schema. Fortunately, however, we do not have to decide which schema is correct in order to get ahead with our studies of psychological space.

Psychologically, there are two related, but roughly distinguishable ways one can impose spatial schemata on ordinary affairs. There is, first, perceptual space, which provides a frame of reference for everything we see, hear, or touch as we go about our daily business. Perceptual space is the indispensable guide for all our movements and manipulations. But there is also a second schema, which can be called conceptual space. This includes the space that physicists and astronomers talk about, but also something much more familiar to a layman. Our psychological worlds do not end with the furthest reach of the senses. Behind that wall there is a room full of familiar things, and beyond that a yard, also familiar, and the whole is embedded in the matrix of a town, which in turn fits into a region located on a continent that is part of a sphere that rotates around the sun. This extended image of space is built up slowly by experience, by fitting smaller regions together into larger ones, by asking questions, by studying maps. It is never perceived directly, however, as a face, a room, or a doorway can be perceived. People can tell us about it, can even draw pictures of it, but they are conceptual, not perceptual pictures.

But the trouble with this distinction is that so much of conceptual space keeps intruding into perceptual space. It is almost impossible to keep them separate. As soon as one begins to consider even the simplest problems, one discovers that space perception is riddled with inferences, hypotheses, assumptions, meanings, expectations, that derive from conceptual space. Figures 10 and 11 in Chapter VII provide two simple examples of a conceptual influence on perception. The great puzzle is why our conceptual space seems to affect some perceptions and not others.

Perceptually, an amazing thing about space is its immobility. Look at some object. Now look to the right of it. Now to the left. The object does not move, but sits solidly still in one place while you move your eyes or your head. You perceive a stationary object—a truly marvelous accomplishment. You do not find this strange?

Recall what happens to optical images in your eyes. Patterns of light and shadow must flash rapidly across your field of vision every time you shift your eyes. Your sensations are in kaleidoscopic flux, yet your perception of the world around you remains quite stable. When your eyes move to the right, the effect on your visual sensations should be exactly the same as if your eyes remained fixed while the entire scene swung to the left. In principle you should be able to perceive it either way: with you fixed and the world moving, or with the world fixed and you moving.

You see the world as fixed because this is your tacit theory of space—if "theory" can be used so loosely. In order to believe in your theory, you have to learn a very precise and delicate relation between the movements of your eyes and the changes in your visual experience. If you doubt the fragility of your apparently fixed, stable objects, do this: Take a pair of binoculars and once more scan back and forth across some object. Now you will find—unless you have used the binoculars a great deal—that the object moves as you change your angle of regard. The magnification provided by the binoculars alters the customary ratio of movements to visual changes. With this delicate perceptual-motor system out of balance, you can move mountains by turning your head. Perceptual mountains, that is. Your conceptual mountains remain stationary even while your eyes report they are moving.

Binoculars are not the only way to put the perceptual-motor system out of adjustment. Try the following illusion: Take a strip of paper about two inches wide and eight inches long and fold it three times as shown in Figure 15. Place it on the table resting on the two folds, with the outside flanges sticking up. Now close one eye. Imagine that the two corners labeled x in Figure 15 are not down on the table, but are actually standing up above it, as if they were on the top edge of a standing screen. (A similar reversal is more easily achieved while looking at the two-dimensional drawing in Figure 15, but with a little persistence you can also reverse the three-dimensional object.) When you have succeeded in getting the reversal to occur, slowly move your head to the left and right. If your perception of the paper is reversed, you will see it tilt and twist in a surprising way.[2] Once again, moving your head moves the world.

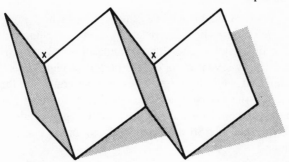

Fig. 15. The Mach-Eden illusion. Fold a strip of paper as shown and examine it with one eye. Imagine that the corners *x*, which in fact lie on the supporting surface, are on the top edge of a standing screen, and that the illumination comes from the opposite side. While the three-dimensional figure is reversed, head movements produce apparent movement in the object itself.

This phenomenon can be made to seem even more dramatic if you will hold the paper, one end in each hand. Now, with the figure reversed, rotate your hands toward your body. The paper almost feels alive as it twists in the opposite direction!

Anyone who argues that all percepts must be familiar and meaningful has trouble understanding illusions like this one. Where could we have learned to see such improbable motions? Nowhere, of course. In this case it is not the percept itself that is learned and probable and familiar; what we have learned is a way to process the incoming information. Whatever it is that we do when we see three-dimensional objects, whether it is learned or inborn, we persist in doing even when the outcome is surprising and unfamiliar. Any learning that is involved in space perception has to do with the operations we perform; we do not simply memorize new connections between visual stimuli and motor responses. We learn to make the transformations which are usually most successful in reducing the gap between our perceptual and our conceptual space.

The fact that the apparatus by which we learn about the world is itself in part a product of learning is demonstrated by our ability to relearn according to new rules. If the outcome of our perceptual transformations persists for a long enough time in looking strange and unusual, we may eventually come to terms with it. The remarkable extent of human plasticity was demonstrated by G. M. Stratton as early as 1896.[3] Stratton constructed an optical headgear that rotated the visual field 180 degrees; not only was the world turned upside down, but left and right were reversed. It was a clumsy thing consisting of a tube eight inches long mounted in a plaster cast, but he wore it for eighty-seven hours over a period of eight days, replacing it by a blindfold while he slept. His right eye could see through the tube, although the inverted field was greatly reduced in size; his left eye remained covered by the plaster cast. In spite of the inconveniences of this gadget, Stratton was able to make some instructive observations.

On his first day in topsy-turvy land he was thoroughly disoriented. His feet were above his head; he had to search for them when he wanted to see if he could walk without kicking things. His hands entered and left his field of view from above instead of from below. When he moved his head, his visual field swung rapidly in the same direction. He could not easily recognize familiar surroundings. He made inappropriate movements and could scarcely feed himself. In spite of nausea and depression he kept going and gradually he began to get accustomed to his rig. By the second day his movements had grown less laborious. By the third he was beginning to feel at home in his new environment. By the fifth day the world had stopped swinging when he moved his head; he was thinking about his body in terms of new images and was often able to avoid bumping into objects without thinking about them first. Most of his world was still upside down, but this didn't bother him much any more. Stratton commented that he did not modify his old conception of space; he simply suppressed it and learned a whole new set of visual-motor relations. His old, familiar conception of the world was no help to him. In fact, the conflict between the old and the new was the major obstacle he had to overcome. When the experiment was finished and he took the lenses out of the tube, he was again disoriented and bewildered for several hours before he became accustomed to the normal view of things.

Stratton's experiment has been repeated; there is no doubting the validity of his observations. The most extensive studies of this type have been reported by Ivo Kohler,[4] who used either left-right or up-down reversals, but not both at the same time. The up-down reversal is easier to adapt to, but in both cases a person learns to make correct movements days or even weeks before he begins to perceive a scene as if it were normally oriented. Even then there are puzzling effects when one part of the scene looks normal but another part looks reversed; perceptual adaptation becomes complete only after many weeks of wearing the lenses.

These experiments demonstrate that a completely new relation between the visual world and the world of muscular movements can be learned in a relatively short period of time. The visual-motor relation we are accustomed to is not inviolate. It is simply something we have learned to live with.

The importance of movement can be emphasized by a short detour into fantasy. Imagine a special tree that through some kind of druidical magic is half animal and half plant. This wonderful tree has sense organs—receptors sensitive to light, sound, odor, taste, touch, static position—connected by sensory nerves to a large and elaborate brain. The tree has everything that an animal has, except that it lacks a motor output. There are no motor nerves, no muscles, no glands. In short, the tree cannot *do* anything about the information it picks up. It must stand rooted in one spot, as trees have always done, moving only with the wind.

Here is the question: Would this strange tree have any advantages over an ordinary tree?

Any knowledge the imaginary tree might acquire would, of course, be useless. What good would it do the tree to see lumberjacks coming? What advantage can it gain from knowing the forest is on fire if it can do no more than feel pain? Without muscles, the tree cannot speak; it has no way to communicate its knowledge to other trees or to share in their experiences.

But to discuss the tree in these terms seems to imply that a motionless tree can accumulate knowledge. The implication may go too far. A tree that cannot move can know almost nothing, even though it has all the marvelous equipment of receptors, nerves, and brain. A basic difficulty the magical tree can never overcome is that it cannot move its sense organs. Animals can move, not only to approach the things they want and to avoid the things they fear, but also to change the location of their eyes and ears. This simple fact has a tremendous influence on the way they must organize their experience.

A tree with eyes might see a house nearby, but the tree could never suspect that the house had another side concealed from view. To discover the thickness of reality it is necessary to move around in it. We must be able to walk around the house and then, somehow, to construct a single object that accounts for all the different views we had of it. A tree with eyes but unable to move would not need an explanation for such diversity as movement generates; it would never see deeper than the flat surface of appearances. The tree's world would have the same flatness a child sees when it looks at the stars as tiny holes in the great black dome of the night.

Moreover, our tree would not be able to distinguish size from distance. When things approached the tree they would be seen as expanding in size. The tree would have no way to learn that it takes a long time to move through a long distance. And without motions through distances, the tree would have no use for time, and hence no way to date its memories. In place of three dimensions of space and one of time, the motionless tree would have but two dimensions of space. In fact, if the tree's eyes were exactly like ours, it might see nothing but movements: when a visual image is completely stabilized on our retinas so that it continues to stimulate the same visual receptor cells in spite of our eye-movements, the image will disappear entirely in twenty or thirty seconds.[5] It is another case of sensory adaptation. For our visual system to work at all, it must experience continuous change in the images that fall on it. This change comes automatically when we move about.

A sentient but immobile intelligence would not develop anything resembling the state of consciousness that men, and probably other mammals as well, take for granted. Only an active being can possess knowledge of an objective reality as something distinguishable from its own private pains and joys.

Our conception of space and time is reserved for creatures who can move about in space and time, who need space and time to reduce and simplify the confusion of appearances reported by their moving sense organs. To attain the conception of a stable environment of objects when the only evidence we have is a haphazard flow of energies into our receptors is one of the great triumphs of childhood. Yet we scarcely notice that it happens. Space and time were always there, as far back as we can remember. In the words of the great German philosopher, Immanuel Kant, space and time are a priori categories of experience, given by the nature of the mind itself. But of course! Before we had the concepts of space and time as a coordinate system to organize our experience, we had no intelligible cognitive structure. Of course we cannot remember or imagine what it was like not to have such a frame of reference. But that does not mean there was never a time in childhood before we had discovered these majestic coordinates of the adult mind.

Sensitive trees are pure fantasy. Nothing of the kind could ever exist. Or could it?

Before we move on too quickly, we should pause to consider the frog. Oddly enough, in the visual modality, at least, there is a crude resemblance between a frog and a tree with eyes.

A frog's head and eyes do not move to notice events or to search for objects or to look where it is going. They move, but only to compensate for movements of its body, for instance, when a wave rocks its lily pad. The frog's eyes are actively stabilized. It has, at least to a first approximation, the kind of immobile visual apparatus that the magical tree would have. It is true, of course, that frogs can move and trees cannot. But on land, frogs move by sudden jumps. Since they are equally at home on land or in water, they do not care where they come down. What a frog sees during its jumps we will never know, but we can probably assume that on land most of the frog's looking is done while it is stationary. The resemblance is imperfect but a frog is enough like the imaginary tree to make the comparison interesting.

What does a frog see? The most striking thing about its vision is that the frog never responds to stationary objects. It will automatically try to eat any buglike object that is about the right size, and moves. But the frog would starve to death in the midst of plenty if its prey were motionless. It does not see color. The lens of its eye is the fixed-focus type and leaves the wretch nearsighted on land, farsighted under water. Its visual acuity must be very poor; it cannot see details the way we do. In short, the frog, like our tree, has a very limited kind of vision. All the evidence says that frogs have not the faintest inkling of the elaborate spatio-temporal world we humans inhabit.

It is possible to get some idea of what a frog can see by recording electrical potentials from its visual nervous system. With a microelectrode properly placed in the optic nerve, the experimenter can vary the pattern of light entering the frog's eye until he discovers what it takes to stimulate a particular nerve fiber. With this technique it has been found that there are four different groups of fibers.[6]

Each group is activated by a different kind of stimulation in the eye. Apparently, therefore, there are four separate operations on the image in a frog's eye; the outcome of each different operation is transmitted to the brain by a different group of fibers.

One operation detects the occurrence of any sharp edge separating light from dark. If such an edge moves into the field of vision and stops, one group of fibers starts to fire nerve impulses up to the brain. A second operation detects small, moving spots; this is the bug-detector. Another operation detects the presence of a moving edge. A fourth detects the onset of darkness in any large area of the visual field. These four operations comprise the total vocabulary of visual forms and events in a frog's world. Obviously, anyone who insists on talking about perception as a compound made up of many elementary color patches will find little to say about a frog.

These studies prove that it is possible to get some use out of a stationary eye after all. Granted, it is nothing at all like our own visual experience; but notice how the stationary eye is used. It waits inert until one of four things happens and then it responds appropriately. To everything else a frog is blind. In other words, a frog has four a priori categories of experience; certainly its visual experience is not constructed by some kind of Wundtian association of simple sensations. The frog is on the side of Immanuel Kant and against the British empiricists.

Before we conclude that frogs are hopelessly special and unique, we should recall that there is a long, largely German, tradition in philosophical psychology according to which perception is to be considered in terms of the operations of testing and sorting, rather than in terms of associating elementary sensations. Perhaps a frog is not an unusual, but an unusually simple, case.

If a frog's eye can perform four separate operations, presumably a mammalian eye can perform many more. Can one specify what they might be?

Perhaps a few of them can be illustrated. For example, operations on the image in the human eye probably should include the rules of grouping discovered by gestalt psychologists. The gestalt psychologists have not generally talked about their work in this context, however, so we must interrupt our argument briefly to illustrate the sort of puzzles they like to study.

An important question for gestalt psychology is to understand why some parts of the visual world hang together as unitary configurations and other parts do not. Located irregularly in space, denser below the natural plane of our eyes, are middle-sized clumps of stuff that resist our pushes, that go all together when they do move, that have colors and textures and shapes that persist in time. We usually see these clumps as figures which stand out against their backgrounds. Gestalt psychologists have listed a number of factors that affect the passively perceived patterns:[7]

Proximity. The smaller the interval between them, in space or time, the greater is the tendency to group two things together as a unit. The effect of proximity is illustrated in Figure 16.

Similarity. If two things are similar, we tend to perceive them as belonging together. The effect of similarity is illustrated in Figure 17.

O O   O O   O O

O O   O O   O O

O O   O O   O O

O O   O O   O O

O O   O O   O O

Fig. 16. Proximity causes us to group the dots into three pairs of vertical columns.

Fig. 17. Similarity causes us to see vertical, rather than horizontal, lines of dots.

It is a simple matter to put the different factors in competition with each other. For example, in Figure 18 the columns of similar dots are farther apart, or, if you prefer, the columns that are closest together consist of dissimilar dots. Such patterns are fickle; they shift easily whichever way they get the most attention.

Common fate. If things move together, at the same time in the same direction, we group them together as a unit.

Set (Einstellung). An observer who has seen things grouped in one manner will remain set to see them that way even when the conditions are slowly changed until the original grouping is no longer appropriate.

Direction. If one pattern continues in the same direction as another, the two patterns will be grouped together (as, for example, when two lines intersect to form four line segments).

Closure. Things will be grouped together if this produces a closed, stable, balanced, symmetric, "good" figure.

Habit. Things will be grouped together if they are familiar in that grouping. For example,

NOONNOONNOONNOONNOON

would, according to the factor of similarity, be seen as pairs of N's alternating with pairs of O's, but reading habits enable us to see this configuration either as an alternation of NO and ON, or as a sequence of NOON's. In this example, habit and similarity conflict, but we can tip the scales in either direction by allying proximity with one or the other:

N OO NN OO NN OO NN OO NN OO N,

or

NO ON NO ON NO ON NO ON NO ON,

or

NOON NOON NOON NOON NOON.

All of these factors are purely sensory—no movements by the

Fig. 18. Proximity and similarity are here put in opposition. The resultant grouping is unstable.

observer are required. Our intelligent tree might be able to notice such clusterings and groupings in its environment on the basis of these gestalt factors.[8] But it would have little reason to suspect the existence of objects and no real use for the objective hypothesis even if it did suspect. Many other factors become effective, many other perceptual operations are required, as soon as we begin to move about and to obtain simultaneously varying information about an object from two or three sense modalities at the same time. Then we must, if only for the economy in our cognitive bookkeeping, reduce all our many different impressions to a single object that is the source of those impressions. We can summarize a great variety of stimulations by a single conception of an object and so simplify our idea of the world we live in. We need not memorize separately all its different aspects, distances, illuminations, motions, warmths, and so on, in order to remember an object and to recognize it when we see it later.

These gestalt factors describe some of the ways we transform our perceptual experience. They indicate some of the operations we use to impose structure, coherence, and organization on our perceptual flux. The same can undeniably be said of a frog. In a sense, therefore, we can imagine a certain functional similarity between a frog's perception of space and our own. But the differences far outweigh the similarities. We have greater acuity, a wider variety of operations, a way to cope with moving sense organs. We have color perception, depth perception, stereoscopic perception. And most important of all, a human eye is backed up by the vast resources of a human brain. This marvellous organ enables us to learn or invent new operations, and new ways of combining the results of old operations. Whereas a frog is forever limited to its four, we can devise new operations, new tests, new categories.

Instead of worrying about magical trees, therefore, it might be much more to the point to wonder how a child experiences space and how he acquires, combines, and builds his vocabulary of perceptual skills. Unfortunately, children cannot say and adults cannot remember how a child's conception of space differs from an adult's. The most we can do is to patch together various scraps of evidence in as plausible a guess as we can formulate.

Some psychologists have tried to infer the child's world from his drawings. To anyone who objects that a child is too poor a drafts-

man to show us what he really sees, they reply that it is not lack of
skill that makes the child's drawings what they are. An adult who
draws with his left hand can produce unskilled drawings, but they
are totally different from a child's. There is a lack of differentiation
in a child's drawings that cannot be explained as mere clumsiness.
The child seems to have something very different in mind.

Rudolf Arnheim has summarized the development of drawings as
a succession of stages.[9] At first the child gestures, scrawling with motions that make his feelings visible. Then, says Arnheim, he discovers
the circle, the closed contour that isolates the space inside from the
space outside. These circular scribbles have the character of objects,
and a child will use them to represent all objects, indiscriminately.
At this stage, for example, one circle may represent both head and
body, as though the two were not yet clearly differentiated for the
child.

Fig. 19. Do children really see people this way?

Next he begins to combine circles and straight lines, but his first
serious experimentation with linearity is usually confined to the horizontal and vertical directions. Only later does the child add oblique
angles. Eventually he begins to fuse several units into a continuous,

more differentiated contour. By this time a fairly advanced level of perceptual-motor skill has been attained.

At first a child draws everything the same size; a house, a man, a cow will all be equal in height. Any child who lived in such an elastic space would never be able to find his way around, but when he draws pictures he seems to tell us that all objects are equal, that they are all isolated from each other by a standard distance and never overlap, that they all present their most typical and familiar aspect toward the artist's eye, that the child can even see through the surface to the parts inside.

It is impossible to believe that such pictures faithfully represent what a child perceives; indeed, many children spontaneously express dismay that their pictures look so strange. Instead of perceptions they are loaded with conceptions, only slightly less stylized than the pictograms that must have served as the earliest kind of writing. It is as if the child drew up a verbal list of all the objects he wanted to include in a finished picture, then drew each independently, according to his own conception of the object. Adult notions of perspective, of light and shadow, of foreshortening, of interposition of a near object in front of a distant one—which are part of the repertory of the adult draftsman—are completely missing from children's drawings. It is not that the child wants it this way, but unequipped with this repertory, the child cannot conceal the underlying conceptual nature of his drawing.

With these drawings we seem, therefore, to have passed beyond the realm of space perception, beyond the tacit and immediate processes that guide us through three dimensions, and into a realm of purely conceptual space, a synthetic realm filled with isolated, equal-sized, stereotyped, almost Platonic objects.

The two realms must be related, yet distinct; compatible, yet self-sufficient. If it ever becomes absolutely necessary to draw a sharp line between them, we will be in serious trouble. Like so many of the terms psychologists use, the distinction is meaningful but vague. Exactly how these crude notions of perceptual and conceptual space should be replaced by scientific terms more precisely defined is one of the thorny questions facing psychologists of the future.

CHAPTER IX

FRANCIS GALTON,
ANTHROPOLOGIST

One of the most important books in the history of Western thought is Charles Darwin's *The Origin of Species by Means of Natural Selection.* This book, which freed intelligent men of an ancient superstition and signalized the scientific maturity of the life sciences, influenced the development of modern psychology as much as any other single event in the nineteenth century. It would be impossible to understand what psychologists today are trying to accomplish or why they go about it as they do unless one first understood something of the importance of evolutionary theory for our contemporary vision of man and his destiny.

The appearance of Darwin's book in 1859 set off controversy of the most intense and exciting kind. Within a year of its publication a debate at Oxford between Thomas Henry Huxley—who fought for science, Darwin, evolution—and Bishop Wilberforce—who defended the Book of Genesis—caused a public sensation in England. Wilberforce asked Huxley whether it was through his grandmother or his grandfather that he claimed descent from an ape, thus phrasing the central issue in terms every man could understand. Huxley replied that an ape would be preferable to the Bishop as an ancestor, and with that the battle began. Science and religion were at it again.

Although we tend to think of biological evolution as Darwin's theory, its origins are quite ancient. Its systematic development in modern times is often said to have begun with George Louis Leclerc, Comte de Buffon, whose forty-four volumes of *Natural History* published in France between 1749 and 1804 attempted to tie together isolated facts and observations into a connected story. Buffon's highly readable style did much to popularize nature studies, but he is usually remembered as a poor scientist. Nevertheless, he saw that the historical development had to be accounted for and that an Aristotelian argument in terms of final causes would not suffice.

It was Erasmus Darwin who, toward the end of the eighteenth century, considered almost every important idea that has since been put forward as an explanation of the way one species can be transformed into another, including the ideas for which his two grandsons, Charles Darwin and Francis Galton, later became famous. Erasmus Darwin's belief that all warm-blooded animals developed from "one living filament" endowed with animality by the Creator deserved a better reputation than it gained. Perhaps his Victorian grandsons failed to mention him because they were embarrassed by his penchant for irregular romantic adventures, but more likely the reason was that his name became linked in the public mind with an evolutionary theory put forward by the Chevalier de Lamarck.

Lamarck's was a behavioral theory of evolution. The giraffe reached up for the highest branches until, after many generations, he stretched his neck to its present odd proportions. The crane got its long legs through generations of stretching them while standing in the water, and the snake lost its legs entirely after generations of retracting them in order to move through the grass without being detected. The behavior of one generation affects its bodily structures; these small changes are then passed on to its offspring. This process continues generation after generation until the cumulative effect is sufficient to create a recognizably new species. The doctrine is usually referred to as "the inheritance of acquired characteristics," and its best-known advocate today is the Russian, Trofim Denisovich Lysenko. Unfortunately, Lamarck's examples made the theory of evolution sound slightly ridiculous and when the famous French naturalist Baron Cuvier refused to entertain an evolutionary hypothesis because the evidence was so inadequate the theory seemed to have suffered a mortal blow.

Although evolution was not scientifically respectable during the first half of the nineteenth century, people persisted in talking about it. Auguste Comte advanced an evolutionary hypothesis for social development. Herbert Spencer accepted Lamarck's ideas and searched for a philosophic justification for the concept of progress. Charles Darwin set about collecting the evidence that would be needed to convince such men as Cuvier. Patrick Mathew and Edward Blyth developed the idea of natural (as opposed to artificial) selection. Just a year before *The Origin of Species* was published Alfred Russell Wallace sent Darwin a paper setting forth a theory of man's origins based, like Darwin's theory, on natural selection. Respectable scientists tried to keep the lid on, but inside the evolutionary kettle pressure was slowly building up. Darwin's book in 1859, with its mass of detailed evidence and argument collected throughout a quarter of a century, was the explosion that at last forced man to revise his conception of himself. Prior to 1859 biological evolution had been a controversial speculation; after 1859 it was a controversial fact.

Important as they were, however, Darwin's ideas would not concern us here had they not influenced the young science of psychology so strongly during its formative years. Consider some of the more obvious lines of influence.

The most direct consequence of seeing man in the framework of an evolutionary theory was the emphasis it placed upon his relation to other animals, especially to the great apes. Darwin, foreseeing the violence that would result from applying the theory to man, concentrated his argument in *The Origin of Species* on the lower animals almost entirely. The evasion fooled no one. Finally, in *The Descent of Man* (1871), Darwin applied his argument to the most interesting animal of all—and showed him to be merely another temporary phase in the story of life. The process of biological evolution is going on now as it always has, and it affects man as it affects all animals.

To most psychologists it was immediately obvious that the techniques they used to study the most highly evolved animal would now have to be generalized and extended to other animals as well. The available evidence for the continuity from animals to man was largely anatomical, but one could dream of showing similar continuities in the development of behavior and even in the development of the mind itself. One effect of evolutionism on psychology, therefore, was the introduction of a new universe of subjects into the psychological laboratory. And so animal psychology was born.

A second consequence of evolutionary thinking was a shift in emphasis, a change in what psychologists considered their goal to be. Whereas the introspective psychologists considered their major task to be the analysis of the contents of consciousness and relating them, where possible, to physiological processes, Darwin's theories were phrased in terms of the struggle for survival. After Darwin, the question, "What *functions* does consciousness serve?" seemed much more fundamental than the question, "What *elements* does consciousness contain?" The very fact that an animal had evolved through thousands of generations implied that the changes were adaptive, that the modified animal was better prepared than its ancestors to fight the battles of life in the present environment. The adaptation of an organism to its environment became a central concern of all the life sciences, psychology as well as biology, and the inner contemplation of mental images began to lose its appeal.

A third, rather unfortunate consequence of Darwin's book was the growth of a philosophy that has since been called social Darwinism. In his discussion of evolution Darwin emphasized the competition among different animals—each would tend to increase its number in a geometric progression if it were not held in check by the competition for food. In this struggle the weak would perish and leave the strong to continue the species. This Malthusian emphasis on struggle, coupled with a belief that acquired characteristics can be inherited, caught the public fancy. It was interpreted to mean, for example, that capitalistic competition was the source of all social progress. In America social Darwinism as preached by Herbert Spencer ("Survival of the fittest") and William Graham Sumner ("Millionaires are a product of natural selection") provided the newly-rich industrialists with scientific proof that their great wealth was fair payment for their superior talents.[1] But they were badly misled by the language Darwin and Spencer used. "Survival of the fittest" carries a suggestion that the strong, healthy, aggressive organisms will always survive, whereas the truth seems to be that usually the most fertile, not the strongest, are most likely to escape extinction.

Another important effect of evolutionism on modern psychology was the emphasis it put on variation, on individual differences. Clearly, if every offspring is identical with its parents, evolution will not occur. There are, however, several sources of variation. In the first place, the offspring are different from their parents because they have had different experiences. Darwin and his contemporaries thought the effects of these experiences were inherited, but genetic research has since discarded this possibility. A second reason offspring are different from their parents is that they receive a random combination of the genes from each parent—and this kind of random variation *is* inherited. Moreover, a third reason the offspring are different from their parents is that unpredictable mutations occur in the genes themselves; the mutations are also inheritable. The important point is this: Any hereditary variation that gives its possessor an advantage in fertility, that increases the probability his offspring will live to reach sexual maturity, will automatically increase the fraction of animals possessing that variation.

Variation is an essential component of any evolutionary theory. Thus, where Wundt searched for the general, universal principles governing all minds, psychologists interested in evolution began to catalogue all the ways minds could differ from one another.

Evolutionism gave a statistical flavor to psychological thinking that has increased with every succeeding generation of psychologists. When one goes beyond the question, "What is the average value?" and begins to ask about the range of variation that can occur, to ask how one kind of variation is related to another, to ask whether an observed variation should be attributed to chance, and so on, the need for sophisticated tools of statistical analysis quickly becomes apparent.

No one better represents an evolutionary attitude toward psychology than Galton. Evolutionary ideas were not quite what Wundt had had in mind for his new psychology. But if the psychology of Wilhelm Wundt offered little room for questions growing out of evolutionism, then it simply had to be loosened up until room was found. And the person who showed most clearly how this could be done was the ingenious Englishman, Sir Francis Galton.

Francis Galton, the last of nine children, was born in 1822 at the Larches, near Sparkbrook, Birmingham, England. His father was a successful and prosperous banker.

Young Frank was extremely intelligent. If we can believe the records of his boyhood achievements, his IQ must have been nearly 200—which places him in a class with some of the most intelligent ᴍen who ever lived.[2] His father decided that the boy should become a doctor, should have a profession that would enable him to earn his own living if that became necessary. At sixteen, therefore, Galton became a House Pupil at the Birmingham General Hospital. At this tender age he walked rounds with the doctors, dispensed to out-patients, read medical books, set broken bones, amputated fingers, kept hospital records, vaccinated children, pulled teeth, and read Horace and Homer on alternate days. But a hospital is not a pleasant way of life, and only his father's determination kept him at it.

After a year of hospital horrors he went to King's College, Lon-don, where he attended medical lectures, absorbed the scientific at-mosphere, and confirmed his opinion that doctors, like parsons, are far too positive. He moved on to Trinity College, Cambridge, where he put a plaster bust of Newton opposite the fireplace and studied mathematics. The standard program at Cambridge consisted of hard work and competitive examinations; the standard consequence was bad health and mental depression, with degrees for those strong enough to survive. Galton, undoubtedly one of the most intelligent men of his time, managed to graduate, but not with honors. Once more he returned to the study of medicine, but his father's death re-leased him from a profession he had come to hate.

After a tour of Egypt and Syria—the Mohammedans impressed him—he made a serious attempt to settle down. For a time he was in danger of following his elder brothers into the life of an English country gentleman. But his wanderlust, a romantic, Victorian interest in distant and exotic things, defeated him. Six fallow years ended in 1850, when he invented a teletype printer and set off to explore Africa. He filled a book with his adventures, and won a medal from the Royal Geographic Society.

In the 1850's he was a geographer. His own explorations were ter-minated by marriage and bad health, but he served on countless com-mittees, wrote a book for explorers called *The Art of Travelling,* organized expeditions for others, and read countless reports until at last his restless attention began to wander once more. From geogra-phy to meteorology was a short step. He designed instruments to plot weather data (mechanical inventions of every description were a lifelong hobby), made the first serious attempt to chart the weather over large areas, and his charts led him to discover and name the anticyclone (a remarkable theoretical insight based on the crudest kind of data).

He read relatively little and then only what was necessary for the problem at hand, but when his cousin, another nonacademic scientist, published *The Origin of Species,* Galton read it and became immediately a strong supporter of the new theory.

Sir Francis Galton

As an ex-doctor and ex-biologist, Galton was at first interested in the biological details. The genetic hypothesis Darwin advanced was that the organs of the body secrete gemmules, little vestiges of themselves, into the blood. The blood, he hypothesized, carries the gemmules to the sex glands. The sex glands use the gemmules to build sex cells. Therefore, the sex cells contain a master plan for building another organism just like the parent. Darwin used his gemmule hypothesis to explain the inheritance of acquired characteristics. If the organs of the body are changed by events during the life of the parent, the changes must appear in the gemmules, then in the sex cells, and finally in the offspring. This was the theory whose validity Galton questioned.

He was not convinced that acquired characteristics can be inherited. To test Darwin's theory, he transfused blood between black rabbits and white rabbits and found that the transfusions have no effect on the color of the offspring. Therefore, the imaginary gemmules could not be an explanation of the mechanism of heredity. In spite of these results, however, both Darwin and Galton continued to look to the blood for an explanation. Gregor Mendel might have helped them, but his work went unappreciated for thirty-five years. And Darwin had explicitly rejected the early experiments of the Frenchman Charles Naudin which had shown the parent strains blending in the first generation but reappearing again in the second, experiments which were less elegant but which anticipated Mendel's results. Blood was too much a part of the everyday language of kinship for anyone to assume it was completely irrelevant to the hereditary mechanism.

The genetic side of Darwin's theory did not detain Galton for long; it was the social implication that really fired his imagination. In his travels he had seen many different societies of men. He knew something of the variation in human physical characteristics and he suspected the differences in mentality were even greater. "It is in the most unqualified manner," he wrote, "that I object to pretensions of natural equality."[3] It seemed obvious to him that the great variation among men—physical, mental, and moral—must be inherited. And it was equally obvious that the human strain can be improved, just as livestock is improved, by artificial selection. It was necessary merely to decide what characteristics one wished to establish, to develop techniques for measuring the extent to which an individual possessed them, and to control breeding in the light of the results of the measurements. To achieve this end he officially founded the science of human eugenics and contributed to the eugenic dream of a superman. By selecting men and women for rare and similar talents and mating them together generation after generation, an extraordinarily gifted race would evolve. Even moral and religious sentiments could be improved by rigid selection.

The evidence he gathered—for he was not one to sit quietly by when there were observations to be made—was presented in four important books on the inheritance of mental traits in man, books calculated to support his eugenic creed with scientific facts: *Hereditary Genius* (1869), *English Men of Science* (1874), *Human Faculty* (1883), and *Natural Inheritance* (1889).

The purpose of *Hereditary Genius* was to show that eminence follows family lines far too frequently to explain it on the basis of environmental influences. In tackling this question he assumed implicitly that eminent men are naturally superior and that superior men are naturally eminent—no mute, inglorious Miltons worried him. His quaint and optimistic identification of talent with success was illustrated when he wrote: "If a man is gifted with vast intellectual ability, eagerness to work, and power of working, I cannot comprehend how such a man should be repressed."[4] Once the Great Man is born he must inevitably realize his genius for the profit of all mankind. The only difficulty, as Galton saw it, was to get him born. Thus breeding better men was the central task for social progress.

To test the eugenic thesis, he necessarily became entangled in problems of measurement. And, after measurement, statistics. In *Hereditary Genius* he relied upon his own subjective estimates of eminence as his method of measurement, and he stated his conclusions in statistical form: Great men have a higher probability of producing great sons than do average men. There were forty-eight eminent sons for every one hundred eminent fathers, a figure so high that he considered giving some of the credit to the mothers, but not high enough to make him consider seriously the advantages of environment, education, and opportunity that such sons might enjoy. His own education, for example, he regarded as largely a waste of time. For Galton, the Great Man provided a hereditary nucleus around which ability clustered with a closeness that rapidly diminished as the distance of kinship from its center increased, as the bloodline thinned out.

The *Inquiries into Human Faculty and its Development,* published in 1883, established Galton as the pioneer of scientific psychology in England. The book is a collection of miscellaneous essays loosely connected by their preoccupation with psychological subjects. He approached psychology with the attitude of a physical anthropologist. He wanted the same kind of data about the dimensions of a man's mind as anthropologists were already collecting about man's anatomy. And he fully expected to find that the mental measurements, when they could be made, would turn out to be closely related to the body measurements. He realized that if they were to provide a complete description of a man, anthropometric measures of stature, weight, skin color, etc., would have to be supplemented by psychometric measures of the senses, the memory, the imagination. But to the day he died he was unwilling to admit that the size of a man's skull had no value as a measure of his intelligence.

His task, therefore, was to develop a set of psychological measurements that could be made quickly and accurately on thousands of people. This gave him an excuse to be an inventor again, and with great enthusiasm and ingenuity he set about devising instruments to measure the senses. He invented a whistle (the length of a closed pipe was varied by a threaded plug in the end of it, and calibrated to a tenth of a turn) to measure the highest frequencies of acoustic vibration that men can hear. He invented a simple photometer to test how accurately people can match two spots of color. He used a calibrated pendulum to measure how quickly people can respond to lights and sounds. He selected a series of weights and measured kinesthetic sensitivity by having people arrange them in order from lightest to heaviest. He invented a bar with a variable distance scale that he could use to test people's ability to estimate visual extensions. He used a rotating disc to test the capacity for estimating the perpendicular. He invented a device—not entirely successful—to measure the velocity of movement attained when a person strikes a blow. He tested smell by having people arrange in order bottles containing material with the same odor but of different intensity. All his tests were simple and relatively inexpensive. They were to be used by anthropologists, as they used scales and measuring tapes, to gather data from large numbers of persons.

Galton's study of psychology was not limited to these sensory phenomena. His next interest was in mental imagery. He became one of the first persons to use the form of persecution known today as the psychological questionnaire. He asked his victims to imagine their breakfast table. Was the image dim or clear? Bright or dark? Extended or clear only in spots? Colored or not colored? His first subjects were scientific acquaintances, since he thought they would be competent to give the most accurate answers. He was astonished to learn that most of them had no clear imagery, and some considered it fanciful when others spoke as if they did. But when he turned from scientists and academicians to ordinary people leading ordinary lives, he found they had perfectly distinct images, full of detail and color. Women and children were especially emphatic in their reports of concrete, detailed imagery. Perhaps, he speculated, imagery is antagonistic to the kind of abstract thought that scientists practice; the ability to form clear images may atrophy from disuse.

He noted that there were large differences in the flexibility of images among persons who reported having them. Some respondents said that their first image was the clearest and that further images would blur and confuse the details. Others claimed to have complete mastery over their images, to be able to call up the face of a friend at will and to modify it in any manner that occurred to them. Following Galton's description of the tremendous variations among individuals in the clarity and flexibility of their mental imagery, it was a rash philosopher indeed who would persist in supposing that anything universally valid could be said about such a general faculty as Imagination, or that there existed a typical Mind that all human minds resembled.

Galton also tackled the problem of measuring the association of ideas; his motto was, "Whenever you can, count." His first attempt consisted of walking 450 yards down Pall Mall, fixing his attention on every successive object that caught his eye until it suggested one or two thoughts to him. The first time he did this he was amazed to notice that samples of his whole life had occurred to him; many incidents he thought long forgotten were fleetingly represented in his associations. Several days later he repeated the walk. His admiration for the teeming activity of his mind was seriously diminished when he discovered that his associations were in large measure repetitions of the associations he had had during his first attempt.

To get a better grip on these fleeting ideas he devised a scheme that involved writing words on small slips of paper. Later, after he had forgotten the particular words, he laid one of the slips partly under the edge of a book. Then he leaned forward until he could read the word he had written. In one hand he held a watch to time his reactions and with the other he wrote quickly the first two ideas that the word suggested. And this was how he invented the word association test—the first attempt to subject associationism to experiment. Wundt quickly adopted the experiment, improved it by limiting the response to a single word, and made it a part of the methodological equipment of his laboratory in Leipzig.

In summarizing his studies of associations, Galton wrote:

> Perhaps the strongest of the impressions left by the experiments regards the multifariousness of the work done by the mind in a state of half-unconsciousness, and the valid reason they afford for believing in the existence of still deeper strata of mental operations, sunk wholly below the level of consciousness, which may account for such mental phenomena as cannot otherwise be explained.[5]

Which was a surprising thing to say in an age when many psychologists considered an unconscious mind to be a logical contradiction.

He spoke of the ideas in full consciousness as being in the "presence-chamber" of his mind; nearby was the "antechamber of consciousness" full of related ideas waiting to be summoned into the presence-chamber.

Galton was never satisfied with a problem until he discovered something to count, some proportions to calculate, or some averages to compare. The recourse to statistical analysis was a persistent feature of his work on psychological questions. In this respect he continued and expanded the ideas of the Belgian, Adolph Quetelet. Quetelet analyzed data on the stature of ten thousand people and drew a chart showing the number found at each height. A few persons were very short, a few very tall, but the majority in his sample clustered around the middle of the range. Thus, his curve had the shape of a bell, as shown in Figures 20 and 21, an example of the

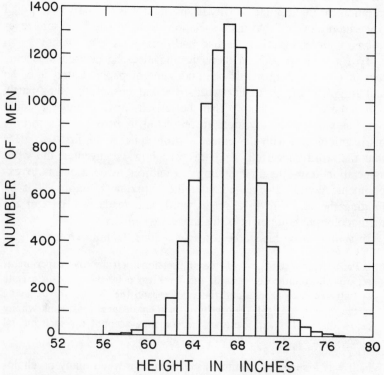

Fig. 20. The number of men of each height is indicated by a vertical bar. The measurement was made on 8585 English-born men.

Fig. 21. The data of Fig. 20 are here replotted as a frequency curve to emphasize its bell shape.

normal probability curve. Such a result, Quetelet argued, was to be expected if all men were cast in the same mold, but emerged with purely accidental differences. Galton accepted the argument as a basic principle of anthropometry and assumed it must hold true for mental as well as physical traits. Since the shape of the curve was relatively simple and remarkably stable from one trait to another, the entire distribution of measurements could be summarized by two numbers: one representing the average value, the other the range of variation or dispersion around the central value. The problem of measurement, therefore, was to collect a large enough sample from which to plot the curve, and obtain from it reliable estimates of the average and of the variance around the average.

In order to collect the data he needed from large numbers of people, Galton in 1884 put together his Anthropometric Laboratory as a demonstration for the International Health Exhibition in London. For 3*d.* one gained entry to a long, narrow room where an attendant supervised instruments for measuring height, weight, span, breathing power, strength of pull and squeeze, quickness of blow, hearing, seeing, color sense, and other personal data. One passed along the line watching his data card fill with numbers, then departed with a good, clean feeling of having contributed to science by being measured accurately in many surprising ways.

The little laboratory attracted much interest and manufactured large quantities of data; the question was what to do with all the numbers that had accumulated on all the cards. As a first step, Galton charted the data as Quetelet had done and found the usual bell-shaped probability curves; the shape was the same for psychological as for anatomical measurements. The curves were interesting and instructive, but even after they had all been plotted it was obvious that there was a great deal more information on the data cards than he knew how to extract. Every person who had passed through the laboratory had contributed several different measures. What were the relations among them? Given two sets of measurements, how could one represent the fact that persons who scored high on one test tended to score high on the other? For example, tall people tend to weigh more than short people; how should the strength of the tendency be measured?

The problem of relating two sets of measurements also arose in a most critical fashion in his studies of inheritance. In these studies, he had two probability curves, one based on measurements of the parents, the other on measurements of their offspring. To establish the fact of inheritance, he had to demonstrate that there is a relation between the parents' measurements and their children's measurements. For example, tall parents tend to have tall children; how should the strength of this tendency be measured?

Galton had data on the heights of all the members of several families. He cast these up in the form of a table, with the possible heights of the parents (the average of each set of two parents represented a fictional "mid-parent") along the side, and the possible heights of the children along the top of the table. In the cells of the table he entered the actual number of children whose height was given by the column heading and whose "mid-parent's" height was given by the row heading. He carried this table with him everywhere he went; when he had a few moments free he would try to discover the reason for the paradox he saw there.

The puzzle is this: If two tall persons marry and have children, the children will usually not be as tall as the parents. The children will usually be taller than the average height of the general population, but they will be nearer to the average than their parents. The corresponding statement is also true of short families; two short parents will usually have short children, but the children will tend to be nearer the population average than are their parents. At first it seemed to Galton that the entire population must be converging slowly toward an average height; after a few more generations of this sort of regression toward the average everyone would be of equal stature, and all variation would have disappeared. But this, as he soon realized, is nonsense. If it were going to happen at all, it would have happened long ago. Is there some biological process that holds variation in check, that drags the offspring back toward mediocrity? Or was there something faulty in the mathematical analysis of the data that was leading him to look for natural forces that do not exist?

One morning he was studying his table while he waited in a railway station. Suddenly he recognized a pattern in the crude data. If he took the average of each *row,* and plotted it on a graph, the succession of points formed an approximately straight line. But if he took the averages, in the same way, of the successive *columns* in the table, the points also formed a straight line. The two lines were different, but they intersected at the average value for the entire population. (This situation is illustrated in Figure 22 for four tables of hypothetical data.) Moreover, he saw that the variation in the different rows was nearly constant, as was the variation in the different columns, but the row and column variances were less than the over-all variance of the entire population. In short, he saw for the first time what now is called a "normal correlation surface." After this amazing insight it was only necessary to express the relations mathematically; the task was accomplished later by Galton's student, Karl Pearson.[6] The puzzling regression toward the average turned out to have a mathematical, not a biological origin.

The situation Galton was struggling with can perhaps be visualized more easily if one imagines an ellipse that surrounds the data. If the ellipse is long and thin, as it would be in the lower right

Fig. 22. Hypothetical data are used to illustrate how the two regression lines change. In the upper left the two variables are independent (knowing the value of one variable does not help you guess the value of the other), the correlation coefficient is r = 0, and the regression lines are at right angles, on top of the coordinate axes. In the lower right the two variables are closely related, the correlation coefficient is r = 0.92, and the two regression lines are very close together. (After H. M. Walker, *Elementary Statistical Methods.* New York: Holt, 1943.)

corner of Figure 22, the correlation between the two variables is quite close. If the ellipse is a perfect circle, as in the upper left corner of Figure 22, there is no correlation between the variables; they are independent, and one cannot be used to predict the other. If the ellipse is of intermediate width, there is some correlation, but not perfect predictability. The correlation, if it exists, may be either direct or inverse, positive or negative. All these possibilities were captured by Karl Pearson in a single number, the "Pearson product-moment correlation coefficient," which varies from $+1$ when the correlation is direct and perfect, through 0 when there is no correlation, to -1 when the correlation is inverse and perfect. The correlation coefficient r is given for all four examples in Figure 22.

Galton's insight led to the development of a measure of correlation, a measure that has since become one of the most important tools in the entire field of applied mathematics. Covariation is a central concept, not only for genetics and psychology, but for all scientific inquiry. A scientist searches for the causes of events; all he ever finds are correlations between antecedent and consequent conditions. To have a simple measure of correlation that can be used to test one's theoretical deductions has enormously facilitated the extension of scientific research into areas where perfect, one-to-one, causal relations are almost never noted, but where degrees of correlation may give some clue to the causal processes that are at work. Galton's insight has been, and continues to be, essential for vast stretches of modern social and behavioral science, and is useful in countless ways to engineers and natural scientists as well. Many of the statistical tools that later generations of psychologists would need grew in large measure out of these pioneer studies.

Galton pointed in the direction psychology was soon to go. The problems that psychologists were to become interested in were problems posed in the context of evolution—adaptation, variation, covariation, heredity versus environment, comparisons of species, studies of children. And so Wundt's science began to change its appearance almost as soon as it was born. As Boring describes it:

> The Americans travelled to Leipzig to learn about the new psychology from Wundt; they came back fired with enthusiasm for physiological psychology and experimental laboratories; they got their universities to let them give the new courses and have the new laboratories; they extolled their German importation; and then, with surpris-

ingly little comment on what they were doing and probably but little awareness of it, they changed the pattern of psychological activity from the description of the generalized mind to the assessment of personal capacities in the successful adjustment of the individual to his environment. The apparatus was Wundt's, but the inspiration was Galton's.[7]

Where Wundt preserved the past, Galton built a foundation for the future. Although he spent only fifteen years actively engaged in pursuits we would recognize as psychological, Galton is the source of much more modern psychology than is Wundt. Partly, of course, he rode on the crest of the evolutionary wave that was changing men's vision in all the biological and social sciences. But what is more impressive to the modern eye, and probably more important for his influence on psychology, is the amazing intelligence and creativity of this gentle Englishman who always seemed to know which way to set out in search of the truth.

CHAPTER X

---·◆·---

RECOGNIZING AND IDENTIFYING

Recognition seems so simple, direct, immediate. The skillful processing of information that must be involved is not itself apparent, for the object seems familiar as soon as the eyes encounter it.

In part, recognition seems so immediate because we spend most of our time in familiar surroundings. We work in the same rooms, see the same people, walk the same streets, live in the same houses for long periods of time. The perceptual information we receive each ordinary day is usually repetitious and redundant. We come to know the things we will encounter even before we encounter them.

Put us on unfamiliar ground, and we are much slower to realize what an object is. We hesitate, look several times, and make mistakes. For an adult it is impossible to imagine any environment that would be completely new and foreign to everything he has ever seen before, that would mislead him with respect to every assumption he made. Even a foreign language is not so completely foreign as that. But a little novelty makes us much more keenly aware of the hypotheses we hold and the inferences we make. As long as they work, we do not notice that we make them. It is when they fail that we become puzzled and search for reasons. After a few failures, we are in a much better frame of mind to accept the proposition that recognizing objects is an elaborate and delicate skill, even though we acquired the skill too long ago to recall how we did it.

When we encounter a common object—a hat, say—we either recognize that it is a hat, equivalent to millions of other hats, or we

147

may recognize that it is Arthur's hat, a particular hat with its own identity, a hat we have seen many times before. To recognize that an object is a hat is to assign it to a class. To recognize Arthur's hat is to recognize an individual object. The class of all hats contains Arthur's hat as a member.

Classes of individual objects can be created in many different ways; putting things into their proper niches in a cognitive filing system is one of the most common of human activities. In general terms, a well-defined class exists if there is a *test* for inclusion. When the test is passed, the object under scrutiny is admitted to the class; when the test is failed, the object is rejected. The simplest tests involve a single perceptual attribute. For example, given normal color vision, we can create the class of blue objects by simply looking at them or, in special cases, comparing them side by side with samples known to be blue. But complicated tests involving many attributes are also useful.

The clearest way to conceive of the psychological processes of recognition and identification is in terms of such tests. One can imagine that the sensory input is matched, simultaneously and successively, against many remembered images or schemata. When the present input and the stored simulacrum match, the test is passed, and the object is included in the class of all objects that meet the test. The analysis of classes is more a task for logic than for psychology; many subtle and difficult problems are involved. Yet the psychologist cannot abdicate completely, for classification is too pervasive a psychological operation. As William James remarked, "Every new experience must be disposed of under *some* old head. The great point is to find the head which has to be least altered to take it in."

Experiments can be done to see how people learn the appropriate tests that determine class membership. One can, for instance, take a set of geometric shapes varying in several aspects—size, contour, color—and define a new concept in terms of a simple subset of the shapes. Figure 23 is an example. The geometric figures are shown to a subject one at a time; he is told about each one whether or not it is, say, a member of the "droomy" subset. Typically there is a period, after he has seen a few examples, when he is able to recognize the droomy figures, but he cannot give any explicit verbal rules for what he is doing. If he persists in his effort to formulate a definition, he will eventually be able to say, "All the large green ones are droomy." In ordinary affairs, however, we are often content to leave the definition tacit.[1]

THESE ARE TERRACHOS:

THESE ARE NOT TERRACHOS:

WHAT IS A TERRACHO?

Fig. 23. These nonsense figures—with nonsense names—might be used to study how people discover the attributes that define a class of objects. Given enough instances and counter-instances, people can eventually say that "terrachos" have large surrounds and unfilled centers: the shapes and the locations of the centers are not relevant.

A most important class of objects is the class of all the things one has seen before, the class of familiar things. Psychologists have studied this class with special care. A person is shown a set of objects —geometric figures, for example—and then the ones he has seen before are mixed in with a large number of similar objects that he has not seen. His task is to identify the familiar ones. If the strange objects are very close in appearance to the familiar objects, the subject may do poorly. Usually the best condition for experimentation is at an intermediate level of difficulty; the investigator selects objects strange enough to induce mistakes in identification, but not so indistinguishable from the prototype as to produce utter confusion. One learns little about the way the subject is performing if he is always right, or if he responds entirely at random.

People are characteristically able to recognize a figure as familiar even though they have forgotten it—forgotten it in the sense that they would not have been able to name or draw it if they had been asked to recall or reproduce all the figures they had been shown.

Thus, *recognition* is generally considered to be an easier test of memory than either *recall* or *reproduction*.

An almost universal reaction to the task of remembering figures is to give them descriptive names. The figure will be called "the large green triangle," and it is often difficult to tell whether it is the perception, the description, or both that a subject remembers. Even with nonsense figures he will search for verbal descriptions: "Square with one of its sides gone," or "Z backwards," and so forth. These verbal tags may either aid or interfere with recall and reproduction of the figure,[2] but they seem to have relatively little effect upon recognition. In Figure 24, for example, if a person describes the left figure as a picture frame, he will draw what he sees differently than if he merely describes it as two carpenter's squares placed together. His ability to recognize it when he sees it again, however, may be little affected by the way he described it.[3]

Fig. 24. What we remember may depend on what we call it.

If a subject's task is not deliberately made difficult by forcing him to recognize nonsense figures briefly seen when they are hidden among many similar nonsense figures, but instead he is given familiar objects or pictures, we find that people have a truly amazing capacity to create and remember a rather special class of objects-seen-recently. Colored pictures clipped from magazines and mail order catalogues, when pasted on cards, provide a suitable set of materials for making the test. Show a person several hundred of them at a regular but leisurely rate, asking him to name each one as he sees it. Then select, say, twenty of those he has seen and mix them haphazardly with another set of twenty pictures that he has not seen. The subject's task is to sort them into two piles, those he has already seen and those that are new. He will make almost no errors.[4] Apparently, people have a remarkable capacity for keeping a set of visual impressions alive and accessible. An informal way to demonstrate this fact to yourself is to purchase two similar magazines from a newsstand, thumb idly through the pages of one, then the other, and ask yourself how many of the advertisements in the second magazine were also in the first. You will find that you make almost no mistakes. Observations such as these make some psychologists feel that storing things away in memory must be very simple and easy; the major source of errors and failures must lie in the processes of retrieval.

Memory is not the only place that recognition processes can go astray. Expectations can also mislead us; the unexpected is always hard to perceive clearly. Sometimes we fail to recognize an object because we did not get a good look at it, or we saw it under conditions that camouflaged it, or it appeared in an incongruous place at a time we least expected it. It may even happen that we fail to recognize a perfectly common and familiar object whose name we would never otherwise forget, when it appears in an alien context.

Suppose a tachistoscope is used to display an object for a very brief period of time, so brief that the watcher fails to recognize it. Start with a very short exposure time, in which the watcher sees almost nothing, and then lengthen the time on successive exposures until he finally recognizes the object. Tachistoscopic exposures can force the person to make mistakes, and from his mistakes one can infer some of the factors that operate to determine his responses. And from the duration of exposure required for veridical perception of the object the difficulty of the recognition task can be inferred.

Now, suppose playing cards are shown in the tachistoscope. The experimenter measures how long a person must see an ordinary card to identify it correctly. Then, without warning, an unusual card is slipped in, say, a *red five of clubs*. The exposure duration becomes longer and longer until finally, at a very long exposure duration, the person realizes what it is. When he does recognize it, there is apt to be a strong emotional response, swearing, expressions of amazement, accusations that the experimenter has changed the card, and so on. Someone who had identified it as, say, an ordinary five of clubs when the exposure was quite short will stick with this identification as the successive exposures get longer and longer. He is set to see a black five of clubs; he persists in seeing what he expects to see long after he should recognize it for what it really is. He is trapped and misled by his own expectations.[5]

It is not difficult to trick and mislead people in various ways, but the real purpose of such experiments is to demonstrate that people have very definite expectations about what is going to happen. In most situations our expectations work excellently and save us a tremendous amount of time and effort. For example, suppose the objects being presented are monosyllabic English words. A listener who knows in advance that the word he will hear must be one of two particular words will be able to recognize it correctly at very faint intensities. The same listener, however, when told that the word will be one of a group of one thousand alternative words, will be completely unable to recognize the word correctly at this same intensity level.[6] The physical stimulation to which he is exposed is the same in both cases; the only difference is what he expects. What he can recognize clearly when it is one of two possibilities is completely obscured when it is one of a thousand. It is not enough therefore to state the physical magnitude of the acoustic waves; if we wish to predict whether a person will recognize the word accurately, we must also specify what it is that he *expects* to hear.

The size of the set of alternative objects (or, equivalently, the probabilities of the alternative objects) that are exposed is, therefore, an important attribute of a recognition task. What will be recognized depends on what might have been, as well as what actually is. The number of alternatives that any system can handle is, in general, a basic measure of the *information capacity* of the system.[7] This measure was applied first to machines and later adopted by psychologists to describe people. It was developed for communication engineering. A communication system must be designed to transmit a variety of different messages. The larger the number of alternative messages that it can transmit in a given interval of time, the larger the information capacity of the system and the more expensive it will be to build and maintain.

In the simplest examples, if a system can handle N alternative signals in one unit of time, it can handle $N \times N = N^2$ in two units of time, N^3 in three units of time; and, generally, N^m alternatives in m units of time. One feels intuitively that a measure of the total amount of information transmitted by the channel should increase linearly as a function of the time. Whereas N^m (the number of alternative messages) increases exponentially as m (the length of the message), the logarithm increases linearly. Therefore, it is convenient to use the logarithm of the number of alternatives as the measure of amount of information per unit time. In m units of time, the channel could transmit $\log N^m = m \log N$ units of information. If logarithms are taken to the base two, the unit of measurement is the *"bit."* When it is said that the capacity of a communication channel is H bits per second, this means that it is capable of transmitting any one of $2\frac{H}{\triangledown}$ alternative messages every second. This unit for measuring information is universally used by engineers who work with communication and computing systems.

It is possible to ask a person to serve as a communication channel and to study how many alternative messages—how many bits of information—he can transmit.[8] The input to the channel then consists of the objects that the experimenter presents; the output is the subject's response when he identifies the objects. The better the correlation between the input and the output, the more information the subject transmits. This application of information theory to the test is somewhat irregular, since one usually imagines persons sitting at either end of the system—source and destination—with the electronic equipment between them. In the psychological laboratory, however, the stimulating and recording equipment are at either end, with a person serving as the channel between them. Logically, however, the mathematics that describes the former can also describe the latter situation.

Estimates of the largest amounts of information an average person can transmit per unit time, run around 25 to 35 bits per second.[9] In an absolute sense 2^{30} is a very large number, and we can feel proud of ourselves for doing so well. But when we remember that telephone and radio channels send tens of thousands of bits per second and that the capacity of television channels runs into the millions, we begin to suspect that man evolved under pressures other than acting as a communication channel.

The information-processing bottleneck in a human being may mean simply that he is not able to respond fast enough to report all the information that his receptors are taking in. One can test this possibility by presenting a single object to be recognized, drawn from a large set of alternative objects, then giving the subject all the time he needs to report as accurately as he can what it is that he saw. When this experiment is done, the amount of information he can process is still sharply limited; the exact amount transmitted, however, depends upon the way the various alternatives are presented.

If the alternative stimuli are all exactly the same except for differences in a single sensory aspect—size, brightness, and the like— the subject will have a difficult time recognizing which stimulus he is looking at. When a single aspect is varied, therefore, a subject typically gives back about 3 bits of information. That is, he can distinguish without error which of $2^3=8$ different values is being presented. If he is asked to distinguish between more than eight values, he will try, but he will make enough mistakes so that the net result will still be, effectively, eight distinguishable values. This limit is not specific for visual recognition; similar informational capacities characterize other sense modalities if the stimuli to be identified differ in only a single aspect. Apparently we have encountered a rather general bottleneck in human information processing capacity.[10]

Clearly there is a discrepancy. It is known that a person can recognize which of many thousands of different pictures he has seen before; in this circumstance he is certainly not limited to seven or eight alternatives. How can these apparently contradictory observations be reconciled?

A person is limited, as has been noted, in his ability to recognize objects that differ from one another with respect to a single aspect. The pictures that he can recognize so easily, however, differ from one another in many aspects. Here perhaps is the source of the discrepancy. If so, it can be studied quite simply by adding more aspects, one at a time, to distinguish the objects the subject must identify.

For example, if the subject is asked to identify simple tones, it turns out that he can reliably distinguish among about four different loudnesses when the intensity is varied, or he can reliably distinguish among about five different pitches when the frequency of vibration is varied. But suppose one varies both aspects at once, intensity and frequency. We might expect to find that the four loudnesses could still be distinguished at each of the five pitches, which means $4 \times 5 = 20$ recognizably different auditory objects. This would be a significant increase in recognition ability—an improvement due directly to the introduction of additional aspects to distinguish the stimuli. In fact, however, the gain is not quite as great as it might theoretically be; instead of twenty there are only ten or twelve recognizable tones when two aspects are varied. In other words, when the subject has to judge two aspects at once, he may not do quite as well on either of them as he could if he judged them separately; nevertheless, the number of recognizably different objects is increased.

The same thing happens if one adds a third and a fourth aspect with respect to which the objects can differ. The amount of information contained in the subject's responses goes up, but not as rapidly as it might. By the time one gets to objects that differ with respect to half a dozen aspects, the accuracy of judgment drops for each separate aspect to just about the equivalent of a binary choice. That is, when pitch is all that a person must judge, he may be able to recognize any one of five or six different values; but when he must judge variations in half a dozen aspects simultaneously, he may be able to recognize only one of two pitches—either high or low. Nevertheless, with six of these binary decisions the person is able to distinguish $2^6 = 64$ different objects, a tenfold improvement over his performance for variations in a single aspect.[11]

These studies of our ability to recognize and identify auditory objects are not completely academic. They relate quite intimately to the way we communicate with one another. In our natural speech we generate phonemes that differ from one another with respect to at least nine or ten aspects—some linguists call them distinctive features—and the differences are usually binary or, at most, ternary. Thus, for example, in English there is a binary distinction between vowels and consonants. Among the consonants a binary distinction exists between stops and continuants. Among the stop consonants we have a binary distinction between voiced and voiceless. Among the voiced stop consonants, a ternary distinction between front, middle, and back. And so we eventually come to /b/, the initial phoneme in the word "boy," which is a front voiced stop consonant. All the other phonemes, of which English has about thirty or forty, can be classified in a similar manner. When we recognize one of these acoustic objects, therefore, it means that we have made several rough, binary decisions about the nine or ten distinctive features involved in the system of English phonemes.

Considerations such as these suggest that our perceptual equipment is designed to make many measurements simultaneously, but to do a fairly crude job on each one. This contrasts with the kind of scientific measuring equipment that measures one thing at a time, but measures it with great precision. The complementarity is scarcely surprising—scientists develop their measuring devices in order to study things that are not immediately obvious to ordinary observation. Meters must make the discriminations that the unaided senses cannot.

It also seems reasonable that higher organisms should be open to a wide variety of events. If a compromise is necessary, it seems far wiser to make rough decisions about everything than to make very acute distinctions as to a few aspects while ignoring completely the information provided by others. We do have some ability to trade breadth for accuracy, of course. This trading relation is a part of the subjective phenomenon called attention.

Psychological measurements of information demonstrate that there is an enormous reduction in the amount of information when it passes through a human nervous system. A television channel sends us millions of bits of information in picture and sound, yet all we can take in is a fraction of a fraction of one per cent. There is a tremendous opportunity for selection by the perceiver of the information that he needs. This selection is not, of course, random or fortuitous. What information the viewer gets from all the dancing dots of lights on his picture tube will be determined by the way his perceptual mechanisms work. For example, the gestalt principles underlying the formation and segregation of wholes in the visual field can—when applied to this situation—be regarded as principles whereby the vast flood of transmitted information is reduced to the few drops of psychological information that a person can absorb. Suppose we reconsider some of the gestalt factors with this in mind.

The first thing to note about a television picture is that much of the information in it is highly redundant. A man stands, for example, near the center of the screen and talks to us. The background is completely stationary for many seconds. Successive frames of the picture are almost completely identical with preceding frames. One wonders why it should be necessary to send a picture of the same background over and over, frame after frame. Why not send it once and forget it until something happens to justify change? Or, if a contour is approximately straight, why not simply transmit a straight line, which can be represented by its two end points, thus dispensing with the necessity of transmitting the information along the contour. The economy of rectilinear contours is illustrated in Figure 25.

Such economical systems are conceivable but it would take a great deal more information-processing in the television transmitter and in the home receiver than is presently necessary. It seems sim-

Fig. 25. The contours of a sleeping cat are efficiently preserved by a few points with straight lines between them. Where a contour is relatively straight, the information it conveys is predictable and redundant. The most important information required to identify such a visual object is associated with the points where its contour changes direction. (From F. Attneave, Some informational aspects of visual perception, *Psychological Review,* 1954, 61–183–193.)

pler to send tremendous quantities of redundant information than to do the elaborate processing that would be required to remove the redundancy.

But suppose we now imagine the gestalt laws to be descriptions of how we take advantage of this redundancy when we look at the picture. For a simplified example, imagine that the spatial distribution of a set of points has to be described in such a manner that the description can be transmitted and the points placed in their correct positions at the receiving station. If the points are located in clusters, it may be more efficient to transmit first the location of a cluster and then the position of the points in that cluster.[12] Within any one cluster the number of alternative positions the points could occupy is less than the number of alternative positions they might occupy within the total display; hence, the amount of information transmitted could be reduced. But notice the principle whereby the economy was achieved: the points had to be grouped on the basis of proximity. And proximity is one of the gestalt factors.

Take another example. If some of the points are one shape and some another, it will be efficient to transmit first the positions of all points of one shape, then the positions of all the points of the other shape. In that way it is not necessary to send the shape description along with the location of every point; the shape description is sent just once for an entire group. But notice the gestalt principle involved: Grouping by similarity.

From this point of view, gestalt factors describe the ways we eliminate redundant information, the ways we encode visual information more efficiently. In short, they simplify our cognitive bookkeeping. The kaleidoscopic flux of our experience is laced through with the correlations we call objects, and it is the task of our perceptual system to discover and identify the correlations, dependencies, and redundancies that signal an object's appearance. In the process of accomplishing this task it seems that the amount of information we are able to handle must be quite small. Because we are limited, the small amount of information that we can handle must be carefully refined to represent just those aspects that are significant for guiding our behavior.

A television set may process millions of bits of information per second, but it is not capable of *recognizing* anything. Before a television system could decide between third base and a package of cigarettes, it would need to be a great deal more complicated than it is. It would, in fact, need exactly what we have—a highly skilled brain for processing sensory information in order to extract the significant features.

If the world around us were completely unpredictable, if what happened at one time and place had no correlation with what happened at any other time and place, we would not be able to develop our conception of a stable environment filled with solid, reliable objects. The objects provide the correlation, the redundancy, the predictability we must have before we can introduce order and structure into our conception of the world and of ourselves. In order to discover those correlations we must have sense organs and a nervous system that are constructed in certain ways not yet understood, to perform certain functions now only dimly conceived. But somehow those functions must include more than a passive sensing of the input; only an active, moving, remembering organism would perform those functions in the way we do.

And we must practice. From the first day we open our eyes we must practice the skills needed to keep the world organized in space and time, the skills that extract critical information from the intricate flux of energy that activates our ever-moving receptors. Anyone who reflects upon the complexity and beauty of these processes which support all our cognitive life will surely find his wonder and amazement growing as rapidly as his knowledge and understanding.

CHAPTER XI

---◆---

MEMORY

"She sent out for one of those short, plump little cakes called 'petites madeleines,' which look as though they had been moulded in the fluted scallop of a pilgrim's shell," wrote Marcel Proust. "And soon, mechanically, weary with the prospect of a depressing morrow, I raised to my lips a spoonful of the tea in which I had soaked a morsel of the cake. No sooner had the warm liquid, and the crumbs in it, touched my palate than a shudder ran through my whole body, and I stopped, intent upon the extraordinary changes that were taking place. An exquisite pleasure had invaded my senses, but individual, detached, with no suggestion of its origin."

The incident of the madeleine surrounds Proust's famous work, *Remembrance of Things Past,* as a frame surrounds a painting. Proust asks himself what this unremembered state could have been; he tastes the tea again and again, trying to stir the image, the visual memory linked to that taste. Suddenly the memory returns, a scene from his childhood, long forgotten but now vividly remembered, and with it his story begins. Seven volumes later he returns to the incident to explain its real significance.

Perhaps nowhere in literature has more talent been lavished on the description of a memory. And nowhere else can a contrast be drawn so clearly between an artistic and a scientific approach to mental events. Proust's little cake set off a psychological accident, so unique, personal, unexpected, and unexplained as to seem the complete antithesis of all we have learned to call scientific. The con-

160

trast does not concern the truth of Proust's account—one can grant that there is a sense in which it is true even though it may never have occurred. The contrast is in his method of displaying the truth.

Consider the difficulties that would face any scientist who wanted to study such mental phenomena. His first difficulty would be that he has no way to capture the thing he wishes to study. He can only sit and wait, hoping for the improbable. "There is," comments Proust, "a large element of hazard in these matters, and a second hazard, that of our own death, often prevents us from awaiting for any length of time the favors of the first." But even if he should live long enough, a scientist would still be in trouble because he would still have to contend with the privacy of his own experience. Once he has produced his specimen he must examine it alone. No one can help him, no one can verify the accuracy of his observations, no one can repeat his experiment. Indeed, no one can prove he ever had the experience he claims to remember. And, finally, the event must be described and communicated by language; how many scientists have sufficient skill to capture the subtle shades of their subjective states?

These elusive phenomena seem to be essentially unscientific. A prudent psychologist might well decide to leave such fragile flowers to Proust and his fellow artists. A scientist would do better to study the workaday memory that guides our plans, feeds our inferences, answers promptly when it is called and stands still long enough to be measured. Proust recognized the importance of workaday memory, too, but he insisted that there was something special, something tremendously significant for the artist in the kind of memory stirred by his taste of the little cake. He seemed to warn psychologists that they ignore or deny these intimate memories at their peril, for they are closely integrated with the set of memories that we refer to as our personal identity.

There is a kind of double awareness that sometimes accompanies a vivid recollection of the past. "During the instant that they last," said Proust, "these resurrections of the past are so complete that they do not merely oblige our eyes to become oblivious to the room before them and contemplate instead the rising tide or the railway track edged with trees; they also force our nostrils to inhale the air of places which are far remote, constrain our will to choose between the various views they lay before us, compel our entire being to believe itself surrounded by them, or at least to vacillate between them and the present scenes, bewildered by an uncertainty similar to that which one sometimes experiences before an ineffable vision at the moment of losing consciousness in sleep."

Should this kind of experience be dismissed because it is so difficult to study? As Proust suggests, it is similar to a dream, a psychological phenomenon whose importance Freud has made overwhelmingly clear. In its most intense reality, such an experience is called an hallucination; it is common in cases of epilepsy, and can be produced under hypnosis. One of the most startling instances, however, was Wilder Penfield's[1] demonstration that weak electrical stimulation of the surface of the brain, in the temporal lobes, can sometimes cause a previous experience of the person to intrude into his field of awareness. In Penfield's words, ". . . the 'double consciousness,' the going 'back to all that occurred in my childhood,' is an hallucination in which the patient re-experiences some period of time from his own past while still retaining his hold on the present. . . . During it a patient may hear music, for example. But, if so, he hears a single playing of the music, orchestra, or piano, or voices; and he may be aware of himself as present in the room or hall. He may hear voices, the voices of friends or of strangers. If they seemed familiar to him during the interval of time now being recalled, they are familiar to him now. If they were strange then, they are strange now. He may see the people who were speaking and the piano being played by the man who played it then. He may, on the other hand, see things that he saw in an earlier period without being aware of sound. If he felt fright then, he feels fright now. If he felt a pleasurable admiration then, he feels it now."

Apparently it is possible, under appropriate conditions, to see ourselves participating in past and present events simultaneously. The experience is surprising because the re-creation of the past is real, complete and detailed. It is difficult to believe that we can remember so much so vividly, as though a permanent record of our stream of consciousness had been stored away somewhere. Compared with the inadequacy of the memory that serves our daily rounds, this total recall of a past episode is startlingly different. It makes us suspect that we have a great deal more brain power than we are using; one's first wish is to master this mental record and bend it to his service. Why can we not use this wonderful storage device to recall telephone numbers when we want them? Or to memorize speeches, or to remember a friend's birthday? Why must complete recollection be so useless, involuntary, and unpredictable?

Penfield's observation suggests that we might be able to gain control of these personal memories if we knew more about their biological basis. At present, however, prospects in that direction are not hopeful. The only biological mechanism for memory that we know much about is the chromosome, which is assumed to be the carrier of genetic information—the thing that enables us to remember how to develop into a man and not into a horse or a fish. A chromosome appears to consist of a string of genes, which are the physical carriers of inherited features. Each gene is probably a large protein molecule—the genetic memory, therefore, is contained in the particular structure of a single molecule. One might imagine, correspondingly, that psychological experiences are translated into similar molecular structures in some unknown way—there are enough molecules in the human body to support as large a memory as anyone could hope for. There is nothing inconceivable about such a possibility.

But perhaps a molecular theory of personal memory is wrong, perhaps some other technique of information storage is used by the nervous system. Concerning this possibility the vast neurological literature is amazingly unhelpful. It is known that considerable damage can be done to the tissues of the brain without producing any measurable impairment of memory and that particular memories do not seem to be stored in particular places. Moreover, it is known that nerve cells can be made to excite each other in cycles: neuron A excites neuron B, which in turn excites C, which may return and excite A again. But these cycles can last, at best, only a few seconds. They are not the kind of thing that might last a lifetime, that could persist through sleep and waking, through electric shocks, surgical insult, and the interference of other activity in adjacent neurons.

In the absence of evidence, therefore, the most anyone can offer is speculation. One plausible theory currently available says that when activity passes repeatedly over a particular synapse—the boundary between one neuron and the next—the resistance to conduction over that synapse is lowered. In the future, therefore, the same stimuli will be more likely to pass again over the same synapses and so will lead again to the same subjective experience and to the same objective behavior. But the theory of lowered synaptic resistance faces certain objections. A synapse is only a micron or so in size; a change at the synapse must be a change in a thin layer of protein molecules. The tissues of the body are being constantly renewed and rebuilt; it is hard to believe that delicate adjustments of synaptic resistance could long survive the processes of metabolism.

The famous psychologist and neurologist Karl Lashley spent more than thirty years in search of the engram, the permanent impression that experience is supposed to leave somewhere in the nervous system.[2] He began with a widely shared impression that the engram must be a path through the brain that connects sensory organs to muscles and glands—the memory of each particular sensory-motor association would be represented by an anatomically distinct path through the brain. Lashley tried to study these hypothetical paths by interrupting them surgically at different places in the brain. Human beings are naturally reluctant to serve as subjects in such experiments; Lashley practiced his brain surgery on lower animals. He began with rats, but the results were so surprising that he repeated his studies later with monkeys and chimpanzees. He trained his animals in various tasks ranging in difficulty from simple sensory-motor associations to the solution of difficult sequential problems. Then he cut, destroyed, or removed a portion of the animal's brain. After recovery from the operation, he tested the animal's memory for what it had learned.

Lashley experimented on all parts of the brain. He placed his lesions in the part of the brain that controls motor performance and so managed to produce paralysis, but he did not destroy the engram. He took out large amounts of tissue from the so-called association areas, but memory was not impaired. He cut all the connections between the sensory and the motor areas of the brain, but again the engram remained intact. A brain operation can affect an animal's behavior in many ways but it does not seem possible to destroy particular memories by injuring the brain in particular places. The best he could do was to show a gross correlation between the total amount of brain tissue destroyed and a general impairment in the animal's performance. But *where* the tissue was destroyed was relatively unimportant. In summarizing his work Lashley said, "This series of experiments has yielded a good bit of information about what and where the memory trace is not. It has discovered nothing directly of the real nature of the engram." And then he added, wistfully, "I sometimes feel, in reviewing the evidence on the localization of the memory trace, that the necessary conclusion is that learning just is not possible."

Not all workers in this corner of psychology are as discouraged about the possibilities as Lashley was, but his experiments do seem to have ruled out most of the simpler explanations which might be proposed as a biological basis of personal memory. Either large parts of the brain work together in complex patterns during recall, or memories are multiply represented in several different regions of the cortex, or individual neurons may be capable of far more precise differentiations than are now understood, or biochemical processes of still unspecified nature take place somewhere scientists have not yet thought to look. But perhaps the simplest way to summarize the situation is to admit with Lashley that we know almost nothing at all about the underlying processes whereby the nervous system stores and maintains such large quantities of relatively precise information.

If we cannot evoke memories when we want to study them, if we are completely ignorant of the place and nature of the biophysical processes that support them, what is left for a psychologist to study? Does this mean that we cannot proceed with our psychological studies? Not at all. Research into human memory is one of the oldest and most active branches of experimental psychology.[3]

By sheer chance Proust tasted his madeleine and so revived a system of memories long since abandoned. An electric current happened to release an otherwise inaccessible pattern of neural activity. It is as if the memory had continued to hold a full record of things past, but had become isolated. It was not so much forgotten as misplaced, until by a lucky accident a part of the memory system was pulled into consciousness and the rest trailed after.

Perhaps the difficulties we have in remembering things are not concerned so much with getting them into our memories as with getting them back out again later. In this respect our personal memory would seem to confirm a simple relation that usually holds for other storage systems, namely, retrieval is more difficult than storage. If one thinks of memory as a place where things can be stored, one should expect retrieval to be the major problem. It is simple to put documents into a filing case, furniture into a warehouse, information into a notebook, articles into a scientific journal, or books into a library. If we never expect to see the things again, it is easy enough to dump them like junk into a junk box. The problem appears only later when we try to find them.

When we organize a storage place according to rules and make records of where everything went, we are attempting by a little effort now to forestall an enormous effort later, when the time comes to retrieve something. Because this organizing and record-keeping must go on at the same time the thing is being stored, we seem to have trouble getting it into storage. When we are unable to remember something that happened to us, it may be either because we did not store it carefully, or because it has disappeared from where we put it, or because we have lost the records of where it went. Thinking of memory in terms of these analogies to other storage problems may make the process seem overly concrete, but it helps us to understand many of the characteristics of learning and forgetting.

When one takes the time and trouble to anticipate the retrieval problem, one passes out of the domain of accidental but often vivid recollections and into the world of workaday memory—a kind of memory that is less dramatic, but considerably more reliable.

How does our workaday memory function? Ordinarily we do not take our experience neat, but work it over before we try to store it away. Vivid, detailed, photographic resurrection of the past is not the most efficient way to remember. Everyday remembering is more like a syllogism than a photograph: we usually follow a sequence of steps to the past; only rarely do we conjure it up in an instantaneous panorama. An adult uses symbols—usually verbal symbols—to organize his memory so that he can find what he wants in it. We constantly translate our experience into symbols, store them in our memory, and retrieve the symbols instead of the experience itself. When the time comes for recall, we try to reconstruct the experience from the remembered symbols.

Frequently, what we store away so painfully in our workaday memory is a rule that will enable us later to construct—or to reconstruct—what we want to know. To illustrate the efficiency of these rules, consider a highly oversimplified way to test your memory. Imagine you are a subject in a psychological experiment. The experimenter says, "I am going to give you some numbers. For each one I say to you, say a number back to me. Use any numbers you like. Only please be consistent. Whenever I give you the same number again, give me back the number you said before. Is that clear?"

"No."

"I will give you a number, for example, 73. Then you give me a number, for instance, 528, or whatever you like. But I want you to remember what you say so that if I ever give you 73 again, you will give me 528 again."

With a task like this you would never give the experimenter 528 as a response to 73. It is far better to pick some simple number, such as 1. Make that your reply to everything, thereby lightening the load on your memory tremendously. You may expect the psychologist to complain.

"Look," he may say, "I want to test your memory. This is no test at all. You must give me a different number every time I give you a different number."

Humor him. Take his number and repeat it. You will still be able to remember your number every time. Moreover, you will be able to remember his number if he gives you yours. Or, if he still is not satisfied, construct your reply by adding a constant to his number. In either case, the situation is completely under control and you can handle an immense variety of stimuli without a single error. You do it by remembering a rule rather than by remembering what you actually said. If you tried to remember literally everything he said and every haphazard reply you made, the task would be overwhelmingly difficult.

If this example seems too artificial, then perhaps it can be transmuted into something more interesting by a series of easy steps. Suppose the psychologist utters not numbers, but words, and asks you for different words in reply. Again, you should adopt a rule. One of the simplest would be always to give the opposite of his word. If he says, "White," you say, "Black." If he says, "Boy," you reply, "Girl." To be sure, this rule will not always work. If he says, "Book," or "Chicago," you are stuck. Thus you may need an additional rule to the effect that when there is no opposite, you will use the commonest associate you can think of, or you will give a word that rhymes, and so on. Unlike the rules in the numerical example, the rule for words is not infallible. But it works far better than if you tried to remember each word-pair separately. You can probably give several hundred such replies and remember them with less than 5 per cent error. And the beauty of it is that you merely make use of what you have already learned in order to avoid having to learn something new.

Suppose you did not do it this way. Suppose instead, you had a sound recorder in your head and could at any moment listen to every word you and the psychologist had said to each other. Even suppose you could turn the recorder on or off at will. And suppose you had no rule for giving replies, but gave them haphazardly because you relied upon this remarkable recording device. Then each time the psychologist said a new word to you, you would start your recorder playing at the beginning and listen to see if you had ever been given that word before, and, if so, what you had replied. The more words he gave, the longer it would take you to play the record through, and the slower your response would become. You would be quickly overloaded; you would remember so much that you could never find what you wanted when you needed it. Soon you would be almost as poorly off as if you remembered nothing. A verbatim recording of the stream of consciousness may indeed be preserved in the brain somewhere, but it is of very little use to us for most of the memory tasks we must constantly perform.

The truth is, your psychologist was too lenient. His tests left you free to choose replies according to your own strategy. He could make it much more difficult if he also told you what you were supposed to say in reply to his stimulus words. When he determines both members of the pair, it may take work to find a mnemonic rule. But your general strategy should be something like this: Look for a third word or image such that his stimulus word suggests it easily, and such that it in turn suggests the response you are supposed to give. For example he might give you the pair "Sugar-Lame." You must remember it well enough to be able, when he tests you later by saying, "Sugar," to reply, "Lame." If you discover the word "cane," it can serve as a mediator: "Sugar-cane" and "cane-Lame" are familiar associations that you have already learned before the experiment began. Given a good mediating word, therefore, you can perform the task easily. Very little of the time you would spend memorizing pairs of words would ordinarily go to engrave new associations into your brain tissue; most of it would be spent searching for some familiar association that satisfies a simple rule.

It should be remarked, incidentally, that it is not sufficient merely to know a mediator unless you actively think of it. The active arousal of the mediator seems to be an indispensable part of the process.

The usefulness of images and words to establish connections among apparently unrelated concepts is well known to authors of popular texts on *How to Improve Your Memory,* but it has not been studied extensively in the psychological laboratory. However, the effectiveness of this simple principle can be demonstrated in the following way.[4] A list of word pairs is presented, one pair at a time. For each pair the subject forms a clear visual image, the more bizarre the better. Ordinarily a person will spend about twenty-five seconds finding a satisfactory image and forming the association, but after some experience he can work accurately with about five seconds per pair. The list is not repeated. At the end of the presentation the subject is given one member of each pair and is asked to write down the other. In one study, lists of up to five hundred pairs were remembered about 99 per cent correctly.

These examples indicate how useful rules and strategies can be to a person trying to remember something, and how they can have advantages not shared by a literal, photo-phono-graphic record. That is not to say that eidetic imagery—the so-called photographic mind—is not an extremely useful gift to have.[5] Rather, the point is that ordinary people can do extraordinarily well if they are permitted to use meaningful words and images as mediators. For some situations it is actually more efficient to remember a rule to generate X than to remember X itself.

If all this testing and searching and rule-making is supposed to go on while we are depositing new information in our memory bank, it seems likely that we must have at least two different kinds of storage. One, a long-term memory system; the other, a temporary memory that can hold information for a few seconds while we do whatever rehearsing or information-processing is necessary to transfer it into the long-term store.

One can isolate the temporary memory system and study its properties independently simply by crippling the rehearsal needed for making the transfer. Give a person three consonants—CHS, or MXB, for instance—and then immediately have him count backwards by threes until you are ready to test his recall. The counting breaks up his normal processes of transfer from temporary to more

permanent memory, so that twenty seconds later the string of consonants, which would ordinarily be perfectly recalled, is forgotten
more than 90 per cent of the time.[6] A curve showing the temporal
course of this very rapid fading is plotted in Figure 26. If we do not
process the information within a few seconds, it is lost.

RECALL INTERVAL IN SECONDS

Fig. 26. When rehearsal is prevented, information drops very rapidly out
of temporary memory. Subjects could not remember three consonants
for more than a few seconds when they had to count backwards during
the interval between the presentation and the test of recall.

This rapid fading is important for many things we do. For example, when we add a column of figures we must keep a subtotal
in mind just long enough to add a new number to it, then forget it.
If the memory of each subtotal did not fade, we would accumulate
a great deal of useless and distracting information. Similarly, the
fading protects us from remembering all the apparent nonsense that
goes on while we are dreaming. It is possible, of course, to train
oneself to remember dreams; one learns to rehearse them immediately on awakening. And some dreams are so important to us that

we wake up spontaneously thinking about them. But most of the time dreams are forgotten because we cannot perform the necessary processes required to fix them more permanently. Our ability to decide what we will try to remember and what we will permit to fade is one of our most powerful tools for selecting a personal world out of what William James called "the primordial chaos of sensation."

The particular associations that people exploit when they try to fix a memory permanently are apt to be somewhat personal and idiosyncratic, but the general strategy they follow is fairly clear. New experience is categorized in terms of familiar concepts shared by the culture and symbolized by the language; then the symbolically transformed experience is related to, and interwoven with, other things previously learned and remembered in terms of these categories and this language. In a new situation it is sometimes difficult to know how best to exploit previous learning, but after a little thought we can usually discover a rule that transforms the novel into the familiar.

But we must not assume that all our memories are so well behaved. The very personal memory that Proust revived with the madeleine is of a different character entirely. In an interesting comparison of Proust and Freud, Ernest Schachtel[7] has called attention to the fact that these Proustian flashes characteristically revive some childhood scene, as though a psychological barrier separated the adult from his early experience. In order to become an adult, to adopt adult habits of thought, it is necessary to forget one's childhood. "The biologically, culturally, and socially influenced process of memory organization," said Schachtel, "results in the formation of categories (schemata) of memory which are not suitable vehicles to receive and reproduce experiences of the quality and intensity typical of early childhood. The world of modern Western civilization has no use for this type of experience. In fact, it cannot permit itself to have any use for it, it cannot permit the memory of it, because such memory, if universal, would explode the restrictive social order of this civilization."

These intimate memories of childhood are obviously of great concern to students of personality, many of whom believe that the adult personality sets like plaster after the first few years of life. Freud particularly emphasized the social necessity of repressing childish memories of sexual pleasure, in order to enable the adult to function effectively in Western culture. But Freud's observation does not explain why all our childhood memories, sexual and asexual alike, are so thoroughly forgotten. In the course of growing up there are several cognitive revolutions that completely reorganize a child's intellectual life. As new and more efficient cognitive systems emerge, the peculiarly intense memories of a child find no place in them. The child is not forgotten; it is simply isolated from the day-to-day experience of the normal adult, because the child existed before the categories of the adult mind had been achieved.

An attentive reader will not have overlooked the metaphorical basis of this discussion—the assumption that memory is a place where information can be stored, just as a warehouse is a place where merchandise can be stored. This seems to make memory a substantial thing that a person possesses in the same way he possesses a head and two hands. Although the metaphor may help us to organize and understand many phenomena of memory that are psychologically significant, it is difficult to suppress a certain uneasiness about this reification of the memory process. To avoid this metaphor, many psychologists prefer to speak of memory as something a person does, rather than something he has. This attitude leads to another set of questions about the effects of past experience on present behavior.

CHAPTER XII

IVAN PETROVICH PAVLOV,
PHYSIOLOGIST

"I propose to prove," said Claude Bernard in 1865, "that the science of vital phenomena must have the same foundations as the science of the phenomena of inorganic bodies, and that there is no difference in this respect between the principles of biological science and those of physico-chemical science."[1] This is *materialism*. At the time Bernard wrote, materialism was generally considered a necessary assumption for any scientific inquiry into living systems. When you study Bernard's book carefully, however, you discover that the great French physiologist was less concerned to reduce all vital phenomena to matter and energy than to show that they are—potentially—as intelligible as the more familiar physico-chemical phenomena. No divine soul or free will capriciously altered his measurements, no supernatural or inexplicable forces intervened unpredictably to spoil his experiments. Bernard fully expected to see vital phenomena reduced to materialistic terms, but this meant less to him than the broader principle that scientific methods can be successfully applied to living organisms. Vital phenomena are governed by laws—laws true always and everywhere.

The positivistic faith (that science can be applied to man and all his affairs) and the materialistic faith (that the results will be expressed as physico-chemical laws) are not always kept apart; they were never closer than when Bernard wrote. In Germany, for example, the science of physiology was controlled by four men: Hermann Ludwig von Helmholtz, Emil Du Bois-Reymond, Ernst Brücke, and Carl Ludwig. These four formed a private club in Berlin whose members were pledged to destroy vitalism, a pledge that one of them phrased so: "No other forces than the common physical-chemical ones are active within the organism. In those cases which cannot at the time be explained by these forces one has either to find the specific way or form of their action by means of the physical-mathematical method or assume new forces equal in dignity to the chemical-physical forces inherent in matter, reducible to the force of attraction and repulsion."[2]

This pledge expresses materialism in a pure form, flatly denying that life might involve vital forces transcending "the force of attraction and repulsion." It is curious to see how easily positivism, which began in violent opposition to any metaphysical dogma whatsoever, slips over into this kind of materialism—into the metaphysical dogma that true existence is reserved exclusively for physical and chemical objects. There is no way to know in advance what kinds of laws will prove necessary as science advances, yet a materialist feels comforted to think that the new laws will always look just like the old ones.

During the last half of the nineteenth century the Helmholtz school of medicine, brandishing its materialistic credo, completely dominated physiological and medical thinking. It was into this intellectual atmosphere that scientific psychology was born.

And it was in this intellectual atmosphere that the pioneer psychologists were educated. Freud was Brücke's student; Pavlov studied under Ludwig; Wundt was Du Bois-Reymond's student and Helmholtz's assistant. With physiology reduced to chemistry and physics, the next step was to reduce psychology to physiology. In that way the students were expected to carry on the work of their teachers. Freud to the end of his life talked about the mind in hydraulic, mechanical, electrical, and physical metaphors. Pavlov would never concede that his physiological interpretation of conditioning experiments was merely an elaborate figure of speech. And even Wundt, who tried to break with the positivistic tradition, founded his new psychology by writing a text, not on psychology, but on physiological psychology.

But the students were not always loyal to their teachers. Wundt deliberately defected. Freud tried to remain loyal, but supplied the revolt with powerful ammunition. Of all the pioneer psychologists the one most faithful to the materialistic standards of nineteenth century science was Pavlov, probably because he never realized that he had become a psychologist.

When materialists try to defend the idea that living systems are nothing but machines they generally begin with the most automatic and involuntary activities they can think of. Those are the reflexes and instincts. Exactly what an instinct is has been the focus of much argument. Some people use the term to mean all the driving desires and passions of the flesh; others mean any reactions an organism is born with and so does not need to learn; and still others take the position that an instinct is any highly automatic, involuntary, sequence of responses. The importance of instincts for a materialist conception of man has waxed and waned from one generation to the next. The reflex, however, has played a more constant role.

A reflex is an involuntary, unlearned, predictable response to a given stimulus (or class of stimuli), a response that is not influenced by any conscious thought or resolution, but that can usually be seen to have some clear purpose in protecting the organism or helping it to adjust to its environment. The study of reflex action has a long history.[3] Probably the first person to give a systematic discussion resembling our modern conception of the reflex was the French philosopher René Descartes. A mechanistic description of the body was a fundamental part of the Cartesian philosophy, which distinguished sharply between the mortal body—a machine—and the immortal soul that transcended space and time yet was somehow capable of controlling the material body. The automatic actions that the soul was unable to control voluntarily were what Descartes called reflexes. The seventeenth century's ideas about physiology were rather crude, however; Descartes spoke of animal spirits being reflected (hence the term reflex) into the muscles by an image in the pineal gland.

In the years that followed, a brilliant array of men—philosophers, physicians, natural scientists—contributed to the growing knowledge about the structure and function of the nervous system. The most significant step forward was probably the discovery, early in the nineteenth century, that the nerves attached to the spinal cord had a clear division of function. Sir Charles Bell in England and François Magendie in France were able to show that the nerves entering the back side of the spinal cord were important for sensory processes, and nerves entering the front side were important for muscular movements. Thus some of the neural pathways involved in reflex action were first revealed.

One of the most attractive figures in this story was the enthusiastic Scottish physician Marshall Hall, who had a rare gift for thinking clearly and simply in his experiments, his theories, and his writings. Hall's major argument was that reflexes are unconscious, an argument that struck at the well-established myth that all nervous activity is, or could be, conscious. Hall won his point so thoroughly that half a century later Wundt took it for granted that his new psychology could have nothing to do with reflexes. If they were unconscious, they were not accessible to introspection and so must be relegated to physiology. This convenient distinction between unconscious physiology and conscious psychology exploded, however, when Freud showed how much of our mental life is unconscious and when Pavlov adopted the reflexes as the fundamental building blocks for all behavior.

After Pavlov many psychologists, especially some American behaviorists, went to the opposite extreme from Wundt and based all psychology on reflexes. Their theories would have been nonsense, of course, if all the reflexes had to be inborn. Reflexes could not possibly play such an important role unless they could somehow be modified as the result of experience. But how can experience modify a reflex? This was the crucial question Pavlov tried to answer.

Ivan Petrovich Pavlov was born in 1849 in Ryazan, a provincial town in central Russia. He was the first of many children, most of whom died in infancy. His grandfather was a peasant and his father a priest; in nineteenth-century Russia that had a rather special meaning.

The social structure of Russia prior to the middle of the nineteenth century was exceedingly simple. There were effectively two social classes: the gentry, or aristocracy, which held all wealth and privilege, and the peasantry, which made up about 90 per cent of the population. (The clergy served the peasantry and were close to them.) The Russian government was equally simple; it consisted of a military aristocracy that did little more than maintain order at home and wage war abroad. During the nineteenth century, however, a third, intermediate class, the intelligentsia, began to emerge from the educational system fostered by Alexander I. It consisted of members of the aristocracy who had fallen upon hard times and members of the peasantry whose talent and energy had lifted them above their class into an intellectual life centered around the universities. The intelligentsia was a uniquely Russian institution, a social class united solely by bonds of education and moral passion. Insofar as they filled a position intermediate between the gentry and the peasantry, the members of the intelligentsia might be compared with the middle-class bourgeoisie in the rest of Europe. But the comparison would be quite misleading. The Russian intelligentsia did not play any commercial role; its special dedication was to reform the Russian government.

Ivan Petrovich Pavlov

As a son of a clergyman, Vanya was permitted to attend the local theological seminary, where his interest in science was encouraged, and in 1870 he was able to continue his studies at the University of St. Petersburg (now Leningrad). In that way he joined the socially intermediate class, too well-educated and too intelligent for the peasantry from which he came, but too common and too poor for the aristocracy into which he could never rise. These social conditions often produced an especially dedicated intellectual, one whose entire life was centered on the intellectual pursuits that justified his existence. And so it was with Pavlov, whose almost fanatic devotion to pure science and to experimental research was supported by the energy and simplicity of a Russian peasant. Those traits characterized the man and his work throughout his life.

In the theological seminary Pavlov was encouraged to follow his own intellectual inclinations, a freedom denied in most Russian schools at that time.[4] His early reading included Herbert Spencer, who became one of his favorite authors, and Charles Darwin, whose teachings and personality he idolized to the end of his days. While still a boy of fifteen he read a Russian translation of George Henry Lewes's *Physiology of Common Life* and became intrigued with a complicated drawing of the digestive system that Lewes had reproduced from Claude Bernard. Pavlov's interest in the physiology of digestion, which culminated in a Nobel prize forty years later, began when he looked at Bernard's drawing and asked himself how such a complicated system could work.

At the University of St. Petersburg the teacher who influenced him most was Ilya Cyon, the professor of physiology. Cyon was an artistic experimenter with exceptional skill in surgery; he wrote a first-rate text on experimental techniques in physiology; his lectures were both masterful and inspiring. "Never can such a teacher be forgotten," said Pavlov. It was Cyon who started Pavlov, then still an undergraduate, on his first physiological experiment. Upon graduation Pavlov was to have become a research assistant, but when Cyon was dismissed for political reasons, Pavlov resigned in protest.

Pavlov's determination to become an experimental physiologist seems never to have wavered. After one taste of research all the practical issues—his position, salary, living conditions, even the clothes he wore—became little more than unavoidable annoyances intruding upon the only part of life that really mattered. In the early years his single-mindedness protected him from the anxieties of poverty; later it protected him from the distractions of fame and administrative responsibility.

In 1881 he married Seraphima Karchevskaya, who devoted her life to protecting him from all mundane intrusions. She discovered her responsibilities rather suddenly when Ivan Petrovich turned up without the money to pay for their wedding or their return fares to St. Petersburg. So she paid their expenses out of her own savings, and the two of them arrived penniless in St. Petersburg. Pavlov's entire income was fifty rubles a month, but he refused to let Sara find a job. He borrowed two hundred rubles, and somehow they managed to exist. It was characteristic of him that Sara often had to remind him when it was time to go and collect his salary.

Only unwavering faith enabled his wife and friends to put up with him. His complete inability to manage his financial affairs was not his only peculiarity: he was equally difficult in other matters. For example, he liked to take long walks with his wife, but he set such a strenuous pace that she often had to run to keep up. During her first pregnancy this exertion caused Sara to miscarry. When he realized what had happened, of course, Pavlov was greatly dismayed. During her second pregnancy, therefore, he was determined to be more careful. So he swung over to the opposite extreme and even insisted on carrying her in his arms up to their fourth-floor apartment. In every way he was the tender, thoughtful husband. But when the child was born, he had no money to support it.

He once accepted an invitation for Sara and himself to attend a party at a professor's home. She was to go alone; he would join her there as soon as he could get away from a scientific meeting. It was a rare treat for her. She had a new dress, she was in excellent spirits, witty, animated, talkative. When Pavlov arrived later the host jokingly reproached him for having hidden so lovely a person from them all. Pavlov frowned. He had a headache. He was going home at once. Sara could stay if she liked. She left with him, told him everything she had said at the party and promised never to go anywhere again without him, but he sulked for two days. "This was so painful to me," she wrote later, "that I told myself that I would not take so much interest in dresses and that I would make a vow of silence. This attitude on my part brought extremely good results. Ivan Petrovich was spared sleepless nights and saved from unpleasant and painful thoughts."[5] In the words of James Thurber, a woman's place is in the wrong.

The Russian peasant custom of swaddling their babies for long periods, alternating with joyous episodes of play and affection, has been blamed for generating personalities that alternate between stolid, patient, self-restraint and explosive, emotional release.[6] Whether or not swaddling has anything to do with these extreme fluctuations is debatable, but certainly Pavlov's behavior often fell into this pattern. He would flare up at trivialities. If his surgery went badly, he might blame his assistant, waving his arms and swearing profusely. Once he hotheadedly whipped a dog whose whining bothered him, then admonished the assistant never to whip a dog because it might spoil his experiment. During the revolution he scolded one of his assistants for arriving ten minutes late for an experiment; shooting and fighting in the streets should not interfere when there was work to be done in the laboratory. Usually these outbursts were quickly forgotten. When a student discovered that no grudges were held, that no subtle meanings lurked behind the professor's words, he was usually grateful to know exactly where he stood and what he was expected to do. Pavlov was never reluctant to tell him.

His anger would become serious only when he thought his rigorous standards of pure science had been violated. If he suspected that a student had values he set above research, that an interest in night life, say, prevented him from arriving promptly at the laboratory, the student might never be forgiven. If someone defended a stupid experiment out of pity for the person who performed it or, worse yet, reported results that Pavlov could not confirm, he could be uncompromising in his opposition and his criticism. He himself was completely direct, completely honest, and he expected no less from others. He may not always have been considerate of the feelings of other people, but his honesty and integrity in research, in personal relations, in his political convictions, were beyond dispute.

During his entire career he worked on only three experimental problems. The first concerned the function of the nerves of the heart; he presented some of this work as his thesis for the degree of Doctor of Medicine, which he received in 1883. The second problem was the activity of the principal digestive glands; his brilliant experiments on digestion brought him world-wide recognition. The third was his study, from 1902 until his death in 1936, of the functions of the higher nervous centers in the brain. His use of conditioning as a way to attack this problem remains his greatest scientific accomplishment. His persistence, his energetic devotion to a few well-defined problems that he pushed as far as he could, was characteristic of him both as a scientist and as a personality.

His work on the digestive system followed two major lines: an analysis of the nervous control and regulation of the digestive glands, and a study of the normal function of the glands under ordinary conditions. His remarkable success in these experiments was due in large measure to his use of chronic, rather than acute preparations. In an acute experiment the anesthetized animal is operated upon, and the experimental observations are made immediately while the organs are surgically exposed. But he had discovered that the surgery itself tended to inhibit the secretion he wanted to study. In order to eliminate any unnatural effects of the operation, therefore, he undertook the more difficult task of creating chronic preparations—animals whose digestive processes could be studied under normal living conditions. The purpose of the operation was to make the digestive process visible to the scientist; experimental observations were not begun until the operation was over and the wound had healed. These chronic animals—in Pavlov's laboratory they were always dogs—were available for prolonged and diverse experiments and, more important, they functioned in the natural manner that he was trying to understand.

The general approach he used in preparing his chronic animals was to divert the secretion of a particular gland through a tube to the outside of the animal's body where it could be collected and measured. Once the flow of the digestive juice could be directly observed and measured, it was possible to explore the conditions that affected it, that increased or decreased the rate of flow. Sometimes the operations were very difficult, because it was crucial that the nerves and blood supply not be injured. His ingenuity in solving these problems and his amazing skill in performing the necessary surgery became a legend among physiologists.

The results of these experiments, along with Pavlov's theoretical interpretation, were summarized in 1897 as *The Work of the Digestive Glands.* In that book he mentioned certain irregularities and interruptions in what seemed to be the normal functioning of the digestive glands, and he attributed them to psychic causes. For example, he noticed that sometimes the glands would start to work before the food was given to the dog; the dog began to secrete digestive juices as soon as it saw the man who customarily fed it. This observation, which could only have been made with chronic animals, led to Pavlov's discovery of the conditional reflex.[7] He debated with himself for several years whether or not these irregularities—he called them psychic secretions—should be studied by experimental methods. It was 1902 before he determined to track them to their source.

His first experiments were done simply by showing the dog some bread in his hand and then giving the bread to the dog to eat. Eventually the dog would begin to salivate as soon as it saw the bread. But if bread was repeatedly shown and withheld, the dog would gradually stop responding to the visual stimulus. The dog's salivation when bread was placed in its mouth was a natural reflex of the digestive system—what Pavlov called an inborn or unconditional reflex. Salivation at the sight of the bread, however, was not an inborn reflex, but was something the dog learned to do. Pavlov called the response at the sight of the food a conditional reflex because its occurrence was conditional upon a prior association between seeing the food and tasting it.

Pavlov thought of, and occasionally discussed, the difference between these two kinds of reflexes by analogy with a telephone system. For a reflex to occur when the appropriate stimulus is given, he believed, there must be a neural path connecting the receptor organ to the gland or muscle that makes the response. For the inborn reflex that path is already completed at birth and corresponds to a direct telephone line. The path of a conditional reflex, however, must be created by making a connection through the central switchboard, by creating an engram in the central nervous system.

He soon discovered that conditional reflexes are affected by everything that goes on around the animal. In order to eliminate as many haphazard influences as he could, he put the dog and the experimenter in separate rooms. The dog was loosely strapped into a test frame where, like a swaddled Russian baby, he remained patiently immobile for hours at a time. Pavlov devised elaborate systems of tubes for presenting the stimuli and observing the secretory response (usually salivation) from outside the animal's room. And he substituted arbitrary conditional stimuli—a bell or a light—in place of the sight of bread in his hand. He discovered that any stimulus whatever could be made the occasion for conditional salivation.

In this way he arrived at the experimental procedure known as conditioning: a bell (conditional stimulus) is repeatedly sounded just before food (unconditional stimulus) is placed in the mouth to produce salivation (unconditional response), until eventually the sound of the bell causes salivation (conditional response) before the food is presented. This was the weapon with which Pavlov attacked the terrible riddles of the central nervous system.

He took special pride in the fact that his method was completely objective. In 1903 in one of his first public descriptions of this research he emphatically rejected any of the subjective methods of psychology. "In our 'psychical' experiments on the salivary glands,"

Fig. 27. Pavlov's arrangement for studying the conditional salivary reflex in dogs.

he said, "at first we honestly endeavored to explain our results by fancying the subjective condition of the animal. But nothing came of it except unsuccessful controversies, and individual, personal, uncoordinated opinions. We had no alternative but to place the investigation on a purely objective basis."[8] For Pavlov, a single line separated physiology from psychology, objective from subjective, and science from metaphysics. But his own work helped to destroy this simple distinction by giving psychologists another way to study their subjective problems objectively.

Around 1907 Pavlov came into public conflict with Bechterev. Vladimir M. Bechterev provides an interesting contrast to Pavlov in several respects.[9] Bechterev, the son of a minor government official, was an idealist far more typical than Pavlov of the Russian intelligentsia of the time. Both men, like many young Russian scientists in those days, went abroad for advanced studies;[10] Pavlov took it as just another step in a direction he was already going, but Bechterev spent the remainder of his life working out ideas acquired during his year in Leipzig. Whereas Pavlov stayed entirely within a rather narrow part of experimental physiology, Bechterev ranged all over the intellectual map, using both experimental and clinical methods to study problems in neurology, physiology, psychiatry, psychology, even sociology. Bechterev cut a fine figure in academic gatherings, for he was picturesquely Russian in a dignified and eloquent fashion;

Pavlov was totally oblivious of all appearances. One suspects that the battle between them was less caused than released by their scientific disagreement; the real animosity derived from their temperamental inability to understand one another.

Bechterev approached the conditioning experiment with different interests from Pavlov's. He was quick to appreciate the importance of Pavlov's discovery and to carry it over into psychological research; he saw it as the proper way to convert Wundt's physiological psychology into a truly objective science. As an experimental psychologist, however, he was less concerned to condition the digestive glands than the voluntary musculature. In that respect his interests closely paralleled those of American behaviorists. He trained dogs to raise a paw when a stimulus was presented, and he spoke of the result as an associative reflex. As a clinician, however, he was more interested in human patients than in dogs. In 1910 he published his ideas in a book, *Objective Psychology,* which went through several revisions; in subsequent editions the term psychology was eventually dropped and he wrote simply of *Reflexology.*

Bechterev's view of conscious phenomena was just as materialistic as was Pavlov's. It was not on that score that their quarrel arose. The spark that set off the explosion was Pavlov's discovery that he could not duplicate an experimental result reported by one of Bechterev's students. The famous Pavlov could easily have ignored the circumstance, but that was not his way. He became convinced that Bechterev was "debasing science," an offense he could never forgive. Pavlov attacked; Bechterev defended himself as best he could.

It had previously been discovered that stimulation of a particular point in the brain caused an animal to secrete saliva. The controversial claim from Bechterev's laboratory was that when this particular point in the brain was cut out, the conditional salivary reflex was abolished. In Pavlov's laboratory, however, it was not abolished. The argument dragged on for two years until finally Pavlov challenged Bechterev to demonstrate the claim experimentally. Bechterev accepted the challenge. Accordingly, the salivary centers in the brains of two dogs were taken out by surgical operation; Bechterev then publicly demonstrated the absence of a conditional salivary response by placing a glass jar containing lumps of sugar in front of the dogs, who did not salivate at the sight of the sugar. Bechterev seemed to be vindicated. But Pavlov and his followers were not impressed; they were not even sure the dogs really saw the sugar. Pavlov rose, took a flask of weak acid solution and splashed it several times into the dog's mouth. This simple procedure was sufficient to condition the dogs (acid, like food, naturally elicits the salivary reflex). After that, the mere sight, smell, or splash of the acid would arouse a conditional salivary response. The brain surgery had had no effect at all. On the spot, and in the presence of a large audience, Pavlov had demonstrated his objection to Bechterev's work. In spite of the dramatic outcome, however, the argument dragged on; the role of higher brain centers in conditioning is still not well understood. No doubt it is true that many of Bechterev's experiments did not come up to the standards of experimental precision and control demanded by Pavlov, yet even today many psychologists, especially in America, feel that in the larger issues there is much to be said on Bechterev's side of the argument.

After 1917 the Bolsheviks had a chance to discover how difficult Pavlov could be to live with. He regarded the revolution as one of the greatest misfortunes sustained by Russia. He could not understand these new leaders who never acted from a sense of guilt. In a public speech he commented on the great social experiment that the Bolsheviks were conducting; for such an experiment, he said, he would not sacrifice a frog's hindleg. In 1922 he asked Lenin to transfer him somewhere abroad. But dialectic materialism needs a scientific base far more than most forms of government, and Pavlov's theories were recognized as a potential source of great educational reforms. Lenin wrote a considerate refusal and offered to increase his food rations. When a commissar phoned to say he should send for the chicken and eggs that he was allowed, Pavlov said, "No, I refuse. As long as you do not give them to every one of my collaborators, I will not take them."

In 1927 when the sons of priests were expelled from the medical schools, he resigned from his chair as Professor of Physiology, saying, "I am the son of a priest and if you expel the others, I will go, too." And when the so-called Red professors were forcibly admitted into the hitherto autonomous Academy of Science, Pavlov wrote strong letters of protest to Stalin and was the only Academician to vote against them. In order to demonstrate his disapproval of the Soviet regime he stayed away from Russian scientific meetings, even though the Congress of Physiologists regularly elected him honorary chairman *in absentia.* (In 1930, however, they passed him by and in his place elected the entire Political Bureau of the Communist Party.)

In 1930 the central theme of a popular play, *Fear,* by Afinogenov, dealt with an eminent professor of physiology who had unconsciously played into the hands of the enemies of the Soviet state by working out a theory that fear was the essential motive in the behavior of the Soviet people.[11] His theory was exposed in a public meeting by an old Bolshevik woman whose political experience compensated for her lack of formal education. She concluded her indictment of the professor with a cry to the audience to be merciless toward the real enemies of the state. The professor, converted, promised to give a public criticism of his malicious theory and to hand over all the keys to his research institute. Of course, nothing was said in the play about the Pavlov affair, but the parallel would have been hard to miss.

In 1933 apparently Pavlov had become convinced that the new government was going to survive, that it had in fact united the Russian people, and that the lavish support of science, which, in Pavlov's positivistic opinion, would in the long run resolve all social problems, meant that the government shared his own high regard for scientific truth and freedom. For the final three years of his life, therefore, Pavlov and Soviet Russia lived together in peace. Since his death in 1936 his research has been continued, his memory preserved, and his writings used to justify new scientific projects in physiology and psychology. When Russians talk about Pavlov today, the difficult interlude from 1917 to 1933 is no longer mentioned.

Why was the conditioning experiment so important? Because of its apparent simplicity, a tremendously important, voluminously discussed, little understood phenomenon, something that philosophers and psychologists had called association, was here captured in simple, objective, experimental terms.

Ordinary human behavior is so enormously complicated that a scientist has great difficulty in knowing where to take hold of it. The first step is to find a satisfactory unit of analysis, a simple building block with which the complicated patterns of our daily conduct can be constructed. Presumably, complex behavior could be analyzed into unconditional and conditional reflexes. Pavlov's genius was to show how those simple elements could be isolated, analyzed, and controlled in the laboratory.

But, if the conditional reflex is so simple, what was Pavlov doing between 1902 and 1936? The simplicity of this reflex unit has not prevented experimenters from finding many aspects of it worthy of careful study. Pavlov's experimental situation seems simple only by comparison with the overwhelming complexity of our uncontrolled behavior. Consider a few of the dimensions that must be explored.

First, there is the time dimension: How long should the experimenter wait between successive trials? If he varies the time at which the conditional and unconditional stimuli are turned on (or turned off), what happens? Is it possible to use an empty interval of time itself as a conditional stimulus? Many experiments had to be done on these questions of timing alone.

But that was only a start. There are several aspects of the unconditional stimulus that had to be investigated: What inborn reflexes are available for an experimenter to work with? Can a well-established conditional stimulus serve as an unconditional stimulus for a higher-order reflex? What happens when the amount of the unconditional stimulus is increased? What is the effect of withholding it repeatedly, or according to some fixed or random schedule?

Similar questions can be posed about the conditional stimulus: What physical energies can be used as conditional stimuli? How sharp a distinction can an animal make between the conditional stimulus and all other stimuli?

The response also suggests several experimental questions: Is a conditional response exactly the same as an unconditional response? What apects of a response—reaction time, probability, magnitude, variability, duration—should be recorded? What other responses normally accompany the unconditional response?

And some of the most important questions concern the animal: Does conditioning depend upon its state of deprivation—hunger, thirst, and the like? Or upon the time of day? Are some animals easier to condition than others? What are the effects of previous experience? Can conditional reflexes be abolished by destroying various parts of the nervous system? What would happen with a species of animal other than Pavlov's beloved dogs; with men, for example?

These questions suggest some of the variables that had to be studied. The simplicity of the conditioning situation is only relative. The important thing, however, is that all these questions can be answered—answered in objective terms. What is needed is patient experimentation, and that is exactly what Pavlov and his small army of students and assistants provided. After twenty years of research Pavlov was ready to report his preliminary answers to some of these questions, along with his theory as to why the answers came out as they did. In 1923 he published a collection of speeches, articles, and reports under the Russian title *Twenty Years of Objective Study of the Higher Nervous Activity (Behavior) in Animals;*[12] the anthology was ill-assorted, but Pavlov hoped it would to some extent foreshadow the book he was planning to write later. His more systematic report appeared in 1926 under the Russian title *Lectures on Conditional Reflexes.*[13] The delay between the time Pavlov began to study conditioning and the time he published these books was less the result of his advancing age—although he was near seventy-five—than of the great scope of the problem and his feelings of scientific responsibility for the validity of everything he published.

When a conditional salivary reflex is established by repeatedly pairing some arbitrary stimulus with food, there is characteristically a generalization from that particular conditional stimulus to others that resemble it. For instance, if a tone of 1000 cycles per second is established as a conditional stimulus, other tones spontaneously acquire similar properties. The ability of the other tones to evoke the conditional reflex diminishes in proportion to the intervals between these tones and 1000 cycles. Similarly, if touching a definite circumscribed area of skin is made into a conditional stimulus, touching other skin areas will also elicit some conditional reaction, the effect diminishing with increasing distance of these areas from the one for which the conditional reflex was originally established. This phenomenon, called stimulus generalization, is of great psychological significance; it illustrates how reactions acquired in one situation can be transferred to similar situations. If such transfer did not occur, animals, man included, would profit little from experience.

From an experimental point of view, the generalization experiment provides a way to measure how similar two situations are for the animal; the greater the similarity, the greater will be the stimulus generalization. Moreover, the experiment can be used to study how accurately the animal can perceive differences in its environment. Psychologists seized upon stimulus generalization as an especially clear instance of a very important psychological process[14] (cf. Chapter VI).

To Pavlov, however, stimulus generalization was a direct indicator of physiological processes taking place in the brain. He believed that there are two complementary processes, excitation and inhibition, perhaps corresponding to two different chemicals, that compete for control of the various parts of the brain. When a conditional reflex is formed, the conditional stimulus acquires excitatory powers; the differentiation of that particular stimulus from all others depends upon the development of inhibition for all nonreinforced stimuli.

Different stimuli affect different points on the surface of the brain. Stimulus similarity is, in Pavlovian theory, a matter of distance in the brain; the more alike two things are, the closer their neural representations will be and the greater the interaction between them. When a point is given excitatory (or inhibitory) properties by the conditioning procedure, stimulation of the point will produce a wave of excitation (or inhibition) radiating into the adjacent brain tissue, which thus lends its excitatory (or inhibitory) properties to similar stimuli. When a conditional discrimination is firmly established, only a small region of the brain corresponding to the conditional stimulus will produce a response. Inhibition lies over the rest of the brain like winter over the empty plains of central Russia, limiting all activity to the lonely stockades.

Just prior to the time Pavlov began his research on the higher nervous centers in the brain, interest in the activity of the lower nervous centers in the spinal cord had developed independently in England. C. S. Sherrington and his school carried out a brilliant analysis of the interactions among the various spinal reflexes;[15] their results are today a generally accepted part of physiological knowledge. It is interesting historically that Pavlov's work, similar in purpose and equally brilliant, has had almost no influence upon other branches of physiology. Pavlov's principal impact has been felt in psychology. The fact is a bit ironic, considering his low opinion of psychology as a science, but the reason is not difficult to find. Pavlov did not make any direct observations of the processes going on in the brain. He based his opinion of them entirely upon inferences from what the animals did in his experiments. What he looked at directly was not the animal's brain, but the animal's behavior. Consequently, all his statements about waves of excitation and inhibition that irradiate over the surface of the brain are little more than plausible fictions; if you opened up the skull you would not know how or where to look for them. His description of the animal's behavior in the conditioning experiment, however, is wonderfully acute. Since experimental psychologists, inspired in no small measure by Pavlov's success, have pursued the objective description and analysis of behavior, Pavlov's work has had its major effect on behavioristic psychology, rather than on physiology.

From a psychological point of view one of his most interesting discoveries was experimental neurosis. If a dog is forced to learn a very difficult discrimination between two stimuli, it may become extremely disturbed. The first systematic observations of this emotional reaction were made in 1914. A dog was trained to salivate when it saw a circle. Then an ellipse was presented without any reinforcement by food; the discrimination was easily established. On subsequent days the difference between the ellipse and the circle was reduced progressively. Finally the two were so much alike that discrimination failed. After three weeks of unsuccessful training the whole behavior of the dog changed abruptly:

> The hitherto quiet dog began to squeal in its stand, kept wriggling about, tore off with its teeth the apparatus for mechanical stimulation of the skin, and bit through the tubes connecting the animal's room with the observer, a behavior which never happened before. On being taken into the experimental room the dog now barked violently, which was also contrary to its usual custom; in short it presented all the symptoms of a condition of acute neurosis.[16]

Pavlov explained these symptoms as a conflict between the excitatory and inhibitory processes. Ordinarily the nervous system can establish an equilibrium between them, but when the sources of excitation and inhibition get very close together, the equilibrium breaks down and a generally excited or inhibited state appears.

The explanation is ingenious but somewhat unreal. Considering the amount of frustration normally involved in a conditioning experiment —the restraint in the test frame, the monotonous repetition of particular stimuli—the addition of a difficult discrimination seems but a small part of the animal's discomfort. If Pavlov's excitation and inhibition had been less metaphorical, it would have been easier to test his theory directly. But it is not a physiological theory at all; it is a psychological theory disguised in physiological language.

Pavlov's interest in experimental neurosis increased as he grew older; he devoted the last decade of his life largely to psychiatric problems.[17] When at last he began to think seriously about human behavior Pavlov recognized that the enormous complexities introduced by language required new explanations. To his earlier distinction between inborn and conditional reflexes, therefore, he added verbal symbols. The conditional reflexes that he had so long studied in animals comprised a "first signaling system." Men, he said, have evolved another, a "second signaling system" of verbal symbols. Although he was not able to develop this proposal himself, it has stimulated considerable speculation and research by subsequent generations of Russian psychologists.

Pavlov's contributions to science are everywhere known and admired, but their implications for social policy and their effects upon our conception of human nature are often deplored. Many people have been frightened by grim visions of a brave, new world where machines will condition every child into submissive uniformity. Such fears are fed by ignorance, but some fairly able spokesmen have given voice to them. George Bernard Shaw once called Pavlov a scoundrel and his teaching a crackle of blazing nonsense from beginning to end.[18] Similar appreciations have been expressed by many other humanists.

Pavlov has often been classed with Freud as a major source of anti-intellectualism in the twentieth century. In their hands Sovereign Reason, benevolent ruler of the eighteenth-century mind, crumbled into unconscious reflexes and instincts, automatic processes that are the very antithesis of ratiocinative thought. Reason seemed to refute itself. Yet both men, Pavlov and Freud, were true children of the Enlightenment; both believed that the search for knowledge must never stop, that only knowledge allows reason to function, that only reason can make men free. Both were loyal to the highest values of their positivistic education. What they both attacked was not sovereign reason, but foolish optimism about the inevitability of human progress. To dismiss them as anti-intellectuals is a dangerous oversimplification.

No doubt Pavlov himself would prefer to be classed with his hero Darwin, with the famous biologist rather than the famous psychologist. And there is reason to respect his wish. Where Darwin showed how living organisms can adapt to their environments by changing slowly from one generation to the next, Pavlov showed how a living organism can adapt by changing rapidly during its own lifetime. And, like Darwin, Pavlov angered the nonscientists whose preconceived notions were threatened by his discoveries. But such anger is the way we pay our greatest men. It is a special tribute reserved for those whose work is truly significant.

CHAPTER XIII

THE SEARCH FOR
BEHAVIORAL ATOMS

"If I attempt to analyze a man's entire mind," said Edward Lee Thorndike, a psychologist who for forty years was an intellectual leader on the faculty of Columbia University's famed Teachers College, "I find connections of varying strength between (a) situations, elements of situations, and compounds of situations and (b) responses, readinesses to respond, facilitations, inhibitions, and directions of responses. If all these could be completely inventoried, telling what the man would think and do and what would satisfy and annoy him, in every conceivable situation, it seems to me that nothing would be left out. . . . Learning is connecting. The mind is man's connection-system."[1]

Such was the associationist position in 1931. It was a linear descendant of an older associationism that began with John Locke and that inspired British empiricists for two centuries. But there was a crucial difference. Instead of connections between ideas, Thorndike talked about connections between situations and responses. In this way he accepted into his psychological theory a physiological frame of reference.

Thorndike stood in a proud tradition, and he spoke for a sizable constituency among America's academic psychologists during the twenties and thirties. If the mind is man's connection-system, then the program of research that lay ahead was clear. Isolate the elementary connection processes, and you will have under your control the very stuff that minds are made of. Pavlov had shown one way to study the formation of connections in animals. Similar analysis should be possible for human behavior, too.

Consider a person who deliberately and intentionally sets out to memorize certain verbal responses to a given set of verbal stimuli. To be definite, imagine an English-speaking student of the French language who undertakes to memorize a new section of French vocabulary. What he will try to do is to learn the meanings of French words; for a beginning student, learning the meanings involves learning what English words he should say, or think of, when he sees the French words. He will go over his list several times, each time looking at the French stimulus, making his English response, and checking to see if he is right. Psychologists call this paired-associates learning.

The student will usually continue until he can give a correct English equivalent for every French word on his list. Attaining a criterion of one errorless recall of the entire list ordinarily satisfies him that he has mastered his lesson. He goes on about his other business until, perhaps, he is tested by his instructor. Then, alas, he discovers that he can no longer give the expected response to every French word. He recalls some words; others he has forgotten.

We normally think of this familiar situation as a build-up and then a slow decay, a strengthening followed by a weakening of the English-French connections, or associations. If there is no rehearsal, then the longer the interval between the building and the testing, of course, the more the associations will fade and the poorer recall will be.

Our description seems to give an adequate account of what happened to the student, but note that there is no mention in it of anything corresponding to a place where his memories of the French-English pairs must be stored. If one thinks of learning as a process of establishing connections between stimuli and responses, then the connection either exists or it does not exist. If it exists, it exists at a strength that waxes and wanes as a function of many different variables. But to know where it exists is not essential. Remembering, that is, making an appropriate response when a stimulus is repeated, is something we do, not something we have.

This approach has the great advantage of being related directly to observable events, to observable stimuli and responses and their co-occurrences. No reliance is placed upon hearsay evidence about visual images, or rules, or mnemonic tricks. Because of the emphasis upon stimulus and response, this hardheaded approach is commonly referred to as the stimulus-response or S-R approach.

Psychologists have invented many different theories to account for our ability to profit from experience; it would be quite misleading to suggest that everyone would defend an S-R theory of learning. But many would, and do. S-R theory has long been a popular approach in America, and a kind of stereotype has developed around it. According to E. R. Hilgard, whose textbooks have for many years settled these matters for American students, S-R theories are characterized by (1) their emphasis upon peripheral muscular mechanisms —chained reflexes, movement-produced stimuli, anticipatory responses—rather than upon central brain processes as the source of behavioral integration, (2) their insistence that what we learn are not passive facts, but active responses, and (3) their faith that trial-and-error rather than insight is the basic mode of learning.[2] An S-R theorist has little use for quiet introspection; the organisms he studies are on the move, struggling, responding, changing constantly.

It is always dangerous to create an imaginary synthesis of the aims and accomplishments of many people, especially when they differ among themselves as violently as S-R theorists often do. But the convenience of the speculation can scarcely be resisted. We shall pretend, therefore, that the S-R stereotype represents something that many psychologists would agree with in spirit, if not in detail. But a cautious reader will remind himself that S-R theory is not really as monocratic as we shall make it seem.

The first self-conscious efforts to create a formal, mathematical theory along S-R lines were Clark L. Hull's *Mathematico-Deductive Theory of Rote Learning* (1940) and his *Principles of Behavior* (1943). Hull was a behaviorist, working in the tradition of Pavlov and Watson, with little respect for mentalistic concepts such as understanding or consciousness. His ambition was to specify rigorously a small number of mathematical variables inside the organism that would account for all of the observed correlations between stimulation and response.

The cornerstone of Hull's theory was the following idea: whenever a response to some stimulus has the effect of reducing a biological drive, the strength of that stimulus-response association will be increased. The idea that we repeat actions that were successful before is, of course, quite ancient. The daring feature of this hypothesis is that, true to the behaviorist tradition, nothing is assumed about *understanding* the connection between the response and the satisfactions that follow it. If an organism is hungry in situation S, say, and if some response R is followed immediately by food, then the habit of responding R in situation S will be *automatically* reinforced. On closer inspection one recognizes that the situation is compounded of many different stimuli: of internal stimuli produced by hunger; of current environmental sights, sounds, and odors; of persisting traces of previous environmental stimuli; and of stimuli resulting directly from the organism's own movements. A description of a particular instance of learning must specify all the connections formed between each of these varieties of stimulation and the sequence of responses that leads to the goal. But the critical assumption is that all these S-R bonds are formed blindly and automatically, without intention or insight.

Fig. 28. Schematic and highly idealized curves for learning and forgetting. During the initial study period the probability of a correct response increases to nearly 1.0; while the person is engaged in other activities, the probability slowly decays.

By making certain simple assumptions about the amount of the increase in habit strength produced by every successful experience, Hull was able to write mathematical expressions to describe the quantitative changes that measure the amount of learning. This mathematical formulation had at least one enormous advantage over theories stated in a purely verbal form: it could be proved wrong. If you cannot discover your mistakes, you cannot correct them. Hull showed the way toward greater rigor in psychological theory; the use of mathematical notation to describe the learning process has grown in popularity ever since.

In his conception of the psychological nature of man, however, Hull advanced little beyond what Herbert Spencer had said seventy years earlier. Hull's achievement was to bring Spencer's genetic philosophy into direct and meaningful connection with quantitative data from the experimental laboratory. Rather than criticize his theory, therefore, we should look at the kind of experimental data that the theory was intended to explain.

Hull wrote equations for the strength of S-R connections. Where does one find a typical S-R connection to study? And, having found it, how does one proceed to measure its strength?

In the simpler forms of S-R theory little is said about the way we organize experience or discover rules that simplify a learning task. To any psychologist who defines learning in terms of the strength of an association between a stimulus and a response, remembering things according to rules is more appropriately classified as thinking or problem solving, not simple learning. What an S-R theorist asks is, "Where do the basic associations come from?" What is the origin of the already present associations that a person presumably exploits when he uses rules or images to facilitate new learning? Mnemonic tricks are merely ways to exploit old connections so as to save the trouble of making new ones. One would like to study the more basic, probably simpler kind of learning first. But how? How can a learner be forced to form new connections?

One strategy is to strip all meaningful associations away, to give the subject something so strange and unfamiliar that he cannot have any old associations to it and so is forced to form new ones. As early as 1885 the German psychologist Herman Ebbinghaus introduced the nonsense syllable as a way to obtain a large number of relatively homogeneous items for the person to learn; they are homogeneous because, being meaningless, they escape the learner's preestablished habits of thought.[3] There is an infinite variety of unfamiliar nonsense. The kind that psychologists have standardized, following Ebbinghaus, is a three-letter, consonant-vowel-consonant (CVC) "syllable." (CVC sequences that spell familiar words are frequently considered ineligible.)

In a typical experiment on serial rote memorization, for example, a subject may be presented with a list of ten or twelve nonsense syllables, one at a time. They appear at regular intervals, usually in the window of a mechanical device designed for this purpose. (In one simple version a cylindrical drum papered with the syllable list slowly rotates behind a covering hood arranged to expose the syllables in a window one at a time—see Figure 29.) As each syllable appears in the window, the memorizer is supposed to pronounce (or spell, since some syllables may be unpronounceable) the *next* syllable on the list. The first time around, of course, he will not anticipate any of the syllables correctly, but gradually, after repeated trials, he will do better and better until eventually he will be able to anticipate each syllable before it appears.

Fig. 29. A teaching machine that presents nonsense syllables one at a time.

Psychologists soon discovered that some nonsense syllables are more nonsensical than others. For example, "BAL," "BIZ," "DUL," "JAN," "TAL" have associations for almost everyone who speaks English, but "CEF," "GIW," "MEQ," "XAD," "ZOJ" do not often stir our memories. In order to eliminate mnemonic tricks, therefore, it is generally assumed that nonsense syllables having low association

values should be used. A sample task consisting of twelve units might
be the following:

YIC

QOM

GEP

DUZ

RIJ

NAW

XOL

HUQ

TEF

ZIK

VOB

PAH

At first glance it would appear that all previous training in the
use of words and sentences has been rendered worthless and inopera-
tive. Now, surely, any learner must start afresh and form new associations for us. But never underestimate a subject's cleverness. One
person made up the following sentences in order to memorize the
above list of syllables:

Why, I see

qom

gets

duz,

right?

Nah!

You need excellent

hucksters

t' have

sick

vob.

Pah!

True, it sounds like an argument between a lunatic and a mis-
anthrope, but it is not difficult to remember; from it the original
syllables can easily be reconstructed. The first time he memorizes
such a list, a typical subject spends much of his time composing just
such mnemonic crutches to guide his recitation. Syllables with low

association values are more difficult to learn because it is harder, and takes longer, to construct the meaningful translation.

Even these Spartan measures, therefore, do not frustrate what has been called the learner's effort after meaning. A psychologist who is convinced that the real process of learning consists of lowering resistance to the flow of nerve impulses along certain pathways leading from the receptor that senses the stimulus to the muscles that make the response will look upon these verbal shenanigans as a pure nuisance. Of course, it is possible to ignore them, to deal only with an average number of correct responses on successive repetitions of the list. But if we want to examine a particular stimulus-response connection, averages do not tell us much. Some other approach is needed. If nonsense syllables do not eliminate the use of mnemonic tricks, then they are too complicated and something still simpler should be learned. Perhaps nonsense syllables are still too much like meaningful words. To get something completely nonverbal, the task has to be simplified. Perhaps the study of motor skills can furnish what is required.

Such skills, it must be admitted, are seldom learned without any taint of verbal guidance. Even if one ignores as obviously too verbal two such carefully analyzed skills as typewriting and radiotelegraphy, it remains that a verbal description of the general strategy a learner should pursue can be a tremendous aid. If you want to teach someone to hit targets that are under water, a verbal explanation of the principle of refraction can speed the learning considerably. Or if you tell a person who is learning to ride a bicycle that he should turn the front wheel in the same direction he is falling, you may shorten his learning time considerably. But verbal hints and helps are not easily discovered for every situation, and in any case it is always possible to withhold them, thus apparently forcing the learner to work without symbolic aids. Here, it would seem, is a place where the elementary connections can be studied. And, to a limited extent, this is true.

But the picture is still not as clean and neat as one might wish for the purposes of an analysis of stimuli and responses. A skilled motor performance usually runs on continuously in time, and it is not obvious where it should be dissected into discrete stimuli and responses. It is not only that both the stimulus and the response are continuous functions of time; the problem is further complicated by the fact that the consequences of the responses are fed back and modify the stimulus. Thus, one can no longer equate stimulus and response with antecedent and consequent, respectively.

The skill involved in steering a car along a winding road provides an obvious example. The road is a continuously varying stimulus that swerves left and right. The driver makes a continuously varying response as he moves the steering wheel left and right. But if he moves the wheel too far in one direction, the error shows up in the path of the car; the stimulus to turn back is correspondingly greater. The stimulus is not the road or the direction of the car; the stimulus is the discrepancy between the two. And the driver's response is to keep that stimulus as small as he can. The complete stimulus-response-feedback loop is closely analogous to what is called a servo-mechanism, and it is a good deal more complicated than the simple S-R atom we started looking for.[4] Apparently, the situation has still not been sufficiently simplified.

Fig. 30. Representation of an automobile and its driver as a servomecha-nism. The driver compares the direction of the road with the path of his car, and adjusts the steering mechanism to reduce the discrepancy be-tween them.

What is necessary is to strip the learning situation to its bare essentials. It is a typical story in science. To study gravity, one must ignore the falling leaves and the drifting clouds and the winged birds that fly upward—one must get to the naked essentials that are re-tained when a body falls freely through a vacuum. What the S-R theorist is trying to do is to find an experimental situation that, like bodies falling in a vacuum, will provide simple, quantitative laws for the basic, underlying processes in learning. Once the laws governing this fundamental S-R process are understood, complications can be added as they are required.

Consider the following simplification of the learning situation: A subject sits with one finger touching an electrode and a second electrode strapped to his wrist. When the experimenter closes a switch a painful electric shock results. The experimenter never closes the switch to deliver the shock, however, without first turning on a tone just a half second before. In the beginning the subject does not respond to the tone, but after a few trials in which the tone is followed by shock, he learns to straighten out his finger, thus lifting it from the electrode and avoiding the shock. So an association is established between the tonal stimulus and the response of straightening the finger.

This kind of learning is, of course, conditioning.[5] It resembles the general pattern of experimentation used by Pavlov, but a human subject has replaced Pavlov's dog. The electric shock is an unconditional stimulus; the withdrawal by straightening and lifting the finger to escape the shock is an unconditional response; the tone that comes on a half-second before the shock is a conditional stimulus; and the withdrawal by straightening and lifting the finger when the tone sounds and before the shock occurs—the response that avoids the shock—is a conditional response.

The principal difference between this procedure and Pavlov's is that here the unconditional stimulus is not given if the conditional response occurs soon enough to avoid it. The difference is important. The procedure just described above is often called *instrumental* conditioning (the response is instrumental in avoiding the shock), to distinguish it from the classical form of Pavlovian conditioning, where the unconditional stimulus is always presented on every training trial.

Here we have reached something basic. The instrumental conditioning experiment is extremely simple, it does not depend upon verbal instructions, and there is a close parallel between the results obtained from humans and animals. Some proponents of S-R theories assume that the conditioning experiment is the prototype of all learning. For more complex situations the theoretical task is to discover how the behavioral processes can be analyzed into these basic components. That analysis often requires considerable ingenuity, especially in the realm of verbal learning, but S-R theorists are confident it can be carried through successfully. "After all," they might say, "analysis into basic units is essential to all scientific progress: look at the analysis of matter into atoms, or the analysis of organisms into cells. Everywhere in science it is the same. We must find the proper elements and then discover the laws of their combination. That was, after all, what Wilhelm Wundt wanted to do; the trouble with Wundt was that he chose the idea instead of the S-R bond as his element."

But there are still problems that must be solved before one can accept this argument. For example, suppose in the finger-withdrawal experiment just described, one asks the subject after one or two hundred conditioning trials, to turn his hand over (as shown in Figure 31). Now, with his hand in this new position, if he straightens his finger it will still be touching the electrode and he will not avoid the shock. To avoid or escape the shock when his hand has been turned over the person must bend his finger, the exact opposite of the movement he had been conditioned to make. What will happen? Will he make the same *response* and extend his finger? Or will he perform the same *act* and flex his finger?

TRAIN   **TEST**

Fig. 31. Arrangement used to demonstrate response generalization.

About seven out of every ten subjects flex the finger, even after many long trials in which they have been conditioned to extend it.[6] Twenty-five per cent do nothing at all, and about 5 per cent persist in making the extensor movement. The subjects themselves can provide no explanation; they report later that the finger acted in the way it did more or less of its own accord. Moreover, there is no satisfactory way to discriminate in advance between people who will flex the finger and people who will continue to extend it. But the gross statistical fact can scarcely be avoided: For most subjects, the result of the conditioning procedure has been to condition the *act* of withdrawal, not the *response* of finger extension. This outcome can be called response generalization—the S-R bond has generalized from the extensor response to the flexor response—but whatever one calls it, it makes a conditional reflex in a human subject appear somewhat more complicated than before.

When you stop to think about it, this conditioning experiment is an unusual way to get a person to lift his finger at the sound of a tone. As R. S. Woodworth pointed out, an occasional subject will misunderstand the experiment and assume that the experimenter wants him to keep his finger on the electrode and take the shock. If his finger does withdraw before the shock, he feels silly and ashamed and increases his effort to keep it in place; and he does not develop a conditional response even after many sessions. Why does the experimenter let this misunderstanding persist? He could simply say to the subject, "I will give you strong shocks preceded by tones. I wish to discover how long it will take you to learn to avoid the shock by raising your finger when the tone comes on." But if he said that, his experiment would lose all point![7] Once again, verbal processes seem able to interfere with the basic process being studied. In an effort to escape the interfering effects of a human subject's symbolic habits the investigator has worked himself into the position of trying to fool the subject about what he is supposed to do.

Lest one becomes discouraged about conditioning human beings, however, a word of warning is needed. The fact that this particular experiment is not as simple as it looks must not be interpreted to mean that human beings are invulnerable to Pavlov's procedures. All the evidence suggests that we can be conditioned, that we are being conditioned every day. We seem to be especially vulnerable when we are not actively aware of the conditional situation and when the response is made by our autonomic nervous system.

The autonomic nervous system controls the vegetative functions of our glands and smooth muscles, vital functions that involve few conscious decisions on our part. Pavlov, for example, worked with responses of the digestive glands; his Russian successors[8] have extended his method to responses of other digestive glands, to stomach contractions and contractions of blood vessels, to heart rate and metabolic rate, and so on. It seems plausible that many of the emotional symptoms of psychoneurosis are created by the pervasive action of the reflexes encompassed by Pavlov's laws on these autonomic processes of the body.

The finger-withdrawal experiment, however, involves a voluntary response of the striped musculature, which is under the control of the central nervous system. In man, the enormous central nervous system—brain and spinal cord—supports symbolic processes that introduce a whole new level of complexity into the control of our behavior. It is this very complexity that seems to thwart our efforts to find a pure example of an S-R connection.

Where can one find learning that is mediated by the central nervous system and yet is not impossibly complicated by all the verbal, pictorial, and formal symbol-systems that are such characteristic ornaments of the human mind? An obvious answer is, in the study of other animals. And, in fact, that is where many psychologists have turned.

The consequences have been rather curious. Animals provide fascinating problems for a psychologist. However, many psychologists who study animals have no profound interest in them except insofar as their behavior can be related to human psychology. Such psychologists would prefer to study the creation of new S-R connections in man, but in order to demonstrate the learning process in its raw and primitive form they are forced to use inarticulate subjects. Admittedly it is a dangerous business to argue by analogy from one species to another, yet many distinguished psychologists are convinced that the fundamental laws of learning are so simple and universal that they can be studied anywhere in the animal kingdom, or, at least, anywhere among the vertebrates. So, in this excellent company, let us descend one more step in our effort to simplify the study of the learning process.

One of the first attempts to use animals in a psychological study of learning was Thorndike's early (1898) experiment with cats in a puzzle box.[9] Thorndike put his cats into a rough wooden crate built of slats. The box had a door that was held shut by a button and a catch. If the cat could either turn the button or pull a loop that hung inside the box and that was connected directly to the catch, it could escape. The cats wanted out; they seemed to dislike the confinement. To reinforce this dislike, Thorndike deprived them of food prior to the tests and then fed them when they escaped.

On their first confinement in the box, the cats, particularly the young ones, scrambled around vigorously, attacked the bars, cracks, corners, and, eventually, the loop or the button until they accidentally worked the escape mechanism. There was no intelligent study of the situation, no insight, no plan: merely random, trial-and-error movements. But once the response that led to escape had been made, the cat could begin to strengthen the connection between its response and the escape mechanism, and to eliminate the responses that did not lead to escape. As the successful association grew stronger on repeated trials, the time it took for the cat to escape grew shorter, but the irregular nature of the function (see Figure 32) is eloquent testimony to the haphazard, trial-and-error nature of the learning process.

Fig. 32. There were large variations from trial to trial in the length of time it took this cat to escape from Thorndike's puzzle box.

Here is a good example of experimental evidence that encourages S-R theorists to believe that learning is nothing but the formation of connections between stimuli and responses. Given that experimental paradigm, it is then possible to search for laws governing the rise and fall of associative strengths. Thorndike proposed two fundamental laws:

The Law of Exercise. The more often a given situation is followed by a particular response, the stronger will be the associative bond between them. Exercise—use, repetition, practice—makes perfect.

The Law of Effect. If a response produces a good effect and leads to a satisfying state of affairs, it will tend to be repeated when the situation arises again. It is a variant of this law that Hull later adopted as the foundation of his S-R theory of learning.

Both of Thorndike's laws are excellent descriptive statements. Animals, including men, tend to repeat activities that are profitable or rewarding, and the more often they repeat them, the better they perform. There are exceptions, but on the whole these phenomena characterize much of the behavior we want to understand.

A large part of scientific psychology in America in the twentieth century has been based on, or directed at, these two laws. The conclusion seems to be that if they are interpreted literally as causal explanations, they are not true. Thorndike himself discredited the Law of Exercise by demonstrating that when a learner is denied information as to whether he succeeds or fails, all the exercise in the world cannot result in learning. On the other hand, the Law of Effect has had a more checkered career; it is not yet obvious that nothing will come of it. What is involved is a particular type of feedback loop; the satisfying effect of a response is fed back to strengthen it on future occasions. A major difficulty arises, however, in the attempt to define what is meant by a "satisfying state" of a response. Hull defined it as a reduction of a biological drive, but this additional assumption raises as many questions as it answers. (We will return to this problem in Chapter XVI.)

A strong case can be made that the satisfying state of affairs does not determine what the animal will learn, but rather will determine what the animal will do. Edward C. Tolman[10] has argued that animals will acquire information, will learn what to expect when certain signs occur, in situations where no apparent reward is offered. The learning becomes evident only later when a reward is introduced that motivates the animal to use the information it has acquired. But the reward does not itself automatically stamp in the connection between a stimulus and a response. What happens is quite complex, and no simple generalization can adequately summarize the hundreds of experimental studies that have been directed toward the problem of rewards and punishments and their effects on both learning and performance.

Let us return to the cats in the puzzle box. Many years after Thorndike's original study the work was repeated with better equipment.[11] The box was arranged with a pole in the center. If the cat pushed against the pole and tilted it, an electric contact was made that released the door. Moreover, a camera was set to take a photograph of the cat at the instant the successful response occurred.

The pictures revealed a surprising thing: the cat's movements at the instant of escape were highly stereotyped for many trials in a row. For example, one of the cats, cat T, on the first trial happened to activate the mechanism by lying down, pausing, then rolling over until it hit the pole. The cat then repeated almost exactly the same elaborate pattern of actions on succeeding trials. Tracings from the photographic record are shown for the first eight escape trials in Figure 33. Other animals regularly brushed against the pole, or always chewed it, or always hit it with their tails, or always stepped on the base. A particular movement pattern would be repeated until by accident it failed to hit the post (or occasionally, the release mechanism in the box failed to work), and then the cat might discover another way to get out and would persist in using those movements for the next five or ten trials.

The regularity of these stereotyped movements has led to the suggestion that what the cats learned initially was an association between the stimuli provided by the box and a very specific pattern of movements, not an association between the stimuli and a purposeful act. The association seemed to be formed after a single successful pairing of stimulus with response. According to Edwin R. Guthrie, in the course of many successive trials the animal built up several alternative movements that opened the door, and so appeared to be acquiring a specific skill. Thus, he argued, the act is slowly learned, yet the individual associations that comprise the act are each learned in a single trial.

Other psychologists have questioned Guthrie's conclusions, however. In maze learning, for example, one might suppose that an animal could learn a thoroughly stereotyped set of movements that would take it from the starting box through the maze to the goal box. But Karl Lashley showed that if rats which have acquired such a maze habit are operated upon, and their motor coordination is so disturbed by surgery that they are no longer capable of making the same movements, they will still be able to run the maze correctly. They may have to roll or somersault or drag paralyzed limbs, but they do not make mistakes. They have learned an act that takes them to a particular place; they have not learned a set of specific limb or muscle reactions.[12] The cats in the puzzle box are an exception to the general

Fig. 33. Escape behavior in cats is highly stereotyped. Here are tracings to show the position of cat T at the instant he activated the release mechanism on the first eight trials. (From E. R. Guthrie and G. P. Horton, *Cats in a Puzzle Box*. New York: Rinehart, 1946.)

picture one gets from other research on this problem. Perhaps the cats cannot learn an act, but are forced to learn a response because the escape mechanism is so arbitrary, so impossible for them to understand. What alternative would they have but trial-and-error?

Many psychologists, even those who admire the hardheaded, quantitative posture of S-R theory, have come to a reluctant judgment that simple S-R connections are often more plausible than real. The apparently simple connection of a response to a stimulus situation has not been a convenient element to use in the general analysis of behavior. Faced with this dilemma, one must either broaden the meaning of stimuli and responses so as to include perceptions and acts, which is to retreat from the hardheaded objectivity of true behaviorism, or propose an alternative element that will be easier to define and study. Many psychologists have broadened their definitions of stimulus and response to include unobservable events and processes that play much the same role in their theories as perceptions, images, ideas, and intentions played in the older psychologies. That is, they have adopted a contradictory position which might be called subjective behaviorism.

Those who resist such contradictions have tried to find alternatives that will enable them to hold on to the ideal of a radically objective behaviorism. One of the most attractive alternatives has been B. F. Skinner's formulation of operant conditioning.[13] Skinner points to the crushing difficulties encountered in finding a stimulus for every response. He proposes instead to distinguish two classes of response, elicited and emitted. Responses elicited by known stimuli are respondents; they can be studied by the traditional S-R approach. Operants are responses emitted without any known stimuli. Since there is no known stimulus for an operant response, it is logically impossible to talk about the strength of an S-R bond. As an alternative, therefore, Skinner proposes to measure the rate at which the operant is emitted and to explore all the variables that can be shown to affect the rate of responding.

In a typical experiment with operant conditioning, a hungry animal—usually a rat or pigeon—is placed inside a small, soundproofed compartment (known in laboratory jargon as a Skinner box) and taught to make a simple response, to press a bar or peck a key in order to obtain food. The grand convenience of this experimental situation derives from the fact that the relation between the animal's response and the presentation of food is completely arbitrary and at the disposal of the experimenter. Once an operant response is established, the rate at which it occurs can be influenced by a reinforcement which itself is contingent upon the response rate. Different reinforcement schedules can be invoked at various times or in the presence of different stimuli, depending upon the purpose of the experiment.

PECKING   **FEEDING**

Fig. 34. A hungry pigeon learns to peck at a key, then is reinforced by presentation of grain in the food tray.

For example, when the key is illuminated by a red light, a pigeon may be reinforced, say, after every fifth peck, or haphazardly at a rate not faster than once a minute, and so on. But when the key turns green, perhaps, no reinforcements are given for pecking. In this example, the pecking response would soon come under the control of the red and green lights, which are called discriminative stimuli. In this way Skinner can bring an operant response under the control of a discriminative stimulus, a stimulus such as the red or green light that indicates when the response may be reinforced. The S-R connection is thus preserved, but in a broader and more flexible conception of the learning process.

These efforts to find a fundamental unit of behavior are continuing vigorously into the second half of the twentieth century. The time to summarize them is not yet at hand. And even after the guide posts are agreed upon there will still be a long road to travel between the operant response of a pigeon or a rodent and the discursive intelligence of a modern, civilized man.

Many learning experiments seem rather trivial, especially when isolated from their theoretical contexts. Indeed, it should probably be admitted that many of them would seem trivial in any context. But that must not mislead us. A most valuable strategy for the scientist is to take a plausible hypothesis and push it until it becomes ridiculous. Only in that way can he discover the range and power of his hypothesis, perhaps even find a better one. The ancient belief that learning is associative and that the mind is man's connection-system is a plausible hypothesis. But until it has been pushed as hard as possible one cannot tell how much truth there is in it.

Eventually this tedious pushing and testing may produce a valid scientific law, one whose importance could be literally overwhelming. Our entire way of life is predicated upon our ability to learn. Not only do we rely on learning to give us the basic skills with which we earn our daily bread, but also to educate our children for citizenship in a free society. It is a solid axiom of the great liberal tradition in England and America that education is the best tool for social progress. We believe that people learn their system of values, learn to love themselves and others, learn to channel their biological drives, even learn to be mentally ill. When we begin to analyze the learning process, therefore, we are probing the ultimate sources of our humanity. No one can now foresee what benefits or dangers may someday come from these fumbling efforts with caged animals and nonsense syllables—but we had better be prepared for success.

CHAPTER XIV

———— ◆━◆ ————

ANIMAL BEHAVIOR

Tony, the fox terrier, when he wants to go out into the road, puts his head under the latch of the gate, lifts it, and waits for the gate to swing open. Now an observer of the dog's intelligent action might well suppose that he clearly perceived how the end in view was to be gained, and the most appropriate means for effecting his purpose. The following chain of ideas might be supposed to pass through the dog's mind, not, indeed, in a clear-cut logical form, but at any rate in a rough and practically serviceable way: "Why does that gate remain shut? The latch holds it. I'll lift the latch. Now it is no longer held, therefore it swings open."

The English psychologist C. Lloyd Morgan doubted that any such thoughts ever entered his fox terrier's head; to prove it he described how the dog happened to learn the trick. "I was sitting at a window above the garden," he continued, "and heard the dog put out of door. I therefore watched him. He ran up and down the low wall, and put his head out between the iron bars, now here, now there, now elsewhere, anxiously gazing into the road. This he did for quite three or four minutes. At length it so happened that he put out his head beneath the latch, which is at a convenient height for his doing so, being about a foot above the level of the wall. The latch was thus lifted. He withdrew his head, and began to look out elsewhere, when he found that the gate was swinging open, and out he bolted. After that, whenever I took him out, I shut the gate in his face, and waited till he opened it for himself and joined me. I did not give him any assistance in any way, but just waited and watched, sometimes putting him back and making him open it again. Gradually he went, after fewer pokings of his head out in the wrong place, to the one opening at which the latch was lifted. But it was nearly three weeks from my first noticing his actions from the window before he went at once and with precision to the right place. . . .

"Now what I am particularly anxious to enforce," Morgan concluded, "is that what we need is careful investigation in place of anecdotal reporting.[1]

This passage, an anecdotal refutation of the anecdotal method of studying animals, was written in 1894. Morgan's efforts to establish a true science of animal behavior were inspired by the theory of evolution. Charles Darwin had focused attention on the problems of adaptation—progressively improving adaptation—of the animal to its environment. Animals adapt to their environments through their *behavior;* behavior thus becomes a central problem for all zoological sciences. At the time Morgan wrote, the future development of biology seemed to hinge upon the creation of a new science, a science of comparative behavior equal in scope and precision to the older science of comparative anatomy.

Earlier attempts to develop a comparative psychology, however, were more gossip than science. Animal trainers, zoo keepers, veterinarians, hunters, animal lovers generally: all had surprising yarns to spin of characteristically human achievements by animals. When these anecdotes had been carefully collected, classified, annotated, and published, the result was a welter of partly true, partly wishful, always interesting misinformation. Even the great Darwin treated such stories as if they were scientific evidence and used them to argue in favor of the evolution of man's mental powers.

Into this situation Morgan tried to introduce a scientific precept known as the law of parsimony. As he applied it to the study of animal behavior, the law decreed that, "In no case may we interpret an action as the outcome of the exercise of a higher psychical faculty, if it can be interpreted as the outcome of the exercise of one which stands lower in the psychological scale."[2]

Subsequent generations of psychologists have called this Lloyd Morgan's canon and have assumed that what he must have meant was that anthropomorphism—attribution of human characteristics to gods or, as in this case, animals—is unscientific. A glance into Morgan's books, however, is enough to refute this assumption. Like all his contemporaries, Morgan took it for granted that since the only psychical faculties we can know anything about directly are our own, "introspection must inevitably be the basis and foundation of all comparative psychology."[3] Any human introspections would necessarily be anthropomorphic; all that Morgan hoped for were a few reasonable rules for playing the anthropomorphic game. The systematic, but probably impossible, effort to avoid projecting any human mental functions into animals did not really reach full strength until the advent of behaviorism. But that was at a later time and in another land.

Willingness to attribute human intelligence to animals is sometimes carried to fantastic extremes. Around the beginning of the century an eccentric German named von Osten decided that higher animals are as smart as men and took it as his mission to demonstrate the truth of his belief.[4] For the first pupil he chose a horse that for some reason had struck him as especially clever. He spent about two years educating it. In order to communicate, the horse shook its head appropriately to say "yes" or "no": for all other answers it tapped on the ground with a foreleg. By the end of the second year the horse, known then as Clever Hans, could read and, by tapping, write; could understand the four fundamental rules of arithmetic; could change common fractions into decimals and back again; and could give the day of the month. Moreover, Clever Hans could tell time and would even shake his head to indicate that an error had been made in playing a musical chord on the piano.

Many people were dubious. But Herr von Osten did not exploit his horse financially and was quite willing to let others ask the questions. A charlatan would hardly have dared to give such cooperation to his critics. Clever Hans seemed truly clever. Because this was obviously an important matter, a commission of eminent zoologists and psychologists was appointed to study the horse. The commission felt that in the course of its prolonged examination any possibility of trickery had been completely ruled out. Thus science put its awesome authority behind Herr von Osten's claims for the intelligence of higher mammals. Clever Hans's admirers were jubilant. Aesop could scarcely have asked for more.

But there was trickery involved. Oskar Pfungst uncovered it only a few weeks after the distinguished commission gave its testimonial. Pfungst showed that when questions were written on cards and selected from a pile so that no one but Clever Hans knew what the question was, the horse could not answer anything at all. It would begin to tap and would continue indefinitely, looking intently at the questioner, as though waiting for some sign to stop. Pfungst discovered that the horse was looking for very small movements of the questioner's head. For the questioner to know whether the horse was giving the right answer, he first had to work the problem himself, then to count subvocally as the horse tapped out its answer. After the last of the expected taps the person would relax ever so slightly, thus inadvertently and unconsciously making a tiny movement. This was what Clever Hans was waiting for. Once he had discovered this secret, Pfungst could get any answer he liked. It was not, to use Lloyd Morgan's terms, the higher psychical faculty of reasoning, but the lower psychical faculty of perception, that made Clever Hans so remarkable.

We should not assume, however, that the turn of the century was a time of universal gullibility about the capacities of lower animals. Clever Hans got a great deal of notoriety from the newspapers, but simultaneously in less publicized quarters the real science of animal behavior was moving ahead at a remarkable pace. The cautious, insightful description of animal behavior was actually flourishing in one of its finest periods around the end of the nineteenth and beginning of the twentieth centuries. Nearly all the great biologists, both in Europe and America, were among the contributors. But then, just as the scientific study of animal behavior was beginning to prosper, the stream of research dried up, first in biology and later in psychology. The systematic description of natural behavior and the comparison of different species with one another and with man lost its impetus. After a brief period of advance, comparative psychology languished for more than a quarter of a century.

Why the sudden change in direction? Had Darwin's ideas been discredited? No, their value for dissolving old mistakes had never been more apparent. Had the work proved too difficult? No, the necessary methods had been slowly developing and progress was by and large encouraging. Had animals become uninteresting? Not at all. A topic that had fascinated men for centuries could scarcely lose its charm in a brief decade.

The true reason seems to have been that biologists were diverted into even more promising lines of research. The diversion arose from the rediscovery of the laws of heredity that Gregor Mendel had first described in 1865. In 1900 Mendel's laws were rediscovered independently by Correns in Germany, by DeVries in Holland, and by Tschermak in Austria. The true significance of the discovery could be recognized in 1900, and a science of genetics could be created to develop and extend the fundamental laws. Moreover, there already existed a relatively advanced science of the cell, cytology, that could be used to explore the actual mechanisms underlying the laws of heredity. It was around 1900 that cytologists formulated the correct hypothesis that the chromosome—a rod-shaped structure they had seen in the nucleus of the cell—plays an important genetic role. In 1902, independently of each other, the German Boveri and the American Sutton perceived the parallel between what a chromosome does under the microscope and what Mendelian genes do in breeding experiments. On the basis of this parallel, cytology and genetics were unified into a single body of knowledge. All this was profoundly exciting. Little wonder that biologists shifted from studies of animal behavior to the new opportunities in genetics.

For biologically oriented psychologists, a second diversion followed: Pavlov developed his objective method to investigate the conditioning of responses to new stimuli. The discovery of conditioning and the behavioral laws that grew out of the conditioning experiments had important consequences in at least two directions:

in ecology, the part of biology that deals with processes outside the skin; and in physiology, the part of biology that deals with processes inside the skin.

The Russian discoveries introduced an analytic approach in place of the ecological study of animals in their natural habitats. The reflex became the basic unit of analysis. According to Pavlov, complex behaviors are built up automatically from simpler reactions by the process of conditioning. "It is obvious," he said, "that the different kinds of habits based on training, education and discipline of any sort are nothing but a long chain of conditional reflexes."[5] For example, Tony, the fox terrier, was simply acquiring a chain of conditional reflexes when he learned to lift the latch and open the gate; the fact that a detailed analysis of Tony's behavior into the component reflexes would obviously be a tedious task was beside the point. It seemed far wiser and simpler to study the basic atoms of behavior in a laboratory, where conditions could be properly controlled and precise measurements made, than to try to tease out all the unpredictable things that might be important in the animal's natural habitat.

In the United States it was John B. Watson who, more than anyone else, made Pavlov's work the basis for a new kind of psychological theory. Conditional reflexes gave him a technique to study association and learning without recourse to introspection. He undertook to demonstrate, for example, that emotional responses in babies are simply a form of conditional reflex.

Behaviorism corrected many of the worst tender-minded mistakes of the older psychologists. It imposed a rigorous discipline upon its adherents. To illustrate: When behaviorists applied Morgan's canon of interpretation to human beings, they reasoned that what a man does should not be explained in terms of higher mental processes until an explanation in terms of simpler processes—which often meant Pavlovian reflexes—had been shown to be inadequate. No longer would an introspective report be accepted as scientific evidence; all the older work had to be discarded to make way for a fresh start.

By the 1930s this revolution had led to a curious situation in American comparative psychology. Animals represented biological objectivity; a psychological law seemed truly basic only if it held for man and beast alike. In fact, however, behaviorists were still psychologists at heart, and, like most psychologists, were interested more in people than in animals. Consequently, although they were willing to study animals, they did not really care what animals. They chose the rat, a creature as good as any for their purposes, and more convenient than most. Thousands of behavioral experiments were done with rats; for decades the rest of the animal kingdom was largely forgotten. Thus behaviorism provoked the wisecrack that a psychologist differs from a magician because he pulls habits out of a rat. Indeed, some behaviorists claimed to pull the whole science of psychology out of a rat.

One rationalization for concentrating on a single species was that all behavior consists of reflexes; a reflex is much the same in one animal as in another. The important thing to study was how new reflexes are built out of old ones; this could be done as well with rats as with any other infrahuman vertebrate. In all this there remained only a hollow echo of an older, ecological conception of comparative psychology.

But just when comparative psychology seemed to have expired, it began to revive. The new ideas came largely from biologists. In Europe the revival took place under the name of ethology.[6] Without waiting to see whether conditional reflexes might be the atoms of all behavior, ethologists set out to discover what behavioral facts they had to explain. Whenever possible they preferred to study a species under its normal living conditions. It quickly became apparent that many of the tasks psychologists used were unnatural; the same animals that looked so stupid in a laboratory might behave most ingeniously when tested in their natural surroundings. In particular, social adaptation was discovered to be crucially important —yet animal society had been largely ignored in the psychological laboratories where animals were normally housed and tested in isolation. This revival of comparative studies had a salutary effect. A series of new and exciting discoveries about animal behavior and animal society have provided a broader and more realistic context for psychological research.

Since much of the interest in ethology has come from ornithologists and bird watchers, it is appropriate to introduce a bit of bird behavior as an example. For many years even the animal psychologists who did not like rats still tended to concentrate on mammals; psychological publications about the animal kingdom were mainly devoted to the small, mammalian duchy adjacent to *homo sapiens*. But mammals are very brainy beasts, and this concentration produced a distorted view of instinct, the nature and importance of which is clearest in lower animals. The study of birds has gone a long way toward correcting this false perspective.

Parental behavior in the ring dove *(Streptopelia risoria)* provides a particularly good example because it has been carefully analyzed and because so many different factors—instinct, social interaction, hormones, learning—can all be seen at work in the small and intimate universe of a dove's nest.

Doves and pigeons belong to the same order of birds; the little members are doves and the big ones pigeons, but the distinction has never been very sharp. The ring dove is a small, buff-colored bird with a black collar (hence the name) that normally lives in southeastern Europe and Asia. The male and the female are, to an untrained observer, indistinguishable. As in most birds, the breeding behavior of the ring dove goes through a succession of stages: courtship, mating, nest building, incubation, brooding over and feeding the young. If a pair is left together this cycle repeats about every five weeks. If the birds are kept in isolation, however, every trace of the cycle disappears; a female will not even lay an egg unless she has seen a male nearby. Apparently the appropriate visual stimulation is necessary before her pituitary gland can secrete the hormones required to start the cycle going.[7]

Ring doves normally lay two eggs in a clutch, and both parents share in the duties of incubating the eggs and brooding over the young. As soon as the eggs are laid the wonderful biochemical pacemaker that supplies the right hormones at the right time in the cycle now irritates the skin on the dove's breast. The cool, smooth surface of the eggs promises relief; the doves open out their feathers and settle down in comfort for the two-week period of incubation.

When the squabs hatch out they are fed in a manner that seems to be almost unique to pigeons and doves. Some birds, like ducks and geese, are able to pick up food as soon as they hatch. Others, like thrushes and blackbirds, hatch out naked, blind, and helpless, unable to do more than lift their heads and open their beaks so that the parents can drop food into them. Pigeons and doves are hatched in this helpless state, but the parent bird does not have to leave the nest to forage for food; another hormonal miracle anticipates the new conditions and fills the parent's crops with a secretion—the so-called cropmilk—that can be regurgitated to feed the young squabs. After the dove has been sitting on the eggs for about a week the walls of its crop begin to thicken as the cropmilk begins to form. The crop, a pouch in the walls of the esophagus where ordinarily food can be stored and prepared for entry into the true stomach, eventually fills up with milk and becomes so distended that the pouches on either side of the bird's throat can easily be felt with the fingers. Feeding behavior in the ring dove can occur only when those pouches are distended with cropmilk.

The problem is how to get the cropmilk out of the crops and into the squabs. It is solved by regurgitation, but the details are slightly complicated: Feeding can be initiated either by the parent or the squab. When the squab takes the initiative, the vomiting movements by the parent are triggered—released, the ethologists would say—by rapid head movements of the squab against the breast of the parent. The squab tries to raise its head, but its neck is so weak that the head wobbles back and forth unsteadily and eventually touches the skin over the distended crop. At this point the parent looks down, an act which brings its bill in contact with the rapidly moving head of the squab. When the bills meet, the parent grasps the bill of the squab, the squab thrusts its head deep into the parent's throat, and the regurgitation movements begin. Regurgitation movements consist of opening the bill as wide as possible, assuming a horizontal position with the neck rigid and slightly bowed, and making convulsive movements of the shoulders and nodding movements of the head and neck. The duration of this activity can range from one up to fifteen seconds.

Being touched on the full crop has an emetic effect on the ring dove, as the young squab can initiate the feeding activity by touching the parent's crop. It is also possible for the parent to initiate feeding. The parent can peck gently at the bill of the squab, thus arousing it to make the characteristic head movements that trigger the activity pattern. The parents often take the initiative in this way as the squabs grow older. When the squabs are four to eight days old the parents do not brood continuously; they may feed the squabs by coming to the nest and pecking the squabs' bills, which releases the feeding behavior. As the squabs grow older the parent's hormones continue their work and the crop glands begin to shrink; the crop

gradually begins to hold less of the cropmilk and more of the grain
that the bird is eating. In this way the squabs are gradually shifted to
the adult diet. After ten or fifteen days, the feeding behavior stops
entirely.

Here one sees an instinct at work. It is a fragile bit of machinery,
at the mercy of hormonal changes and social interactions that must
cooperate in exactly the right sequence if the young birds are to
survive. A question that usually arises when one sees such a won-
drous bit of biological engineering is the extent to which it can be
modified by experience. Is it, in truth, rigid, preformed, predetermined by the way ring doves are built? Or is it, at least in part, a
learned adjustment to the demands of the environment? In a very
careful series of experiments the American psychologist D. S. Lehrman proved that learning does occur and that the normal pattern of
parental behavior is, at least in part, the result of previous experience.[8]

What happens the first time a parent sees a newly hatched squab?
After watching many new parents in this novel situation, Lehrman
discovered that the feeding activity is always initiated by the squab;
an inexperienced parent never tapped the squab to stimulate it to
make the necessary head movements. This observation convinced
him that the experienced parent learns how to arouse the squab at
feeding time, that the instinctual act of feeding the young is normally
modified by experience. In order to test his argument, Lehrman took
two groups of ring doves, one with experience feeding the young,
the other without experience. He injected both groups with prolactin,
a pituitary hormone that stimulates secretion of cropmilk. After
seven days of prolactin, all the doves had crops distended with
cropmilk. They were then exposed to young squabs (borrowed from
another family, of course). The experienced birds approached the
squabs slowly, pecked at their bills gently to arouse the head movements, and so completed the feeding response. The inexperienced
birds, however, did not know how to use the squabs to relieve the
tension in their crops; since they were not broody and thus not in
position to be touched by the squabs, none of the innocents showed
the so-called instinctual pattern of regurgitation feeding. (Normally,
an inexperienced parent will have secreted progesterone, the hormone that produces broodiness. A broody parent sits on the young
and so is in position to receive tactual stimulation from the haphazard movements of the squab's head.)

In this particular instance, therefore, the instinct works by a peripheral mechanism—tension in the crop that must be relieved—and not through some inherited pattern laid down at birth in the bird's central nervous system. By comparison with higher mammals, the effects of learning are relatively slight, the effects of hormones are rather direct, and the stimuli that release the behavior are rather simple. But even here the instinct is not a blind, mechanical pattern that runs off mechanically without respect for environmental conditions.

Admittedly, it would be foolish to generalize from the parental behavior of a ring dove to any other species, or to any other instinctual pattern. But a careful inspection of this relatively simple case should convey some impression of how difficult it is to distinguish between those two ancient, theoretical competitors, heredity and environment.

Consider, for purposes of comparison, how these same parental duties are discharged by a mammal. Mammals are more complicated than birds and take longer to develop. Part of the development is postponed until after birth, which is why the problem of parental care is particularly important for the survival of mammalian species.

A convenient example is the rat.[9] The rat's parental behavior is maternal behavior, since the female provides all the care for the young. (Baby rats are born during the night, an inconvenience that usually leads investigators who study them to keep their rats in a room where, by the modern miracle of electricity, the day-night cycle is reversed.) At the time of birth the mother rat is amazingly skillful at removing the foetal membranes, which she immediately eats, and at biting off the umbilical cord. This skill is just as apparent with the first litter as with all subsequent litters. The cleaning of each young pup is accomplished by much licking and cleaning, which is the mother's reaction to complex nutritional needs. For the young pups this mauling about is a necessary part of the birth process and serves to stimulate the circulation of blood.

At about the time of birth—a little before or a little after—the mother usually builds a nest out of whatever materials are available. Although it may vary greatly in its structural details, a rat's nest is a notoriously untidy thing. Some rats build no nest at all; others pile up all the straw or bits of paper they can find and so make a very large nest. A really eager builder may even pick up her own tail in her teeth and deposit that on the nest, too.

Nursing is not very complicated. The mother responds to the presence of young in the nest by simply crouching over them; most of the work is done by the pups. Young rats will try to crawl under any warm object, a kind of reaction known among ethologists as a taxis. Once under the mother, the pup finds a nipple by searching movements of the head. When a nipple is found the pup catches hold very strongly; if the mother is startled and leaves the nest, she will usually drag two or three youngsters along with her.

The part of this maternal behavior that has been studied most extensively, probably because it is easiest to see, is the mother's retrieving behavior. Whenever the pups are scattered the mother tries to collect them and put them back in the nest. This retrieving behavior is strongest at first. As the young rats become more and more active, the mother's efforts to keep them nursing in the nest become progressively less enthusiastic and eventually cease. During the time it is present, however, retrieving behavior presents a good opportunity to study instinctive behavior in a mammal.

A significant thing about mammalian instincts is the relative complexity of the stimuli that can release them.[10] With the feeding response of the ring dove the releaser was simply the squab touching the distended crop; with the retrieving response of the rat, things seem much more complicated. Consider the following evidence:

First, it is possible to cut the olfactory nerve in the female rat so that she cannot smell anything. When the nerve is cut, however, the retrieval responses remain unimpaired. This means that if there is some simple releasing stimulus, it is not an odor.

Next, one may take another group of mothers and try vision. The female can be blinded, but this does not interfere with retrieving either. Again, if there is a simple releasing stimulus, it is not something the rat sees.

Next, if one takes a group of mother rats and cuts the nerves to their mouths so that they cannot feel or taste the pups they are retrieving, once more there is no effect on the retrieving responses. If there is a simple releasing stimulus, it is not a touch or a taste.

If the releaser is not an odor, a taste, or a visual object, what is it? The answer is that all these aspects are involved. If one puts lavender on the pups to make them smell strange, or if they are dead and cold, or if their visual appearance is altered, the female will still retrieve them, but not as rapidly as she would normally. Since the instinctive behavior is triggered by a group of factors, taking away only one at a time does not stop the instinct from coming into play. This degree of complexity and redundancy, which is characteristic of mammalian instincts, may be related to the larger mammalian brain and to greater modifiability through experience.

There is no sense in which one can imagine this rodent behavior evolving out of the pattern described in the ring dove; nevertheless, the comparison between them is probably not unrepresentative of the picture one could gather from a broader sample of birds and mammals. A general rule of thumb is that mammals are more complex, more flexible, and more intelligent—all presumably correlated with the enlargement of the mammalian neocortex.

There are, of course, astonishing differences in parental behavior even among the mammals. A rat is not especially typical of anything but rats. For comparison it is interesting to look at how our nearest relatives, the primates, take care of their young.[11] An infant monkey makes an especially good subject because it is enough like humans, perhaps, to enable psychologists or biologists to generalize what can be learned from observing it. On the other hand, unlike the completely helpless human infant, the baby monkey is active and ready to go the instant it is born. As soon as its shoulders and arms are free of the birth canal it reaches out and grabs anything it can reach —which is usually the hair on its mother's body. Since the monkey would normally be born in a tree, this grabbing reaction has obvious advantages.

As soon as the baby is born the mother carefully licks and cleans it; the source for this instinctive reaction is much the same as in the rat. Once clean, the baby is grasped somewhat haphazardly over one arm and must turn itself about until it discovers the nipple. Although an infant is strong enough to walk as soon as it is a few hours old, it normally spends its early days at its mother's breast. It is possible, however, to separate a newborn monkey from its mother and to raise it under experimental conditions in the laboratory. This has been done by Harry F. Harlow and his collaborators at the University of Wisconsin, with somewhat surprising results.[12]

Harlow constructed what he called surrogate mothers. A good surrogate mother was made of a block of wood covered by sponge rubber and sheathed in terrycloth. A bad one was made of wire hardware cloth. An infant monkey was then left free to go to either of the mothers it wished. For half of the infants the good mother gave milk; for the other half, the bad mother gave milk. In both cases, however, the infant monkey spent most of its time—as shown in Figure 35—clinging to the terrycloth mother. Those who were forced to do so would spend just enough time on the bad mother to nurse, but then would return to cling to the terrycloth mother. If something frightened the infant, it would run for comfort and protection to the mother that felt good, not to the wire mother that nourished it. Given a choice between a mother that fed it and a mother that provided comfortable tactual stimulation, the monkey clearly preferred tactual stimulation.

At the time these studies began it seemed curious but interesting that the attachment of a young monkey to its mother depended so much on a tactual element. The experiment was continued, however, until the young monkeys grew into adults, some singly, others in pairs, with their terrycloth mothers. In some respects a laboratory mother looked more satisfactory than a natural mother would have been; it was always available and it never cuffed or scolded. But as the youngsters grew up, it became increasingly apparent that they were all very unhappy, asocial, aggressive, maladjusted monkeys. The most significant biological handicap they suffered was that none of them, male or female, was able to copulate. They all looked interested, but they did not know what to do.[13] Inadvertently, the Wisconsin psychologists had deprived the infant monkeys of far more than they intended when they removed them from their mothers.

What is it that a reacting mother gives and an immobile mother does not? In a normal situation a baby monkey will begin to reach out for things when it is two or three weeks old. When it tries to grab food the mother usually seems annoyed and tries to discourage it, but this kind of maternal tuition does not begin in earnest until the baby starts to explore the world for itself. The mother teaches her baby to hang tightly to her body with both hands and feet as she is moving about. And she teaches it not to wander too far away and not to approach strange objects. The method of teaching is quite simple; she cuffs the youngster whenever it is disobedient. All of this training the Wisconsin monkeys missed.

Ordinarily the babies will cling to and remain dependent on their mothers for some time, perhaps even until another baby is born. But

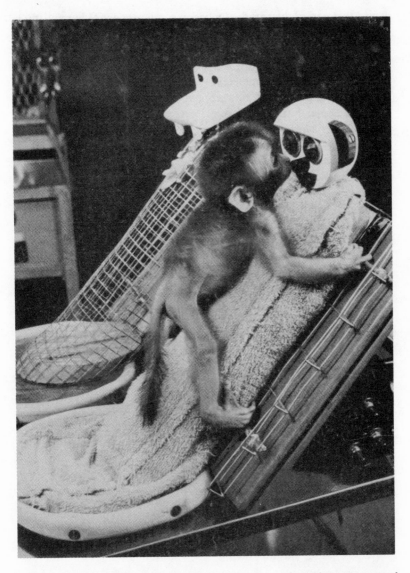

Fig. 35. Infant monkeys much prefer surrogate mothers that are covered with terrycloth. This monkey spends most of his time clinging to the cloth mother, even though his milk is provided through the nipple on the wire mother in the background. (From H. F. Harlow, Love in infant monkeys, *Scientific American,* June 1959.)

during that period they gradually become independent of her and, most important, learn how to adapt their behavior appropriately to the other monkeys in the social group. The experience with the mother, the play and grooming with other young monkeys, the discipline by the older and stronger monkeys—this pattern of growing up is essential for the production of a normally curious, happy, well-adjusted monkey. Social relations among monkeys depend upon stable patterns of behavior—grooming, sexual presentation and mounting, threatening—that are released when the proper social cues are given by other monkeys. Monkeys whose social experience has been sharply restricted do not develop the usual social responses to those cues.

Parental behavior is only one facet of animal life. There are many others—mating, migration, fighting, communication, territoriality, to name a few—and each must be studied in many different species. Perhaps all the effort that will go into mapping this vast domain will reward us with a better understanding of our own psychology. But in science such practical justifications of one goal in terms of another have a way of becoming irrelevant as the work progresses.

Why study animal psychology? Not to learn about man, even though we may. If we see ourselves mirrored there, it is good, but not necessary. The only true reason for studying animals is to learn about animals, about the lives and struggles of our fellow creatures.

CHAPTER XV

SIGMUND FREUD, PSYCHOANALYST

It comes as something of a surprise that Freud—sensitive prober of dreams, outspoken defender of sexuality, patient interpreter of the neurotic and the insane—should have regarded his life's work as an inevitable extension of the positivistic tradition in which he was trained as a medical student. No one revolted more effectively, or showed more clearly the narrowness of the mechanistic conceptions of man that dominated European thought in the nineteenth century. Yet throughout his life he considered himself faithful to the precepts of Helmholtz. He was a rebel, but he was a loyal one. In order to appreciate just how much of a rebel he was, it is necessary to resurrect an earlier conception of human nature.

Some historians say that modern intellectual history began sometime in the seventeenth century when—largely as a result of Descartes' teachings—mathematics replaced theology as the Queen of the Sciences.[1] Men became convinced that natural laws are always true everywhere and that the human mind is capable of understanding them. Faith in the powers of human reason persisted without effective scientific criticism for about two hundred years and provided the moving spirit of that great, optimistic period of modern history called the Enlightenment. Anyone who might have questioned sovereign reason was refuted immediately by examples from the natural sciences.

But what about man's own affairs? Can men live together rationally? If reason can comprehend the cosmos, does that mean it can serve equally well as a guide in social and economic matters? Can a society, having no mind of its own, be rational? It was generally assumed that either a rational God would do the necessary thinking for society or, in more positivistic quarters, that if every individual member of society did the most intelligent thing he could possibly do, given his personal circumstances, the cumulative effect of so much rationality would itself be rational. In other words, if every individual would make his decisions in a reasonable way so as to advance his own best interests, he would simultaneously advance the interests of society generally.

The whole matter was reduced to its crudest fundamentals by Jeremy Bentham near the close of the eighteenth century. Although Bentham was somewhat extreme, his arguments were only exaggerated versions of views widely held in his time. "Nature has placed mankind under the governance of two sovereign masters, pain and pleasure," said Bentham. "It is for them alone to point out what we ought to do, as well as to determine what we shall do."[2] In England and France Bentham's philosophy, called utilitarianism, was a close partner of positivism. Along with materialism, empiricism, and evolutionism—the nineteenth century bristles with isms—Bentham's ultilitarianism was especially attractive to those who wished to discuss man in the language of the natural sciences.

The utilitarian philosophy consists of four simple propositions:[3]

1. All that anybody wants is to be as happy as possible, to maximize his own happiness.

2. It is morally good for him to maximize his happiness as effectively, as intelligently, as he can.

3. Society must be organized so that maximizing his own happiness is always the most beneficial thing for his fellow men.

4. It is possible to calculate the quantities of pleasure and pain (by Bentham's "felicific calculus") expected from different kinds of behavior, and to arrange society so as to produce the greatest happiness for the greatest number.

Bentham coupled these utilitarian propositions with a firm belief in empiricism and the laws of the association of ideas. It was central to his thinking that men should be simple machines whose choices and decisions could be anticipated perfectly and allowed for in a set of laws and social institutions that would automatically maximize the amount of happiness available for everyone.

It is not our task to criticize Bentham's ethical assumption that, because it is desired, happiness must be desirable. The fact remains that Bentham and his followers were remarkably influential in nineteenth-century England; utilitarianism was one of the intellectual foundations of British democratic thought and, by and large, its consequences were liberal and humanitarian. Each person was considered free to enter into any social contract that made him happy. Nevertheless, it was psychological nonsense; and it is remarkable that such an odd conception of man (as a felicity computer) captured the leading minds of the day. John Stuart Mill and Herbert Spencer both defended the "maximum happiness principle" and made it a part of their social philosophy. There were critics, but the utilitarians were able to remain in the ascendancy. In the hands of Jevons, Walras, Menger, Marshall, and others, utilitarianism later became the foundation for much of modern economic theory. Even those who questioned the ethical assumption that it is good to pursue happiness were inclined to accept the psychological assumption that each man automatically and inevitably pursues his own pleasure.

Psychological objections center around the fact that happiness depends far more upon what you expect than upon what you get. There is no absolute scale of happiness along which every possible event can be measured. The human ability to experience happiness is limited, it does not go on increasing indefinitely. There is no evidence that the rich are always happier than the poor. Indeed, there is not even any evidence that social progress promotes happiness, that Parisians are essentially happier than African Bushmen.

Not until the nineteenth century was drawing to a close did utilitarianism lose its iron grip on the scientific mind. One of the most effective attacks on it was initiated by a French sociologist, Emile Durkheim, who asked how such a theory could account for suicide.[4] Obviously, suicide is not motivated by happiness; it seems reasonable to suppose that a person who takes his own life is unhappy. If this is so, and if Bentham was right that unhappiness results from a loss of valuable possessions, then one should expect to find that the suicide rate increases during periods of economic depression. And this is in fact the case. But Durkheim turned up another fact that was more puzzling, namely, that suicide is frequently caused by sudden success during periods of unusual prosperity. This is difficult for a utilitarian to explain. Why should a man who is just beginning to prosper consider killing himself? Prosperity should make him happy.

Durkheim argued that happiness has little to do with it. Unexpected wealth can disorient a person with respect to all the social values that had previously governed his life; sudden wealth can weaken or destroy his former ties with a social group. The resulting loss of his goals and values, the resulting state of social disequilibrium—Durkheim termed it *anomie*—might in severe cases lead to suicide. And for the same reason a sudden loss of wealth is also dangerous; it weakens a person's ties with his social group. It is a loss of love, of sympathetic acceptance into the lives of other people, not a loss of material possessions, that can make a man take his own life. To strengthen his argument, Durkheim demonstrated that suicide is relatively rare among the perpetually poor, who are necessarily well integrated into their own social groups.

Durkheim considered himself a thorough positivist, carrying on the scientific traditions of the nineteenth century. He used empirical data on suicide rates and he analyzed them statistically with scientific precision; certainly there was nothing metaphysical in his method or his results. Yet his explanation in terms of loosening the sympathetic ties of the individual with his group has an almost spiritual character. How does one measure anomie in centimeters, grams, and seconds? If Durkheim was right—and his evidence was compelling—then somehow society has claims upon us far subtler and more complex than anyone in the eighteenth century would admit. To preserve a positivistic tradition, to make possible the continuation of the study of man and his affairs in scientific terms, the materialistic conception of science had to be enlarged.

Durkheim was one of several who, around the turn of the century, helped to expand our conception of science as it applies to human beings. Others included William James, Henri Bergson, Max Weber, Benedetto Croce, Vilfredo Pareto; beginning about 1890 a rebellious generation of genius completely reoriented European social thought.[5]

And the most important of these young rebels was the Austrian Jew, Sigmund Freud.

Freud was born at Freiberg, Moravia, in 1856. Except for the first three and the last two years of his life, however, he lived in, and was a part of, Vienna.[6] His father, a tall, kindly man who was said to resemble Garibaldi, was an unsuccessful wool merchant; when his business failed in Moravia he moved his growing family to Leipzig, then to Vienna. Their life was not easy, for anti-Semitism was rampant in Imperial Austria. Nevertheless, Jews had been granted citizenship and one who was willing to step into the gutter to let a Christian pass could earn a meager living.

At seventeen Sigmund entered the University of Vienna, a somewhat reluctant medical student in negligent pursuit of anatomy, botany, chemistry, physics, physiology, and zoology. We get glimpses of him studying Aristotle's logic, engaging in violent arguments with fellow students and obstinately refusing to apologize for his rudeness in philosophic debate. During this period he received a thorough grounding in the positivistic science of the nineteenth century. First he concentrated on biology, and as a research project dissected more than four hundred male eels in search of their testes. Next he moved on to physiology and the spinal cord of the fish; he spent countless hours hunched over a microscope in Ernest Brücke's laboratory. In 1881 he received his M.D. degree, but even that did not interrupt his devotions at the microscope. Finally Brücke explained to him that a penniless Jew could never become Professor of Neurology. It was a rude shock, but of course Brücke was right; the Vienna that was to give lessons to Adolf Hitler was a difficult place for a Jew, even one as brilliant as Freud.

Yet he must have known what was coming, for his decision to study medicine in the first place had been based on the assumption that he could, if necessary, practice for a living. So he left the scientific life of the university and hung out his shingle as a clinical neurologist. It was a difficult thing for him to do; even though he became famous for his neurological research, he was never greatly attracted to the practice of clinical neurology. Fortunately for him, however, most of the patients who went to see a neurologist were actually psychoneurotic.

In June 1882 he became engaged to Martha Bernays, who was as penniless as he. Although he loved her passionately, it was necessary repeatedly to postpone their marriage until he could earn enough money to support her. For four intense, frustrated years he worked and saved and waited. There was hardly a moment in the long engagement when the first thought in his mind was not how soon he could convert it to marriage. Finally he could wait no longer; in September 1886 they were married. The young couple managed to exist through their first months together by borrowing, by pawning their watches, until finally the tide began to turn. But the terrible poverty of those early years left a lasting impression on him.

It was during that difficult time that he became friendly with Joseph Breuer, who loaned him money and discussed interesting cases with him. Breuer had discovered a new way to use hypnosis in the treatment of hysteria. Hysteria is a form of neurosis in which there are bodily symptoms, paralysis and abnormal sensations, that cannot be attributed to any obvious abnormality of the nervous system. Actually the discovery was made by one of Breuer's patients, a stubborn young woman known to history only as Fräulein Anna O., who insisted that talking about her problems while she was hypnotized would relieve her anxieties and temporarily cure her hysterical symptoms. Freud was very interested in Anna O. and tried to use Breuer's technique with other patients.

Although at this time Freud was publishing important work in neurology, his interests were steadily shifting toward his psychological studies with Breuer; in 1895 they published a book, *Studies on Hysteria*. By the time it appeared, however, Freud was already breaking off his personal friendship with Breuer and was well along toward replacing hypnosis by free association as a better method for treating hysteria. His adoption of free association was a critical step in the development of psychoanalysis.

In free association a person starts with some element of emotional significance and lets, or tries to let, his ideas flow spontaneously until, for one reason or another, they seem to break off. He then takes another item and repeats the process. Speaking freely of whatever enters one's head is not easy. Even without intending to, a person protects himself in certain matters. These points of resistance became the focus of Freud's inquiry and his basis for psychotherapy. The great advantage of free association over hypnosis is that these areas of resistance can be located and explored; the patient himself is forced to recognize consciously the nature of his problem.

Freud also discovered that a rich source of emotionally significant ideas, suitable to start the process of free association, can be found in a patient's dreams, which often contain valuable clues to the psychological problems underlying his sickness.

As a positivist, committed to the belief that everything has a cause, he knew that events in a dream cannot be as senseless as they seem. They must be the result of something going on in the person's mind, if not consciously, then unconsciously. He decided that there must be truth in the ancient theory that dream images are symbolic. They do not symbolize future events, of course; they refer to personal matters, things that can arouse strong emotions. It seemed to him that the purpose of a dream is to preserve sleep. If the emotionally charged images were to appear undisguised in the dream, they would be so disturbing that they would interrupt the sleeping state. So they appear only indirectly in a harmless, symbolic form. Instead of dreaming about a penis, the dreamer may substitute the image of a gun, a snake, a fountain pen, the number three, and so on. For masturbation the dream symbol may be climbing a tree, or playing the piano. By recognizing these substitutions, therefore, it is possible to recover the true meaning of the dream.

It is a little hard, of course, to believe that a sleeping mind can perform all these complicated substitutions in its state of reduced activation. To Freud this meant that the unconscious is much cleverer than we usually give it credit for. It is possible to argue, however, that the symbols are not disguises at all, but are more like slang, or figures of speech. C. S. Hall[7] has pointed out that a dreamer may have a disguised dream of an incestuous relationship one night and a perfectly barefaced dream of incest the next night. If the symbol is hiding something obnoxious, why is it hidden one time and not another? But even though his hypothesis that symbols are protective disguises may be more imaginative than necessary, it remains that Freud discovered in dream analysis a very useful way to explore a person's emotional life.

Freud tried to get his neurotic patients to remember the events that had caused their symptoms; free association provided a method to probe their memories. The associations did not stop with a painful event, but often extended back into early childhood. Moreover, many of the most significant memories were of sexual experiences. Freud gradually became convinced that sexual disturbances are the essential causes of neurosis. In particular, he observed that his hysterical patients always reported a premature sexual experience during their childhood. He was convinced of the validity of his method, and in all good faith he presented this observation publicly as his theory of hysteria. But then the truth dawned on him: most of the reported childhood seductions had never occurred. They were fantasies nourished by unconscious processes unrelated to ordinary reality. This realization was a severe jolt to his pride, but when he had time to ponder its implications he was not ashamed of his blunder. It had forced him to recognize the fundamental nature of infantile sexuality and so led him to one of his major contributions to psychological theory.

In the summer of 1897 Freud decided to apply his technique to himself. There were several reasons: his father's death had occurred a few months earlier and Freud wished to explore the emotions it had aroused; he was concerned by his increasing hostility toward an old friend; he wanted to be able to understand his patients better. He worked principally with his dreams, seeking to discover the unconscious processes that formed them. It was lonely work, but he slowly made progress. He recognized the truth about his father and separated it from ideas that he had projected into his image of his father. He remembered sexual feelings toward his mother and jealous rivalries with other children. And he rediscovered a nurse who had caused him most of his later troubles. The results were not magical, but he persisted and eventually mastered many of the problems that had disturbed him. For the rest of his life he spent the last half hour of each day in self-analysis.

In 1900 he published his major account of this work in *The Interpretation of Dreams*. It was written during the period of his self-analysis and is profusely illustrated with his own dreams. The book was received with thunderous indifference by both neurologists and psychologists; it took eight years to sell the first printing of 600 copies. Nevertheless, *The Interpretation of Dreams* is Freud's most important work. In particular, the seventh and last chapter contains the theory of mind that he was to amplify and develop in the period ahead.

For ten lonely but productive years he worked almost alone on his new ideas. In 1904 he wrote *The Psychopathology of Everyday Life* in which he described the now famous Freudian slip, and in the following year the *Three Essays on Sexuality*. But not until 1906 did he begin to attract colleagues and followers, and he did not gain international recognition until 1909, when he was invited to the United States, with Alfred Adler and C. G. Jung, to give a series of lectures at Clark University.

Those years were also filled with much bureaucratic activity centered around the founding of international societies and their journals. Freud tolerated no dissent from his emphasis on sexuality as the great motivating force behind all abnormal psychological processes; anyone who disagreed was excommunicated. In the second volume of his fine biography of Freud, Ernest Jones has sympathetically described these political struggles, with their attendant concern that psychoanalysis would be rejected by gentiles.

Sigmund Freud

The psychoanalytic movement was launched much as a political party would be launched, or as a new church might be founded. Thus when Freud broke with Adler in 1911 and with Jung in 1913 it was more than a scientific disagreement about the evidence and the conclusions that could be based on the evidence; it was also a personal quarrel, a political defection, and a religious heresy.

In 1914, pressed by fear that psychoanalysis would be discredited because its major proponents could not agree among themselves,

Freud wrote a polemical *History of the Psychoanalytic Movement:* "Psychoanalysis is my creation," he said. "For ten years I was the only one occupied with it. . . . Nobody knows better than I what psychoanalysis is." One can sympathize with his attitude toward quarrelsome disciples. But the important distinction between a political movement and a scientific theory should never be forgotten; the success of one does not test the truth of the other.

Freud continued to live in Vienna, practicing as a psychoanalyst and writing many books of an increasingly speculative nature. In 1910 he wrote a psychoanalytic biography of Leonardo da Vinci. In 1913 he wrote *Totem and Taboo,* an imaginative anthropological adventure. He extended psychoanalysis further into the realm of social theory with *The Future of an Illusion* (1927) and *Civilization and Its Discontents* (1930). When the Nazis absorbed Austria in 1938, he escaped to London, carrying under his arm the manuscript of a book on *Moses and Monotheism.* The following year he died at the age of 83.

It is sometimes said that anybody who had as much interest in sex as Freud, must have led a lusty and exciting life. As near as one can tell from published biographies this is simply not true; in his private life he appears to have been a complete puritan. He was so inhibited, in fact, that some writers have speculated that his sexual theories were rationalizations of his inability to love other people.[8] No insatiable lust inspired him; his mission was to save civilization. In his prime he dreamed of being a modern Leonardo, the creative genius; in his old age he saw himself as a modern Moses, the great lawgiver. He expected others to follow him and to sacrifice their independence and intellectual freedom for him. Certainly he must have been a difficult man to work with. He had his faults, for which his friends paid dearly, but lechery was not one of them. The sexual license that has so often been justified in terms of his theories must have been hateful to him, a sad mockery of his life and ideals.

Freud introduced a number of new terms for the theoretical constructs he used to describe the human mind.[9] He believed that the total personality is organized into three major systems:[10] the *id,* which is concerned with the immediate discharge of energy or tension; the *ego,* which regulates the interactions of the person with his environment; and the *superego,* which represents the moral and judicial aspects of personality. These three systems are in constant interaction.

In his early work Freud used a simpler twofold distinction between the conscious and the unconscious mind. Later, the unconscious became the id, the conscious the ego; and the superego was added to his theory as a new concept. This remarkable and imaginative man never shirked the burden of self-criticism and revision, and his theories grew and evolved continually for almost half a century. In describing psychoanalytic doctrine, therefore, it is always necessary to specify whether the ideas come from the early or the late Freud.

Dynamic aspects of personality depend upon a supply of instinctual energy from the id; Freud made the same distinction between the mind and its source of energy that an engineer would make between an engine and its fuel. Although he modified his theories several times, toward the end of his life he recognized two great groups of instincts that provide energy for the id. One group serves the purposes of life: their energy is called *libido*. The life instincts are a constant source of emotional tension, whose conscious impact is painful and unpleasant. One of Freud's first and most fundamental assumptions was that all activities of the mind are driven by the need to reduce or eliminate this tension. Because a conscious experience of pleasure was supposed to accompany all tension reduction, Freud called this fundamental assumption the *pleasure principle*. The second group of instincts, introduced later and never so well described, are in the service of death. These destructive instincts represent Freud's attempt to explain the sources of energy for aggression, for sadism and masochism, for suicide. That he toyed with so odd a conception as an instinct for death and destruction indicates how deeply he was impressed by the irrational hatred and violence he saw everywhere around him.

In a very young infant the functions of the id are purely automatic. But when reflex action fails, as eventually it must, frustration causes emotional tension to build up. The baby must then learn to form an image of the object that reduces its tensions. At first, this image, which is generated by the *primary process,* is offered as a kind of substitute satisfaction whenever frustration occurs. This use of imagery is pure wish-fulfillment. Freud believed that wish-fulfillments, or attempted wish-fulfillments, persist into adulthood; dreams were his prime example.

The ego is the executive branch of the personality. It operates according to a *reality principle,* rather than the pleasure principle.

When reflex action and wish-fulfilling imagery have both failed, the child begins to develop a secondary process: the thinking, knowing, problem-solving processes necessary to produce the desired object itself. As a consequence of the secondary process, a plan of action is created and tested. The testing is called *reality testing*. Most of the psychological functions that had been studied prior to Freud's work—sensation, perception, learning, thinking, memory, action, will, and so on—are pure ego functions in Freudian terminology.

The ego has no energy of its own, so it steals energy from the id by a process known as *identification*. The theft is perpetrated as follows: The id invests its instinctual energy in the images that its primary process creates, but the id has no way to distinguish between its own wish-fulfilling imagination and the veridical images of perception. To achieve gratification the id's fomenting energy must be invested in an accurate image of a tension-reducing object; the imagination image that the id desires and the perceptual image of the goal object must be in good agreement. When the internal image corresponds closely to the perceptual object, the idea can be identified with the object, and the idea's psychic energy can be transferred to it. This identification process enables the energies of the id to be guided by an accurate representation of reality, and makes possible the further development of the ego.

The superego, which develops at a later age, is said to include two subsystems, an *ego-ideal* and a *conscience*. Both are assimilated by the child from examples and teachings provided by his parents. The ego-ideal is the child's conception of what his parents will approve; his conscience is the child's conception of what they will condemn as morally bad. The ego-ideal is learned through rewards, the conscience through punishments. The superego, in short, is the repository of social norms—Freud's way of dealing with the kinds of problems that Durkheim discovered in his studies of social action.

It should be noted that the superego was Freud's way of going beyond the felicity calculators that utilitarians had believed in. The id wants happiness and the ego does the calculating—that much of the older theory he preserved intact—but the superego is something more, something that holds the happiness-calculator within bounds set by society, something that introduces the social norms that are so necessary for our understanding of human society. Much that was most revolutionary in Freud's thinking had to do with how these social restraints become internalized to form the superego.

The process of investing instinctual energy is called *cathexis*. The id has only cathexes, but the ego and the superego can use the energy at their disposal in either of two ways, for cathexis or *anticathexis*. Anticathexis, which manifests itself in terms of self-frustration, is the way the ego and the superego keep the id in check. Perhaps the most important example of anticathexis has to do with memory. A person may fail to recall something, Freud would say, because the memory trace is not sufficiently charged with energy— it is too weakly cathected. But sometimes his memory may fail because the cathexis is opposed by an even stronger anticathexis; in that case a memory is said to be *repressed*. The repressive mechanism is one way—a very common way—the ego protects itself against painful memories and the discomfort or anxiety they would arouse.

Anxiety is a crucial concept in psychoanalytic theory, especially when the theory deals with neurosis and psychosis.[11] Freud distinguished between objective, neurotic, and moral anxiety. Objective anxiety is a painful emotion aroused by the recognition of a real, objective danger. Neurotic anxiety is aroused by a recognition of danger from instinctual forces—by fear that the anticathexes of the ego will not be strong enough to prevent instinctual energy from being discharged in an impulsive action. When neurotic anxiety is focused upon a particular object or situation, it is called a *phobia;* when a person is unable to specify what is causing his discomfort, his anxiety is called *free-floating*. Moral anxiety is aroused by the recognition of danger from the conscience, and appears as feelings of guilt or of shame at what one has done or, more often, what one is contemplating doing. A virtuous person with a well-developed conscience always experiences more shame, more moral anxiety, than a less virtuous person.

To protect itself from anxiety, the Freudian ego develops various defensive methods or mechanisms.[12] We have already mentioned identification. When identification is used as a defense mechanism, the person identifies himself with someone who seems desirable or admirable, with someone who would not be vulnerable to the danger that is causing the subject anxiety. We have also mentioned repression, which simply prevents an anxiety-arousing situation from becoming conscious. Other mechanisms include *sublimation* (a socially more acceptable goal is substituted for one that cannot be directly satisfied), *projection* (attributing the source of the anxiety to someone or something else external to the person), *reaction formation* (concealing a disturbing impulse by converting it into its opposite), *fixation* (refusing to take the next step in normal development because of anxiety aroused by fear of the new and the unknown), *regression* (retreating to an earlier stage of development when there was greater security, when this anxiety did not arise). A large part of the theoretical machinery developed by Freud and his followers is concerned with the various strategies whereby a person tries— usually irrationally and unsuccessfully—to escape from the intolerably unpleasant emotional experience of anxiety.

J. S. Bruner has aptly called this a dramatic theory of personality:

> Freud's is a theory or a proto-theory peopled with actors. The characters are from life: the blind, energetic, pleasure-seeking id; the priggish and punitive superego; the ego, battling for its being by diverting the energy of others to its own use. The drama has an economy and a terseness. The ego develops canny mechanisms for dealing with the threat of id impulses; denial, projection, and the rest. Balances are struck between the actors, and in the balance is character and neurosis. Freud was using the dramatic technique of decomposition, the play whose actors are parts of a single life.[13]

Because neurotic patients taught him that their troubles began in childhood, Freud developed an elaborate theory of how children grow up, how their sexual instincts develop and mature. The evidence for his theory of development came largely from retrospective accounts by adults; at first it had little support from actual observations of children. Even so, by placing his usual heavy emphasis on sexuality he forced child psychologists to recognize something that it had always been easier to ignore: Sweet, innocent, little children are just as sexual as anybody else. Sex does not spring suddenly into existence at puberty; it is there all along. Many people found psychoanalytic theory most shocking at this very point. One distinguished critic complained that in the study of infantile sexuality, "Freud went down deeper, stayed down longer, and came up dirtier than anyone else." But such complaints miss the point of Freud's insight. He was not talking of dirty habits in nasty little brats; he was telling the story of a force of nature.

Freud was the first psychologist who took systematic account of the pleasures and problems every child has with the apertures of his body. He believed that a child's sexual gratifications come from different openings—different *erogenous zones*—at different ages. In unfortunate circumstances, a child can become fixated at an infantile stage and thus develop personality traits corresponding to that particular level.[14] According to Freud, the first erogenous zone is the mouth, where a baby first gets pleasure from sucking, then from biting. If any psychic energy becomes fixated on the *oral zone* during the ingestive, sucking stage, it will produce a dependent personality in the adult. If trouble arises later during the oral biting phase, the person will become aggressive in an oral sense: verbal scorn, sarcasm, cynicism are typical expressions of oral agression. These problems can appear first when a child is being weaned, so the weaning practices of mothers have assumed great theoretical interest.

In the normal course of development, however, sexual gratification shifts from the mouth to the other end of the alimentary tract; the child will begin to experience pleasure in the *anal zone*. Again there are two modes of functioning: holding back and giving up. If there is important conflict during the period of toilet training, a person may grow up with an anal expulsive character—messy, dirty, wasteful, extravagant—or with an anal retentive character—neat, clean, compulsive, fastidious.

The next Freudian stage occurs when erotic impulses migrate to the sexual zone and the child enters the *phallic stage*. Masturbation and incestuous longings for the parents, who are a child's first love objects, must be brought under control; how that is achieved is one of the central features of Freudian theory and usually a central problem that has to be worked through and accepted by the patient during psychotherapy.

When a little boy begins to feel sexual impulses toward his mother, Freud said, he becomes jealous of his rival, the father. Since this family crisis was discussed in terms of the Greek legend about Oedipus, who killed his father and married his mother, the boy's dilemma is generally referred to as an *Oedipus complex*. According to Freud, a boy normally becomes afraid that his father will castrate him as punishment for his incestuous desires; this *castration anxiety* eventually forces him to repress both his desire for his mother and his hostility toward his father. When the repression is complete, the Oedipus complex finally disappears. At this point he may identify with either the father or the mother, depending upon whether the masculine or the feminine components of his personality are dominant. In this process of identification the boy adopts the parental values and morality that will constitute his superego as an adult.

The little girl is not so thoroughly explained. She is supposed to develop *penis envy,* a female counterpart of the boy's castration anxiety, and she too may resolve her conflict by identifying with either parent. But many clinicians feel that Freud's theory is weakest in dealing with feminine psychology.

It is interesting to note that here, as elsewhere, Freud had an attitude characteristic of the nineteenth-century middle class, which was more concerned with having than with being. His deepest fears were always of losing something one has, a love object, a feeling, or the genital organs.[15] Thus castration anxiety and penis envy seemed to him the most powerful emotional forces that any child would have to cope with.

If, by a miracle, one manages to get through all these Freudian stages with some psychic energy left, he will, after a normal period of latency from about five to twelve years of age, pass into a final, adult phase of genital sexuality. People who negotiate the course successfully, however, seldom turn up in a psychoanalyst's office asking for help. Hence there is little psychoanalytic description of what the genital stage of adult sexuality is like.

Freud's theories often seem absurd, if not downright false, to readers who encounter them first in a brief summary such as this. It is an easy exercise for a detached outsider to be critical; Freud has little to say to someone who is not personally involved in psychoanalysis. Those who are involved, however, are usually less confident in their criticisms. Once the psychoanalytic expedition back into childhood begins, once the personal commitment to the therapeutic process is given, once one tries to look honestly at oneself, it is no longer so obvious what is reasonable and what is absurd. There is some merit to the claim that the criticism of psychoanalysis is best left to those who have experienced it. In this respect, at least, it is more like a way of life than like a scientific theory.

Freud's first and major contribution was his psychological theory of personality and neurosis, but he was also, particularly in the later years of his life, a social theorist of considerable importance. His first efforts in that direction were presented in *Totem and Taboo,* published in 1913. His point of departure was the family, the basic building block of all larger social groups, and a powerful influence on the psychosexual development of the child. His social argument— a modern version of the ancient doctrine of original sin—rested on a vast elaboration of the Oedipus complex, an elaboration that made the complex as important in the development of society as in the development of an individual personality. *Totem and Taboo* is an allegory about a "primal horde" and the banding together of the sons to slay their father and eat of his flesh. But Freud did not intend to be allegorical; he insisted that he was describing actual events that must have been repeated thousands of times before civilization could have been achieved.

It was Freud's idea that the uncivilized sons hated and feared their uncivilized father because he monopolized the women. After they killed him they felt remorse perhaps, but, more important, they recognized that they needed to replace him with a new moral authority or they would all perish in bloody strife of brother against brother. So they began to discipline themselves. Their first step was to impose a taboo on incest, outlawing the possibility of competition with the father for the mother and sisters. Only with an incest taboo is it possible for males to live together peacefully in a single family group. This first and most fundamental prohibition was later followed by others, which became equally binding. These socially necessary restraints have never been completely accepted, however, so the battle has to be fought all over again in the development of every male child.

It is curious how culture-bound Freud was when he ventured into anthropology. Bronislaw Malinowski, who tried to use psychoanalytic concepts in his anthropological studies of the family, once commented that Freud, in a most attractive but fantastic hypothesis, equipped his primal horde with all the bias, maladjustments, and ill tempers of a middle-class European family let loose in a prehistoric jungle.

The implication of Freud's argument is that guilt (anxiety aroused by threats from the superego) is the motive force behind all social solidarity.   Locke, Spencer, and the utilitarians explained social integration in terms of a social contract between individuals free to maximize their own happiness; Durkheim discussed the social facts that exist external to the actor yet somehow tie him to his group by providing norms and ideals; William James made habit the great flywheel of society that keeps us all within the bounds of ordinance; in place of these theories Freud proposed to substitute a vast burden of guilt shared by every civilized person.

The id impulses spring up in all of us; we want to destroy authority and enjoy our sensual pleasures. But in a civilized person the thought arouses guilt; self-indulgence is repressed to protect the ego. Thus social restraints are imposed by a superego that holds over us the unbearable threat of guilt, of moral anxiety. The more a social group imposes constraints upon the sexuality of an individual, the more powerful his superego must become and the greater must be the guilt he experiences. His feelings of guilt may increase beyond all tolerable bounds, until they usurp all his psychic energy and leave him helpless.

Is there some way to prevent this? Could we organize a society around love and reason, rather than around fear and guilt? On this question Freud was basically pessimistic. He had seen too much persecution of his own people, and he had listened to too many neurotic patients describe their inner thoughts ever to be lulled into thinking that men are gentle, friendly creatures who fight only when they are attacked. The great optimist Herbert Spencer could argue all he liked that the predatory habits of modern men were only vestigial survivals that would soon vanish in the upward sweep of evolution; Freud saw only the increasing burdens that modern society was placing on the ego, burdens that would create an ever-increasing measure of guilt and aggression.

When we compare his conception of man with the hopeful mood of the Enlightenment in the eighteenth century, it is obvious why he has so often been called the great anti-intellectual, the great destroyer of faith in rationality. Yet Freud never wavered in his faith that the search for truth must continue. He wrote:

> We may insist as much as we like that the human intellect is weak in comparison with human instincts, and be right in doing so. But nevertheless there is something peculiar about this weakness. The voice of the intellect is a soft one, but it does not rest until it has gained a hearing. Ultimately, after endlessly repeated rebuffs, it succeeds.[16]

Freud struggled to see man as he is, not as he ought to be or as Freud would have liked to imagine him. As one trained in the Helmholtz school of medicine, he carried on this struggle in a positivistic spirit with what he felt were scientific methods of observation and analysis. He was convinced that all mental events are completely determined—even mistakes have a cause. And to the end of his life he used the mechanical, electrical, hydraulic terminology of his positivistic teachers. Thus we must classify him as loyal to the positivistic tradition. But in spite of his loyalty, he was a powerful and damaging critic. After he had completed his demonstration of the importance of unconscious, instinctual forces in human conduct, the old faith in the inevitability of human progress through man's constant growth of knowledge and understanding sounded like an innocent myth concocted to amuse little children. Few men have influenced us so deeply.

CHAPTER XVI

———◆◆———

GOADS AND GUIDES

Emerson once said that every man is as lazy as he dares to be. It was the kind of mistake a New England Puritan might be expected to make. It is not that we don't dare, but that we don't care to be lazy. If we really set our minds to it, we could all be a lot lazier than we actually are.

How lazy can a man get? The absolute limits, of course, are imposed by his body: At the very least he must obtain and consume food and drink; he will occasionally have to move out of harm's way; he must deposit his wastes at some distance from his place of repose; he will have to cover himself when it gets too cold and move out of the sun when it gets too hot; and while this is not vital in quite the same sense, he will one day surely advertise to attract the attentions of a mate. Yet in a friendly, nurturant environment these minimal demands of biology would fill only a fraction of his waking hours. From all we might learn in a textbook of physiology, a man could dare to be very lazy indeed.

In some idyllic lands blessed by natural advantages of food and safety, living may approach much closer to this biological minimum than it does in ours. But even at its simplest, human life boils at a temperature several degrees hotter than absolute lethargy. Trouble begins when we get mixed up with other people, all of whom take as much pleasure in laziness as we do. We have to compete with them for food and drink, we find they have already appropriated all the desirable clothing and shelter, and they insist that our wastes be deposited far from their places of repose, too. Moreover, they usually have strong opinions about proper ways to deal with these problems. What is dangerous, and requires real daring, is to be lazier than your neighbors think you should be. There are, in short, social as well as biological limits on just how lazy bone-lazy can be.

And, even when we have scrambled inside the bounds of social propriety, there are still other goads at work inside us. Something keeps us going: curiosity, play, humor, stories, boredom. The mind is a restless organ. Even Emerson would have admitted that the devil finds work for idle hands.

The study of motivation is the study of all those pushes and prods —biological, social, psychological—that defeat our laziness and move us, either eagerly or reluctantly, to action. Psychologists sometimes talk as though the study of motivation were their own private hunting ground, but it is a much larger, looser domain than that, extending from biochemistry on one end to sociology, economics, and anthropology on the other. A grand variety of mechanisms participates, and no single theory will ever account for them all.

This diversity has not always been apparent, however. The history of the subject has been a story of persistent search for a simple and sovereign principle to explain everything we do. Pleasure, instinct, mental faculties, volition, passion, reason—these are among the candidates put forward for the title.

Following Darwin, instinct became a favorite explanation. This conveniently vague notion said that men act as they do because they are born that way, because they cannot help themselves. When psychology first tried to become scientific, therefore, it was natural to try to catalogue all the instincts men were born with.

An especially enthusiastic cataloguer was William James. He held the unusual but interesting opinion that men are born with many, many instincts that remain active only long enough to establish necessary habits and then, if development proceeds naturally, fade quietly away. In 1890 his list mentioned the following:

> Sucking
> Biting
> Chewing
> Licking
> Grimacing

Spitting
Clasping
Pointing
Carrying to mouth
Crying
Smiling
Turning head
Holding head erect
Sitting up
Standing
Creeping
Walking
Climbing
Vocalizing
Imitating sounds
Imitating gestures
Rivalry
Pugnacity
Anger
Resentment
Sympathy
Hunting
Fear of noises,
    strange men,
    strange animals,
    black things,
    high places,
    etc.
Hoarding
Constructing
Playing
Curiosity
Sociability
Shyness
Secretiveness
Cleanliness
Modesty
Shame
Love

Sex
Jealousy
Parental love

All these and more were supposed to be transitory human instincts. With so many inherited reactions goading him on, a child would have little time to be lazy. "Repose," said James's close friend Justice Oliver Wendell Holmes, as if to correct Emerson, "is not the lot of man."

James's list was not the last word, of course. Every new author proposed his own version. In 1908 a particularly famous list by William McDougall paired off seven human instincts with their corresponding primary emotions as follows:[1]

The instinct of flight and the emotion of fear,

repulsion	and	disgust,
curiosity	and	wonder,
pugnacity	and	anger,
self-abasement	and	subjection,
self-assertion	and	elation,
parental care	and	tenderness.

In addition to these seven, McDougall believed there were other instincts that did not arouse such specific and well-defined emotions: reproduction, gregariousness, acquisition, and construction.

The full flavor of these discussions cannot be conveyed by mere lists. One needs to read the detailed descriptions of each instinct and the careful comparisons of one author's list with another's to appreciate how the various goads to action were supposed to be grouped under these headings. The discussions contained many acute observations and much wise counsel, but they were lost in the loose and shifting framework of the competing catalogues. And the lists continued to multiply. One careful survey[2] found that by 1924 at least 849 separate instincts had been proposed by different writers on the subject! No student could absorb all the subtleties of this vast and tangled subject; it was easier to invent your own classification than to try to understand the other fellow's.

By the 1920's American psychologists determined to dump these overblown theories and start anew. Much behavior that was being called instinctive was actually acquired through learning. And accounting for everything that happened in terms of its own specific instinct dissolved the difficult art of explanation into an easy game of definitions. In order to fight their way back to scientific realities, therefore, psychologists began to talk about physiological drives instead of inherited instincts. Instincts have since recovered some of

Fig. 36. A phrenological chart. Phrenologists not only constructed long lists of mental faculties, they located them on various parts of the skull. This attempted classification was a forerunner of the lists of instincts that psychologists later adopted.

their lost respectability, especially for describing animal behavior—examples of a new approach to instinct have already been displayed in Chapter XIV—but they will never again run quite as free as they did in the days of James and McDougall.

While instincts were at their peak of popularity, the Viennese shadow of Sigmund Freud was beginning to fall on American shores. Freud is usually called an instinct theorist, but the accuracy of the description is uncertain. The German word he used was *Trieb;* at the time, "instinct" seemed a reasonable translation. When instincts lost their monopoly, however, it became apparent that Freud had been talking about something much closer to a sexual drive than to a sexual instinct. Nevertheless, the translation stuck and many Americans have ever since thought of Freud as a proponent of instinctive sexuality. Motivational terminology becomes confused so easily; it is almost as if we wanted to keep our terms vague and general enough to match our imperfect understanding of these very complex problems.

Freud's ideas about instincts were revised several times during his long career. Here is one of his final statements on the matter:

> It is possible to distinguish an indeterminate number of instincts and in common practice this is in fact done. For us, however, the important question arises whether we may not be able to derive all of these various instincts from a few fundamental ones. We have found that instincts can change their aim (by displacement) and also that they can replace one another—the energy of one instinct passing over to another. This latter process is still insufficiently understood. After long doubts and vacillations we have decided to assume the existence of only two basic instincts, *Eros* and *the destructive instinct*.[3]

This urge to derive the various instincts from a few simpler, basic processes was shared by Freudians and non-Freudians alike.

The aching void left in American psychology by the passing of the traditional theory of instincts was filled for many by Freudian explanations. Most hardheaded, laboratory-oriented psychologists, however, held out for something more tangible. For them the gap was filled by physiological theories, especially those of Walter B. Cannon and his associates at the Harvard Medical School.[4] But in many respects the two alternatives, Freud's and Cannon's, were much alike. Cannon's work on motivation seemed to provide a physiological foundation for those life-preserving instincts that Freud had lumped together under the general name of Eros.[5]

At the focus of Cannon's theory was the concept of *homeostasis*. The cells and organs of the body require very specific conditions of temperature, blood sugar, acidity, water balance, carbon dioxide, and so on. Mammals have evolved an almost endless variety of regulating mechanisms designed to maintain what Claude Bernard called the internal environment of the body. According to Cannon, when the internal environment begins to drift beyond tolerable limits, it acts as a stimulus for receptor organs located in specific parts of the body. These local irritations drive us into action until they are removed. As you get hungry, for example, your empty stomach begins to contract; these contractions are the source of stimuli for your hunger sensations. You eat, in short, to escape discomfort. When you go without water, your throat gets dry and produces a sensation of thirst. You drink to eliminate this unpleasant sensation.

These regulating mechanisms provided an objective basis for a theory of motivation; instead of postulating instincts for chewing and swallowing, psychologists began to look for homeostatic drives of hunger and thirst. And they tried to extend Cannon's ideas to account for other kinds of motivation; sexual behavior, for example, was represented as an attempt to relieve local irritation or pressure in the genitals.

Since Cannon's time scientists have learned how to talk about homeostatic drives in the language of servomechanisms. A servomechanism is a self-regulating system designed so that the difference between the actual and the intended state of the system is fed back as input, and the system becomes active, and remains so, until the difference is eliminated. Perhaps the most familiar example of a servomechanism is a thermostat that turns on a heater whenever the temperature falls below a predetermined level, then turns it off again as soon as the temperature rises above that level. The feedback loop that is involved is indicated in Figure 37. In a biological servomechanism, the organism becomes active whenever the sugar or the water is running low, and it stays active until food or drink reestablishes homeostatic equilibrium.

It soon became apparent, however, that the mechanisms of hunger and thirst are much more complicated than Cannon imagined. Hunger and thirst both activate very elaborate sensory and response systems that are under the control of neural and hormonal factors. Moreover, it takes a relatively long time before the ingestion of food and water can have any physiological effect, before eating and drinking can reduce the local irritations. For a simpler example of a homeostatic system that guides overt behavior it would be better to examine a temperature-regulating mechanism.

THERMOSTAT   FURNACE

TEMPERATURE
OF AIR

Fig. 37. The feedback loop that regulates room temperature.

There are several servosystems that enable warm-blooded animals to keep their body temperatures at a constant level. Over a wide range of environmental temperatures these regulating systems do their work without conscious attention on our part. However, when it gets so hot or so cold that these autonomic systems are no longer adequate, we begin to search actively for a more temperate environment. The receptors that guide us in this search are located in the skin; we persist until they tell us that we are once again within a tolerable range of environmental temperatures.

This behavioral system for controlling body temperature can best be studied in the laboratory. Suppose rats are placed in a cold environment and permitted to press a lever to turn on a heat lamp for a few seconds. The feedback loop that is created in this way is indicated in Figure 38. There is little delay in this feedback. When it is turned on, radiant energy starts almost immediately to raise the skin temperature; when it is turned off, the skin temperature begins abruptly to fall again. Rats will learn to push the lever under these conditions. Moreover, they push the lever at an average rate that keeps their skin temperature constant.[6] That is to say, when they get only a little heat per press of the lever, they press at a rapid rate. When they get a lot of heat per press, their rate slows down. If one thinks of the calories they absorb as a kind of reward, a payment for their work on the lever, then the more they are paid, the less they work! Clearly, the rats are not trying to hoard calories as a miser hoards gold; they are simply trying to keep their body temperatures in homeostatic equilibrium.

RESPONSE   ELECTRIC
LEVER   HEATER

TEMPERATURE
OF SKIN

Fig. 38. The feedback loop that is created when a cold animal learns to press a lever that temporarily activates a heat lamp.

At the time Cannon put forward his speculations about homeostasis it was already a well-established fact, both inside and outside the laboratory, that behavior can be guided by giving or withholding particular kinds of stimulation: food and water, warmth, electric shock, and so on. Psychologists wanted to know why. Why do some stimuli control behavior when others do not? The concept of homeostatic drives seemed to provide an easy answer: Stimuli are effective in controlling behavior to the degree that they serve to satisfy these drives and restore the organism to homeostatic equilibrium.[7]

In particular, Cannon's work seemed to provide a solid physiological basis for Thorndike's Law of Effect, which had become a pivotal issue in S-R theories of learning. Thorndike had said that we form only those stimulus-response connections that can lead to satisfying effects; many were willing to turn his law about and assume that effects are satisfying only if they can lead us to form stimulus-response connections. With this inversion it seemed possible to give an operational definition of motivation in terms of its reinforcing properties: a motive was anything that could be used to make an organism learn, that could reinforce a change in behavior. All that was missing was a theory to explain the mechanism of reinforcement, to explain why some effects are satisfying and others are not. And that is precisely what Cannon's drive theory seemed to offer. It is not surprising, therefore, that these ideas about homeostatic drives found an attentive audience among American psychologists[8] and that research in this direction was quickly and vigorously pursued.

Unfortunately for the cause of simplicity, however, the evidence soon indicated that local irritation is only one of several goads to action. For example, a man whose stomach has been removed surgically cannot have stomach contractions, yet he can feel hunger. And persons born without salivary glands always have a dry throat, yet know when they are thirsty. Although the underlying concept of homeostasis seemed valid enough, Cannon's initial suggestions as to how these homeostatic systems guide behavior soon proved to be inadequate. Drives are not mere sources of irritating stimuli; neural and hormonal interactions of the most intricate design seem to be involved.

A variety of regulatory mechanisms may play a role over and above the local irritations that Cannon considered. Perhaps disequilibrium is signalled by variations in the pleasures of sensation, perhaps there is a direct effect on the central nervous system, perhaps there are hormonal changes in the blood stream, perhaps some connection is learned between a particular stimulus and an eventual change in homeostasis. Perhaps. Much research has been and is being done to evaluate these and other possible explanations. At present the consensus seems to be that most homeostatic drives arise through the internal environment acting on the central nervous system.[9] But it is difficult to be much more specific without going into great detail for each drive.

Let us focus on a simple, behavioral fact: It is possible to train hungry animals to perform simple tricks by reinforcing their behavior with sweetened water. Why does sweetened water have this effect? Perhaps the sugar is absorbed into the blood stream, reduces the hunger drive, and thus relieves local irritation; the sweetened water is reinforcing because it removes a source of discomfort. The fact that so much time is required for digestion and absorption, however, makes this explanation dubious; for the reinforcement to occur promptly, as soon as the correct response is made, a neural process in the central nervous system—more rapid and symbolic—would have to be involved.

Some psychologists believe that reinforcement can be produced by the sheer pleasure of a sweet taste. In support of this belief they point out that animals appear to be as well reinforced by a saccharine solution, which has no nutritive value, as by a solution of glucose or sucrose. A sweet taste is rewarding whether or not it relieves the hunger drive. But why is it rewarding? Are animals born that way? Or do they learn to like sweetness because it is so often associated with the alleviation of hunger?

Questions such as these bring to mind the ancient doctrine of *hedonism*, the notion that we do the things that increase our pleasures and decrease our pains. At the root of this doctrine, no doubt, is an appreciation of the sensory pleasures aroused by genital stimulation, by the taste of sugar, by certain fragrant odors, and the like, and the sensory discomforts of heat, cold, shock, and so on. But no one who has argued for hedonism—Epicureans, Stoics, Utilitarians, Freudians—has ever argued for a purely sensory hedonism. It is rational, not sensory hedonism that has been defended. Rational hedonism assumes that an intelligent person will take the long view, will postpone small pleasures now in the hope of greater pleasures later. In Freudian language, the pleasure principle gives way to the reality principle. Certainly rational hedonism is the only form of this doctrine one can imagine applicable to man. But many of the experiments on the physiological bases of motivation are performed with lower animals whose ability to postpone their pleasures must be severely limited. Sensory hedonism may, therefore, be an important factor controlling the behavior of simpler organisms.

Hedonistic theories of motivation always seem to involve a semantic trick. A hedonist tells us, for example, that we do not really enjoy smoking; what we enjoy is the pleasure of smoking. With every pleasant activity the hedonist associates something called pleasure— or value, or utility—which then becomes the real motive for the activity. "Don't spend your time smoking," he seems to say. "It is only a means to attain pleasure. Let it go and devote yourself directly to the true end, pure pleasure itself." As if you could experience the pleasure of smoking without smoking.

Yet divorcing the experience of pleasure from the pleasant experience may not be as ridiculous as it sounds. In 1954 two young psychologists, James Olds and Peter Milner, working together at McGill University in Montreal, stumbled across what seemed to be the pleasure center in a rat's brain.[10] They had pushed an electrode—

two wires extending down into the brain from a plastic base mounted on the skull with jeweler's screws—into the hypothalamus, an old and vital region deep in the center of the brain. They were using the electrode to see what effects electric currents might have on the rat's behavior. Their happy innovation was to give the rat control of the electric stimulus; they let the animal press a lever that turned on the electrical stimulus to its own brain. The experimental arrangement is pictured schematically in Figure 39.

Under these conditions, and with exactly the right placement of the electrode, a rat will work hard to get the electric current, just as if it were a conventional reward. When the current is disconnected, the rat stops working. The electric stimulation can be powerfully attractive; a hungry rat may even refuse to eat if it is given a chance to stimulate itself instead. Exactly what goes on in this reinforcement center—if that is what it is—is not yet clear; this remains one of the most intriguing and, potentially, most important questions in the field of physiological psychology.

Although there are many deep issues still unsettled, it appears that slow but steady progress is being made in the effort to understand the physiological drives.

But that is not enough. There is more to life than keeping one's blood chemistry in equilibrium.

Homeostatic drives play only the most general role in human conduct. They do not even account for all the motivated behavior observed in animals; manipulation, exploration, playfulness are motivated activities unrelated to homeostasis. Like the force of gravity, homeostatic drives are always around to trip us up if we become careless or unlucky. They goad us to action because they are part of being alive. But they are not the central focus for most of us most of the time.

The larger and more baffling problem is to understand what guides human action, what organizes it and assigns priorities. As a consequence of certain natural pleasures and many acquired tastes, we eventually come to make fairly predictable appraisals of the values of objects and activities in our daily lives. These are the values that guide us and channel our energies in one direction rather than another.

When one begins to ask about values one discovers that an old and elaborate theory of value already exists. The theory was not invented by psychologists, but by economists. Many psychologists have thought that it might be refitted for their purposes without too much trouble.

Fig. 39. Diagram of circuit used in self-stimulation studies. When the rat presses the lever an electric current stimulates its hypothalamus. The response is simultaneously recorded via a separate wire. (From J. Olds, Pleasure center in the brain, *Scientific American*, October 1956.)

Beginning around 1870 a revolution in the classical science of economics led such men as W. Stanley Jevons and Alfred Marshall in England, Auguste Walras in Switzerland, and Karl Menger in Austria to try to analyze the psychological background of a consumer's motives, decisions, and actions. It was an abstract, mathematical kind of psychology that they adopted, based on the faith that men are rational and that rational men always try to maximize their happiness—or, as it was often called in honor of Jeremy Bentham, their utility.

A psychological assumption of crucial importance for these mathematical economists was that the satisfaction we get from any commodity—its value to us—grows more and more slowly as we acquire more and more of it. This situation is illustrated graphically in Figure 40. The first apple we get is the most satisfying; a man who already owns ten apples receives less satisfaction from his eleventh; and a man who has a thousand cares little for one more. For historical reasons that would interest only an economist, this relation between quantity and satisfaction is usually referred to as the theory of marginal utility. It was a crucial assumption to economists because they could use it to explain why people wanted to exchange goods with one another—which is, after all, the lifeblood of an economic system. If you have too many apples and I have too many peaches,

Fig. 40. Illustrating the economic principle of marginal utility: The increase in utility (satisfaction) per unit of the commodity decreases progressively as the amount of the commodity increases. A consumer will continue to buy this commodity until he gets so much of it that his increase in satisfaction per dollar becomes less than it would be for some other commodity.

then according to the principle of marginal utility we can both increase our satisfaction by exchanging some of our fruit.

In many respects this economic theory was a mathematical formulation of the pleasure principle, since behavior was explained in terms
of a single motive, namely, the increased satisfaction of the individual. It was also a mathematical statement of the homeostatic
principle, because the principle of marginal utility plus the effort to
maximize satisfaction defines a point of equilibrium toward which
a person would gravitate. Only one detail seemed to keep economists
and psychologists apart: the economist's theory was normative, not
descriptive.

If your system of values is firmly established and you are trying
to maximize your satisfaction, economic theory is your best guide;
if you don't want to maximize your satisfactions, you should look
elsewhere for guidance. By approaching the problem in this spirit,
economists had the option of remaining indifferent to what people
actually did in economic contexts. The theory indicated what rational
people should do; what people actually did was their own foolish
business. Unfortunately, it was exactly that kind of foolish business
that psychologists were most interested in. It was the economist's
assumption of rationality that most sharply distinguished his approach
from that of a psychologist who wanted to understand all choices,
not only the rational ones.

But perhaps a few minor modifications would enable psychologists
to salvage a part of this elegant economic theory for their own use.
What assumptions are involved? Theories fashioned along these lines
generally begin with a person who is faced by a large, but well-defined
set of alternative actions from which to choose. Moreover, this hypothetical person is able to decide, for any two of these alternatives,
which one he would prefer; he has a preference ordering from the
most valuable down to the least valuable alternative in the set. He
knows, for example, that possessing five hundred apples and five
hundred peaches is preferable to possessing one thousand apples and
no peaches.

Assumptions of this kind are a glorious convenience for an economist, but they take for granted the very thing that a psychologist
would like to explain. Consider the difficulties. In the first place,
a flesh-and-blood consumer, unlike his theoretical counterpart, knows
that large quantities of luck are needed to achieve economic suc-

cess. Second, he almost never understands or tries to formulate explicitly all the alternatives that face him. Third, he seldom possesses either the ability or the patience to calculate his optimal course of action.

Certain of these objections are harder to meet than others. Perhaps the easiest is the one involving luck. Luck and uncertainty can be blended into an economic theory by using the mathematical theory of probability. As every gambler knows, the value of an outcome partly depends on the probability of attaining it. In the long run, a not-so-valuable outcome that is reliable may be worth more than a very valuable outcome that is highly improbable. To balance values against probabilities, economic theory introduces the concept of expected value. The expected value of a particular action is what one would receive on the average if one took that action again and again throughout a long sequence of choices. The expected (or mean) value of an action is obtained by listing all n of the possible outcomes, by assigning to each outcome $i = 1, 2, \ldots, n$, a value $v(i)$ and a probability $p(i)$, then averaging:

$$\text{Expected Value} = p(1)v(1) + p(2)v(2) + \ldots + p(n)v(n).$$

By using expected values rather than absolute values, it is possible to preserve most of the economic theory intact. One merely assumes that people try to maximize their expected happiness, and all runs as smoothly as before. Uncertainty of success, therefore, is not the principal stumbling block in combining economic and psychological theories of choice.

Another obstacle that a psychologist must overcome if he hopes to adapt the economist's theory to his own ends is that the theory assumes people know things they don't know. An example has been given: In introducing the notion of expected value, it is implicitly assumed that one knows the probabilities for every outcome that might result from one's actions. But often there is no possible way of knowing the true probabilities. All that the person usually knows is his subjective appraisal of the probabilities; he may in fact be far off the mark.

But all is not yet lost; the theory may still be adaptable to our psychological needs. Since the true probabilities are unknown, we must follow the next best course. Suppose, therefore, that subjective instead of true probabilities are used in the above equation. The result should then be closer to what the person subjectively expects; it will be wrong, but it may be more closely related to his choices than the true value. Because this is an attractively precise kind of theory, several experimental attempts have been made to test whether, under appropriate conditions, people really do try to maximize their subjective expected value.[11] But it is a difficult question, and the verdict is not yet in.

Whether or not a situation can be found in which people try to maximize their subjective expected value, there are clearly many situations in which they do not. For example, if people are paid for guessing correctly which of two lights is to flash next, then over a long string of trials their guesses will roughly match the probabilities. If one light comes on at random 80 per cent of the time, people will guess it about 80 per cent of the time.[12] If, however, they had wanted to maximize the amount they were being paid, they would have chosen that light at every trial. Unless there are important non-monetary rewards involved, therefore, people do not naturally follow what most economists would consider an optimal strategy in this situation.

Even if one disregards the element of risk and the knowledge of probabilities there are other difficulties that the economic theory raises when it is used for descriptive purposes. Consider the assumption that a man has complete information about all the alternative courses of action that are open to him. In most practical situations this assumption is simply not true. A housewife does not learn the price of potatoes in every store in town before she makes her purchase. A real estate agent cannot know the price every potential customer would be willing to pay for a particular house before the agent makes the sale.

George Katona, a psychologist who looks at economic behavior through a magnifying glass called the University of Michigan Survey Research Center, has pointed out that what people do depends upon their level of aspiration.[13] They decide on a value that would be satisfactory and then accept the first offer that exceeds it. In experimental studies it has been shown that, if they are successful, people tend to raise their aspiration level next time; if they fail, they tend to lower the value they regard as satisfactory.[14] Herbert A. Simon, a behavioral scientist at the Carnegie Institute of Technology and a close student of administrative behavior, has suggested that this strategy of searching for something good enough—even though it may not be the best possible—should be called *satisficing*.[15] Satisficing does not always extract as large a return as maximizing would, but it is a much easier strategy to follow.

A person who has decided what will be good enough for him can then use this rude decision as a test. Each alternative that presents itself can be tested to see if it matches up to the standard. If it does, he accepts it. If not, he looks further. If a long search turns up nothing good enough, he may revise his level of aspiration.

The alternative choices available will depend partly upon what luck provides, partly upon the personal efforts of the satisficer. If he finds himself in an undesirable situation, he can take action to change or abandon the situation; he is not required to sit quietly until it goes away. This capacity to modify the environment develops progressively up the evolutionary scale, until in man it is so highly developed that the very operation of natural selection can be controlled. Let us consider briefly how the capacity operates.

Assume one is dealing with an organism complex enough to maintain an implicit image of the satisfactory states of its world—of itself and its environment. When the state that is perceived to exist does not fall within the bounds of satisfaction, the organism becomes active. If the activity changes the situation in a satisfactory way, it ceases and, presumably, the successful action is remembered for future reference. If the activity does not create a new situation more to the organism's liking, other actions may be initiated. If failures persist, it may be necessary to lower the level of aspiration, to revise the conception of what is desirable in order to bring it more in line with what is attainable. Such revisions, however, are often accompanied by strong emotions.

This description of the adjustment process is quite abstract. It describes the way we cope with our homeostatic drives as well as it describes the way we work toward any other valued objective. The underlying notion is that of a discrete servomechanism, with the one —very important—difference that the threshold for activation can vary as a function of success or failure. In very general terms, therefore, this description preserves the general philosophy of the early, biological accounts of motivation, but does so in terms of guidance and adjustment, rather than in terms of energy.

Leaving aside all the biological problems of energetics and focusing simply on the psychological problems of direction and control, it seems that several independent accounts of motivation—from physiology, from psychoanalysis, from economics—tend to converge. The organism struggles to reduce the mismatch between its own criteria and perceived reality. Of course, consensus is never a guarantee of validity. Even the most rapt admirer of this general picture has to admit that there are many blanks at critical points. How is value conferred or withheld as a result of experience? How do we decide what is good enough? How do we compromise between the claims of the present and our hopes for the future? How do we save, plan, and postpone?

When these questions are faced squarely, the picture begins to look very sketchy indeed—hardly more than an outline of a picture that may someday be drawn. Instinct, drive, reinforcement, pleasure, utility, level of aspiration—these will fit somewhere in the finished product, but exactly where is still an open question.

CHAPTER XVII

———◆———

THE TYRANNY OF THE FUTURE

What do people want? As regards Americans around the middle of the twentieth century, what they want is all too familiar. Listen to Rosser Reeves, a high-powered salesman whose business it is to know what people want:

> We know, for example, that we do not want to be fat. We do not want to smell bad. We want healthy children, and we want to be healthy ourselves. We want beautiful teeth. We want good clothes. We want people to like us. We do not want to be ugly. We seek love and affection. We want money. We like comfort. We yearn for more beautiful homes. We want honesty, self-respect, a place in the community. We want to own things in which we can take pride. We want to succeed in our jobs. We want to be secure in our old age.[1]

These are proven demands of the market place. Never mind whether it is good to want such things, or whether we even have a right to want them. The point is that these are the things people in America work for, spend money on, devote their lives to. Surely here is where a psychologist should start to fashion his theory of human motivation.

This list, however, seems little better than our grandfathers's lists of instincts. If one is to make scientific sense out of these human desires, one will first have to discover the underlying dimensions of similarity among them.

Notice first of all that these American demands are all perfectly explicit, conscious, and socially acceptable. One may suspect that beneath these manifest desires is concealed a less admirable core, but this is a difficult issue.

267

Next, notice how typically American the list is. Imagine collecting a similar catalogue from Neanderthal men or the Tartar hordes. Americans find it difficult to believe that their own longings for particular things are learned, that the American conception of the good life is not universal and inevitable, that human nature has its own dimensions in India, Brazil, Nigeria.

Consider the salesman's list in a broader context: In many parts of the world obesity is judged beautiful. In extremely cold regions where clothes are seldom removed, body odors are simply ignored. Concepts of health and disease, of normal and abnormal, vary widely from one culture to the next. Teeth we think beautiful do not look beautiful to everyone. And so on down the list. Each thing we think so desirable is desirable because we have learned to desire it. In another culture we would have learned to desire other things. Even within our own relatively homogeneous society different social groups have very different dreams of the future.

As a start, therefore, one asks how this learning takes place. Where and when in the life of a youngster does stern society sit him down and explain what to crave and what to despise?

One answer runs something like this. Homeostatic drives are primary, and all the environmental conditions that are consistently associated with the satisfaction of primary drives will thereby acquire a secondary power to satisfy us. Mother's smile becomes rewarding because it accompanies the satisfaction of so many of her child's primary motives. And by generalization the value of mother's smile extends to other smiles, to all smiles, to social approval in its broadest sense. Similarly, power over others becomes a social motive because it was first associated with the various biological satisfactions that others can provide. Avarice is a social motive because money is associated with the satisfaction of many other motives. And so on and on. It is apparently true that every social value can be traced back, in theory, at least, through some such hypothetical chain of associations, to primary, homeostatic drives. These biological primitives constitute—in theory—the latent core around which cluster these manifest desires that an advertiser can exploit.

There is little that is objectionable in such a theory until it is claimed that social action is *always* energized in this manner. No doubt it is true that some adult values are acquired by repeated association with eating, drinking, sexing. But many psychologists feel that the insistence—typified by orthodox Freudian theorists—that all human behavior, normal and abnormal alike, draws its energy either directly or indirectly from these life-preserving, species-preserving mechanisms imposes on us an unprofitable burden of explanation. According to this theory, the reasons for everything we do must somehow be traced back historically to our sex glands and to homeostatic changes in the chemistry of our blood.

It detracts little from the importance of homeostasis and the pleasure principle to argue that some important social motives are acquired and mediated by very different processes, symbolic processes that must take place in the central nervous system.

One objection to the borrowed-energy theory is that it encourages us to think of social motives as if they ran a course entirely parallel to homeostatic drives. For example, an organism works to reduce its primary drives, to bring its tensions to an absolute minimum, to return to homeostatic equilibrium. If social motives are learned by association with primary drives, it seems reasonable to assume that they will also manifest this self-terminating characteristic. When this pattern of tension-reduction is imposed on social motives, however, it leads to an odd distortion. The simple truth is that social action does not always reduce tensions. To imply that it must suggests that persistent diligence and hard work are symptoms of maladjustment, that exciting stories and martial music will never be popular, that sport, humor, and dancing are signs of insanity, in short, that nirvana is the only goal anyone could imagine in this life. But this is nonsense. No sane person would reduce all his motivation to a minimum. Emerson was wrong when he said that every man is as lazy as he dares to be. Instead—when homeostasis gives us a chance—we constantly seek out new tensions to keep us occupied and entertained.

If we slavishly follow an analogy to biological drives, we are likely to assume that social motives can be satiated, as hunger, thirst, and sex can be. And on that assumption we must be surprised to find that millionaires want to make money, that neurotics never seem to get all the love they desire, that famous people like to see their names in newspapers, and so on. Social motives grow by what they feed on; the more we succeed, the higher we set our level of aspiration.

The mistaken notion that social motives can be satiated has even confused some economists and led them to prophesy that when the market was saturated—when 80 per cent of the American families owned refrigerators, or 70 per cent owned automobiles—the economy would slump to a level set by the rate of replacement. They failed to include the wages of optimism. Families with a refrigerator wanted a better one; families with one car wanted two cars; families with both a refrigerator and a car wanted their own house. Homeostasis follows an entirely different course.

The orthodox notion that we must have motives to energize our social actions—just as homeostatic drives energize our search for food, drink, and a mate—has been losing adherents for many years. Probably it would by now be abandoned, except that the defectors have been unable to agree among themselves on any single theory to replace the simple homeostatic analogy. When we desert it, therefore, we set out upon an uncertain journey of exploration; what follows here is only one of several directions that we might have chosen.

Suppose one asks, not where the energy for social action comes from, but where it is going. A psychologist can take the biological source of our vitality for granted; given that we are alive, metabolism provides our energy. The psychological problem is how we organize and guide a flow that must inevitably continue until our final tension-reduction in the grave. What determines how we will use our brief gift of time?

Most human endeavors are guided not by learned motives, but by learned values.[2] There are important differences. Motives are a source of energy, values a form of knowledge. Motives like to push us from the past, values try to draw us into the future. Many psychologists feel that these differences are purely verbal, that motive and value are two sides of the coin. Perhaps this is true. There is as much of philosophy as of science in these distinctions. Here, however, we shall try to keep separate our energies and our concepts.

Let us turn, therefore, to the question of how we acquire and use our conception of the values and cost of things.

Along with every name and every skill a child learns he also absorbs an evaluation. Along with "What is it?" goes "Is it dangerous? Do you like it? What good is it? How much does it cost?" These evaluations are different in every society, and a person who does not know them cannot function in a manner acceptable to the members of that society. In short, costs and values constitute a kind of personal and cultural knowledge that we have all acquired through many years of experience.

In our society there are several different realms of value corresponding to different social functions. Within any single realm it may be possible to develop a consistent system of values, but the demands from separate areas may conflict in ways that seem impossible to reconcile. Value systems can be classified as theoretical, economic, esthetic, religious, social, political; men can be classified according to the ways they assign priorities to one or another of these six realms.[3]

Why do we have to learn these value systems? What purpose do they serve? The answer springs directly from the fact that we are constantly being put into situations where we must express a preference, must make a choice between two or more courses of action. If we believe in social motives, we say that we choose the course of action that mobilizes the greatest amount of energy. If we believe in values, we say that we choose the course of action that we expect will lead to the most valuable outcome. But whatever the explanation, the need to choose is inescapable.

The act of choice is often embedded in great conflict and uncertainty. We like to smoke; we value our good health; we are told the two are incompatible. What do we do? We have learned that freedom of speech is good, but we are convinced that someone is using it for evil ends. What do we do? We treasure all the human values that marriage represents, yet we chafe under its contraints and responsibilities. What do we do?

In these and in thousands of similar conflicts, what we must do is decide which values are greater, which are more important. And to facilitate the constantly recurring processes of choice, we try to organize our values into a coherent, usually hierarchical, system. It is a great help, of course, if the values involved are conscious, if we can make them explicit and talk about them. But even that is not enough to resolve all our problems, because our decisions are usually made in a complicated and idiosyncratic context of past achievements and future ambitions.

Since these comparisons must be made so frequently, it would be a wonderful simplification if we could always use a single, simple quantity as our measure of value. Money is the most obvious candidate, and we use it wherever we can. Indeed, Americans are often accused of putting too much faith in dollars and cents, of imposing a public rate of exchange where private opinion and personal conviction should be sovereign. But even for Americans, money is not always a meaningful measure of value. Psychological value depends upon the situation we find ourselves in and the way we expect the situation to develop. It is not a price tag fixed once and for all, the same for every customer, every day. There are times when a man would offer his kingdom for a horse.

If one tries to analyze conflicts of value, one finds that the simplest involve a triadic system of relations.[4] There is the person himself and two other persons, things, or activities that are causing him trouble. If one represents the possible values as plus or minus, then the diagrams in Figure 41 help keep distinct the three simplest situations that lead to conflicts. Perhaps the easiest to sympathize with is a person who wants two things that are mutually exclusive; the child wants his dime but he wants the candy, too. A bit more special, perhaps, is a person who must choose between two things that are both unpleasant for him; the student who dislikes studying, but also dislikes failing is caught in this dilemma. In the third case, a person likes one thing and dislikes another, but cannot separate them; the hostess who wants to invite a friend to a dinner party, but cannot tolerate her friend's husband, knows what kind of conflicting evaluations must be settled in this situation.

In all these simple conflicts the person is faced with two alternatives. The child is comparing his situation when he has a dime and no candy with the alternative situation when he will have the candy but no dime. The student is weighing the advantages of leisurely failure against stressful (and uncertain) achievement. The hostess contemplates her dinner party with both Jane and John, or without either of them. The choice is between two situations, and the situations differ in only the two respects, X and Y.

Most choices, however, are a good deal more complicated. They can involve several alternatives that differ from one another in many aspects, where each aspect has several intermediate shades of value between all good and all bad, and where the choice may have consequences that will reverberate far into the unforeseeable future. Simply keeping track of the various possibilities and all their distinguishing features can be quite an intellectual feat; the additional task of deciding how to reconcile conflicting values may completely overload one's cognitive machinery. And on top of the cognitive problem, there may be important values that we refuse to formulate explicitly—that are banished into the limbo of unconsciousness.

Fig. 41. Types of conflict. A person faced with a choice between two mutually exclusive alternatives may have difficulty deciding which of two positive values to accept (*a* is "approach-approach" conflict), or which of two negative values to reject (*b* is "avoidance-avoidance" conflict). Or, if the two things are inseparable, he may find it difficult to decide whether the positive value of one overcomes the negative value of the other (*c* is "approach-avoidance" conflict).

It is scarcely surprising, therefore, that we adopt strategies for cutting through this complexity, for reducing the cognitive strain of making a rational decision. Probably the simplest strategy is to flip a coin; the reasoning here is that if you really cannot decide, the coin at least serves to get you back in action. A subtler variation on this scheme is to flip the coin and notice carefully whether you are relieved or disappointed by the way it falls; that bit of self-deception can sometimes help you to discover what you really want.

But random choices are too easy; they disregard all the relevant information. Less drastic is to disregard a part, but not all. A favorite strategy of this type is to ignore most of what one knows about the ways in which the alternatives differ from one another, to pretend that only one or two aspects of the situation are relevant. For example, when a group chooses a leader it should consider such values as power, ability, prestige, and the like; for each value the candidates may rank differently. But these several rankings are difficult to remember and think about. Instead of weighing Abel's skill against Baker's influence against our personal friendship for Charlie, we lump these different value scales into a single figure of merit that covers everything. Instead of deciding which candidate would be the best leader in given situations, we convince ourselves that the one we favor is the best for every conceivable situation. This phenomenon has been called the *halo effect;* because we know that a person is good in one important aspect, we put a halo of goodness over his other aspects as well.[5] It makes the world a great deal simpler when the good guys are always smart, honest, beautiful, and brave, while the bad guys are always stupid, crooked, ugly cowards.

Out of thousands of inner battles we try to evolve a workable hierarchy of our own. Repeatedly, day after day, we face conflicts and make decisions that force us to search for rules, for strategies, for a structure that will reduce the complexity and ease our burden of decision. Little wonder, therefore, that we prefer a single, simple ordering. We may even come to feel that there is a kind of inconsistency in multiple orderings, that all values *ought* to be measurable with a single yardstick.

The urge toward greater consistency among our various scales of value can itself assume the energizing properties of a social motive. When we find ourselves being inconsistent, it usually annoys us and we are likely to search for ways to eliminate the source of our inconsistency. Indeed, some psychologists have suggested that an effort toward consistency plays much the same role in our cognitive life that homeostasis plays in our biological drives.[6]

When a person feels himself caught in an evaluative inconsistency, there are usually several avenues of escape open to him. He can revise his evaluation of one or the other objects involved. He can modify or deny the incompatibility or the inseparability of the two objects. He can withdraw entirely, or he can bring to bear additional factors that enrich or redefine the objects involved. Exactly what he will do in any particular situation cannot be predicted without an exact knowledge of his particular circumstances.

Consider the following situation: There is an object that you want, but you must work hard to earn it. You decide the cost is justified, and you go ahead. So far you have faced a conflict squarely and have resolved it reasonably. However, when you finally attain the thing you wanted, you discover that you were wrong. It is not valuable after all. Your effort has been wasted. Now you are faced with this inconsistency: The object is worthless, but you worked hard to get it. What do you do?

In this situation most people persuade themselves that the object really is valuable. Consider the alternatives. It is too late, of course, to separate the two conflicting aspects: to stop working for the object, or to try to redefine or withdraw from the situation. All that is over and done. The only consistent escape left is to overvalue your goal or to undervalue your work. To undervalue your work may have extended consequences for everything else you do; the possibility is too grim to face, hence you end up overvaluing the object. Otherwise said, when you find that your scale of values for labor and your scale of values for a commodity are badly out of line, you try to bring them into agreement so as to be consistent, to profit from the cognitive simplification that a single ordering implies.

What you should do, if you can, is to admit that you wasted your time, and face the inconsistent values squarely. If you don't, if you take the easier way of revising your values to make what you have done seem consistent and reasonable, you will increase your chances of making exactly the same mistake again on another occasion. A person who cannot cut his losses and get out may soon find himself totally unable to profit from experience; he will come to love the worthless things for which he has suffered.[7] But facing one's conflicts squarely is usually easier to say than to do.

Sometimes people acquire values so deeply at odds with everything else they believe that no simple resolution of their conflict seems possible. In that case they may actually deny their disturbing values, may refuse to formulate them explicitly as part of their conscious picture of themselves. It was Freud who explored the depths of our capacity to deceive ourselves about what we value and what we fear. When these unconscious systems become involved, a whole new dimension of complexity is added to our problem.

Consider an example. Suppose you are told that a certain man is a trained athlete, that he has won prizes in several sports, and that he places the highest value on physical fitness and stamina. Under most conditions you would probably assume he was a thoroughly masculine type of person. But suppose you ask further and discover that he is thirty-five years old, without heterosexual experience, living with his mother, and sponsoring boys' clubs. Then the very same athletic values may take on exactly the opposite appearance; you may begin to wonder whether the man has a homosexual component, strong but latent, in his personality. You may begin to suspect that his interest in athletics is what Freud called reaction formation: perhaps the athletic activity conceals, yet simultaneously indulges, some deeply disturbing impulses he does not dare to admit consciously. If you are correct, the athlete has a conflict that he cannot face squarely. His tragedy is too large to play on the same mental stage he uses for his ordinary decisions. A reconstruction project of considerable magnitude would be required before he could even recognize, much less resolve his dilemma.

In short, it is not always easy to discover what you want, or to face what you discover. Only under the best possible conditions can you hope to resolve all claims in a reasonable and consistent way. Even if all your values can be stated explicitly, and even if you limit your attention to one decision at a time, the task is still formidable. But add the inescapable fact that each choice interacts with others now and in the future, that what you do presently determines the possibilities open to you later, and even the simplest decision will be seen to involve contingencies far too fine to contemplate. Who is wise enough to know what will be best for him in the long run? We can hope for little more than rude and abstract generalizations.

If we decide upon a particular course of action, it may be necessary to pursue it for long stretches of time—for days, months, even years. Some few decisions dedicate us to a particular path throughout an entire lifetime. Sticking to a long, elaborate program of activity is something we human beings can do—not as well as we would like perhaps, but far better than any other living organism. We manage it principally by using linguistic symbols to control our behavior, by constructing elaborate verbal plans that we remember and use to guide successive steps along the way.[8]

That is not to say that man is the only planful animal. Anyone who has worked around monkeys or apes has observed them constructing and executing simple plans. The chimpanzee that hears a visitor approaching, and dashes quickly to the drinking fountain to fill its mouth with water, then runs back to its regular position where it waits patiently for an unsuspecting target to come within range—this chimp has conceived and carried out a plan just as surely as any human bureaucrat ever did. Even in lower animals there seem to be plans, although they are usually rather inflexible and are probably better regarded as instincts. Organisms that live entirely in the present, uninfluenced by the past and unprepared for the future, are low on the evolutionary scale.

Many animals can follow simple plans, but man has carried a planfulness to its most extreme form. Language is a critical element in this development, but language is not the sole reason for man's superiority.

When the gap between actuality and desirability grows so large that no simple reflex can repair it, we are forced to break up our task into a sequence of subtasks. In learning to perform such analysis man has been particularly favored, oddly enough, by his possession of an opposable thumb. The human hand is often praised as a marvelous tool and credited for much of man's success as an evolutionary experiment. Our ability to hold an object in front of our wonderful simian eyes, to carry things with us, to feed ourselves, to grasp tools —the significance of these skills for the evolution of modern man is by now a familiar story. But the development of the hand also had great psychological significance. The hand is our basic tool. As a tool, it intervenes between the man and his task. Instead of moving directly to the desired object, he reaches out, grasps, and hauls in; a series of steps is substituted for the immediate response. The way we us our hands introduces a sequential character into our behavior. In order to exploit this marvelous new tool, the human brain came under selective evolutionary pressure to develop new ways to organize the sequential aspects of behavior. Here, then, was the beginning of our unique ability to analyze problems and to coordinate long sequences of actions, to subject ourselves to the guiding influence of long-term plans.

Hands: Chimpanzee and human

Most plans are hierarchically organized. We hold some image of the state we hope to achieve. By comparing this image with perceived reality we notice the major discrepancies, we analyze our task into several main parts, and we decide on an order for doing them. We then begin to execute the first part of our plan; other parts are relegated to the status of intentions. But each subpart in turn is usually too complex for a simple reflex; again we must analyze and postpone some parts while we start to work on others. Thus it sometimes happens that we find ourselves working at unpleasant tasks, doing things we dislike or disapprove of, because they fit into a larger, hierarchically organized plan whose eventual value will, we assume, justify all our temporary discomforts. It is this ability to postpone gratification that distinguishes rational from sensory hedonism, that justifies Freud's reality principle as a supplement to his pleasure principle. Our willingness to renounce the pleasures of the moment and to submit to the tyranny of the future is one of the best measures of our humanity.

The capacity to postpone rewards has been studied in some detail. In rats, for example, delays longer than a few seconds considerably reduce the effectiveness of the reward to reinforce the animal's behavior.[9] In children, the willingness to reject a small reward now on the promise of a larger reward later is known to develop with age; children are more likely to wait for a larger reward when parents are present than when they are absent; children who are socially responsible and reliable are more likely to postpone their rewards than are juvenile delinquents.[10] The acceptance of delayed gratification can also be studied by survey research;[11] many people plan far in advance for their large purchases—for houses, college education for their children, life insurance, cars, even for major appliances. Their plans and attitudes are often a more reliable indicator of future consumer buying than are such purely economic indicators as disposable personal income or savings.

There can be little doubt, therefore, of the psychological validity and importance of our expectations and the plans whereby we hope to achieve them, but they are so heterogeneous that only the most general and obvious comments can be made about them.

Suppose, for example, that we ask how much detail people include in their plans. There can be no universal answer, for this is one important way in which people differ. But one can point to variables that are probably involved. The amount of detail included in a plan will depend upon the importance of success; upon the amount of time available; upon the skill and competence of the person doing the planning. The first two are obvious enough, but the third merits further discussion.

There is little need to plan in detail an activity that you know you are competent to perform, that you have successfully performed many times before, that no longer holds any power to surprise you. If you are going to visit a friend, you need not decide in advance where to place your feet each step along the way. As one gets into more and more detail, the need for explicit planning declines correspondingly. Our most deliberate plans are constructed in terms of strategy, not tactics; in terms of molar acts, not molecular responses. One goes just far enough in elaborating a plan to reassure himself that he is competent to perform each subpart. Thus a person with considerable experience and competence in a particular area will not need to plan as carefully or in as much detail as would a novice. The old hand knows what he can do and how the parts must fit together; all of that must be painstakingly explored by the beginner.

A major component of our plans, therefore, must be our conception of our own competencies. As usual, the simplest example is an economic one. When we plan to buy something, the amount of money at our disposal sets a very clear, unambiguous limit on our ability to obtain the thing we want. Thus money serves as a kind of generalized competence, since it enables us to purchase the abilities of others and incorporate their extended competence into our own plans. People save money, often with no specific or immediate goal in view, but simply for a rainy day, for an emergency, for their old age, for any of a dozen vague reasons; but basically because it increases their potential competence to execute any of a variety of plans that they may someday formulate.

For most people there is a special kind of satisfaction and security associated with competence; in the absence of any very specific aim, they will work simply to increase their general level of skill and information. Reading, play, talking, going to school, traveling, hobbies, curiosity in general, all can contribute directly or indirectly to greater competence.

Professor R. W. White, the clinical psychologist, has referred to this urge for greater competence—the urge to be effective—as effectance motivation. He writes:

Of all living creatures, it is man who takes the longest strides toward autonomy. This is not because of any unusual tendency toward bodily expansion at the expense of the environment. It is rather that man, with his mobile hands and abundantly developed brain, attains an extremely high level of competence in his transactions with his surroundings. The building of houses, roads and bridges, the making of tools and instruments, the domestication of plants and animals, all qualify as planful changes made in the environment so that it comes more or less under control and serves our purposes rather than intruding upon them. We meet the fluctuations of outdoor temperature, for example, not only with our bodily homeostatic mechanisms, which alone would be painfully unequal to the task, but also with clothing, buildings, controlled fires, and such complicated devices as self-regulating central heating and air conditioning. Man as a species has developed a tremendous power of bringing the environment into his service, and each individual member of the species must attain what is really quite an impressive level of competence if he is to take part in the life around him.[12]

White's description emphasizes how very important the development of competence is for young children. He does not mean that a child at play is grimly storing up skills for the rainy days ahead; the child plays, masters, and enjoys the efficacy that mastery brings. An organism that depends as heavily as we do upon flexibility and adaptability needs to be born with the kind of hunger for competence that White describes.

But a teacher is all too prone to exaggerate the importance of competence. Room for individual differences in these matters is enormous. A feeling of effectiveness can be valuable and rewarding, but it is more valuable to some than to others. And it is only one aspect of the vast and intricate structure we blandly call human nature. In an adult the child's urge for competence can become a need for achievement, for power, for security; it may even atrophy and disappear.

If there is one thing above all else we should learn from a study of human values, it is to respect their diversity. It is essential to leave one's ideas open to the great variety of possible motivations, to the endless subtle ways that people can project their past into a vision of the future. No single food delights every palate, no single slogan stirs every imagination, no single key unlocks every heart. The African does not share your dreams—and neither does your neighbor next door.

———◆◆———

CHAPTER XVIII

ALFRED BINET, PSYCHOLOGIST

During the early years of the French Revolution a remarkable man named Philippe Pinel became chief physician at a Paris hospital filled with madmen. As a beginning Pinel proposed to take off their chains. When the President of the Commune heard this reckless proposal he came in person to reassure himself. The lunatics greeted him with shouts, curses, and the clanking of chains.

"Citizen," he shouted to Pinel above the din, "are you mad yourself that you would unchain such beasts?"

"I am convinced," said Pinel, "that these mentally ill are intractable only because they are deprived of fresh air and their liberty."[1]

It speaks volumes for Gallic intelligence that Pinel was allowed to conduct his experiment. For the first time the insane were treated, not as criminals, not as if they were possessed by demons, but with the restraint and kindness that sickness requires. Pinel's reforms turned a madhouse into a mental hospital and laid new foundations for the psychiatry of the future.

If insanity is a sickness, it would seem to be a sickness of the brain. In order to cure it, therefore, one must understand how the brain works. This line of reasoning, as old as Hippocrates, but especially appealing to positivistic thinkers in the nineteenth century, led to many important discoveries about the psychological effects of organic injuries and diseases in the nervous system. Psychiatrists who worked in this tradition found their major ally was the neurologist, and their favorite theories of insanity were theories of neural damage.

In spite of noteworthy successes, however, not all mental disorders could be traced directly to organic causes. The difficulties with a purely organic theory first became obvious, not in the study of psychosis, but in the study of neurosis. (As a rough and ready rule: If cognitive disorders predominate, it is usually psychosis; if emotional disorders predominate, it is usually neurosis; if moral disorders predominate, it is usually psychopathy.)

Once again a Frenchman led the way. The particular kind of neurosis that was to prove so very instructive was called *hysteria*. A patient with hysterical symptoms seems to have a great and senseless variety of bodily ailments. Parts of his body may be paralyzed so that he cannot move them or cannot feel anything in them, his vision and hearing may be impaired, his memory may be faulty, and the like. Hysteria was once considered a woman's disease, but this theory was discredited when the neurologist Jean Martin Charcot discovered male patients suffering from all the classical symptoms. For many years Charcot shared with his fellow neurologists the assumption that hysteria was a disease of the nervous system. There seemed little reason to doubt it—all the symptoms appeared to be organic in nature.

But then the neurologists learned about hypnosis. Some of Charcot's assistants at the famous neurological clinic he had created at the Salpêtrière in Paris became interested in hypnotism; they began to try it on one another and on the patients. They discovered that they could produce all the symptoms of hysteria in a normal person and then could cure him instantaneously, first by hypnotizing him and telling him he could not move, or could not feel, or could not see, and so on, then by awakening him from the hypnotic state. Even the great Charcot was unable to tell the difference between simulated, hypnotic symptoms and true, hysterical symptoms.

The possibility of psychological involvement in these apparently organic ailments put the whole problem of hysteria in a new light. Charcot began to examine hysterical symptoms in great detail; he soon discovered convincing evidence that they are not due to peripheral organic injury. For example, a neurologist knows from his study of anatomy which parts of the body are served by which nerves. In particular, he knows which areas of the skin will become insensitive if a particular nerve branch is damaged. When a patient complains that he cannot feel anything in his hand, a neurologist can usually diagnose which nerve must have been damaged, by carefully mapping out the insensitive area. If the area of anesthesia does not make anatomical sense—if it follows the pattern of a glove, say, rather than the true pattern of the nerve endings in the skin—the complaint cannot be attributed to organic damage to the peripheral nerves in the arm. Charcot discovered that hysterical symptoms usually made this kind of neurological nonsense, and that the same nonsense could be produced by hypnosis. In certain cases, apparently, it was even possible to relieve hysterical symptoms by hypnotizing the patient and telling him his symptom would vanish. The older view that mental illness is caused by damage to the nervous system clearly needed to be revised to include psychological causes. How that revision was to be phrased, however, remained obscure.

Pierre Janet, a student of Charcot, saw clearly that the emphasis should be shifted from the hysterical patient's symptoms to his state of mind. After observing many hysterical patients Janet concluded that they suffered from mental dissociation. An emotional system of ideas becomes isolated from the rest of his mental life and takes control of part of his body or part of his memory. These insulated subsystems cannot be controlled voluntarily by the patient. Today it seems obvious that Janet's descriptions of hysterical patients moved the problem of accounting for this neurosis from neurology into psychology. But Janet, paralyzed by the positivistic spirit of nineteenth-century medicine, hesitated to give a frankly psychological explanation. Perhaps, he thought, hysterics have an hereditary inability to integrate their experience. He saw the emotional struggles and conflicts that his patients were going through and he described the dissociation that existed in their mental life, but he could not accept the conflicts as the *cause* of the dissociation. That step was left for another student of Charcot—Sigmund Freud.

In spite of their reluctance to accept a purely psychological explanation of mental disorders, Charcot and Janet created in Paris an environment where psychogenic and somatogenic theories could compete, where the precise measurements of the laboratory and the rough-and-ready methods of the clinic could be used side by side. It was in this environment that Alfred Binet learned his psychology and adopted the catholic attitude that he carried into all of his later research. This proved to be perfect preparation for the work he was to perform.

Alfred Binet was born in Nice in 1857.[2] His mother, a talented painter, took him to Paris while he was still a boy; there he received his education at the center of French cultural and intellectual life. After taking his baccalaureate degree from the Lycée Saint-Louis he embarked upon the study of law. He enjoyed life as a law student and often talked about it in later years, but he discovered that his interest in law was only marginal. Instead of devoting himself single-mindedly to his law books, he found himself being pulled in several different directions at once. Paris was then as now an enormously stimulating place for a young intellectual, and Binet's energy could scarcely be contained by any single field of study. In particular, he could not suppress his interest in the natural sciences and especially in medicine. His fascination with medicine was a family affair—his father and his grandfather were both physicians.

Binet was never socially ambitious, but he did form many friendships with fellow students and collaborators, and much of his later research was published with coauthors. Among his friends at the Lycée was Babinski, later to become a famous neurologist; it was probably Babinski who introduced Binet to Charles Féré, an enthusiastic disciple of Charcot. Féré and Binet began to collaborate actively in research on abnormal psychology and hypnotism at Charcot's clinic in the Salpêtrière. And at the same time he was absorbing the medical psychology of Charcot's clinic, Binet was also studying under the direction of his father-in-law, the histologist Balbiani, for his degree in science from the Sorbonne. It is characteristic of Binet's omnivorous intellectual appetite that in 1878, the same year he received his license as a lawyer, he published a scientific article on the psychic life of microorganisms.

During these years Binet's interests shifted more and more toward psychological problems. The shift was stimulated principally by his work with Féré in Charcot's clinic, but his newly awakened curiosity was not confined solely to the psychological problems of the clinical practitioner. He began to devour the British empiricist philosophers. His special interest was in the process of association and, like all of

Binet's interests, it was quickly reflected in print. As early as 1880 he published a short paper on the fusion of images, a subject he was led to directly by reading about the association of ideas.

Although Binet is remembered today principally for his way of testing the intelligence of children, his contributions to psychology were much broader than that. It is the case of a mountain dwarfing some very respectable hills nearby. Binet's first book, *The Psychology of Reasoning* (1886), had as its subtitle, *Experimental Studies of Hypnotism;* it was the result of combining British associationism with French hypnotism. His knowledge of hypnotism derived from the work with Féré; his knowledge of associationism came from reading, not the German Wilhelm Wundt, but the British John Stuart Mill. Binet had no formal instructor in psychology, no one to teach him either the old, philosophical version or the new, experimental kind. What he knew of it he picked up by reading a few books: Ribot, Taine, Hamilton, and others, especially Mill. His training as an experimental investigator was obtained through his studies in biology and medicine, and through his experience in the neurological clinic. He admired British psychology and in later years was probably nearer to Galton than to Charcot in his sympathies. But most of his psychological ideas came from his own thinking and his own observations, a fact which gave his work a freshness and originality that were characteristically his own. Of all his work his first book was the most heavily dependent upon traditional views. As he grew older he came to rely more and more upon his own intuition and experience.

In 1887, with Féré as coauthor, he published his second book, *Animal Magnetism. On Double Consciousness* appeared in an English edition in 1889; and *Personality Deviations,* his fourth book in six years, in 1892. All were written from a clinical, psychiatric view of psychology, but they indicate a period of transition in Binet's life, when his interests were moving from the abnormal to the normal. In spite of the speed with which they appeared, these books were both original and readable. Binet had enormous energy for hard work and a capacity to write about it rapidly in clear and flowing prose. Work cost him no effort. "I work quite naturally," he once said, "as a hen lays eggs."

In the summer of 1892 Binet was on his way to a little beach at Saint-Valery, where he spent his vacations with his family, when he happened to meet the physiologist H. Beaunis on the platform of the railroad station at Rouen. Beaunis was director of the laboratory of physiological psychology that had been created at the Sorbonne in 1889. The two men fell into a friendly argument about hypnosis and in the course of it Binet asked if he might do some work in the laboratory. Beaunis was glad to have this energetic young man as a collaborator, so a decision was made that fixed the future direction of Binet's career. He joined the four-room laboratory first as Beaunis's assistant, then became associate director and finally director when Beaunis retired in 1894. The directorship carried no specific responsibilities and, since he had an independent income, it left him completely free to pursue his own research.

Alfred Binet

The year 1894 was eventful for Binet. Not only did he become director of a laboratory. He also completed his doctorate in science with a thesis on the nervous system of insects. He published two more books: *The Psychology of Great Calculators and Chess Players,* a minor work, with Henneguy, and *Introduction to Experimental Psychology,* which reviewed both the standard methods of measuring sensation, reaction time, and memory, and the newer methods that used questionnaires. This latter part of the *Introduction* anticipated the methods which he was soon to use so effectively in his studies of children. It was in 1894 also that he founded his own journal, *L'Année Psychologique.*

Binet remained the editor and a major contributor to *L'Année* through fourteen volumes until his death in 1911. During those years he wrote a large book on *Suggestibility* (1900) which summarized his work on hypnosis, contributed *The Soul and the Body* (1906) to a traditional philosophical debate, and averaged about ten articles a year in his own and other journals.

Binet worked frequently with collaborators—although his dominating energy frequently antagonized them—but he was not a professor and he did no teaching. Students would have got in his way. He seldom appeared in public, being too busy with research and writing. His only deviation from complete loyalty to psychology seems to have been his tendency to write plays that were successfully produced in Paris. But even his plays usually had a psychological theme.

Binet performed experiments on adult subjects, but he preferred to work with children. There is one advantage (along with many disadvantages) in using the schoolroom for psychological experiments: young subjects are available in large numbers and are accustomed to following instructions. A long series of studies of children during the 1890's provided the necessary background for Binet's most famous work—the Binet-Simon scale for measuring the intelligence of school children.

A mark of a good idea is that it makes one forget how confusing things were before it was invented. Today the Binet-Simon scale seems such a simple and obvious way to measure intelligence that it is hard to believe how many brilliant men were unable to think of it. Francis Galton, for example, wanted to measure intelligence. He developed a collection of tests, and he contributed the statistical tools necessary to analyze the results. But Galton's tests were aimed at psychological processes fashionable in his day. He measured visual and auditory acuity and observed that, "The more perceptive the senses are of differences, the larger is the field upon which our judgment and intelligence can act."[3] It was a good idea, but it didn't work.

James McKeen Cattell was similarly hobbled by the empiricist tradition in the psychology of his day. Cattell, student of Wundt and friend of Galton, was one of the brightest lights in American psychology at the turn of the century. Yet look at the list of tests he proposed to measure intelligence:[4]

1. *Dynamometer Pressure.* How tightly can the hand squeeze?

2. *Rate of Movement.* How quickly can the hand be moved through a distance of 50 cm.?

3. *Sensation-areas.* How far apart must two points be on the skin to be recognized as two rather than one?

4. *Pressure Causing Pain.* How much pressure on the forehead is necessary to cause pain?

5. *Least Noticeable Difference in Weight.* How large must the difference be between two weights before it is reliably detected?

6. *Reaction-time for Sound.* How quickly can the hand be moved at the onset of an auditory signal?

7. *Time for Naming Colors.* How long does it take to name a strip of ten colored papers?

8. *Bisection of a 50-cm. Line.* How accurately can one point to the center of an ebony rule?

9. *Judgment of 10-sec. Time.* How accurately can an interval of 10 seconds be judged?

10. *Number of Letters Remembered on Once Hearing.* How many letters, ordered at random, can be repeated exactly after one presentation?

Cattell described these tests as beginning with bodily measures, then proceeding through psychophysical to mental measures. If indeed there is any continuum of measurements running from bodily to mental, Galton and Cattell explored only the bodily end of it. Today we know that of all Cattell's tests only the last, measurement of memory span, provides any indication of a person's intelligence, and even this measurement is of limited value.

The Frenchmen Binet, Henri, and Simon took up where Galton, Cattell, and others had left off. They pushed boldly along the imaginary continuum toward the higher mental processes, into measures of memory, imagination, attention, comprehension; it was at that end of the continuum that they began to get results. But it took someone with clinical attitudes to attempt such measures; the laboratory scientists knew intuitively that the higher mental processes were too complicated to permit of valid measurement.

In a series of articles in *L'Année Psychologique* from 1894 to 1898 Binet and his assistant Victor Henri described their attempts to measure higher mental processes in children and adults. They were quite clear that sensory and motor measurements were easier to make and less variable when repeated, but, for all their virtues, such tests did not seem to distinguish sufficiently among different people. Binet wanted to measure mental functions that different people performed in different ways, with different degrees of skill. Since memory is an important component of intelligence, everyone agreed that it should be included. But Binet thought it might be possible to make similar measurements on many other psychological functions. For example, why not measure the vividness of imagery, or the kind of imagery that a person has? Why not test his attention, both its scope and its duration? Why not test comprehension of sentences, or synonyms, or ask the person to find logical errors in a text? Many tests of suggestibility were available from the studies of hypnosis; could suggestibility be related to intelligence? Even esthetic judgments could be obtained and scored against the esthetic judgments of experts. Why not ask people to make moral judgments, or judge emotions from pictures of facial expression? Why not study their will by asking them to withstand pain or fatigue? Why not measure the speed with which they could acquire a motor skill?

Why not, indeed? Who could say that all those higher mental functions were not involved in intelligence? No one had ever measured those functions in a large number of different people in order to relate the results to intelligence. The reasons for this neglect were unclear except for the fact that the inquiry did not seem tidy. In the minds of such academic psychologists as Wundt, psychology should begin with the simplest measures of the simplest mental elements. Wundt flatly denied that psychology could study thinking. Even those who were more optimistic felt that psychology could build up toward these more complicated kinds of measures only slowly. Psychology wasn't ready to jump into the middle of the mind without any notion of what might be encountered.

Such a jump is what one might expect from a psychologist trained in the clinic. Because no two patients ever suffer from exactly the same complaints, a clinician is seldom able to repeat his observations precisely; if he is not to lose his way, he must inure himself to the complexities and variabilities that his patients exhibit, and learn to discover order in the most untidy and abnormal kinds of behavior. But the complexities a clinician must learn to live with frequently serve only to convince experimentalists that clinical data are worse than useless.

In 1904 the Minister of Public Instruction in Paris assembled a commission to consider the problem of subnormal children in the public schools. If the children who were likely to fail could be placed in special schools, they might be helped; Binet, whose studies of child psychology were well known, was a member of the commission. As early as 1894 he had begun to try his tests on school children; in

1903 he had reported an intensive study of the intellectual development of his own two daughters.

Binet quickly became disturbed because the discussions of the commission were so vague that everything they tried to do seemed confused and pointless. He took it upon himself, therefore, to provide clear definitions for the terms that were being used to describe subnormal children. He devoted his research thereafter to the problem of finding a scientific basis for a medical classification that would be more useful to educators. His principal collaborator in this attempt was Dr. Simon, a young physician in an asylum for backward children. From 1905 until Binet's death in 1911 at least twenty-eight articles and one book were written by Binet and Simon together.[5]

In 1905, primarily to facilitate the work of the commission, Binet and Simon published their first results. They used a large battery of different mental tests, some hard, some easy. Binet collected tests from everywhere, and his own mind bubbled over with ideas for others. To discover which tests were useful, he and Simon spent endless hours in the schools with the children, watching, asking, testing, recording. Each proposed test had to be given to a large number of children. If a test did not distinguish the brighter from the duller, or the older from the younger, it was abandoned. Tests that worked were retained, even though they often failed to conform with the theoretical principles Binet and Henri had announced ten years earlier. The memory tests worked. And the tests of comprehension worked—comprehension of words, of statements, of concepts, of pictures. Binet did not retain the tests on the basis of a theory; he watched the children and let their behavior decide which tests were good and which were irrelevant. The 1905 version of the "Metrical Scale of Intelligence" simply arranged all the tests that Binet had selected in an order of increasing difficulty. Each child passed as many tests as he could until they became too difficult for him. How far the child got down the list of tests could then be compared with how far other children of the same age usually got.

In 1908 a revised version was published. The tests were grouped according to the age at which 50 to 75 per cent of a large sample of children passed them, from age three up to age thirteen. In 1911, the year of Binet's death, there was still another revision that extended the age up to fifteen years.

According to the 1911 scale an average three-year-old French child should pass half of these tests: he should be able to point to his nose, eyes, and mouth; repeat two digits; enumerate objects in a picture; give his family name; and repeat a sentence of six syllables. By age seven the child should pass half of these tests: be able to show his right hand and left ear; describe a picture; execute three commands given simultaneously; count the value of six sous, three of which are double; and name four cardinal colors. By fifteen the youngster should be able to repeat seven digits; find three rhymes for a given word in one minute; repeat a sentence of twenty-six syllables; interpret pictures; and interpret given facts.

These should give the flavor of Binet's tests to anyone who (though it is hard to imagine how) might have been sheltered from them heretofore. The age group of tests that a child could pass half the time defined his mental age, regardless of what his chronological age might be.

Binet used as the measure of retardation simply the difference between the child's mental age and chronological age. Thus a child who was six years old but passed only the items on the four-year age group would have a mental age of four, and so would be retarded two years in mental development. Binet regarded two years as a serious deficiency. Other psychologists decided later that it was better to use the ratio, rather than the difference between the two ages. Mental age divided by chronological age gives a mental quotient. If the two ages are the same, then the child is average for his age and the quotient is unity. If the child is retarded, the mental is less than the chronological age, and the quotient is less than unity. If he is advanced, the quotient will be greater than unity. When this quotient is multiplied by 100, the result is usually referred to as the intelligence quotient, or IQ. The various confusing arguments about whether the IQ is constant throughout life, or whether it can be raised or lowered with special circumstances, came later and cannot be blamed on Binet. His contribution was a simple, reliable method for determining a child's mental age.

One of Binet's advantages in solving this problem may have been that, although he read English fluently, he did not know a word of German. Some such insulation from Fechner, Helmholtz, and Wundt was probably necessary. If he had known more about what happened east of the Rhine, he might have been more willing to stop short with the study of sensations and reaction times. Fortunately, he was not overly concerned with scientific purity; he had a practical problem he urgently wanted to solve, and he did whatever seemed necessary to solve it. The solution did not come through an elegant experiment conceived in an armchair and conducted in a laboratory. It came through tedious hours spent testing children in the schools of Paris.

Instead of experiments, Binet conducted interviews—in the best tradition of the clinical interview. "For the all-round clinical appraisal of a subject's intellectual level," wrote Lewis M. Terman many years later, "the Binet type of scale has no serious rival. It is not merely an intelligence test; it is a method of standardized interview which is highly interesting to the subject and calls forth his natural responses to an extraordinary variety of situations."[6]

Within ten years of Binet's death in 1911, translations and revisions of the Binet-Simon scale were in use all over the world. The immediate, international enthusiasm demonstrated how great the need for such a measuring device had been. Oddly enough, the scale gained little fame in France. In his old age Simon recalled[7] that it was not until the early 1920's that a French social worker, having visited clinics in the United States, found the Binet-Simon scale frequently mentioned there. On her return to France the social worker was instrumental in reintroducing the test to the land of its birth. During World War II the test became very fashionable in France but under the names of Terman and Merrill, the Americans who revised it for use in the United States!

Binet was not a great man. He was a competent, hard-working psychologist whose career ended abruptly when he was still in his prime and still had much left to do. He trained no students, he wrote no immortal books, and his memory has been little honored by his countrymen. But even though he was not great, he was important—made important by subsequent events.

Over the years the demand for mental tests has steadily grown. The individual differences explored by psychological testing now include innumerable varieties, and the statistical methods of analyzing test data have grown in power and sophistication. The vein that Binet opened up is still being mined today—and still yields ore of the highest grade.

CHAPTER XIX

---—◆•◆—---

THE MIND OF A CHILD

Imagine that you are given a number, somewhere between 0 and 1000, and are told that it represents a person's age in months. How much would you know about the person?

If the number is somewhere in the middle of the range—between 200 and 800, say—it would not tell you very much. Since you do not know the person's sex, education, native ability, or even the society in which he (she) lives, you could not form any clear picture of him (her). If the number gets large enough, of course, you have some feeling for the kind of constraints old age imposes. But you will extract the greatest amount of information from the number when it is small, and the smaller it gets the more accurate you can be.

Small numbers place the person in the time of life called his growth period, when successive phases unfold themselves in regular order. The predictable succession of changes in bodily size and structure, in motor skills, in mental competence and achievement, in social and emotional adjustment is generally familiar to everyone. For those who wish to know more—parents, say, who wonder if their child is developing properly, or educators trying to plan a school curriculum—many detailed facts have been collected and tabulated for ready reference, both in popular guides and in technical handbooks.[1]

A regular procession of structural changes is something we all take for granted. The emergence of motor skills is almost equally reliable.

294

And cognitive development is only slightly more variable. Hundreds of studies—beginning even before Alfred Binet's experiments in the schools of Paris—have demonstrated convincingly that mental growth also pursues an orderly course, that measurable skills appear at predictable ages, that deviations above or below the average are not accidental. Binet calibrated a whole battery of tests, to which many subsequent workers have added, so that today we can sample quite different aspects of the unfolding process of mental growth. With those tests it has become possible to measure the growth of the mind.

But there are still many problems that remain unsettled.

Take, for example, that hotly debated subject, the constancy of the intelligence quotient. Adherents of hereditary theories of mental ability like to think of the IQ as if it were printed indelibly on the chromosomes at the moment of conception. Empiricists, on the other hand, credit experience and education for all our mental accomplishments and recognize no other factors which might limit a child's IQ score. In the twentieth century this ancient argument has come to rest—or roost—on the question of whether or not an IQ score is indeed constant throughout life.

Consider what this constancy would imply. Suppose one thousand children of the same age are tested every year until they are adults. If the intelligence of every child is constant, their rank order from best to worst, from brightest to dullest, would never change—except, perhaps, for random errors inherent in the measuring instruments. The child who ranked 100 at the age of one year would still rank 100 at the age of 20 years.

When studies of this sort are actually done, however, it is found that the rank orderings can change markedly from year to year.[2] One child shows a sudden spurt in skill A while a second is developing skill B and a third seems to be standing still. In the first years of life the scores change considerably; after six or seven years they begin to settle down and our predictions get better and better.

It may be suggested therefore, that the IQ is variable at birth, but becomes more stable as we get older. It is not apparent whether this finding favors either side of the heredity-environment battle. Perhaps one inherits one's constant IQ the way a man inherits his beard—it doesn't appear until the age is right. Or perhaps one needs time to decide what IQ will be necessary in one's social environment.

Increasing stability of the IQ can be explained away by proponents of either theory. Nevertheless, it is fair to say that informed opinion in the United States is currently on the side of the environmentalist— if not completely, at least in spirit and emphasis. Within limits, Johnny can change his position in the rank ordering—although it becomes more and more difficult to do so as he grows older.

Psychologists who have puzzled over the instability of predictions based on the early years do not believe that it can be attributed to poor measurements—not entirely, anyhow. There is reason to think that even the most accurate tests during infancy have little power to predict adult intelligence.

Consider the following argument:[3] Suppose that mental growth is cumulative, so that the level a child attains by the age of nine is simply the sum of all he has achieved in each of his preceding years. If this assumption were reasonable, it would mean that our prediction from age nine to age ten would be very good, since nine-tenths of the basis for the new measurement would be the same as for the old and only one-tenth would be attributable to new growth or experience during the tenth year. And by the same argument, the prediction of the child's IQ score at age two on the basis of his score at age one would be based half on old achievements and half on novel achievements—hence the prediction would be less accurate. On a relative basis, therefore, more could happen to change the relative standings early in life than later on. Every baseball fan who has watched batting averages vary wildly during the early part of the season and then settle down as the players accumulated more turns at bat will understand this explanation of why the test scores should become more reliable as the children grow older.

For older children, at least, mental tests can give a valuable measure of mental age, one that can be usefully compared with chronological age. But there are still other problems we should recognize when we try to understand what an intelligence score means.

By combining all the individual tests in order to obtain a single number that represents a child's status, psychologists have encouraged uncritical people to imagine that mental growth is an undifferentiated process, to think that a child's mind grows like a potato. Even psychologists who should know better have been tempted to plot smooth curves of mental growth, forgetting that they were actually dealing with a composite of many separate curves for separate skills. The practical convenience of having a single number is, of course, too great to resist. But a scientist must look more closely.

As stated earlier, to measure a process is not necessarily to understand it. Mental tests may give a number—mental age—that is highly correlated with mental growth, but they do not contain within themselves any coherent explanation of that growth. One has to take the single number apart to see what it consists of. Why do certain skills emerge before others? Why are some tasks easy and others so difficult? What does a child actually do in the process of finding an answer to a test item? What manner of thing is the mind of a child that his abilities should multiply in this particular fashion? Binet's achievement cried out for support from a more comprehensive theory of mental growth.

A common assumption, already mentioned, is that mental growth is a cumulative affair, that new skills can be added steadily without modifying old skills in any significant way. An alternative assumption is that childhood is a series of abrupt transitions from one fairly stable stage to another which is equally stable but more advanced and (presumably) more complex. According to this view of development, the reason that early measures do not predict later measures of intelligence is that very different psychological processes are involved at different stages; a child might excel at one stage, yet be mediocre at another. These transitions supposedly have the character of sudden and radical reorganizations; they are not a simple summation of new and old. Different kinds of observations are relevant and necessary at different times in a child's life. The cumulative hypothesis is simpler, perhaps, but the hypothesis of distinct stages with critical transitions between them also has much to recommend it.

Undoubtedly the most dramatic illustration of a sudden transition is birth itself. The transition from the foetal stage to an independent and reactive stage of infancy may seem to be a sudden, mechanical process, but evidence indicates that the transition is neither brief nor simple. For months afterward constant stimulation and mothering are required in order to get an infant successfully through this transition.

The tragic effects of maternal neglect at this stage can be seen in very young babies who have lost their mothers. They commonly develop a regressive kind of reaction.[4] In the first stages of this reaction the orphaned infant may fall into a light stupor when given his bottle, so that strong stimulation is needed to keep the infant active and sucking. His muscles become flaccid and his skin begins to turn pale. As the condition gets more serious there may be vomiting and diarrhea, hiccups, and irregular breathing. Still later his skin may become gray and wrinkled. All the symptoms point to a regression by the baby to the prenatal mode of functioning, when breathing and circulation of the blood were the mother's responsibility. Poor breathing and poor circulation may interfere with the normal development of the nervous system, which in turn can have physiological and psychological consequences that persist throughout life. If nothing is done to prevent it, a baby may waste away and die, a fate that was once quite common in orphanages and hospitals. Today doctors know that the regression can be prevented by massage and stimulation, and by vigorously exciting the sucking reflex. The prescription they usually give is TLC—a daily dose of Tender Loving Care.

The transition from foetus to infant is assumed to be merely the first of a long series of passages that the child must negotiate. Students of personality development generally concentrate on the important transitions involved in weaning, toilet training, sex training —on all the little tragedies and comedies that are required in order to develop competence in managing the orifices of the body.[5] Certainly these are the crises most apparent to a mother and probably to the child himself. The way they are handled is believed to have significant influences upon the way the child's personality develops, although opinions are easier to find than proof.[6]

Cognitive transitions are less immediately apparent, but are equally important for the growth of a normal, intelligent, human being. By cognitive transitions are meant changes in the child's manner of knowing—knowing about himself and the world in which he lives. Their subtle consequences often go unnoticed by the parent; the child does not notice them because his new way of knowing destroys the old. But the changes occur, nonetheless.

An adult deals with his world easily, almost automatically, in terms of certain concepts or systems of concepts involving space, time, number, quantity, causality, motion, velocity, and so on. These provide a frame of reference for all his other thoughts. Certain philosophers have assumed that, because these concepts are so important, they must be given immediately to all minds by a kind of a priori intuition. The fact is, however, that the concepts are acquired rather slowly during childhood and pass through several more-or-less predictable stages before attaining the obviously correct form familiar to all intelligent adults. The development of these fundamental concepts has been studied with particular care and ingenuity by Jean Piaget, Professor of Psychology at the Universities of Geneva and of Paris, and by his students and associates.

If Piaget's observations are correct, even so simple an idea as that of an object—a relatively permanent, enduring thing that continues to exist regardless of whether you are looking at it—is one that must be slowly and patiently learned during the first two years of life. An adult considers space and substance to be very different things, but to an infant who has no concept of an object, this difference between space and substance is literally inconceivable.

Consider some of the necessary steps along the path from birth to the final development of an object concept.

What does a baby do when the perceptual image of an object disappears from view? This question is relevant from the first week of life. What does the baby do when the mother's breast escapes his lips? At first his response is undirected, but after the second week a nursling is able to find the nipple and differentiate it from other objects. Now we ask the following question: Can it be assumed that a baby recognizes the nipple or has any conception that the nipple just recovered at this instant is identical with the nipple that escaped a few seconds ago?

Or, to choose other examples: When mother's face disappears from view and then reappears, does baby recognize it as the same face? Where does a baby think the face goes when it disappears?

At first, of course, the baby cannot think about such matters at all, for he does not have the concepts available to think with. Nevertheless, it is possible, as Piaget has demonstrated, to infer something of the nature of the child's world from his behavior. As soon as the child is old enough to follow a moving image with his eyes, we can watch him search for vanished objects and thus learn at least a little about his conception of the things he is looking for.

Few objects are more interesting to a baby than his bottle. Piaget always had a cooperative collaborator when the object that appeared and disappeared in the various tests was a bottle of milk. "At six months and nineteen days," said Piaget of a child he had studied most carefully, "Laurent immediately began to cry from hunger and impatience on seeing his bottle (he was already whimpering, as he does quite regularly at mealtime). But at the very moment when I make the bottle disappear behind my hand or under the table—he follows me with his eyes—he stops crying. As soon as the object reappears, a new outburst of desire; then flat calm after it disappears. I repeat the experiment four more times; the result is constant until poor Laurent, beginning to think the joke bad, becomes violently angry."[7] At this age—around six months—when the bottle disappears from view, it ceases to exist.

A very young child seems to behave as if an object were merely a visual image that enters and leaves the field of view capriciously, appearing for no particular reason and disappearing into the void just as unpredictably as it came. A toy that falls from the child's hand vanishes instantly from the universe. But before the same child is six months old he will begin to coordinate his visual and tactual worlds. He begins to reach toward and grasp things in his visual field. Then a series of skills are learned in quick succession. This learning does not seem to require any biological satisfactions to reinforce it; the child seems to regard competence as its own reward. He learns to move his eyes slightly in advance of an object; hence a rapidly moving object that vanishes briefly and reappears is correctly followed. He begins to practice at making images enter or leave his visual field at will. He learns to reconstruct the whole object when only a part is visible. He learns to pull or push aside things that block his view of an object he is searching for. Each step represents a separate triumph of infantile persistence. But even at this stage the child does not yet seem to dissociate his own actions from the objects themselves.

By the time a child is nine or ten months old he will ordinarily have achieved a rather stable concept of an object. Human beings provide the child the best instances. But even at this late age it is possible to uncover surprising reactions if one looks carefully. For example, the child watches while a toy that he has often played with is put under a cloth. The situation is pictured at the top of Figure 42. After a little experience the child learns to pull the cloth aside and find the toy. But now the same toy is put under another

Fig. 42. A child sees a toy placed under a cloth and learns to find it there. When it is placed under a second cloth, he looks again under the first. (J. Piaget, The child's view of reality, *Scientific American,* March, 1957.)

coverlet at a slightly different place. The child is baffled, looks under the original cloth, then stops searching! As shown at the bottom of Figure 42, he does not look where he saw the object last, but where he found it before.

Piaget describes another example in the following passage:

> Gerard, at 13 months, knows how to walk, and is playing ball in a large room. He throws the ball, or rather lets it drop in front of him and, either on his feet or on all fours, hurries to pick it up. At a given moment the ball rolls under an armchair. Gerard sees it and, not without some difficulty, takes it out in order to resume the game. Then the ball rolls under a sofa at the other end of the room. Gerard has seen it pass under the fringe of the sofa; he bends down to recover it. But as the sofa is deeper than the armchair and the fringe does prevent a clear view, Gerard gives up after a moment; he gets up, crosses the room, goes right under the armchair and carefully explores the place where the ball was before.[8]

How should we account for such odd behavior? Should we shrug and say that children are naturally unpredictable?

Perhaps the simplest explanation would be to say that the child has learned an association between the object and the first place he recovered it. This object-place connection has been practiced and reinforced by success. According to this view, the connection between the object and a new location is much weaker, so it is quickly extinguished, and the child is left with the prior, but strong and irrational association. Indeed, such experiences are not confined to children. A man gets a necktie out of his closet, puts it where he can reach it; but when he is ready to put it on he goes back to the closet to look for it. We all do such foolish things every day. Perhaps the child has merely suffered a common lapse of memory.

But no.

According to Piaget, the difference is that a man is capable of remembering but has momentarily forgotten, whereas the child is incapable of remembering—he does not know he is dealing with a single object. For the child, ball-under-the-armchair is one thing and ball-under-the-sofa is another. Having lost the ball-under-the-sofa, he decides to play with the other ball instead. The association between object and place that the child has established is complete; he does not yet have a clear enough conception of an object to realize that the same ball might be associated with two different places. The child has not forgotten anything. Instead, he is remembering something different from what an adult would remember. In an adult, object-place associations are much more flexible than they are for the child; the same object can be recalled as being in any of several different places. Thus the child's apparently poor memory, and his deficient conception of physical objects are simply two different aspects of the same psychological process. The child has established the various appearances of the ball as forming a class of equivalent objects, but he has not yet thoroughly mastered the concept of a single, identical object.

Recognition that a variety of sensory images can be generated by an identical, individual, physical object is learned so young that we cannot remember how we did it or what life was like without the concept. We can try to imagine a preobjective state of consciousness by observing carefully what happens when, for example, we enter a new visual world through a telescope or under a microscope. But comparisons of this experience with a child's perceptual world can be little more than a suggestive fantasy.

The first two years of life are devoted to the acquisition of many perceptual-motor coordinations. Out of them the child develops a concept of permanent objects—objects existing in a spatial framework defined by his own bodily orientation.

Next the child is ready to develop symbols associated with these sensory-motor objects. As his language begins to develop, he is launched into a new domain of learning, into completely new ways of coping with his environment.

An average child is capable of imitating speech sounds and forming simple words during his second year of life, but not until he is about two years old does he seem capable of sustaining true symbolic processes. This ability can be observed in his play activities as well as in his vocalizations. For a very young child, play is merely a kind of exercise. But as he develops he becomes able to carry out actions that would be appropriate in a situation not actually experienced—for example, pretending to sleep, or pretending that the teddy bear is asleep. Such activities are a form of symbolic play. Once the child has achieved the symbolic processes necessary for enjoying this kind of play, he has developed all that is needed to begin using spoken noises to signify an (possibly but not necessarily) absent thing or situation.

It is at about this stage—when language is first beginning to play an important role—that most children develop a kind of willfullness. They begin to assert their own opinions and to make some of their own decisions. The development of volition and of language must be closely related, since voluntary actions are so often responses to verbal commands generated internally and subvocally. But talking to yourself about what you must do is a very complicated skill, one that children develop only slowly over several years.

It is possible to study the way in which words come to control behavior; Russian psychologists have found this especially interesting.

Imagine two different pictures. One shows a bright red circle on a pale yellow background, the other a bright green circle on a gray background. The child is told something like this: "When I show you the picture with the pale-yellow background, I want you to raise your *right* hand. When I show you the picture with the gray background, I want you to raise your *left* hand." This is a simple task and young children have little trouble performing it correctly.

Now notice what has been done with the verbal instructions. The child's attention has been directed to the part of the picture that is the least impressive, that has the least attention value. We tell him to ignore the strong red and green colors and to pay attention instead to the pale background colors. He may not learn the task exactly the way we described it, however. It is more natural to look at the bright colors. For a child to be able to follow the instructions, he must control his attention by the use of words, by internal commands.

It is easy to test the child and to see which way he has solved the problem. One merely reverses the circles and their backgrounds. If the red circle was at first on a pale yellow background, one now puts a red circle on a gray background and shows this new picture to the child. Will he respond to the bright red circle (which is the natural thing to do) or will he respond to the pale background (which is what we told him to do)? If the child raises his right hand, we know he was paying attention to the dominant red circle; if he raises his left hand, we know he was paying attention to the weaker background color.

Russian psychologists have found that children three years old do not follow the verbal command; they pay attention to the impressive color of the circle instead. At four years they seem confused, now doing one thing, now the other. Not until the child is five will a verbal command produce a stable reorganization of this perceptual field.

Experiments of this sort illustrate the fact that long after a child has mastered the basic skills needed for social communication there are still important changes going on in the way these linguistic skills modify and control other aspects of his cognitive life.

The reorganization of thought in terms of verbal symbols has a number of advantages in terms of easier communication, more abstract kinds of thinking, greater speed and efficiency in processing information, and so on. One of the most important advantages, however, is that after the psychological processes have been brought under the control of verbal symbols it becomes possible for the child to control himself with his own words. Eventually, the child can give himself the orders that he has heard so often from his parents—parental control can be internalized. Then he can begin to explore the realm of self-control, the realm of independent, voluntary behavior that is so important for psychological maturity.

By the time a child is four years old his skill with language will have progressed to a point where one can talk with him and ask indirect questions about his concepts. If the questions are artfully posed, surprising results may turn up. Consider the following example:

> Two small glasses, A and A_2, of identical shape and size, are each filled with an equal number of beads, and this equality is acknowledged by the child, who has filled the glasses himself, e.g., by placing a bead in A with one hand every time he places a bead in A_2 with the other hand. Next, A_2 is emptied into a differently shaped glass B, while A is left as a standard. Children of 4–5 years then conclude that the quantity of beads has changed, even though they are sure none has been removed or added. If the glass B is tall and thin they will say that there are "more beads than before" because "it is higher," or that there are fewer because "it is thinner," but they agree on the non-conservation of the whole.[9]

Children who give this response are following the maxim that seeing is believing, that the world is the way it appears to be. When the beads are poured into B there appear to be more of them; therefore, there are more of them!

Fig. 43. A child of five years agrees that beaker A and beaker A_2 contain the same amount of juice. He then pours the contents of A_2 into another beaker B of a different shape. When asked, he judges that A and B do not contain the same amount of juice. At seven years, however, the child knows that A must equal B.

If the same experiment is tried with a child seven or older, the question will surprise him. He may look around on the floor to see if any beads were spilled. Or he may think the experimenter is joking. Of course, he says, the two are the same. Pouring them from one glass to another does not create or destroy beads. The seven-year-old responds as would an adult.

Suppose, however, that we question him. Our (imaginary) conversation might sound like this:

"How do you know that they are the same?" we ask.

"Because I put the same number of beads in both glasses," he replies.

The four-year-old interrupts. "I knew *that*," he says.

We ask the seven-year-old, "Is that the only reason you said they were equal?"

"You didn't spill any, did you?"

"No," we admit, "we didn't spill any."

We turn to the younger child. "Did you know that we didn't spill any?" we ask him.

"Sure, I knew that."

We press the seven-year-old again. "Is that the only way you knew?"

He considers a moment. "Well . . . if you pour them back into the first glass again, it will come to the same level."

We turn again to the younger child. "Did you know that?" we ask.

"Yes," he replies, "I knew that."

What facts, what evidence, what new data does the older child have to guide him so easily to the correct answer? Surely there must be some crucial fact that the older child observed but the younger child missed. But what can it be? We insist, "What other reasons do you have?"

"The new glass," says the seven-year-old, "is tall and thin, so the level is higher and maybe it looks like there are more. But the amount it is higher is just equal to the amount it is narrower, so there really isn't any change."

We turn back once more to the four-year-old. "Did you know that the new glass made the beads look both taller and also thinner?"

"Yes," he replies, "I could see that."

Try as we may, we cannot discover any objective fact about the beads that the older child knew and the younger child did not know.

Both possessed the same information. Both understood the question. Yet they responded in different ways. Why?

According to Piaget, somewhere between the age of four and seven a cognitive revolution takes place. Instead of dealing with appearances as if they were the true reality, an older child believes in a theory. This theory, which says that physical quantities are invariant under simple changes in shape or location, seems more fundamental to him than the way the world looks. Indeed, it will actually change the way things look. When he knows they are the same, he may find it very difficult to see them as different. But the important point is that the universe of the seven-year-old is not merely the same old universe he lived in at the age of four with a simple addition of certain new facts. His world is organized—seen, remembered, imagined, thought about, behaved in—in a new and better way. Moreover, it is difficult for him to remember how the world appeared to him before he organized it in this new way. Memories stored in terms of the old concepts become almost inaccessible after such revolutions; therein lies the source of much of our childhood amnesia, our inability to recall our earliest experiences.

A seven-year-old child cannot state explicitly in so many words the nature of the theory he has adopted; that must come at a still later stage of intellectual development. And at first his theory may be somewhat limited in its range of applications; it must be discovered all over again in a new context.

For example, suppose he is given two balls of modeling clay which he recognizes as equal. Then one of the two balls is mashed flat. Which contains the more clay? The young child takes this question seriously. If he is impressed by the density per unit area as he holds the ball in the palm of his hand, he may say the ball has more clay. If he is impressed by the visual extent of the clay pancake, he may nominate it as having more clay. As he grows older, however, the day will arrive when he says they must be equal. Yet, on that very day, if we ask him which one weighs the most, (which we can do in the course of playing with a balance), the same child will usually be surprised to find they weigh the same. Moreover, even after both quantity and weight are known to be conserved in spite of the mashing, he may expect the pancake to displace more water from a full glass than would the ball. Conservation of volume is the last to appear; that may not happen until the eleventh or twelfth year.

Boys and girls five years old have many curious ideas about their world. They are not clear about the difference between some and all. Their notions of contradiction, even of negation, are not the adult notions. Time, movement, and speed are mutually confounded in a world where the distance traveled is more important than the time elapsed. Space is plastic, bearing only a crude, topological resemblance to what an adult means by space. It is rather marvelous that such intuitive thinkers manage to survive long enough to grow up and join the ruling majority.

Of course, Piaget does not say that children are incapable of forming the more sophisticated concepts before they are seven years old. He says merely that in the normal Swiss environment they do not develop these concepts until about the age they start to school. What they might be able to do, given appropriate coaching, is still unknown.[10] But this exciting possibility has not yet been carefully explored.

Dependence upon the perceptual field, with little capacity for going beyond or behind it, characterizes a young child's orientation toward space as well as toward quantity. Consider this example: Three cardboard mountains are constructed on top of a square table. A child is brought in and walked around the table, inspecting the mountains from every angle. Then he sits down and watches while a doll is moved around the table. His task is to select out of a set of pictures the one that corresponds to the way the mountains might look to the doll. Now, even though the child understands the task perfectly well, if he is under seven or eight he will select a picture that shows how the mountains look to him and he seems to believe that this is also how the mountains must look to the doll. His own perception is the only reality.

Another way to study a child's orientation in space is to ask which way is up. Under normal conditions this is an easy question to answer, but psychologists know how to make it difficult. The child sits in a chair that can be tilted to the left or right. He looks at a visual display, a room with clear indications of vertical and horizontal. As shown in Figure 44, the room can also be tilted.

The child's problem is to adjust the tilt of his chair to zero, that is to say, to bring himself to a normal sitting position while he is looking at the room. When asked, "Is this the way you sit when you eat your dinner?" the child who has adjusted his chair properly should say, "Yes," without any hesitation.

In this situation some people align themselves fairly accurately with the true vertical, that is to say, with the vertical determined by gravitation. But many do not feel they are vertical until their bodies line up with the visual directions they see in the slanted room. When they are looking at a very tilted visual field they may have

Fig. 44. The girl who is seated in a tilted chair, looking at a tilted room, has been challenged to adjust her chair to the upright. Younger children are more affected by visual cues, tend to adjust the chair off the true upright in the direction suggested visually by the tilted room.

to tilt themselves as much as 35 degrees before they feel upright. The instant they shut their eyes, of course, they know they are tilted.

Children at the age of eight will be strongly dominated by the visual field. They will accept as up whatever *looks* up. But between the ages of eight and about thirteen there is marked learning, so that older children are better able to ignore the visual appearance and to judge on the basis of internal clues.[11]

The final phase of intellectual development begins when the child starts to describe or explain the principles and operations that he has previously learned in a tacit, unverbalized way. From about eight to twelve years the child's knowledge is largely organized in terms of concrete operations to be performed on concrete objects. In many situations the child obviously knows the rules for performing a task, since he can be consistently successful, yet at the same time he does not know them, since he cannot communicate them. A boy who is quite expert at catching a ball will be completely unable to explain anything about its trajectory; a girl who rides her bicycle with great skill will have nothing to say about balance or the center of gravity. Their situation can be rudely described by saying that they know a great deal more than they understand. Adolescence, famous for its social crises and its emotional tempests, is also the period during which the tacit becomes explicit, when what is known becomes understood.

The process of converting tacit into explicit knowledge may continue throughout life as a part of the never-ending education of those who try to stay intellectually alive. Probably there will never come a time when everything will be explicit, when everything that can be known can be written down on paper. But the adolescent is beginning to move in this direction; he is beginning to codify his knowledge, to extend it in ways that only formal, abstract thought can support.

What advantages are there in making tacit knowledge explicit? An obvious advantage is that the knowledge thereby becomes communicable. Science is a prime example of the enormous benefits that can result.

But there are personal consequences as well. When facts are well expressed in terms of a symbol system, it becomes clear that certain relations between propositions are necessary. When this symbol system is imposed upon reality a similar kind of necessity is attached to the physical events. Where, before, a relation may have seemed arbitrary or accidental, it now inherits requiredness from its symbolic representation.

Still another important advantage of symbolic knowledge is that it can be broadly generalized. Quite different situations can, when summarized symbolically, be seen as variations on a single theme. Behind apparent diversity one discovers a formal core, a single scheme, that can be expressed and manipulated symbolically. Once this is seen, knowledge gained in one situation can be transferred immediately to all other situations fitting the same schema. As in the child's earlier intellectual revolutions, this one also extends his ability to see behind and beyond the surface of things. Whereas at first he went beyond sensations to discover perceptual objects, and then went beyond perception to discover physical objects and operations, now he goes beyond physical things to discover the conceptual symbols and transformations of language and logic. Each stage of development carries with it new rewards in terms of greater power, subtlety, and economy of thought.

An example may make these claims more intelligible.[12] A group of children are asked to play a kind of billiard game. Balls are launched with a tubular spring device that can be pivoted around a fixed point and aimed in various directions. The ball is shot against one wall of the billiard table. The wall, like all billiard tables, has a rubber cushion. The ball rebounds out onto the table. The nature of this game should be clear from Figure 45. A target is placed at successively different points on the table and the children are asked to make the ball hit it. Afterwards, they report what they observed.

The psychological question is not how accurately they manage to aim the ball at the target, but how they cope with a simple principle, namely, that the angles of incidence and reflection are equal.

Young children are concerned only with success or failure. They often manage to hit the target, but when asked about it they will usually describe the path of the ball as a smooth curve. They may ignore the angle of rebound entirely. They may realize that moving the plunger changes the direction the ball will go, but they do not explore the matter in a systematic way.

At age eight or so, however, most children attain complete mastery of the concrete operations involved in hitting the target. They clearly recognize the rectilinear trajectory and rebound, and will even

Fig. 45. The equality of the angles of incidence and reflection is demonstrated for children on this billiard table. (The dotted line shows the path of the ball.) Targets are placed on the circles and balls are shot out of the plunger, which can be pivoted and aimed by the child. (After B. Inhelder and J. Piaget, *The Growth of Logical Thinking*. New York: Basic Books, 1958.)

make such spontaneous comments as, "The more I move the plunger this way, the more the ball will go that way." These children see the relation between plunger position and trajectory quite clearly. But they do not attempt to go beyond this observation, which is sufficient for hitting the targets consistently.

Boys and girls do not discover that the angles are equal until they are somewhere between eleven and fourteen. At first the equality seems to them a curious fact, interesting perhaps, but little more. Finally, there is a recognition that the equality of the angles is necessary. The recognition usually follows a comment about lines that are perpendicular to the wall of the table at the point of impact. Suddenly they are convinced that the equality is not accidental. The angles *must* be equal. The necessity of the principle becomes clear to them once they recognize that the ball returns to its starting point when the plunger is perpendicular to the wall. With this insight, they can break up the total angle into component parts and recognize the symmetry around an imaginary perpendicular line. At this point the children have achieved a formal principle that is not restricted to this particular game of billiards. Their new comprehension can now be transferred easily to any new situation that involves reflection.

It is a long and tenuous path that leads from the cradle to symbolic knowledge. The wonderful thing is how often the path is pursued successfully to its conclusion, how seldom any one of a thousand components fails to make its contribution in the right place at the right time. The growth of human understanding in a young child is one of the most intricate, amazing, and beautiful phenomena in nature.

CHAPTER XX

———◆◆———

CLINICAL OR STATISTICAL?

For several years there has been a running battle between the clinical heirs of Sigmund Freud and the statistical heirs of Sir Francis Galton. The Freudians learn about people by talking to them; the Galtonians give tests and compute statistics. When both groups are not both busy doing this, they like to spend their time criticizing each other.

Galton, you will recall, did not set out to understand people. His more modest goal was to measure certain basic capacities that he assumed were important components of intelligence. He devised and standardized simple tests to measure these capacities in large groups of people, and he developed statistical tools to evaluate the correlations among the resulting scores.

Freud, on the other hand, tried to cope with a whole person, not with one of his isolated aspects. He measured nothing. Instead, he dealt with his patients one at a time, and approached each individual, not with a comparative, but with an historical orientation. He developed a procedure to explore his patient's past and provided an extensive, though perhaps overly dramatic theory to interpret what the patient said and did.

Freud and Galton were worlds apart in methods and in philosophy. Yet both scored notable successes, and both attracted vocal and energetic followers. Feuding between two such incompatible views of psychology was almost inevitable.

In 1954 Paul Meehl, a Professor of Psychology at the University of Minnesota, wrote a small book surveying the battleground, evaluating the opposing forces, and estimating the chances for an armistice.[1] By way of introduction Meehl classified the various epithets that are hurled in both directions; this classification is summarized in the Table on page 317. He listed all these terms at the outset "for cathartic purposes so that we may proceed to our analysis unencumbered by the need to say them," which is an academic way of asking the gunmen to check their weapons at the door. The real issues are difficult enough without the emotional intensification that name-calling can provoke.

Think of this argument in terms of the mental health problem. It comes up elsewhere, but it is usually found in purest form among the members on the staff of a psychological or psychiatric clinic. Many decisions must be made about a patient who is disturbed mentally or emotionally. What kind of person is he? What kind of illness does he have? How serious is it? Is he dangerous? Should he be hospitalized? What kind of therapy is indicated? What are the chances that he will cooperate with the therapist? What are the chances that he will recover? How long will it take? Is he getting better? Can he be discharged? Does he need vocational training? Should his family be visited by a social worker? Some of these are questions of diagnosis and classification; others are questions of prediction, questions about the future. They must be asked and somehow answered for every individual who requests treatment. They are usually asked and answered in an atmosphere of ever-growing urgency, as the number of patients and the cost of medical care continue to grow.

In these pages we have persistently skirted around the practical applications of psychology and have focused instead on scientific issues. We will not try here to discuss the many pressing problems of medical psychology; we mention them only to indicate one context in which the clinical-statistical argument can arise. This is not a mere tempest in an academic teapot; the way the argument is resolved can affect the health and happiness of hundreds of thousands of people.

In Meehl's opinion there are, potentially, at least, two different arguments involved. First, there are disagreements about the kinds of data that a psychologist should collect when he is asked to diagnose or predict a person's behavior. On one side, faith rests in the ob-

TABLE OF COMPLIMENTS (after Meehl, 1954)

	That the Clinical Method is:	That the Statistical Method is:
Clinicians say:	dynamic, global, meaningful, holistic, subtle, sympathetic, configural, patterned, organized, rich, deep, genuine, sensitive, real, sophisticated, living, concrete, natural, true to life, understanding	mechanical, atomistic, additive, cut-and-dried, artificial, arbitrary, unreal, incomplete, dead, pedantic, fractionated, trivial, forced, static, superficial, rigid, sterile, academic, oversimplified, pseudoscientific, blind
Statisticians say:	mystical, transcendent, metaphysical, supermundane, vague, hazy, subjective, unscientific, unreliable, crude, private, unverifiable, qualitative, primitive, prescientific, sloppy, uncontrolled, careless, verbalistic, intuitive, muddleheaded	operational, communicable, verifiable, public, objective, reliable, behavioral, testable, rigorous, scientific, precise, careful, trustworthy, experimental, quantitative, down-to-earth, hardheaded, empirical, mathematical, sound

jective, psychometric test: a standardized situation in which a person's responses can be objectively recorded, scored, and compared with statistical norms pre-established on large samples of other people. For example, a long list of opinionated statements may be presented and the person asked to indicate which ones he endorses; he can then be classified according to the degree of agreement between his responses and the responses of the criterion groups on which the test was standardized. On the other side, enthusiasm feeds on non-psychometric data: information gathered from interviews, social histories, police records, ratings by physicians or teachers, marital status, history of employment, and especially from subjective impressions based on appearance, mannerisms, expressed opinions, and so on.

The disagreement does not end there. After the evidence is collected there is a second focus for controversy about what to do with the evidence. One camp likes to base predictions on some perfectly mechanical procedure, such as a regression equation or an actuarial table; no weighing, judging, or inferring is done by any trained clinician. The other camp insists that someone with clinical experience, intelligence, and sensitivity must personally look at the data, comprehend it, and come to a considered opinion about it before a meaningful prediction can be made.

By combining these two disagreements, one gets four different positions that have to be distinguished:

Mechanical predictions based on psychometric tests,

Personal predictions based on psychometric tests,

Mechanical predictions based on nonpsychometric data,

Personal predictions based on nonpsychometric data.

And, in addition, there are various other combinations of these four alternatives that can be defended for one purpose or another. The question, "Which is better, a clinical or a statistical procedure?" is not nearly as simple as it sounds when you first hear it, for in practice one often shades off gradually into the other. In order to sharpen the issues involved, therefore, we shall concentrate here on the opposition between the first and last, between the extreme positions of a pure statistician and a pure clinician.

In the realm of intelligence testing, of course, it is now generally agreed that predictions can follow more or less mechanically from test data. There the Galtonians (with considerable help from a

French clinician named Binet) have carried the day. The present feud, however, is concerned with something even more complex and elusive than the measurement of intelligence—with questions of personality, of mental health, of future behavior—so it seems plausible that purely mechanical methods would lack the sensitivity and power necessary to do the job.

Certainly that is how clinicians feel about it. Any clinician worth his salt soon acquires confidence in his ability to help people, an ability that he feels must rest on his special and superior power for understanding them. And anybody on the receiving end of these investigations will surely feel more comfortable in the tender, understanding hands of a sympathetic clinician than in the electro-mechanical maw of an IBM machine.

In spite of all this confidence in a clinician's good judgment, however, a number of empirical checks have been run that should make us more cautious and humble in our claims. In several careful studies it has been found that a stubbornly statistical approach—objective tests and mechanical predictions—is a great deal more accurate and dependable than it has any right to be. Often an unskilled clerk does even better than the best-trained clinicians. And so the battle rages.

The statistician argues, with good reason, that a clinician cannot hold in mind at one time all the diverse knowledge he has acquired about his patient; by fixing upon one or another item of information as specially significant he distorts the larger picture. Only an actuarial table or a regression equation can incorporate all the data and weigh them appropriately. Moreover, the fact that this chore can be done mechanically by a mere clerk is an unexpected, but highly welcome bonus that leaves the clinician free to do what no test can ever do—to administer therapy. The clinician's objection that statistical equations will never be able to comprehend a patient's inner essence seems completely irrelevant to a statistician.

In the eyes of a statistician, the problem to be solved is the old and familiar one of inductive inference, of arguing logically from observations to conclusions. Because of the vast complexity of the clinical problem and the black depths of our ignorance, the inference must necessarily be tentative and fallible. The problem is even worse when clinical evidence is used to predict future events; such predictions are necessarily vulnerable to all the uncertain and unforeseeable developments that the future may hold. In this situation the mathematical machinery of probability theory would seem to be indispensable. The psychologist must not pretend that he owns a crystal ball. The most that he can do is to classify this patient as similar to others seen previously and to assume that his case will probably develop as most of the others did. The result is a statement of this form: "On the basis of my information about Mr. X, I must classify him in category Y, which has in the past done Z with a probability p."

But probability statements are easily misunderstood. To say that "On the basis of his test performance, the probability is 0.2 that Mr. X will commit suicide sometime within the year," is to invite confusion.

"Nonsense," snorts the clinician, "either he will or he won't. Nobody can commit suicide once in every five lives."

It is possible that part of the conflict could be resolved if clinicians as a group had a better understanding of the logic of probability and of statistical inference. But it is hard to believe that the real source of disagreement does not run much deeper than that.

If a clinician had nothing to do but make predictions, it would undoubtedly follow that he could do it better by using statistical tools. That is exactly the kind of job that the science of statistics is designed to handle and, where data are available for statistical analysis, a clinician's hunches are bound to come off second best. He has about as little chance of beating the equations as he would have of persuading a bank to respect his subjective impression of his cash balance.

Since clinicians are intelligent people, the power of statistical analysis must be apparent to them. Yet they persist in their objections to statistical procedures. Could their stubbornness mean that they are trying to do something more than to predict?

Obviously they are. It is far less important to a clinician to make an accurate, terminal prediction than it is to understand his patient on a moment-to-moment basis and to help him get well again. In this larger, vaguer task of understanding people the objective tests and equations simply get in the way and obscure his view.

Moreover, he is not deeply impressed by a statistician's predictions; even though they are right, he is convinced they are right for the wrong reasons. The tests may work, but no one understands why. If you are going to be effective as a clinician, you must somehow probe behind the observed correlation to find the underlying process that produced it.

Certainly the clinician is right when he says that one can make accurate predictions before one can explain why they work. For example, in our society it would probably be possible to predict a child's success in school from a knowledge of the number of electric motors in his home. But this is obviously not a cause-and-effect kind of relation. No one would expect to raise his child's grades by purchasing more electric motors. Scholastic success and electric motors are both tied to socio-economic status in a very complicated matrix of relations, a social matrix that we understand quite imperfectly. In spite of our ignorance, however, we could, if we had to, use the grades-motors correlation for predictive purposes. Nevertheless, the job of untangling the network of other variables in which this correlation occurs must still remain the central scientific problem. Clinicians like to feel that many of the predictive relations used so successfully by statistically inclined colleagues smell of just this kind of superficiality. You cannot in truth understand a person by asking him to check which of five hundred opinions he agrees with; if such procedures work, it can only be a lucky coincidence. They are of little assistance, clinicians say, in the other, more important departments of this work.

If the clinician and the statistical clerk are doing different jobs, how do they differ? Is it possible to say more explicitly what other things a clinician does? Meehl offers the following formulation: Between observations and prediction there must always be an hypothesis. This hypothesis is not itself a formal consequence of the facts that support it:

> When the hypothesis has been stated, the original data are seen as entailed *by* it, in conjunction with the general laws and the rules of inference. But someone has to state the hypothesis in the first place. It is in the initial *formulation* of the hypothesis that there occurs a genuine creative act with which the logician, as such, has no concern. There is a stage at which someone must have thought up a hypothesis which, in the context of discovery, was, to be sure, suggested by the facts, but is not a formal consequence of them.[2]

For those who adopt the statistical approach, the hypothesis has been formulated and standardized long in advance. In clinical experience, however, the situation is more difficult. The unexpected is the rule rather than the exception; every patient is unique, and well-formulated hypotheses simply do not exist for most of the bizarre and pathetic episodes in which a clinician must participate. His indispensable contribution, therefore, is to formulate hypotheses that can tame the raw designs of madness and capture them in a form to which science might conceivably apply. The basis for his hypothesis is often exceedingly subtle. From a slip of the tongue and an indescribable change in the tone of voice, the patient betrays a sudden anger; from the context the clinician guesses that his patient has a reaction formation against feelings of dependency. (In a different context, of course, the same behavioral evidence might have suggested an entirely different hypothesis.) In the course of an interview the clinician may entertain dozens of such hypotheses that he tries to fit together into his developing concept of this patient.

Formulating appropriate hypotheses as to how a patient's behavior can be classified and what it really means is a clinician's central business; he knows in his bones that it is something no clerk can ever do for him. Unless, of course, the clerk also becomes a skilled clinician. However, once the hypothesis has been invented, it must be subjected to the usual canons of inference and tested by the usual scientific criteria of evidence and probability. The clinical context of discovery may be unique, but the context of justification is not.

In principle, perhaps, all the enormously diverse and imaginative sources of a clinician's hypotheses might be spelled out in sufficient detail so that the entire job, both discovery and justification, could be done automatically. It is at least conceivable. The development of modern computers has put powerful clerical help at our disposal, and clearly we should try to think creatively about how to use it. But such a detailed explication of the clinician's role would be an extravagant undertaking, even if all the appropriate probabilities were known. One major obstacle is that existing descriptions of how a clinician creates his hypotheses are far too vague to program for any computer. Freud once commented that he let his unconscious hover over the unconscious of his patient; others say they learn to read between the lines, or to listen with a third ear, and the like. Such metaphors are suggestive, but they are little help in generating the hypotheses and formulas that a clerk—either human or mechanical—would require in order to replace the clinician. For the present, therefore, the clinician can relax, secure in his knowledge that automation is not yet a threat; and at the same time the statistician can feel vindicated that automation of the clinic is at least conceivable—even if only in principle.

Unfortunately, peace is not purchased so cheaply.

Many clinical psychologists believe there is something intrinsically valuable about the experience of understanding another person, a very different person, in great and intimate detail. Those values are lost when objective tests are substituted for interviews and impersonal equations replace personal comprehension. Until recently, however, most statisticians have felt that their freedom from conceptual luggage of this kind was more of an asset than a liability. But freedom is not to be confused with irresponsibility, and increasing criticism of the extreme empiricism of many psychometricians has been emanating in recent years, not only from the psychological clinic, but from other sources as well.

In order to convey a sense of the immediacy of the problem, this controversy has been described in a context of mental health, for it is there that the issues have been most sharply framed. However, personality tests are widely used outside the clinic—in research, in vocational counseling, in all kinds of personnel selection, in schools — and have come in for heavy criticism in those spheres, too.

Many critics accuse psychologists of pretending that the tests can perform feats that, on the face of it, are impossible. For instance, there is a famous physicist who, whenever personality tests are mentioned, likes to ask whether the felony-proneness test has yet been perfected. As soon as it is, he points out, we can wipe out crime by throwing all felony-prone children into jail for life. It is a crude joke, but it makes a blunt point that enthusiastic psychometricians often forget to mention. There are very real limits on what any personality test can tell us, even if it is the best personality test imaginable.

In 1956 William H. Whyte, Jr., included in his best-selling book, *The Organization Man,* a scathing denunciation of the use of objective personality tests in personnel selection. In Whyte's opinion the psychometric instruments are being used by The Organization as a kind of loyalty test. Since the tests force a man to bear witness against himself, they are basically immoral. Whyte advises his readers to cheat, and gives explicit instructions how to do it.

In order to get a good score—one that will earn you a new job or a big promotion—Whyte's advice is to give the most conventional, pedestrian, run-of-the-mill answers possible. When in doubt, repeat to yourself: "I loved my father and my mother, but my father a little bit more. I like things pretty much the way they are. I never worry much about anything. I don't care for books or music much. I love my wife and children. I don't let them get in the way of company work."[3] If you take the tests in this frame of mind, The Organization will discover unsuspected depths of normalcy in you, and you can look forward to a substantial promotion. You should have no qualms about cheating. Since you are really not that kind of person at all, you may do very well on your new job.

Whyte's tirade is aimed about equally at the psychometricians who create, and at The Organizations who use, the personality tests. Since his argument sounds so plausible and was so widely publicized, one might think that by now the tests would have been abandoned. At the very least, one would expect the tests to begin losing their discriminating power as everyone suddenly adopted the same disguise. In fact, the evidence indicates that people were already way ahead of Whyte. The desire to look good, to endorse what is socially acceptable, has always been a major factor at work in most of these objective tests.

In 1953 Allen Edwards presented clear evidence that the more socially desirable a statement is, the better are the chances that it will be endorsed on a personality test.[4] And even earlier, psychologists had suspected that such attitudes might be biasing the results they were getting.[5] It is possible, of course, to avoid this bias. You can word the questions so that social desirability does not affect the personality trait you are trying to measure. If, for example, you want to measure ambition, you can make half the symptoms of ambition sound socially acceptable and half sound socially reprehensible. Or, if that is impossible, you can include dummy items on the test specifically aimed at measuring a person's defensiveness, then correct his test score accordingly. By using such devices it is easy enough to cancel out the effects of social desirability.

Although not all test-makers have guarded against faking, most of the better-known tests were protected against it long before Whyte even thought about the problem. Few psychologists are so gullible as to accept what people say about themselves without at least a twinge of doubt.

The new twist that Edwards and others have added in recent years is that this bias may be something more than a nuisance. It may, in fact, be measuring something important about the person. Instead of eliminating the effects of social desirability, therefore, a current tendency is to regard the desire for social approval as one of the more important and ubiquitous attributes that an objective test can measure.

Attempts to isolate a social desirability variable, however, have repeatedly got tangled up with another personality variable that also reflects the style of the person taking the test. Apparently some people like to say yes, no matter what you ask them, and other people like to say no. If you try, for example, to measure anxiety by an objective test, and if you happen to phrase your questions so that "yes" means high anxiety and "no" means low anxiety, you will discover that your measure of anxiety is colored by this tendency to acquiesce to anything. All the yeasayers will look anxious; all the naysayers calm and collected. Here again it is a simple matter to eliminate the effect by phrasing the questions properly. Many of the older tests, however, were strongly contaminated by an acquiescence variable.

These two stylistic variables—social desirability and acquiescence—account for many of the individual differences that turn up on personality inventories and questionnaires.[6] To the extent that Whyte's jibes were directed at tests that disregarded response biases of this sort, they performed a valuable service. Fortunately, there are corrective measures available; the objective tests are not quite as vulnerable to cheating as Whyte made them seem.

Response bias is something a psychometrician can make allowances for. But other criticisms are not so easily met. How, for instance, does one answer the indignant gentleman who charges that the whole test movement is a form of pseudoscience, based on spurious and misleading correlations dressed up in quantitative language to swindle the yokels? It is unfortunate that these wild and frequent accusations sound so simple when an honest answer must be so complicated—often too complicated for a busy reader to study carefully. It is easy to raise suspicions that something improper is going on; so much smoke must mean at least a small fire somewhere.

Personality tests are not perfect and they are not always wisely used. But it is foolish to say they are undermining our national

character. To form an intelligent opinion of their value it is necessary to know something about the tests, and particularly how they
are constructed.

Here in rough outline are the steps usually involved in putting
together an objective personality test. First, we assemble a large
group of people known to possess trait A, and another group
known to lack it. (Trait A, which is called the criterion, may be
anything from gall stones to schizophrenia. Our eventual goal is to
predict the occurrence of trait A in other people about whom nothing is known, simply on the basis of their responses to our test.)
Next, we make up a pool of questions, using whatever theory, experience, or intuition we can muster to guide our selection. (This
is where theory could play an explicit role—but in practice it is
usually easier to include everything, even the kitchen sink. The idea
is to collect a basket full of different but similar test items—there is
always safety in large numbers.) Then we ask all the questions of
our two groups, often by printing the questions in booklets and
having people check the answers they prefer. (As we have already
seen, there is quite an art to phrasing the questions. Presenting them
is a tricky business, too, particularly if the tests are to be scored with
a computing machine.) We then break out the statistical techniques
and pore over the results to see which questions were discriminating
—which questions were answered differently by the two groups.
(Here is where we get rid of the kitchen sink—unless, of course, it
happens to discriminate.) If we find enough questions that seem to
predict the criterion, we can announce that we have developed a new
psychometric test. Dozens of shiny new tests are manufactured this
way every year.[7]

Notice that inclusion of an item on the test depends entirely on
whether or not it works. Why it works is, in most instances, an
academic question. We do not need to know why it works to use
it for predicting—often very accurately—who will have trait A and
who will not.

This who-gives-a-damn-why-it-works attitude—it is called the criterion method of test construction—has bothered many people,
including some who are themselves in the psychometric business. It
frequently happens that a test originally constructed to predict trait
A also turns out to be equally useful in predicting trait B. If traits
A and B are intuitively very different psychological variables, we will

be somewhat embarrassed to say exactly what it is that our test tests. But embarrassments of success are easily borne, and for many years nobody worried much about the logic of this situation.

What is lacking is a psychological theory that dictates explicitly which items should be included on the test. Then the criterion would be used, not to validate the test, but to validate the theory on which the test was based. Such an explicit theory—if it were true—would resolve all doubts as to whether or not the test actually measured what it was intended to measure. Questions of validity would be transferred to the larger domain of psychological theory in general, and the tests would become an instrument of research comparable in power and dignity to experiments conducted in the laboratory.

As experience with these tests has accumulated and as new uses for them have been discovered, the need for a theoretical integration and explanation of all the relations among the different tests has become increasingly apparent. The current trend, therefore, is toward the explicit use of psychological theory in constructing new tests.[8] With this changed emphasis the psychometric problem enters a new phase, less technological and more scientific. And as the fundamental concepts of various psychological theories are introduced into the objective tests in this more direct and intimate fashion, the gap between the statisticians and the clinicians—between the statisticians and all other psychologists—will surely narrow. The psychometricians have developed a marvelous research tool, but we are only beginning to understand how to use it properly to test our psychological theories.

CHAPTER XXI

———————◆•◆———————

COMMUNICATION AND
PERSUASION

Social psychology inherits from philosophy the ancient query, What is the social nature of man?

A question so profound obligates the social psychologist to learn a great deal about human societies: he must know and work with facts and theories drawn from art, history, economics, sociology, anthropology, political science, and all the other social and behavioral sciences. It is an ambitious project, yet those who trust science to resolve the central dilemmas of human existence find social psychology one of the most exciting intellectual endeavors of our time. It is a large and explosively expanding field whose boundaries fade hazily into a dozen neighboring disciplines.

To give a flavor of social psychology in a few brief pages, we shall focus on the social process of communication—a process indispensable for any kind of social interaction. A social group affects an individual by communicating with him; the study of human communication is a particularly important section of social psychology. What we will try to do here is to illustrate how a scientific psychologist can use his methods and techniques to study this critically important process.

Let us look at some of the pioneering experiments on persuasive communication.

Go back to early 1945. Germany, after losing the Battle of the Bulge, had few resources left; it was clear to everyone that the

European war was rapidly drawing to a close. Allied commanders were beginning to think more immediately about the war in the Pacific. Eventual victory in that theater also seemed assured, but long months would pass before sufficient strength could be assembled to mount a full-scale invasion of the Japanese homeland. Once the Allies could concentrate their strength on a single front the outcome would be inevitable, but the time required to shift troops from Europe to the Pacific would enable the Japanese to postpone their eventual defeat for months, even years. The troops in Europe were in no mood to face another war on top of the one they were just finishing. They had done their job, they were fed up with war, they expected to be sent home directly. The effect on morale was bad; the U. S. Army issued a directive to impress upon enlisted men the seriousness of the job remaining to be done. Military experts knew they must plan for a long and expensive war; the common soldiers hoped that in a few weeks it would all be over. The debate quickly caught everyone's attention.

In this situation a group of psychologists in the Army's Information and Education Branch saw an opportunity to study an old and controversial issue in the art of persuasive communication.[1] As part of the general campaign to persuade enlisted men that they had a tough job ahead, that the war with Japan would be long and difficult, the psychologists decided they would try to compare two different techniques of radio presentation. In one radio program they would present the story that the Army was trying to tell; just that and no more. In the other they would add something to the Army's argument; they would add some of the counterarguments that they knew were simmering in the men's own talk among themselves. The aim of the experiment was to see whether a one-sided or a two-sided presentation is more persuasive. Is there an advantage in trying to give an impression of fairness, or is it a disadvantage to publicize the other side's case?

Two radio scripts were written and transcribed for broadcast. Program I presented only the reasons for expecting a long war: the vast distances in the Pacific, the large Japanese stockpiles, the quality of the Japanese troops not yet met in battle, the determination of the Japanese people. Program II presented all these reasons in exactly the same way, but it also spent a small amount of time considering arguments on the opposite side: our naval victories, our previous progress even in a two-front war, our ability to concentrate on Japan after victory in Europe, Japan's inferior industrial strength, our increasingly effective air warfare. These additional points were woven into the context of the rest of the program.

Before the programs were presented to any troops, two groups of men were selected and their opinions were determined in a preliminary survey. Once that had been done each group heard one of the programs, after which their opinions were sampled again to see if any changes had occurred.

Since events were moving rapidly, it seemed possible that changes could result from external factors other than the radio programs. It was necessary, therefore, to use a third group of men—the control group—whose opinions would also be measured twice, but who would not hear either of the radio programs. Having a control group would make it possible to say whether the observed changes were attributable to the radio programs or to some other events occurring at the same time.

Throughout these tests and measurements extreme precautions were taken to prevent the men from suspecting that they were being experimented upon.

During the first week of April (while Allied armies were crossing the Rhine) the preliminary questionnaire was administered. A week later (while American troops were mopping up Japanese resistance in the Philippines) the two programs were presented, each to a different group of men during their regular orientation meetings. Immediately after hearing the programs the men answered the second questionnaire.

On both questionnaires there was an item that asked, "What is your guess as to how long it will take us to beat Japan after Germany's defeat?" Before they had heard the program about 37 per cent of the men estimated it would take more than 18 months. On the second questionnaire, 34 per cent of the men in the control group gave the same answer. It seemed reasonable to assume, therefore, that little change could be attributed to sources other than the radio programs. In the experimental groups, on the other hand, those who, after they had heard the one-sided program, estimated more than 18 months, increased to 59 per cent. Those who estimated more than 18 months after hearing the two-sided program also increased—also to 59 per cent.

The increases were significant; both programs were effective in changing the men's opinions. But from an experimental point of view the results were indecisive. Apparently it does not matter whether one side or both sides of an argument are given. In order to understand why this should be the case the experimenters carried their analysis a step further.

When the groups of men were broken down according to educational level, a difference in the persuasiveness of the two programs became apparent. As indicated in Figure 46, it was found that the

Fig. 46. Two-sided presentations are more persuasive with well-educated audiences, less persuasive with people who have not graduated from high school. The length of the horizontal bars represents the net proportion of men in each of the four classifications who revised their estimates in the desired direction after hearing the radio programs.

two-sided presentation was more effective with the better educated men; the one-sided presentation was more effective with the less educated men. Habits of thought acquired in high school and college tended to make the educated listeners resist a one-sided presentation, whereas their less critical, less educated friends were impressed by the one-sided program and were not challenged to think of possible objections to it.

As is often the case in mass communications, however, there was a boomerang effect. It turned up in the form of an apparent contradiction in the data. One of the questions that had been asked about the radio programs concerned the adequacy with which they presented the facts on the Pacific War; men who heard the one-sided presentation replied more often that it did a good job than did the men who heard the two-sided presentation. How could such a contradictory result have occurred? Why did so many men who had just heard a two-sided program feel it was not fair?

When the experimenters poked into this unexpected outcome, they discovered that the source of trouble was their failure to mention the possibility of Russian aid. Apparently, when no counterarguments at all were presented, Russian aid was not missed. But when the program tried to give an appearance of fairness and objectivity, omission of Russian aid became glaringly obvious. And it was especially obvious to those men who considered Russian aid a major factor in shortening the war with Japan; when their best counterargument was not included, they resisted the communication more than if no counterarguments had been mentioned at all.

Similar boomerang effects have been observed in dozens of different studies of mass communications; avoiding them is one of the principal reasons for pretesting a message on a small group of people before broadcasting it to thousands or millions of listeners.

With the rapid growth of the communication sciences since World War II experiments of this sort have become commonplace for both the practical and the theoretical study of mass communications. One of the scientists involved in this particular experiment, Dr. Carl I. Hovland, continued the work after he returned to his regular duties at Yale University. The significant thing about his approach was not that it was aimed at mass media of communication; that had been tried many times before. The novel element was the introduction of experimental techniques, techniques that had been developed first in the psychological laboratory.

What are the advantages of an experimental approach? The answer to this question becomes obvious when we compare experimental with correlational methods for studying the same problem. Consider an example drawn from studies of race prejudice.

Attempts to discover who listens to communication aimed at countering racial antagonisms often take the form of questionnaires administered to carefully randomized samples of people drawn from the general population. The interviews may or may not be conducted in connection with some particular radio or television program. One regular finding in every case has been that (a) the amount of information people have about a minority group, and (b) the extent to which they approve of that group and its aims, tend to be positively correlated. For example, people who listen to propaganda deploring anti-Semitism and who know the most about the Jews are usually those who approve most of Jews and Jewish aims. The correlation agrees nicely with common sense. "To know them is to love them," we say, or, "To understand is to forgive." Consequently, the correlation is often carelessly interpreted to mean that education eliminates race prejudice. Because information and approval are correlated, it would seem to mean that we need only provide more information to create more approval.

When we look at the correlations closely, however, we discover that the facts are misleading. Too often it turns out that the people who know most about Negroes and who approve most of Negroes *are* Negroes.

A spurious correlation can be a dangerous weapon in the hands of a person who does not suspect it, who does not stop to think through the correlation to the underlying causes that produced it. In order to test the suggested relation between information and approval, we must perform an experiment. We must experimentally manipulate one variable (increase the amount of information about an ethnic group) and see if the other variable (approval of that ethnic group) is affected. This has been done and the results are negative. So far, the experimental results indicate that prejudice can seldom be attributed to ignorance.

When they are applicable, experimental methods enable us to test a correlation to see if it is basic or derivative in nature. Thus the introduction of experimental methods into the study of mass communication has been an important contribution to the social sciences.

To understand how experiments can be pursued until they turn into programs of research and lead to new theories, consider a question that arises directly out of the problem of two-sided presentations.

Imagine that both sides of an issue must be presented in a single discussion, but you are in favor of one over the other. In which order should you present the two arguments? Should you get your side in first, while your listeners are fresh and receptive? Or should you present it last, so that no counterarguments can follow and interfere with a listener's memory of it? The advantage of the first position produces a primacy effect in persuasion. The terminal position has a recency effect. The question is, "Which effect is bigger?" This is a problem we can approach by experimental methods.

Take the following episode: "Jim left the house to get some stationery. He walked out into the sun-filled street with two of his friends, basking in the sun as he walked. Jim entered the stationery store which was full of people. Jim talked with an acquaintance while he waited for the clerk to catch his eye. On his way out, he stopped to chat with a school friend who was just coming into the store. Leaving the store, he walked toward school. On his way out he met the girl to whom he had been introduced the night before. They talked for a short while, and then Jim left for school. After school Jim left the classroom alone. Leaving the school, he started on his long walk home. The street was brilliantly filled with sunshine. Jim walked down the street on the shady side. Coming down the street toward him, he saw the pretty girl whom he had met on the previous evening. Jim crossed the street and entered a candy store. The store was crowded with students, and he noticed a few familiar faces. Jim waited quietly until the counterman caught his eye and then gave his order. Taking his drink, he sat down at a side table. When he had finished his drink he went home."[2]

With no more information than that, would you say Jim is friendly or unfriendly? Shy or forward? Social or unsocial? Aggressive or passive? A group of students who read this description of Jim's behavior decided that he was friendly, forward, social, and aggressive; you probably agree with them.

You have a right to be suspicious, however. After all, Jim turned up in a psychology book as part of a discussion on two-sided communications. Perhaps you were cautious and studied the passage closely. If so, you probably noticed a striking change in Jim's personality after he got out of school and headed home. Before school he seemed extroverted; afterwards he had suddenly become an introvert. Although a sizable fraction of the students did not notice it, the account was written with a deliberate intent to be contradictory. Half of the students saw it in the form given above. The other half saw it in the opposite order, with the episode in the candy store preceding the episode in the stationery store. For this second group there appeared to be a remarkable blossoming in Jim's character as the story ends. This second group, which learned about Jim initially as an introvert, judged him to be unfriendly, shy, unsocial, and passive. The two groups had read exactly the same words. The only difference between them was the order in which the two episodes were presented.

The experiment just described gave relatively clear evidence of a primacy effect. The first impression we get of a person or a topic is likely to be the one that prevails.

But how much travel can we expect from this one study? Even when this kind of experimental evidence is available, most people are reluctant to jump to conclusions, to generalize the results to all situations, or to believe in any universal law of primacy in persuasion.

The difficulties are all too plain. We have observed a primacy effect for personality judgments by students. Does that tell us what would happen if different materials were presented, if different media of communication were used, if different people received the message, if the two sides were presented by different people, and so on? Before we generalize to the many situations in which an order effect might occur, we should conduct a program of experiments to explore some of the conditions that might alter any conclusion based on this single study of Jim's hypothetical personality. That program is part of the research that the Yale workers undertook.

As a result of a program of experimental research, therefore, we now know that the most important factor is whether the opposing messages originate from the same source or from different sources. When the two sides come from two different persons, there is usually a recency effect; the second debater has a slight advantage over the first. If the two sides are presented by a single source, most people try to perceive a coherent message; contradictory information introduced later is merely confusing, not persuasive.

But why, we might ask, should there be any effect at all? Given that two arguments are, in an absolute sense, equally persuasive, why should the second be either more or less effective than the first? Suppose we phrase the puzzle this way: Imagine possible opinions represented along a continuum ranging from very unfavorable opinions on the left to very favorable on the right. A person's initial opinion can be represented by a point along that line. He gets the first message; it moves him in one direction or the other. He gets the second message, which is equally persuasive; it moves him right back to wherever he was at the start. Two equal and opposite persuasions should cancel each other out, regardless of the order in which they occurred.

One clue that things are not so simple comes from the observation that the size of the change you will produce in an attitude is usually proportional to the amount of change you try to produce. That is to say, if you are trying to move people in a given direction, you should advocate a position more extreme than the one you actually hold. The bigger the difference between your argument and the listener's initial position, the larger the change you are likely to produce. That effect is itself open to further study and confirmation, but for the moment let us assume a proportionality effect does occur. What consequences would it have for an order effect?

At this point we must keep track of several things simultaneously; mathematical notation becomes very helpful. Let X represent values along the opinion scale. Let X_a represent the particular position that is being advocated by the argument a that is presented, and let X_0 represent a recipient's initial position. Then $X_a - X_0$ represents the magnitude of the change that the argument is attempting to produce in the recipient's opinion. The opinion that he will hold after hearing the argument will be given by

$$X_1 = X_0 + d,$$

where d indicates the difference actually produced by the message. This definition of d is represented graphically in Figure 47.

Now we are able to state precisely our hypothesis of proportionality: the change d produced by argument a will be proportional to the difference $(X_a - X_0)$ between the opinion that the argument advocates and the opinion that the listener holds. Therefore,

$$d = k(X_a - X_0),$$

where k is a constant of proportionality depending upon the persuasiveness of the message, the credibility of the source, and other variables not directly related to our interest in the order of presentation. Presumably, k will usually be a number between 0 and 1. If k is between 0 and 1, then our assumption means that we should advocate a larger change than we really want to produce. Negative values of k would represent a boomerang effect; the listener would change in a direction opposite to the one advocated. Values of k greater

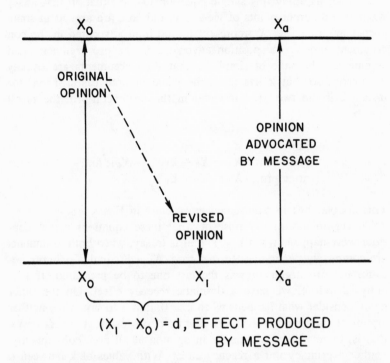

Fig. 47. A person holding opinion X_0 hears an argument advocating opinion X_a and as a result he revises his opinion from X_0 to X_1.

than 1 would mean that the argument produced an even greater change than we intended.

When we combine the two equations we obtain

$$X_1 = X_0 + k(X_a - X_0)$$

as our prediction of the opinion that the person will hold after hearing argument *a*, on the assumption that the change produced will be proportional to the change attempted. (Alternatively, we could rewrite the relation as

$$k = \frac{X_1 - X_0}{X_a - X_0}$$

and use this equation to define a coefficient of persuasiveness k as the ratio of the shift produced to the shift advocated.)

Now let us apply this simple equation to the situation that arises when two different points of view, pro and con, are argued in some particular order. Let X_c represent the position advocated in the con argument and X_p the position advocated in the pro argument, and assume for the sake of simplicity that both arguments are equally persuasive, so that k has the same value in both cases. Then, for instance, if the two are presented in the order con-pro, the result will be:

initially, X_0;
after con, $X_1 = X_0 + k(X_c - X_0)$; and
after pro, $X_2 = X_1 + k(X_p - X_1)$.

This double shift is represented graphically in Figure 48.

To get an intuitive glimpse of what these equations mean, consider what happens when k = 1, that is to say, when both arguments are completely persuasive. In that case, X_2 will equal X_p simply because the pro argument was the last one to be presented. If k is unity, therefore, we have a dramatic recency effect. On the other hand, consider what happens when k = 0, that is to say, when neither argument carries any weight. In that case, obviously, $X_2 = X_1 = X_0$, that is, there will be no change in opinion at all and, consequently, neither a primacy nor a recency effect. With values of k between 0 and 1, there is always some recency effect, the magnitude increasing as the persuasiveness of the arguments increases.

Thus we see that we can tie together two apparently unrelated phenomena, the recency effect and the proportionality effect. From such modest beginnings we might hope that a matrix of further connections will eventually develop.

The fact that a theory is clear and explicit, however, does not mean that it is true. One very suspicious feature of this theory is its prediction that the person who is most strongly opposed to something will be the most persuaded by an argument in its favor. It may apply only to neutral or undecided listeners who are still willing to consider both sides of the question. But these speculations cannot settle the matter. What we need is some evidence. To test the theory we must turn to observations and experiments. What results do we know that might either support or contradict this particular fragment of theory?

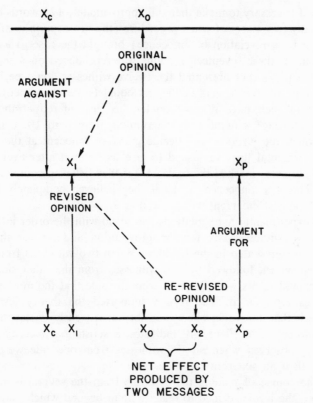

Fig. 48. The recency effect. A person holding opinion X_0 first hears an argument X_c against an issue and so revises his opinion to X_1. He then hears an argument X_p in favor of it and revises his opinion again now to X_2. If the arguments are equally persuasive (in this case k = 0.75) the net effect will be in favor of the argument heard most recently.

There are several studies that might be cited as relevant to the ideas just presented; the following serves to illustrate the kind of data that have been obtained.[3] The communication materials for the study were taken from an actual law case tried early in the nineteenth century, the case of Thomas Hoag, who was indicted for making a bigamous marriage with Catherine Secor. For the purpose of the experiment, the evidence was organized into seventeen sections. The first one of these was the indictment itself, the next twelve sections were the summarized testimony of twelve different witnesses (reworded slightly if necessary to make them all approximately 175 words long), and finally two pieces of court procedure (the prosecution arguments followed by a revelation of innocence) brought the case to a close. Each one of these seventeen sections was reproduced on a separate page; the pages that presented the twelve witnesses could be bound together in different orders in the test booklets. As the experimental juror read each page of his booklet, he encountered at the bottom of the page a numbered line running from 0 to 10. Unlike a trial, where the jurors would decide guilty or innocent at the close, the experimental jury was asked to give its opinion after every witness. The jurors marked the scale at 0 if they believed completely in the defendant's innocence, at 10 if they believed completely in his guilt. A neutral judgment was marked at 5.

The experimental manipulations had to do with the order in which the twelve witnesses, six for the prosecution and six for the defense, were presented in the booklets. When two witnesses from one side were given, followed by two witnesses from the other side, the experimental jurors wound up favoring the side that the most recent witnesses represented. The results supported the theory just outlined, whether the order-effect was introduced early or late in the case. Moreover, as Figure 49 indicates, a substantial recency effect was also observed when all six witnesses from one side were presented, then all six from the other side.

In the course of reading the evidence from the several witnesses, however, the jurors seemed to reach a point beyond which they were no longer susceptible to persuasion. The order effect, although real and measurable, was only a preliminary phenomenon. At first the arguments added and subtracted much as the equations predicted, but behind these local fluctuations there was a more fundamental process of opinion formation going on, a process not described by the equations. Perhaps if one could present the best evidence at the critical instant, when judge and jury were ripe for decision, one would have a far more telling effect than could be produced with the same evidence presented either earlier or later. But what this more basic process consists of remains a question for further research.

A great amount of work is going on aimed squarely at this question. We can do little more than sample it here.

For many years psychologists have known that active participation in the learning process produces faster learning and better retention.

Fig. 49. Experimental demonstration of the recency effect. One group of experimental jurors (open circles) heard six prosecution witnesses followed by six defense witnesses; the other group (filled circles) heard the defense first, then the prosecution. The groups tended to favor the side they had heard most recently. (After N. H. Anderson, Test of a model for opinion change, *Journal of Abnormal and Social Psychology, 59,* 1959, 371–381.)

Every teacher knows that the best way to learn something is to teach it to others. Suppose we try to generalize this observation. Does active participation also produce conviction? To remember an argument does not mean that we must believe it—yet the two may be more closely related than we think. We are accustomed to say that a person expresses a particular opinion because he believes it; perhaps he believes it because he expresses it.

Suppose you could force a person to make your argument for you. Would the fact that he himself had actively expressed it make him tend to believe what he had said? A man who is promoted into an executive position may find that he is required to say things and to support opinions and policies that are really not his own; does he come eventually to believe what he is saying? Does a preacher persuade anyone as much as he persuades himself?

In order to put the matter to an experimental test, the Yale workers performed an experiment in role playing.[4] Young men, college students, were given an "oral speaking test." Each speaker was assigned the task of defending an extreme position on some topic of current interest. At the end of a session all the students answered a series of questions, ostensibly to help in the evaluation of the different speakers, but actually to measure the extent to which their own opinions had been modified. In most cases the students who had actively argued for a particular side showed a larger change in their opinions on that question than did the students who merely listened. They had convinced their listeners to a certain extent, but they had done an even better job of convincing themselves.

Of course, there were exceptions. Some speakers did not show the effect. The experimenters noted that these were usually the speakers who had shown little imagination in elaborating the arguments they had been assigned and who expressed the least satisfaction with their own performance. So a further study was aimed at the questions they posed.

The experiment was repeated, but now some of the students were asked to read a passage aloud to the class, whereas other student speakers saw the script of the talk, but were not permitted to read aloud from it. The results were clear. Speakers who had to improvise their arguments were far more persuaded than were those who merely read the script aloud. Moreover, personal satisfaction with the effectiveness of the performance seemed to have nothing to do with it. It was the amount that a person contributed from his own store of information and anecdote that served to convince him.

One of the slippery characteristics of words is that we tend to believe them, especially when they are our own. In this simple experiment we see at work the kind of process that enables us wholeheartedly to adopt our social roles complete with all the values and opinions that go with them. Attitudes and behavior initially prescribed by some external authority come to be genuinely accepted and adhered to even in the absence of surveillance. If it were not so, civilized society as we know it could scarcely exist.

Why does a public declaration, especially if it seems to come from us personally, have this persuasive effect? One suggestion is that the declaration forces us into an incongruous position, and that the change in attitude is simply an attempt to reduce the inconsistency. Previously, in Chapter XVII, we noted how strong and pervasive is the human urge to make things look simple and consistent.

This high value people set on being consistent in their opinions gives us excellent leverage for persuading them to change their opinions. The recipe runs something like this: If you want someone to revise his considered opinion A, first find another opinion of his, B, and convince him that A and B are inconsistent. Since you now have the tendency to eliminate inconsistencies working in your favor, offer him a simple resolution of the problem that involves changing A. Of course, this strategy will work only on reasonable people. But most people are willing to be reasonable, at least some of the time, about all but a few things.

If you are going to persuade somebody by pitting one of his opinions against another, you will have to know your victim rather well. The argument that traps Jones into feeling inconsistent may not work at all with Smith. When we take this tack, therefore, we are beginning to look at the fine grain, the microstructure of public opinion. If we want techniques that are more effective than mass appeals via mass media of communication, we must learn how to analyze in considerable detail the cognitive structures of the men and women we want to influence.

Thus social psychology comes back once more to a familiar question. If you want to change a person's mind, you must know how his mind was made up to begin with. And that is, after all, the central question for any science of psychology.

CHAPTER XXII

---◆---

IN CONCLUSION

Psychology, said William James, is the science of mental life.

We are now in a better position to appreciate how far the meaning of that definition has shifted since 1890.

Up until a century ago psychology was a branch of philosophy; the great thinkers somehow knew intuitively what was true and spent their days inventing clever arguments designed to prove it. Then, beginning with Fechner and Wundt and some of their contemporaries, they began to buttress arguments with observations and experiments: at that point the shift into scientific modes of thinking began. But it was still a philosophical kind of psychology, concerned primarily with the source and nature of man's conscious knowledge.

In the background, however, a tremendous development was taking place in the biological sciences. At the first sign of trouble with the introspective analysis of mental life, therefore, the philosophical preoccupation with Man as Knower was swept away and replaced with the newer vision of Man as Animal. The new focus was not knowledge, but adaptation, not thought, but behavior. The mental life that psychology now began to study was not something to be experienced, but something inferred from action.

Eventually, however, problems inherent in a purely behavioral conception of psychology also began to appear. So the vision of man was once more revised and extended, this time emphasizing Man as Social Animal—buffeted as much by the strange whims of his fellow

344

men as by the stern demands of physiology. Developments in the social sciences—in anthropology and sociology—enabled psychologists to recognize the extent to which all mental life is conditioned by cultural traditions, by personal participation in the social process. The adaptation that man struggled to achieve was now seen to be largely a social adaptation. The knowledge he accumulated was seen to be largely symbolic knowledge, encoded in whatever language his culture provided. And this concern with socially significant symbols led back once more to a renewed concern with Man as Knower, but now in a vastly expanded context of new methods and new theories.

That is about where psychology stands today—partly social science, partly biological science, and still partly philosophy.

Where is it going in the future?

We can only guess. It is unlikely that we will see any more revolutions that completely redefine what we mean by mental life. Probably we will see increasing specialization as our factual information continues to grow in depth and detail. The dream of a single philosophical principle that explains everything it touches seems to be fading before the realization that man is vastly curious and complicated, and that we need a lot more information about him before we can formulate and test even the simplest psychological laws. Perhaps a whole set of psychological sciences will eventually emerge, although where the divisions between them should be is not yet clear.

How psychology develops in the future will depend to a large and increasing extent upon what it can contribute to our lives, both individually and collectively. As science in recent years has become more and more an instrument of national policy we have tended more and more to support those scientific enterprises that are relevant to our social, economic, political situation. There are today enormous problems facing us—facing all mankind—where psychological knowledge would be invaluable: education, race prejudice, mental health, old age, population control, international cooperation, and many others. These problems do not themselves pose scientific questions, of course; asking the right questions will always be just as difficult in psychology as it is everywhere in science. But if it is possible for scientific psychology to contribute to the solution of practical problems such as these, its future will be bright indeed.

On the basis of the record so far, there is some reason to be optimistic.

GLOSSARY

Acquired characteristic: A structural or functional modification that occurs as a result of an organism's own activities or through the influence of its environment. Contrasts with an inherited characteristic.

Adaptation: In general, an adaptive process is one appropriate for maintaining an organism's vital processes in a given situation. In discussions of sensation and perception, however, adaptation usually refers to some reduction in sensitivity as a result of steady stimulation.

Amnesia: A partial or complete inability to remember.

Anxiety: An unpleasant, apprehensive emotion aroused by the recognition of danger. Anxiety is considered to be neurotic if it grows out of all proportion to its realistic justification.

Associationism: A psychological theory, dating from Aristotle, that explains our complicated mental experiences as the product of combinations of simpler mental elements.

Attention: The active selection of certain stimuli or certain aspects of experience, with consequent inhibition of all others.

Auditory nerve: That part of the VIII cranial nerve that transmits neural activity from the auditory receptors in the ear to the central nervous system.

Autonomic nervous system: That part of the nervous system that innervates glands and smooth muscles. It is involved in the regulation of vital homeostatic processes and in the physiological changes that accompany emotions.

Behavior: An extremely complex pattern of responses that may have special meanings for the organism is often called, somewhat loosely, behavior.

Behaviorism: A psychological theory that emphasizes objective, publicly observable events (usually called stimuli and responses), rather than private consciousness, as the subject matter of scientific psychology.

Brain waves: Electrical activity of the brain, as recorded in an electroencephalogram.

Cathexis: Psychoanalytic term denoting the investment or concentration of instinctual energy in some object or idea.

Central nervous system: The brain and spinal cord.

Cognitive: Pertaining to the various psychological processes involved in knowing.

346

Conditioning: A training procedure, usually associated with the name of I. P. Pavlov, whereby a response is brought under the control of (made conditional upon the occurrence of) a new stimulus.

Discrimination: An organism is said to be capable of discriminating between two different stimuli if it can respond differently to them.

Drive: Urge. A condition that impels the organism to become active until the drive can be reduced. Sometimes used with special emphasis on the physiological needs of the body, as contrasted with social motives.

Ego: The individual's conception of himself. In the psychoanalytic concept of personality structure, the term is used to refer to that part of the mind that controls conscious experience and regulates the interactions of the person with his environment.

Ego-ideal: Psychoanalytic term denoting one's image of self-perfection.

Electro-encephalogram: A record of electrical potentials from the brain, obtained by amplifying and recording the electrical activity picked up by electrodes applied to the scalp. Popularly called "brain waves."

Emotion: Any experience of strong feeling, usually accompanied by bodily changes in circulation, breathing, sweating, etc., and often accompanied by intense and impulsive actions. The opposite of calm relaxation.

Empiricism: The empirical method refers to the pursuit of knowledge by observation and experiment. In psychology, the empiricist theory emphasizes the importance of perception and learning in the growth of the mind.

Engram: A modification that is assumed to occur somewhere in the nervous system as a result of learning and that therefore provides the physiological basis for memory in higher organisms.

Erogenous zones: Areas of the body where stimulation can produce pleasure and, under appropriate conditions, can arouse sexual reactions.

Evolutionism: Any theory that regards the present state of the world as the cumulative result of a long series of small steps. The biological version, usually associated with the name of Charles Darwin, holds that maladaptive variations in the members of a given species will die out and that advantageous variations will be propagated so the species will slowly change over the course of many generations.

Fechner's law: A formulation of the relation between stimulus-intensity and sensory magnitude proposed by G. T. Fechner as an extension of Weber's Law: The subjective magnitude of a sensation is measured by the logarithm of the physical magnitude of its stimulus.

Fixation: Focusing the eyes in such a way that a particular point falls on the fovea. In psychoanalytic theory, fixation refers to the persistence of an unconscious wish for some infantile mode of gratification.

Free association: The spontaneous association of ideas in the absence of any specific purpose or instruction. Insofar as they are able, patients undergoing psychoanalytic therapy are encouraged to associate freely; a block in their revery may signal an emotionally disturbing topic.

Freudian slip: An accident that is not wholly accidental, but that seems to be determined, at least in part, by personal causes unknown to the person who commits it.

Functionalism: In general, any doctrine that emphasizes function, use, adaptation. As a psychological theory, functionalism holds that all mental processes serve an adaptive function for the organism. Often contrasted with structuralism.

Gestalt: A German word, sometimes translated as structure or configuration. As a theory, gestalt psychology emphasizes that organized units, both in perception and in behavior, have characteristic properties that cannot be reduced to the properties of their component parts.

Habit: A response pattern, acquired by learning, that is relatively stable, easily elicited, and hard to get rid of. Most habits are motor acts, but sometimes the term is used more broadly to refer as well to habits of thought.

Halo effect: A common source of error in judging people. Because we rate the person high (low) on some particular trait—or hold a favorable (unfavorable) impression of him in general—we are likely to overrate (underrate) him on other traits.

Homeostasis: Steady state. A term introduced by W. B. Cannon, who wrote, "The co-ordinated physiological processes which maintain most of the steady states in the organism are so complex and so peculiar to living beings—involving, as they may, the brain and nerves, the heart, lungs, kidneys, and spleen, all working cooperatively—that I have suggested a special designation for these states, *homeostasis.*"

Hypnosis: An induced state of heightened suggestibility.

Hysteria: A psychoneurosis, in which (according to psychoanalytic theory) unacceptable impulses are repressed and unconscious, yet presumably find outlet through bodily symptoms—abnormal sensations, paralysis—that occur without any apparent injury to the nervous system.

Id: In the psychoanalytic concept of personality structure, the id is the deepest, unconscious part of the mind, devoted entirely to pleasure and driven by blind, instinctual impulses.

Identification: An unconscious mental process whereby we can, according to the psychoanalysts, invest our instinctual energies in particular images by adopting them as our own, by identifying ourselves with them.

Information theory: A mathematical theory developed by Claude Shannon and Norbert Wiener that enables engineers to measure the average amount of information (in bits/sec) that a communication channel can transmit.

Inhibition: A term broadly used to denote any suppressive interaction between two or more processes, whether in the physiological, behavioral, mental, or social realm.

Ink-blot test: A projective test. The person taking the test describes all of the scenes he recognizes in an ink blot.

Instinct: An organized and often complicated pattern of behavior, characteristic of a given species, that is adaptive in certain environmental situations, but that seems to arise with a relatively small amount of experience and learning.

Instrumentalism: A form of pragmatic philosophy, often associated with the name of John Dewey, that holds ideas to be instruments of action whose usefulness determines their truth. In psychology this doctrine gave rise to functionalism.

Intelligence quotient (IQ): Mental age (measured by some suitable intelligence test) divided by chronological age (where, usually, everyone over some given chronological age—say, 16—is considered to be exactly that age), the quotient then being multiplied by 100.

Interval scale of measurement: The type of measurement that is possible when there exist empirical operations for determining whether two intervals along the scale are equal.

Just noticeable difference (jnd): Difference threshold. The smallest difference between two stimuli that can be reliably detected.

Kinesthesia: Sensitivity to movements by parts of the body.

Law of effect: The hypothesis that responses leading to rewards are learned, while those that do not are extinguished.

Learning: Adaptive change in thought or behavior.

Libido: Psychoanalytic term for sexual energy.

Limen: Threshold.

Materialism: The faith that everything in the universe will eventually be explicable in terms of the existence and the properties of matter. In psychology, this faith usually leads to an emphasis on the importance of the body, and especially the nervous system, as the basis for all mental processes.

Memory: The retention of acquired skills or information.

Motivation: Conditions determining persistent and goal-directed activity. Sometimes used with special reference to social goals and incentives, as contrasted with biological drives.

Motor skill: A capacity for proficient performance—prompt, smooth, accurate—of some practiced pattern of movements: walking, talking, driving a car, playing tennis, chipping flints, etc.

Neurology: The branch of biology that studies the nervous system.

Neuron: A nerve cell.

Neurophysiology: The branch of physiology that deals with the functions of the nervous system.

Neurosis: A common abbreviation for psychoneurosis.

Nominal scale of measurement: The type of "measurement" that is possible when the only empirical operations available are those for determining whether two objects are identical. The "values" assigned are simply names, letters, serial numbers, etc.

Objective: That which exists independent of any conscious experience or personal judgment. Contrasted with subjective.

Operant: A term introduced into discussions of conditioning by B. F. Skinner. It denotes a response that at first may seem to occur spontaneously, but that can, through conditioning, be brought under the control of discriminative stimuli.

Operationism: The doctrine that the meaning of any concept derives from the operations by which it is observed.

Optic nerve: The II cranial nerve that transmits neural activity from the light-sensitive receptors in the retina of the eye to the central nervous system.

Ordinal scale of measurement: The type of measurement that is possible when there exist empirical operations for determining the rank order to be assigned to the measured objects.

Perception: The process of becoming aware of objects and relations in the world around us, insofar as that awareness depends on sensory processes.

Perceptual-motor: Pertaining to the coordination of skilled movements, guided by previous experience and corrected by perceptual feedback as to their effects.

Personality tests: Any psychological test—there are numerous varieties —that endeavors to provide a basis for classifying people into various personality types.

Phobia: A psychoneurotic dread of some particular object or situation.

Physiological psychology: The branch of psychology that treats of the relation between physiological and psychological processes.

Physiology: That branch of biology that investigates the processes and functions of the living cells, tissues, organs, and organ systems of the body—as distinguished from anatomy, which studies their structure.

Pleasure principle: A psychoanalytic name for the hypothesis that all pleasure results from the satisfaction of instinctual drives. The id is assumed to be dominated by the pleasure principle. *Cf.* reality principle.

Positivistic: An adjective used rather loosely in the nineteenth century to describe any discussion of human beings in the language of natural science. According to Ambrose Bierce, "Its longest exponent is Comte, its broadest Mill, and its thickest Spencer."

Posthypnotic suggestion: A specific order, given during hypnosis, to be obeyed after the hypnotic state has ended.

Pragmatism: Defined by William James as "the doctrine that the whole *meaning* of a conception expresses itself in its practical consequences." This doctrine became the basis for a highly influential school of American philosophy.

Preconscious: Those latent ideas and feelings that are potentially conscious, even though the person may not be aware of them at the moment.

Primacy effect: The name used to refer to a situation in which earlier items of a series are remembered better than later items. Contrasts with recency effect.

Projection: A term used in several loosely related contexts. In discussions of perception, it generally refers to the localization of a perceived object at a distance outside of the body. In social psychology, it is the tendency to assume that other people experience the same ideas and feelings that we do. In psychoanalytic theory, projection is one of several ways the ego can defend itself from anxiety—by attributing a repressed idea to someone else.

Projective test: A personality test, so-called because the person unwittingly projects his own feelings, attitudes, preoccupations, etc., into his perception of some ambiguous picture or situation.

Psychiatry: That branch of medicine dealing with the treatment of psychological disorders and abnormalities.

Psychoanalysis: A system of psychological hypotheses originated and developed by Sigmund Freud as the basis of his technique for the psychiatric treatment of personality defects, nervous and mental disorders.

Psychogenic disorders: Disorders having their origin in psychological problems or conflicts. Contrasted with somatogenic disorders.

Psychology: The science of mental life, based on evidence obtained through the observation and analysis of one's own behavior and the behavior of others.

Psychometric: Any quantitative technique of scientific psychology, but especially those used in mental testing.

Psychoneurosis: A psychological or physiological disturbance, less severe than psychosis but severe enough to limit the patient's social adjustment and ability to work, usually attributed to some unconscious emotional conflict. Commonly abbreviated as "neurosis."

Psychopathic: A type of personality characterized by an inability to restrain immoral and anti-social impulses.

Psychopathology: The study of psychological disorders and abnormalities.

Psychophysics: In its narrow and traditional sense, which stems from the work of G. T. Fechner, psychophysics is the name for the several methods that are used to measure thresholds. Recently there have been attempts to apply the term more generally to any study of the relations between psychological phenomena and the physical properties of stimuli.

Psychosis: Insanity. A mental illness characterized by cognitive disorders so severe (often including delusions or hallucinations) that social adjustment becomes impossible and the patient must be placed under medical supervision.

Psychotherapy: The treatment of disease by psychological methods.

Ratio scale of measurement: The type of measurement that is possible when there exist empirical operations for determining the natural zero value and for determining whether two ratios of the measured attribute are equal. Ratio scales are more common in physics than in psychology.

Reaction formation: In psychoanalytic theory, reaction formation refers to an unconscious mental process that converts a personality trait or disposition into its exact opposite.

Reality principle: A psychoanalytic term used to describe the functions of the ego in controlling the pleasure-seeking id impulses by postponing their gratification until external difficulties and constraints can be avoided. *Cf.* pleasure principle.

Recency effect: The name used to refer to a situation in which later items of a series are remembered better than earlier items. Contrasts with primacy effect.

Receptor: A specialized cell that is very sensitive to one kind of stimulation and that, when stimulated, initiates neural activity in a sensory nerve.

Recall: In discussions of remembering, recall denotes the arousal of a memory trace. Recall of verbal materials can be tested by asking a person to name or recite the items he has learned earlier.

Recognition: In discussions of remembering, recognition denotes perception accompanied by a feeling of familiarity. Can be tested by asking a person to identify the familiar objects when they are scattered haphazardly among similar but novel objects.

Regression: In statistics, regression is a general term, originated by Francis Galton, to describe the relation beween two correlated variables. In psychoanalytic theory, regression is the return to younger stages of personality development.

Reinforcement: Strengthening. In discussions of conditioning, a reinforcement is any outcome of an act that tends to increase the likelihood of that act under similar circumstances in the future.

Repression: In psychoanalytic theory, repression is the involuntary rejection of any conscious awareness of a sexual or hostile impulse.

Reproduction: In discussions of remembering, reproduction denotes a particular method of testing memory by asking the person to duplicate, orally or graphically, some previously learned pattern of behavior.

Response: Any pattern of glandular secretions and muscular contractions resulting from activity that arises in the nervous system as a result of a stimulus.

Sensation: The process of sensing, considered abstractly without concern for the stimulus object responsible for the experience.

Sign: A stimulus that can stand for or suggest something that is not itself present as a stimulus.

Signal: A sign that is not a symbol.

Situation: An extremely complex stimulus object that may have special meanings for the organism is often called, somewhat loosely, a situation.

Smooth muscles: Found in the walls of the internal organs and blood vessels, and innervated by the autonomic nervous system; so-called because, in contrast to skeletal muscles, they have a smooth, unstriped appearance.

Social desirability variable: On personality questionnaires, the tendency some people have to give those answers that seem socially most acceptable and commendable.

Social psychology: That branch of psychology that treats of the relation between the individual and his social environment.

Somatogenic disorders: Disorders having their origin in physiological (bodily) abnormalities. Contrasted with psychogenic disorders.

Somesthesia: Bodily sensations, both external (touch) and internal.

Stimulus: Any change in energy that causes an excitation of the nervous system leading to a response.

Stimulus generalization: In discussions of conditioning, stimulus generalization is said to occur when a response that has been conditioned to one particular stimulus is also observed in the presence of different (but usually similar) stimuli.

Stimulus object: Any object that is the source of a stimulus. Often referred to loosely as if it were the stimulus itself.

Stimulus-response (S-R) theory: The theory that all psychological phenomena can be described in terms of stimuli and responses and the correlations between them.

Structuralism: In general, any doctrine that emphasizes structure, form, composition, rather than function. As a psychological theory, structuralism tries to describe the anatomy of conscious experience, to identify mental elements and to state the laws governing their integration. Often contrasted with functionalism.

Subjective: That which exists only by virtue of conscious experience. Contrasted with objective.

Sublimation: In psychoanalytic theory, sublimation is an unconscious process whereby a sexual desire is desexualized and used to motivate art, work, play.

Subliminal: Below the threshold.

Superego: In the psychoanalytic concept of personality structure, the superego includes those prohibitions and ideals—largely unconscious —that comprise the moral and judicial aspects of personality.

Supraliminal: Above the threshold.

Symbol: A meaningful sign, one of a system of related signs whose uses are governed by rules.

Symbolic knowledge: Knowledge that can be expressed in symbols and communicated to other people.

Synapse: The region of contact between neurons in chain.

Tachistoscope: An instrument to present visual stimuli for very short periods of time, usually so short that their appearance and disappearance seem instantaneous.

Threshold: A statistically determined boundary point on a stimulus scale, where one variety of experience changes into another. The absolute threshold is the boundary separating what we can perceive from what we cannot. The difference threshold is the smallest stimulus change that produces a noticeable difference in perception.

Unconscious: An adjective applied to any mental process whose operation can be inferred from a person's behavior, but of which the person himself remains unaware and which he is unable to report or discuss. "The unconscious," according to Sigmund Freud, "is the true psychical reality; in its innermost nature it is as much unknown to us as the reality of the external world, and it is as incompletely presented by the data of consciousness as is the external world by the communications of our sense organs."

Visual field: The more-or-less oval-shaped scene that we can experience visually when our eyes are immobile and fixed on some given point; correlated roughly with the momentary pattern of stimulation on the retina. Sometimes contrasted with the visual world, which is not bounded and which remains stable even when eye or head movements cause the visual field to change.

Weber's law: According to H. C. Warren, *Dictionary of Psychology* (Boston: Houghton Mifflin, 1934), Weber's Law is a formulation of the relation between changes in stimulus-intensity and perception, devised by E. H. Weber, and expressed as follows: "The just perceptible difference of sensation occurs when the stimulus is increased (or decreased) by a certain proportion of itself, that proportion being constant for any given sense." Further experimentation has indicated that the law is only approximately true. The name was suggested by G. T. Fechner; *cf.* Fechner's Law.

NOTES

Chapter 2
WILHELM WUNDT, PSYCHOLOGIST

1. John Locke, *An Essay Concerning Human Understanding*, Book II, Chapter 1, paragraph 2.
2. Edwin G. Boring, *A History of Experimental Psychology*, 2nd ed. New York: Appleton-Century-Crofts, 1950. See Chapter 16 and references cited therein.
3. Wilhelm Wundt, *Outlines of Psychology*, translated by C. H. Judd. Leipzig: Wilhelm Engelmann, 1907. Pp. 31–32.
4. Fechner's Law says that the subjective magnitude of a sensation is a logarithmic function of the magnitude of the physical stimulus that produces it. Cf. Chapter 6.

Chapter 3
LEVELS OF AWARENESS

1. For an enlightening discussion of what it means to say that an electromechanical system thinks, see A. M. Turing, Can a machine think? In J. R. Newman, *The World of Mathematics*, Vol. IV. New York: Simon and Schuster, 1956.
2. W. Grey Walter, Intrinsic rhythms of the brain. In J. Field, H. W. Magoun, and V. E. Hall (eds.), *Handbook of Physiology*, Sec. I: Neurophysiology. Washington: American Physiological Society, 1959. Vol. I, Chapter 11, pp. 279–298.
3. W. Dement and N. Kleitman, The relation of eye movements during sleep to dream activity: An objective method for the study of dreaming, *Journal of Experimental Psychology*, 1957, Vol. 53, pp. 339–346. N. Kleitman, Patterns of dreaming, *Scientific American*, November 1960, 203, pp. 82–88.
4. D. B. Lindsley, Attention, consciousness, sleep and wakefulness. In J. Field, H. W. Magoun, and V. E. Hall (eds.), *Handbook of Physiology*. Sec. I: Neurophysiology. Washington: American Physiological Society, 1959. Vol. III, Chapter 64, pp. 15–53.
5. E. N. Sokolov, Neuronal models and the orienting reflex. In M. A. B. Brazier (ed.), *The Central Nervous System and Behavior*, Transactions of the Third Conference. New York: Josiah Macy, Jr., Foundation, 1960.

6. W. Heron, The pathology of boredom, *Scientific American,* January 1957. P. Solomon *et al* (eds.), *Sensory Deprivation.* Cambridge: Harvard University Press, 1961.

Chapter 4
The Selective Function of Consciousness

1. William James, *The Principles of Psychology.* New York: Henry Holt, 1890. Vol. 1, pp. 288–289.
2. For a critical review, see S. B. Sarason, *The Clinical Interaction, with Special Reference to the Rorschach.* New York: Harper, 1954.
3. W. Wundt, *An Introduction to Psychology,* translated by R. Pinter. London: George Allen, 1912.
4. R. Hernandez-Peon, H. Scherrer, and M. Jouvet, Modification of electrical activity in cochlear nucleus during "attention" in unanesthetized cats, *Science,* 1956, 123, 331–332.
5. E. L. Kaufman, M. W. Lord, T. W. Reese, and John Volkmann, The discrimination of visual number, *American Journal of Psychology,* 1949.
6. G. A. Miller, The magical number seven, plus or minus two, *Psychological Review,* 1956, 63, 81–97.
7. L. S. Kubie, *Neurotic Distortion of the Creative Process.* Lawrence: University of Kansas Press, 1958.
8. R. Reeves, *Reality in Advertising.* New York: Knopf, 1961.
9. K. S. Lashley, Cerebral organization and behavior. In *The Brain and Human Behavior, Proceedings of the Association for Research on Nervous and Mental Disease.* Baltimore: Williams & Wilkins, 1958.
10. Recounted by Andre M. Weitzenhoffer, *General Techniques of Hypnotism.* New York: Grune and Stratton, 1957. P. 83.

Chapter 5
William James, Philosopher

1. M. White, *The Age of Analysis.* Boston: Houghton Mifflin, 1955.
2. L. A. Cremin, *The Transformation of the School: Progressivism in American Education.* New York: Knopf, 1961.
3. R. B. Perry, *The Thought and Character of William James.* Boston: Little, Brown, 1935. Vol. I, pp. 171–172. For a brief introduction to James's life and works, see Margaret Knight, *William James.* London: Penguin, 1950.
4. Cf. William James, *Letters,* ed. by Henry James. Boston: Little, Brown, 1926.
5. William James, What is an emotion? *Mind,* 1884, 9. Cf. Saul Rosenzweig, The Jameses' stream of consciousness, *Contemporary Psychology,* 1958, 3, 250–257.
6. W. James, *The Principles of Psychology.* New York: Dover, 1950. Vol. 2, pp. 449–450.

7. William James, On some omissions of introspective psychology, *Mind,* 1884, 9, 1–26. Cf. R. B. Perry, *In the Spirit of William James.* New Haven: Yale University Press, 1938. Chapter 3, pp. 75–123.

8. W. James, *Essays in Radical Empiricism* (edited by Ralph Barton Perry). London: Longmans, Green, 1912. P. 160.

9. W. James, Reviews of Janet, Breuer and Freud, and Whipple, *Psychological Review,* 1894, 1, 195–200.

10. Jerome D. Frank, The dynamics of the psychotherapeutic relationship, *Psychiatry,* 1959, 22, 17–39.

Chapter 6
SUBJECTIVE YARDSTICKS

1. S. S. Stevens (ed.), *Handbook of Experimental Psychology.* New York: Wiley, 1951. Pp. 23–30.

2. An introduction to sensory psychology providing references leading into the extensive literature on the subject is F. A. Geldard, *The Human Senses.* New York: Wiley, 1953. For a more advanced discussion see W. Rosenblith (ed.), *Sensory Communication.* New York: The M.I.T. Press and John Wiley, 1961.

3. E. G. Boring, *A History of Experimental Psychology,* 2nd ed. New York: Appleton-Century-Crofts, 1950. Pp. 275–276.

4. L. L. Thurstone, *The Measurement of Values.* Chicago: University of Chicago Press, 1959.

5. See, for a discussion of two classes of sensory scales of measurement, S. S. Stevens and E. H. Galanter, Ratio scales and category scales for a dozen perceptual continua, *Journal of Experimental Psychology,* 1957, 54, 377–411.

Chapter 7
THE ANALYSIS OF PERCEPTIONS

1. R. S. Woodworth and H. Schlosberg, *Experimental Psychology,* rev. ed. New York: Holt, 1954. Pp. 286–293.

2. *Gestalt* is a German word that can be translated approximately as "pattern or configuration." Probably the most readable introduction to gestalt psychology is Wolfgang Köhler's *Gestalt Psychology.* New York: Liveright, 1929.

3. H. Fletcher, *Speech and Hearing in Communication,* 2nd ed. New York: Van Nostrand, 1953.

4. E. Oppenheimer, Optische Versuche Uber Ruhe und Bewegung, *Psychologische Forschung,* 1935, 20, 1–46.

5. J. J. Gibson, *The Perception of the Visual World.* Boston: Houghton Mifflin, 1950. P. 211.

6. J. S. Bruner, Going beyond the information given. In *Contemporary Approaches to Cognition.* Cambridge, Mass.: Harvard University Press, 1957. Pp. 41–69.

7. A. H. Hastorf, Influence of suggestion on size and distance, *Journal of Psychology,* 1950, 29, 195–217.

Chapter 8
SPACE

1. M. Jammer, *Concepts of Space*. Cambridge: Harvard University Press, 1954.
2. This illusion was brought to my attention by Murray Eden. Ernst Mach, the famous Viennese physicist and philosopher, studied it as early as 1866, but he was interested principally in the apparent brightnesses and shadows on the surfaces when they were reversed, and did not notice the effects of movement. See Ernst Mach, *The Analysis of Sensations*, translated by C. M. Williams. New York: Dover, 1959. Pp. 209–210.
3. G. M. Stratton, Some preliminary experiments on vision without inversion of the retinal image, *Psychological Review*, 1896, 3, 611–617; Vision without inversion of the retinal image, *Psychological Review*, 1897, 4, 341–360, 463–481.
4. I. Kohler, Rehabituation in perspective, *Die Pyramide*, 1953, Nos. 5–7.
5. R. W. Dichburn and B. L. Ginsborg, Vision with a stabilized retinal image, *Nature*, 1952, 170, 36–38. L. A. Riggs, F. R. Ratliff, J. C. Cornsweet, and T. N. Cornsweet, The disappearance of steadily fixated test-objects, *Journal of the Optical Society of America*, 1953, 43, 495–501.
6. J. Y. Lettvin, H. R. Maturana, W. S. McCulloch, and W. H. Pitts, What the frog's eye tells the frog's brain, *Proceedings of the IRE*, 1959, 47, 1940–1951.
7. The best introduction to the gestalt theory of the formation and segregation of wholes (by immobile organisms) is Laws of organization in perceptual forms, by Max Wertheimer, abstracted and translated in W. D. Ellis, *A Source Book of Gestalt Psychology*. London: Routledge & Kegan Paul, 1938. Pp. 71–88.
8. Perhaps this overestimates once more what the tree could achieve since it has no eye muscles and could not change the direction in which it is looking. The stabilized image would tend to disappear; and it could not move its eyes along a contour, which some psychologists regard as an essential step in our learning to recognize different shapes.
9. Rudolf Arnheim, *Art and Visual Perception*. Berkeley and Los Angeles: University of California Press, 1954.

Chapter 9
FRANCIS GALTON, ANTHROPOLOGIST

1. Richard Hofstadter, *Social Darwinism in American Thought*, rev. ed. Boston: Beacon, 1955.
2. Lewis M. Terman, The intelligence quotient of Francis Galton in childhood, *American Journal of Psychology*, 1917, 28, 209–215. Terman's retrospective techniques of estimating intelligence provided

the basis for a more comprehensive study of the childhood of great men by Catherine M. Cox, *The Early Mental Traits of Three Hundred Geniuses*. Stanford, California: Stanford University Press, 1926. The present discussion of Galton is based largely upon the three volume biography by Karl Pearson, *Life, Letters and Labors of Francis Galton*. London, 1914–1930.

3. Francis Galton, *Hereditary Genius*. New York: Macmillan, 1914. P. 14.

4. *Ibid.*, p. 39.

5. Francis Galton, *Inquiries into Human Faculty and its Development*. London: Macmillan, 1883. Pp. 202–203.

6. Galton's discussion of regression toward the mean can be found in *Natural Inheritance*. London: Macmillan, 1889. Pp. 95–110. For a general history of the development of statistical methods, see Helen M. Walker, *Studies in the History of Statistical Method*. Baltimore: Williams & Wilkins, 1929.

7. E. G. Boring, *A History of Experimental Psychology*, 2nd ed. New York: Appleton-Century-Crofts, 1950. P. 507.

Chapter 10
RECOGNIZING AND IDENTIFYING

1. These experiments are reviewed in Chapter 9 of George Humphrey, *Thinking, An Introduction to its Experimental Psychology*. London: Methuen, 1951. See also J. S. Bruner, J. J. Goodnow, and G. A. Austin, *A Study of Thinking*. New York: Wiley, 1956.

2. J. J. Gibson, The reproduction of visually perceived forms, *Journal of Experimental Psychology*, 1929, 12, 1–39.

3. W. C. H. Prentice, Visual recognition of verbally labeled figures, *American Journal of Psychology*, 1954, 57, 315–320.

4. Cf. R. N. Shepard and M. Teghtsoonian, Retention of information under conditions approaching a steady state, *Journal of Experimental Psychology*, 1961, 62, 302–309.

5. J. S. Bruner and L. Postman, On the perception of incongruity: A paradigm, *Journal of Personality*, 1949, 18, 206–223.

6. Cf. G. A. Miller, G. A. Heise, and W. Lichten, The intelligibility of speech as a function of the test materials, *Journal of Experimental Psychology*, 1951, 41, 329–335.

7. C. E. Shannon, A mathematical theory of communication, *Bell System Technical Journal*, 1948, 27, 379–423.

8. Fred Attneave, *Applications of Information Theory to Psychology*. New York: Holt, 1959.

9. Henry Quastler (ed.), *Information Theory in Psychology*. Glencoe, Ill.: Free Press, 1955.

10. G. A. Miller, The magical number seven, plus or minus two: Some limits on our capacity for processing information, *Psychological Review*, 1956, 63, 81–97.

11. Irwin Pollack and Lawrence Ficks, Information of elementary multi-dimensional auditory displays, *Journal of the Acoustical Society of America,* 1954, 26, 155–158.
12. Fred Attneave, Some informational aspects of visual perception, *Psychological Review,* 1954, 61, 183–193.

Chapter 11
MEMORY

1. Wilder Penfield, Functional localization in temporal and deep sylvian areas. In *The Brain and Human Behavior.* Baltimore: Williams & Wilkins, 1958. Pp. 210–226.
2. K. S. Lashley, In search of the engram. In *Society of Experimental Biology Symposium No. 4: Physiological Mechanisms in Animal Behavior.* Cambridge: Cambridge University Press, 1950. Pp. 454–482.
3. I. M. L. Hunter, *Memory: Facts and Fallacies.* London: Penguin, 1957.
4. Wallace H. Wallace, Stanley H. Turner, and Cornelius C. Perkins, *Preliminary Studies of Human Information Storage.* Signal Corps Project No. 132C, Institute for Cooperative Research, University of Pennsylvania, December, 1957.
5. G. W. Allport, Eidetic imagery, *British Journal of Psychology,* 1924, 15, 99–120. H. Kluver, Eidetic phenomena, *Psychological Bulletin,* 1932, 29, 181–203.
6. L. R. Peterson and M. J. Peterson, Short-term retention of individual verbal items, *Journal of Experimental Psychology,* 1959, 58, 193–198.
7. E. G. Schachtel, On memory and childhood amnesia. In F. Mullahy (ed.), *A Study of Interpersonal Relations.* New York: Grove, 1949. Pp. 3–49.

Chapter 12
IVAN PETROVICH PAVLOV, PHYSIOLOGIST

1. C. Bernard, *An Introduction to the Study of Experimental Medicine,* translated by H. C. Greene. New York: Dover, 1957.
2. Quoted by Ernest Jones, *The Life and Work of Sigmund Freud.* New York: Basic Books, 1953. Vol. I, p. 40.
3. Franklin Fearing, *Reflex Action, A Study in the History of Physiological Psychology.* Baltimore: William & Wilkins, 1930.
4. B. P. Babkin, *Pavlov, A Biography.* Chicago: University of Chicago Press, 1949. See also the biographical sketch by W. H. Gantt at the beginning of his translation of I. P. Pavlov, *Lectures on Conditioned Reflexes.* New York: International, 1928.
5. Babkin, *op. cit.,* p. 48.

6. G. Gorer and J. Rickman, *The People of Great Russia*. London: Cresset Press, 1949.
7. The term "conditioned reflex" which has been in general use for many years is an inaccurate translation of the Russian "ouslovny." Since "conditional reflex" is closer to what Pavlov meant and is also more easily understood, it has been adopted here.
8. Gantt, *op. cit.*, p. 50.
9. P. I. Yakovlev, Bechterev. M. A. B. Brazier (ed.), *The Central Nervous System and Behavior*. Transactions of the First Conference. New York: Josiah Macy, Jr., Foundation, 1959.
10. Pavlov spent a year with Heidenhain in Breslau and a year with Ludwig in Leipzig; Bechterev visited Charcot in Paris, Du Bois-Reymond in Berlin, but spent most of his time in Leipzig with Flechsig and with Wundt.
11. D. Joravsky, Soviet scientists and the great break, *Daedalus*, 1960, 89, 562-580.
12. Translated by W. H. Gantt under the English title *Lectures on Conditioned Reflexes*. New York: International, 1928.
13. Translated by G. V. Anrep under the English title *Conditioned Reflexes*. London: Oxford University Press, 1927.
14. E. R. Hilgard and D. G. Marquis, *Conditioning and Learning*, 2nd ed., revised by G. A. Kimble. New York: Appleton-Century-Crofts, 1961.
15. C. S. Sherrington, *The Integrative Action of the Nervous System*. New Haven: Yale University Press. 1906. Cf. J. Konorski, *Conditoned Reflexes and Neuron Organization*. Cambridge: Cambridge University Press, 1948.
16. Pavlov, *Conditioned Reflexes*, translated by G. V. Anrep. London: Oxford University Press, 1927. P. 291.
17. I. P. Pavlov, *Conditioned Reflexes and Psychiatry, Lectures on Conditioned Reflexes*, Vol. 2, translated by H. W. Gantt. New York: International, 1941.
18. *Everybody's Political What's What* (1944), quoted by Babkin, *op. cit.*, p. 342.

Chapter 13
THE SEARCH FOR BEHAVIORAL ATOMS

1. E. L. Thorndike, *Human Learning*. New York: Appleton-Century-Crofts, 1931. P. 122. Unfortunately, Thorndike never asked whether such an inventory would be of finite length.
2. E. R. Hilgard, *Theories of Learning*, 2nd ed. New York: Appleton-Century-Crofts, 1956. Pp. 9–11.
3. H. Ebbinghaus, *Memory: A Contribution to Experimental Psychology*, translated by H. A. Ruger and C. E. Bussenius. New York: Teachers College, Columbia University, 1913. A review of the field of research Ebbinghaus initiated can be found in J. A. McGeoch and

A. L. Irion, *The Psychology of Human Learning,* rev. ed. New York: Longmans, Green, 1952.

4. The idea that feedback loops (rather than reflex arcs) are the basic building blocks of the nervous system is the fundamental hypothesis of cybernetics. See, for example, N. Wiener, *Cybernetics.* New York: Wiley, 1948.

5. E. R. Hilgard and D. G. Marquis, *Conditioning and Learning* (rev. by G. A. Kimble). New York: Appleton-Century-Crofts, 1961.

6. Delos D. Wickens, The transference of conditioned excitation and conditioned inhibition from one muscle group to the antagonistic muscle group, *Journal of Experimental Psychology,* 1937, 22, 101–123. Also, D. D. Wickens, The simultaneous transfer of conditioned excitation and conditioned inhibition, *Journal of Experimental Psychology,* 1939, 24, 332–338.

7. R. S. Woodworth, *Experimental Psychology.* New York: Holt, 1938. P. 110.

8. K. Bykov, *The Cerebral Cortex and the Internal Organs.* New York: Chemical Publishing Co., 1957.

9. Edward L. Thorndike, *Animal Intelligence.* New York: Macmillan, 1898.

10. E. C. Tolman, *Purposive Behavior in Animals and Men.* New York: Century, 1932. P. 364.

11. Edwin R. Guthrie and G. P. Horton, *Cats in a Puzzle Box.* New York: Rinehart, 1946.

12. K. S. Lashley and D. A. McCarthy, The survival of the maze habit after cerebellar injuries, *Journal of Comparative Psychology,* 1926, 6, 423–432.

13. B. F. Skinner, *The Behavior of Organisms.* New York: Appleton-Century-Crofts, 1938.

Chapter 14
ANIMAL BEHAVIOR

1. C. Lloyd Morgan, *An Introduction to Comparative Psychology.* London: Scott, 1894. Pp. 287–291.

2. *Ibid.,* p. 53

3. *Ibid.,* p. 37

4. For a recent account see D. Katz, *Animals and Men,* translated by H. Steinberg and A. Summerfield. London: Penguin, 1953.

5. I. P. Pavlov, *Conditioned Reflexes,* translated by G. V. Anrep. London: Oxford University Press, 1927. P. 395.

6. N. Tinbergen, *The Study of Instinct.* London: Oxford University Press, 1951.

7. D. S. Lehrman, Induction of broodiness by participation in courtship and nest-building in the ring dove (*Streptopelia risoria*), *Journal of Comparative and Physiological Psychology,* 1958, 51, 32–36. Also, D. S. Lehrman, Effect of female sex hormones on incubation

behavior in the ring dove (*Streptopelia risoria*), *Journal of Comparative and Physiological Psychology,* 1958, 51, 142–145.

8. D. S. Lehrman, The physiological basis of parental feeding behavior in the ring dove (*Streptopelia risoria*), *Behaviour,* 1955, 7, 241–286.

9. B. P. Wiesner and N. M. Sheard, *Maternal Behaviour in the Rat.* London: Oliver & Boyd, 1933.

10. F. A. Beach and J. Jaynes, Studies of maternal retrieving in rats. III. Sensory cues in the lactating female's response to her young, *Behaviour,* 1957, 10, 104–125.

11. C. R. Carpenter, Societies of monkeys and apes, *Biological Symposia,* 1942, 8, 177–204.

12. H. F. Harlow, Love in infant monkeys, *Scientific American,* June, 1959.

13. W. A. Mason, The effects of social restriction on the behavior of Rhesus monkeys: I. Free social behavior, *Journal of Comparative and Physiological Psychology,* 1960, 53, 582–589.

Chapter 15
SIGMUND FREUD, PSYCHOANALYST

1. J. B. Bury, *The Idea of Progress* (1920). Reprinted New York: Dover, 1955. Chapter 3.

2. J. Bentham, *An Introduction to the Principles of Morals and Legislation* (1789).

3. O. H. Taylor, *A History of Economic Thought.* New York: McGraw-Hill, 1960. P. 120.

4. E. Durkheim, *Suicide: A Study in Sociology.* Glencoe, Ill.: Free Press, 1951.

5. H. S. Hughes, *Consciousness and Society.* New York: Knopf, 1958.

6. Ernest Jones, *The Life and Work of Sigmund Freud.* New York: Basic Books, 1953, 1957.

7. C. S. Hall, A cognitive theory of dream symbols, *Journal of General Psychology,* 1953, 48, 169–186.

8. Erich Fromm, *Sigmund Freud's Mission.* New York: Harper, 1959.

9. There are several introductory books on psychoanalysis. Freud's own are the most authoritative: *Five Introductory Lectures on Psychoanalysis* (1910), London: Hogarth, 1947, and the supplementary *New Introductory Lectures on Psychoanalysis,* New York: Norton, 1933. A shorter introduction by Freud is *An Outline of Psychoanalysis,* New York: Norton, 1949. An excellent discussion that brings the ideas up to date is given by Ives Hendrick, *Facts and Theories of Psychoanalysis,* 3rd. ed., New York: Knopf, 1958. A short and readable account for 35 cents is Calvin S. Hall, *A Primer of Freudian Psychology,* New York: Mentor, 1954.

10. S. Freud, *The Ego and the Id* (1923). London: Hogarth Press, 1927

11. S. Freud, *The Problem of Anxiety* (1926). New York: Norton, 1936.

12. Anna Freud, *The Ego and the Mechanisms of Defense* (1936). New York: International, 1946.
13. J. S. Bruner, Freud and the image of man, *Partisan Review*, Summer, 1956, 23, 343. Cf. Francis Bacon's "Idols of the Theatre" in the *Novum Organum*.
14. S. Freud, *Three Essays on Sexuality* (1905). London: Hogarth, 1953.
15. Fromm, *Sigmund Freud's Mission*. New York: Harper, 1959. P. 36.
16. S. Freud, *The Future of an Illusion* (1927). New York: Doubleday, 1957.

Chapter 16
GOADS AND GUIDES

1. W. McDougall, *An Introduction to Social Psychology*. New York: Barnes and Noble, 1960.
2. L. L. Bernard, *Instinct*. New York: Holt, 1924.
3. S. Freud, *An Outline of Psychoanalysis*, translated by J. Strachey. New York: Norton, 1949. P. 20.
4. W. B. Cannon, *The Wisdom of the Body*. New York: Norton, 1932.
5. I. Hendrick, *Facts and Theories of Psychoanalysis*, 3rd ed. New York: Knopf, 1958. Chapter 5.
6. B. Weiss and V. G. Laties, Magnitude of reinforcement as a variable in thermoregulatory behavior, *Journal of Comparative and Physiological Psychology*, 1960, 53, 603–608.
7. C. P. Richter, A behavioristic study of the activity of the rat, *Comparative Psychology Monographs*, 1922, 1, No. 2.
8. For a functionalist version, see H. A. Carr, *Psychology, A Study of Mental Activity*. New York: Longmans, Green, 1925. For a behavioristic version, see J. F. Dashiell, *Fundamentals of Objective Psychology*. Boston: Houghton Mifflin, 1928.
9. C. T. Morgan, Physiological mechanisms of motivation. In M. R. Jones (ed.), *Nebraska Symposium on Motivation 1957*. Lincoln, Nebraska: University of Nebraska Press, 1957. Pp. 1–35.
10. J. Olds and P. Milner, Positive reinforcement produced by electrical stimulation of septal area and other regions of rat brain, *Journal of Comparative and Physiological Psychology*, 1954, 47, 419–427.
11. W. Edwards, The theory of decision making, *Psychological Bulletin*, 1954, 51, 380–417.
12. L. G. Humphreys, Acquisition and extinction of verbal expectations in a situation analogous to conditioning, *Journal of Experimental Psychology*, 1939, 25, 294–301.
13. G. Katona, *Psychological Analysis of Economic Behavior*. New York: McGraw-Hill, 1951.
14. K. Lewin, T. Dembo, L. Festinger, and P. S. Sears, Level of aspira-

tion. In J. McV. Hunt (ed.), *Personality and the Behavior Disorders.* New York: Ronald, 1944. Vol. 1, pp. 333–378.
15. H. A. Simon, *Models of Man.* New York: Wiley, 1957.

Chapter 17
THE TYRANNY OF THE FUTURE

1. R. Reeves, *Reality in Advertising.* New York: Knopf, 1961. P. 73.
2. D. W. Taylor, Toward an information processing theory of motivation. In M. R. Jones (ed.), *Nebraska Symposium on Motivation 1960.* Pp. 51–79.
3. G. W. Allport, P. E. Vernon, and G. Lindzey, *Study of Values,* Rev. ed. Boston: Houghton Mifflin, 1951. See also C. Morris, *Varieties of Human Value.* Chicago: University of Chicago Press, 1956.
4. F. Heider, *The Psychology of Interpersonal Relations.* New York: Wiley, 1958.
5. C. B. De Soto, The predilection for simple orderings, *Journal of Abnormal and Social Psychology,* 1961, 62, 16–23.
6. L. Festinger, *A Theory of Cognitive Dissonance.* Evanston, Illinois: Row, Peterson, 1957.
7. L. Festinger, Some psychological effects of insufficient rewards, *American Psychologist,* 1961, 16, 1–11.
8. G. A. Miller, E. Galanter, and K. Pribram, *Plans and the Structure of Behavior.* New York: Holt, 1960.
9. F. A. Logan, *Incentive.* New Haven: Yale University Press, 1960.
10. W. Mischel, Preference for delayed reinforcement and social responsibility, *Journal of Abnormal and Social Psychology,* 1961, 62, 1–7.
11. G. Katona, *Psychological Analysis of Economic Behavior.* New York: McGraw-Hill, 1951. Also, *The Powerful Consumer.* New York: McGraw-Hill, 1960.
12. R. W. White, Motivation reconsidered: The concept of competence, *Psychological Review,* 1959, 66, 297–333.

Chapter 18
ALFRED BINET, PSYCHOLOGIST

1. R. W. White, *The Abnormal Personality,* 2nd ed. New York: Ronald, 1956. P. 9.
2. F. L. Bertrand, *Alfred Binet et Son Oeuvre.* Paris: Alcan, 1930.
3. Francis Galton, *Inquiries into Human Faculty and Its Development.* London: Macmillan, 1883. P. 27.
4. J. McK. Cattell. Mental tests and measurements, *Mind,* 1890, 15, 373–380.
5. T. H. Wolf, An individual who made a difference, *American Psychologist,* 1961, 16, 245–248.

6. L. M. Terman and M. A. Merrill, *Measuring Intelligence.* New York: Houghton Mifflin, 1957.
7. T. H. Wolf, *op. cit.*

Chapter 19
THE MIND OF A CHILD

1. L. Carmichael (ed.), *Manual of Child Psychology,* Rev. ed. New York: Wiley, 1954.
2. N. Bayley, On the growth of intelligence, *The American Psychologist,* 1955, 10, 805–818.
3. J. E. Anderson, The prediction of terminal intelligence from infant and preschool tests, *39th Yearbook, National Society for the Study of Education,* 1940, Part I, 385–403.
4. M. A. Ribble, Infantile experience in relation to personality development. In J. McV. Hunt (ed.), *Personality and the Behavior Disorders,* Vol. 2. New York: Ronald, 1944.
5. R. W. White, Competence and the psychological stages of development. In M. R. Jones (ed.), *Nebraska Symposium on Motivation, 1960.* Lincoln, Nebraska: University of Nebraska Press, 1960. Pp. 97–141.
6. J. W. M. Whiting and I. L. Child, *Child Training and Personality: A Cross-Cultural Study.* New Haven: Yale University Press, 1953.
7. J. Piaget. *The Construction of Reality in the Child,* translated by M. Cook. New York: Basic Books, 1954. P. 30.
8. *Ibid.,* p. 59.
9. J. Piaget, *The Psychology of Intelligence,* translated by M. Piercy and D. E. Berlyne. London: Routledge & Kegan Paul, 1950.
10. J. S. Bruner, *The Process of Education.* Cambridge: Harvard University Press, 1960.
11. H. A. Witkin, The perception of the upright, *Scientific American,* February, 1959.
12. B. Inhelder and J. Piaget, *The Growth of Logical Thinking from Childhood to Adolescence,* translated by A. Parsons and S. Milgram. New York: Basic Books, 1958. Pp. 3–15.

Chapter 20
CLINICAL OR STATISTICAL?

1. P. E. Meehl, *Clinical vs. Statistical Prediction.* Minneapolis: University of Minnesota Press, 1954.
2. Meehl, *op. cit.,* p. 57.
3. W. H. Whyte, *The Organization Man.* New York: Simon and Schuster, 1956. Pp. 197, 405–410. For a sober rebuttal, see S. Stark, Executive personality and psychological testing, *University of Illinois Bulletin,* 1958, 55, 15–32.

4. A. L. Edwards, *The Social Desirability Variable in Personality Assessment and Research.* New York: Dryden, 1957.
5. L. J. Cronbach, Response sets and test validity, *Educational and Psychological Measurement,* 1946, 6, 616–623.
6. D. N. Jackson and S. J. Messick, Content and style in personality assessment, *Psychological Bulletin,* 1958, 55, 243, 252. S. J. Messick and D. N. Jackson, Acquiescence and the factorial interpretation of the MMPI, *Psychological Bulletin,* 1961, 58, 299–304.
7. O. K. Buros (ed.), *The Fifth Mental Measurements Yearbook.* Highland Park, N. J.: Gryphon, 1959.
8. H. Peak, Problems of objective observation. In L. Festinger and D. Katz (eds.), *Research Methods in the Behavioral Sciences.* New York: Dryden, 1953. L. J. Cronbach and P. E. Meehl, Construct validity in psychological tests, *Psychological Bulletin,* 1955, 52, 281–302. J. Loevinger, Objective tests as instruments of psychological theory, *Psychological Reports,* Monograph Supplement 9, 1957, 3, 635–694.

Chapter 21
COMMUNICATION AND PERSUASION

1. C. I. Hovland, A. A. Lumsdaine, and F. D. Sheffield, *Experiments in Mass Communication.* Princeton: Princeton University Press, 1949.
2. Carl I. Hovland, *et al., The Order of Presentation in Persuasion.* New Haven: Yale University Press, 1957.
3. N. A. Anderson, Test of a model for opinion change, *Journal of Abnormal and Social Psychology,* 1959, 59, 371–381.
4. Carl I. Hovland, I. L. Janis, and H. H. Kelley, *Communication and Persuasion.* New Haven: Yale University Press, 1953. For a review of the concept of role in social psychology see T. R. Sarbin, Role theory, in Gardner Lindzey (ed.), *Handbook of Social Psychology.* Cambridge: Addison-Wesley, 1954. Pp. 223–258.

SOME SUGGESTIONS FOR FURTHER READING

The following suggestions are offered in the hope that some readers may want to learn more about psychology. Two different kinds of suggestions seem appropriate: (1) books that professional psychologists must know and use, books that contain the core of a graduate program leading to an academic degree in scientific psychology; and (2) the more enjoyable, yet equally trustworthy books for the general reader. I have tried to offer both, but to keep them distinct, in the following paragraphs.

First, the basic references. Anyone whose appetite has been aroused by a specific issue, and who wishes to pursue it into that vast wilderness known as the technical literature of psychology, should find that the notes accompanying each chapter will help him to get started in the right direction. In those notes there are repeated references to such basic texts as Boring's *A History of Experimental Psychology;* Carmichael's *Manual of Child Psychology;* Field, Magoun and Hall's *Handbook of Physiology: Neurophysiology;* Festinger and Katz's *Research Methods in the Behavioral Sciences;* Geldard's *The Human Senses;* Hilgard's *Theories of Learning;* Hilgard and Marquis's *Conditioning and Learning;* Hunt's *Personality and the Behavior Disorders;* Lindzey's *Handbook of Social Psychology;* Stevens's *Handbook of Experimental Psychology;* Terman and Merrill's *Measuring Intelligence;* White's *Abnormal Personality;* Woodworth and Schlosberg's *Experimental Psychology;* and many others. Anyone who diligently masters such books as these will have gone a long way toward acquiring the verbal mannerisms of a professional psychologist.

In order to go further, a really determined reader will have to tackle the periodical literature. Guidance in that undertaking should be sought in *Psychological Abstracts,* where most of the world's literature in psychology is regularly surveyed, abstracted, and topically indexed, and in the *Annual Review of Psychology,* which since 1950 has been publishing summaries of work reported each year in the major fields of psychology. Because their facts are packed as tightly as possible, these guides cannot be recommended as easy reading. Fortunately, however, the American Psychological Association has since 1956 published a sprightly and interesting journal of book reviews, a journal entitled *Contemporary Psychology,* where it is possible, almost painlessly, to keep abreast of the more important books in psychology.

But what of the general reader? What books can be recommended to the person who is interested but has no intention of making psychology a career? In answering this question personal taste intrudes to a far greater extent. For example, I am immediately struck by how many more excellent and readable books are available to the general public in the fields of psychiatry and clinical psychology (Freud, Jung, and Adler in paperback decorate every American drug store) than in the more academic fields of experimental, physiological, comparative, differential, and even social psychology. And even within these more traditional fields, it is my impression that the British have done more than we to popularize the subject. With a few exceptions, academic psychologists in the United States have tended to channel their expository energies into the production of textbooks—which may explain why it seems so natural to refer to them as academic psychologists. Even here, however, my personal preference is for a text by a Canadian, D. O. Hebb, *A Textbook of Psychology* (Philadelphia: Saunders, 1958), because it is relatively short (as introductory texts go), because it provides a firm grounding in physiological mechanisms, and because it is written with spirit and imagination.

Accompanying the textbook for most introductory courses is a book of selected readings; my favorite in this category is *Contributions to Modern Psychology,* compiled by Dulany, DeValois, Beardslee, and Winterbottom (New York: Oxford University Press, 1958). But one hesitates to send the general reader to such books as these; the odor of the schoolroom is likely to spoil them for many people.

One attractive and authoritative series of popular books in psychology has been published in paperback by Penguin Books. The series includes such titles as Eysenck's *Uses and Abuses of Psychology;* Hunter's *Memory: Facts and Fallacies;* Sluckin's *Minds and Machines;* and several others equally rewarding.

The amount of psychological writing increases exponentially from year to year, and there must be hundreds of excellent items that never reach my desk. I fully recognize the inadequacy of the following list. All I can truthfully assert is that I have found all the books on it to be both informative and readable; but let no one imagine that all the informative and readable books in general psychology are included:

R. C. Birney and R. C. Teevan (Eds.), *Instinct*. New York: D. Van Nostrand, 1961.

E. G. Boring, *A History of Experimental Psychology*. (Second ed.) New York: Appleton-Century-Crofts, 1950.

J. S. Bruner, *The Process of Education*. Cambridge: Harvard University Press, 1960.

S. Freud, *Five Introductory Lectures on Psychoanalysis*. (Trans. by J. Strachey.) London: Hogarth Press, 1957.

W. James, *The Principles of Psychology*. Reissued in paperback by Dover Publications, 1950.

F. S. Keller, *Learning: Reinforcement Theory*. New York: Random House, 1954.

K. Z. Lorenz, *King Solomon's Ring*. (Trans. by M. K. Wilson.) London: Methuen, 1952.

J. Piaget, *The Language and Thought of the Child*. (Trans. by M. Gabain.) Reprinted by Meridian Books, 1955.

A. Scheinfeld, *Women and Men*. New York: Harcourt Brace, 1943.

B. F. Skinner, *Science and Human Behavior*. New York: Macmillan, 1953.

L. M. Terman and M. H. Oden, *The Gifted Child Grows Up* and *The Gifted Group at Mid-Life* (Vols. 4 and 5 of *The Genetic Study of Genius*). Stanford: Stanford University Press, 1946, 1959.

L. S. Vygotsky, *Language and Thought*. (Trans. by E. Hanfmann.) Cambridge, Mass.: M. I. T. Press, 1962.

M. Wertheimer, *Productive Thinking*. (Second ed.) New York: Harper, 1959.

That should be enough to get started. By the time these have been explored, the reader should have a reasonably clear notion of what kind of psychology he likes and where to go to find more of it.

Index

INDEX